Frommer's

Am 100 Best-Loved State Parks

A Complete Guide
to Some of the Country's
Most Scenic and Affordable
Outdoor Vacations

by Robert Rafferty

MACMILLAN • USA

MACMILLAN TRAVEL
A Simon & Schuster Macmillan Company
15 Columbus Circle
New York, NY 10023

ISBN 0-02-860462-8
ISSN 1081-4922
Editor: Peter Katucki
Assisted by Yvonne Honigsberg, Kim Jesuele, and Robin Michaelson
Map Editor: Douglas Stallings
Design by Irving Perkins Associates
Maps by Johanna Jacob

Manufactured in the United States of America

Dedication

This book is dedicated to the hardworking men of the Civilian Conservation Corps who, between 1933 and 1942, built the physical foundations for state parks all over our nation.

Acknowledgments

Even when there's a single author, a book is always a team effort. A major part of my team was the multitude of state park personnel—from the state directors to clerks—who provided the thousands of details that are essential to make this guidebook useful and beneficial to you, the reader. Without their help and willing cooperation, researching this book would have been an impossible task.

I especially want to thank those park personnel at the state headquarters who helped me select the parks and set up my visits to the nominated parks, and the rangers and other park personnel at the individual parks who took the time to answer my innumerable questions and, with justifiable pride, show me around their parks. My sincerest compliments for a job well done, and a job you continue to do very well with the public every day. You are one of the primary reasons we have great state parks in every state.

My thanks and heartfelt regrets go to those park personnel who worked with me and will now find out that their parks didn't make the book. The 50 states nominated close to 200 parks for this guide. Without exception, all proved worthy of their nomination, and there are undoubtedly hundreds more that could have been nominated, but the competition for *America's 100 Best-Loved State Parks* was fierce and some had to miss the cut. The final selection was mine—a much tougher job than I anticipated—so if you are displeased with the results, blame me, but, please, still accept my thanks.

Another part of the team was the acquiring editor, Lisa Renaud at Frommer's Travel Guides, and my agent, Vicky Bijur. My sincere thanks to both for their guidance and their angelic patience and understanding when disasters—natural and personal—caused inordinate delays in the research and writing. My gratitude is extended to Peter Katucki, the final editor of this guide at Frommer's, who shaped the book to make it the best possible for you, the reader.

Finally, a thank you to the computer division of AT&T for providing me with a notebook computer that proved invaluable for recording research during the many weeks I spent on the road. I had never used a notebook computer before this book, and now it's become one of those items I can't travel without.

Contents

	Visitor Center	Lodge/Hotel	Restaurant	Cabins & Cottages	RV Camping	Primitive Camping	Tent Camping	Group Lodge Dormitories	Group Camping	Marina	Boating	Boat Launch
1. Alabama/*Desoto State Park* 2	✔	✔	✔	✔	✔	✔	✔				✔	✔
2. Alabama/*Gulf State Park* 4	✔	✔	✔	✔	✔		✔	✔			✔	✔
3. Alabama/*Joe Wheeler State Park* 6		✔	✔	✔	✔	✔	✔	✔		✔	✔	✔
4. Alaska/*Chena River State Recreational Area* 9					✔	✔	✔		✔			
5. Alaska/*Chugach State Park* 11	✔				✔	✔	✔		✔			
6. Arizona/*Lake Havasu and Cattail Cove State Parks* 16	✔		✔		✔	✔	✔		✔	✔	✔	✔
7. Arkansas/*DeGray Lake Resort State Park* 19		✔	✔		✔		✔			✔	✔	✔
8. Arkansas/*Petit Jean State Park* 21	✔	✔	✔	✔	✔		✔		✔		✔	✔
9. California/*Anza-Borrego Desert State Park* 26	✔				✔	✔	✔		✔			
10. California/*Calaveras Big Trees State Park* 29	✔				✔	✔	✔		✔			
11. California/*Humboldt Redwoods State Park* 32	✔				✔	✔	✔		✔			
12. California/*Pfeiffer Big Sur State Park* 35	✔	✔	✔		✔		✔		✔			

Handwritten annotations: MAY - JUNE (next to item 1); (So. Liv readers choice) (below item 2)

Non-Motorized Boating Only	Fishing	Beach	Swimming	Waterskiing	Snorkeling & Diving	Picnic Areas	Trails	Horse Trails	Nature Programs	Bicycling	Golf	Tennis	Fitness Center	Playground	X-Country Skiing	Downhill Skiing	Snowmobiling	Gift Shop
	✔		✔			✔	✔		✔	✔		✔		✔				✔
	✔	✔	✔			✔	✔		✔	✔	✔	✔		✔				✔
	✔	✔	✔			✔	✔		✔		✔	✔		✔				✔
✔	✔					✔	✔	✔							✔		✔	
	✔					✔	✔	✔	✔	✔					✔	✔	✔	✔
	✔	✔		✔		✔	✔											
	✔	✔	✔			✔	✔		✔	✔	✔							✔
	✔		✔			✔	✔		✔			✔		✔				✔
						✔		✔	✔	✔								✔
	✔		✔			✔	✔								✔			
	✔		✔			✔	✔	✔	✔	✔								✔
✔	✔		✔			✔	✔		✔									✔

	Visitor Center	Lodge/Hotel	Restaurant	Cabins & Cottages	RV Camping	Primitive Camping	Tent Camping	Group Lodge Dormitories	Group Camping	Marina	Boating	Boat Launch
13. Colorado/*Golden Gate Canyon State Park* — 40	✔				✔		✔		✔			
14. Colorado/*Mueller State Park and Wildlife Area* — 43					✔		✔		✔			
15. Colorado/*Ridgway State Park* — 46	✔				✔		✔			✔	✔	✔
16. Connecticut/*Rocky Neck State Park* — 49					✔		✔				✔	✔
17. Delaware/*Cape Henlopen State Park* — 52	✔				✔		✔	✔				
18. Florida/*John Pennekamp Coral Reef State Park* — 55	✔				✔		✔		✔	✔	✔	✔
19. Florida/*Myakka River State Park* — 57	✔			✔	✔	✔	✔		✔		✔	✔
20. Florida/*Paynes Prairie State Preserve* — 59	✔				✔		✔					✔
21. Georgia/*Amicalola Falls State Park* — 63	✔	✔	✔	✔	✔	✔	✔					
22. Georgia/*Little Ocmulgee Lodge State Park* — 65	✔	✔	✔	✔	✔	✔	✔		✔		✔	✔
23. Hawaii/*Kauai's Northwest Coast Parks* — 68			✔	✔			✔	✔				
24. Idaho/*Bruneau Dunes State Park* — 72	✔				✔	✔	✔		✔			
25. Idaho/*Farragut State Park* — 74	✔				✔	✔	✔		✔		✔	✔

Georgia – Stone Mtn.
S. Liv. Reader's choice

Non-Motorized Boating Only	Fishing	Beach	Swimming	Waterskiing	Snorkeling & Diving	Picnic Areas	Trails	Horse Trails	Nature Programs	Bicycling	Golf	Tennis	Fitness Center	Playground	X-Country Skiing	Downhill Skiing	Snowmobiling	Gift Shop
	✔					✔	✔	✔	✔	✔				✔				
	✔					✔	✔	✔	✔	✔					✔			
	✔	✔		✔	✔	✔	✔	✔	✔	✔				✔	✔			
	✔	✔		✔		✔	✔		✔						✔			
	✔	✔				✔	✔		✔	✔		✔						
	✔	✔	✔		✔	✔	✔		✔									✔
	✔					✔	✔	✔		✔				✔				✔
✔	✔					✔	✔	✔	✔	✔				✔				
	✔					✔	✔		✔					✔				
	✔		✔	✔		✔	✔				✔	✔		✔				✔
	✔	✔				✔	✔											
✔	✔	✔				✔	✔	✔	✔									
	✔	✔		✔		✔	✔	✔	✔	✔				✔	✔			

CONTENTS

	Visitor Center	Lodge/Hotel	Restaurant	Cabins & Cottages	RV Camping	Primitive Camping	Tent Camping	Group Lodge Dormitories	Group Camping	Marina	Boating	Boat Launch
26. Illinois/*Pere Marquette State Park* 77	✔	✔	✔	✔	✔		✔	✔	✔	✔	✔	✔
27. Illinois/*Shelbyville State Park: Eagle Creek and Wolf Creek* 79		✔	✔		✔	✔	✔		✔		✔	✔
28. Indiana/*Harrison-Crawford-Wyandotte Complex* 84					✔	✔	✔		✔		✔	✔
29. Indiana/*Spring Mill State Park* 87	✔	✔	✔		✔		✔		✔			✔
30. Iowa/*Backbone State Park* 90				✔	✔		✔					✔
31. Iowa/*Lake Macbride State Park* 92					✔	✔	✔		✔		✔	✔
32. Kansas/*Clinton State Park* 95					✔	✔	✔		✔	✔	✔	✔
33. Kentucky/*Barren River Lake State Resort Park* 98	✔	✔	✔	✔	✔		✔			✔	✔	✔
34. Kentucky/*Lake Barkley State Resort Park* 100	✔	✔	✔	✔	✔		✔			✔	✔	✔
35. Kentucky/*Lake Cumberland State Resort Park* 102	✔	✔	✔	✔	✔	✔	✔			✔	✔	✔
36. Louisiana/*Bayou Segnette State Park* 106	✔			✔	✔		✔	✔			✔	✔
37. Maine/*Baxter State Park* 109				✔	✔	✔	✔	✔	✔			
38. Maryland/*Assateague State Park* 114	✔				✔	✔			✔			✔

(S.Liv Readers Choice)

Non-Motorized Boating Only	Fishing	Beach	Swimming	Waterskiing	Snorkeling & Diving	Picnic Areas	Trails	Horse Trails	Nature Programs	Bicycling	Golf	Tennis	Fitness Center	Playground	X-Country Skiing	Downhill Skiing	Snowmobiling	Gift Shop
	✔		✔			✔	✔	✔	✔	✔		✔		✔				✔
	✔	✔				✔	✔	✔	✔		✔	✔		✔	✔		✔	✔
	✔		✔			✔	✔	✔	✔									
✔	✔		✔			✔	✔	✔	✔					✔				✔
✔	✔	✔				✔	✔	✔						✔	✔		✔	
	✔	✔				✔	✔			✔				✔			✔	
	✔	✔		✔		✔	✔		✔	✔				✔				
	✔	✔	✔	✔		✔	✔	✔	✔	✔	✔	✔		✔				✔
	✔	✔	✔	✔		✔	✔	✔	✔			✔	✔	✔				✔
	✔		✔	✔		✔	✔		✔		✔	✔		✔				✔
	✔		✔			✔								✔				
✔	✔		✔				✔								✔	✔		
✔	✔	✔	✔				✔		✔	✔								

	Visitor Center	Lodge/Hotel	Restaurant	Cabins & Cottages	RV Camping	Primitive Camping	Tent Camping	Group Lodge Dormitories	Group Camping	Marina	Boating	Boat Launch
39. Maryland/*Deep Creek Lake State Park* 118					✔		✔				✔	✔
40. Massachusetts/*Myles Standish State Forest* 121					✔		✔		✔			
41. Massachusetts/*Nickerson State Park* 123					✔		✔		✔		✔	✔
42. Michigan/*Hartwick Pines State Park* 126	✔			✔	✔		✔		✔			✔
43. Michigan/*Porcupine Mountains Wilderness State Park* 128	✔			✔	✔	✔	✔		✔		✔	✔
44. Minnesota/*Itasca State Park* 132		✔	✔	✔	✔	✔	✔	✔	✔		✔	✔
45. Minnesota/*St. Croix State Park* 134	✔				✔	✔	✔	✔	✔			
46. Mississippi/*Paul B. Johnson State Park* 138	✔			✔	✔		✔	✔			✔	✔
47. Missouri/*Sam A. Baker State Park* 141	✔		✔	✔	✔	✔	✔					
48. Missouri/*Thousand Hills State Park* 143			✔	✔	✔		✔			✔	✔	✔
49. Montana/*Flathead Lake State Park* 146					✔		✔			✔	✔	✔
50. Nebraska/*Fort Robinson State Park* 150		✔	✔	✔	✔	✔	✔	✔				

Non-Motorized Boating Only	Fishing	Beach	Swimming	Waterskiing	Snorkeling & Diving	Picnic Areas	Trails	Horse Trails	Nature Programs	Bicycling	Golf	Tennis	Fitness Center	Playground	X-Country Skiing	Downhill Skiing	Snowmobiling	Gift Shop
	✔	✔				✔	✔		✔	✔				✔	✔		✔	
✔	✔		✔			✔	✔	✔	✔	✔					✔		✔	
	✔	✔		✔	✔	✔	✔	✔	✔	✔					✔			
✔	✔					✔	✔		✔	✔				✔	✔		✔	
	✔	✔				✔	✔		✔	✔				✔	✔	✔	✔	✔
	✔	✔				✔	✔		✔	✔				✔	✔		✔	✔
✔	✔	✔				✔	✔	✔	✔	✔					✔		✔	
	✔	✔	✔	✔		✔	✔							✔				✔
✔	✔		✔			✔	✔	✔	✔					✔				
	✔	✔		✔		✔	✔		✔					✔				
	✔	✔		✔		✔	✔		✔	✔								
✔	✔	✔	✔			✔	✔	✔	✔	✔	✔			✔	✔	✔		✔

CONTENTS

	Visitor Center	Lodge/Hotel	Restaurant	Cabins & Cottages	RV Camping	Primitive Camping	Tent Camping	Group Lodge Dormitories	Group Camping	Marina	Boating	Boat Launch
51. Nebraska/*Eugene T. Mahoney State Park* 153		✔	✔	✔	✔		✔	✔				
52. Nevada/*Lake Tahoe–Nevada State Park* 156						✔					✔	✔
53. Nevada/*Valley of Fire State Park* 159	✔				✔	✔	✔					
54. New Hampshire/*Franconia Notch State Park* 162	✔		✔		✔	✔	✔					✔
55. New Jersey/*Allaire State Park* 166	✔				✔		✔					
56. New Jersey/*High Point State Park* 168	✔			✔	✔	✔	✔	✔	✔			
57. New Jersey/*Wharton State Forest* 170	✔			✔	✔	✔	✔		✔			✔
58. New Mexico/*Elephant Butte Lake State Park* 174	✔		✔	✔	✔	✔	✔			✔	✔	✔
59. New York/*Jones Beach State Park* 177			✔							✔	✔	
60. New York/*Letchworth State Park* 179	✔	✔	✔	✔	✔		✔		✔			
61. New York/*Niagara Reservation State Park* 182	✔											
62. New York/*Saratoga Spa State Park* 184	✔	✔	✔									
63. New York/*Watkins Glen State Park* 187	✔				✔		✔	✔				

Non-Motorized Boating Only	Fishing	Beach	Swimming	Waterskiing	Snorkeling & Diving	Picnic Areas	Trails	Horse Trails	Nature Programs	Bicycling	Golf	Tennis	Fitness Center	Playground	X-Country Skiing	Downhill Skiing	Snowmobiling	Gift Shop
✔	✔		✔			✔	✔	✔	✔	✔		✔		✔	✔			✔
	✔	✔		✔	✔	✔	✔	✔	✔	✔					✔			
						✔	✔	✔	✔	✔								
✔	✔	✔		✔		✔	✔		✔	✔						✔	✔	✔
✔	✔					✔	✔	✔	✔	✔	✔			✔	✔			✔
✔	✔	✔				✔	✔	✔	✔	✔				✔	✔		✔	
✔	✔	✔				✔	✔		✔					✔				✔
	✔		✔	✔	✔	✔	✔		✔	✔				✔				
	✔	✔	✔			✔			✔		✔	✔		✔				✔
	✔		✔			✔	✔	✔	✔					✔	✔		✔	✔
						✔		✔										✔
			✔			✔	✔		✔	✔	✔	✔		✔	✔			✔
✔	✔		✔			✔	✔		✔					✔				

	Visitor Center	Lodge/Hotel	Restaurant	Cabins & Cottages	RV Camping	Primitive Camping	Tent Camping	Group Lodge Dormitories	Group Camping	Marina	Boating	Boat Launch

64. North Carolina/*Jordan Lake State Recreation Areas* 190					✔	✔	✔		✔	✔	✔	✔
65. North Carolina/*Morrow Mountain State Park* 191				✔	✔	✔	✔				✔	✔
66. North Dakota/*Fort Abraham Lincoln State Park* 196	✔				✔		✔				✔	
67. North Dakota/*Lake Metigoshe State Park* 198				✔	✔	✔	✔	✔			✔	✔
68. Ohio/*Maumee Bay State Park* 202		✔	✔	✔	✔		✔			✔	✔	
69. Ohio/*Mohican State Park* 204		✔	✔	✔	✔	✔	✔		✔			
70. Ohio/*Shawnee State Park* 206		✔	✔	✔	✔	✔	✔			✔	✔	
71. Oklahoma/*Beavers Bend and Hochatown State Parks* 209			✔	✔	✔	✔	✔	✔		✔	✔	✔
72. Oklahoma/*Lake Murray Resort and State Park* 211		✔	✔	✔	✔	✔	✔	✔		✔	✔	✔
73. Oklahoma/*Quartz Mountain Resort and State Park* 213		✔	✔	✔	✔	✔	✔	✔		✔	✔	✔
74. Oregon/*Fort Stevens State Park* 217					✔		✔		✔		✔	
75. Oregon/*Jessie M. Honeyman State Park* 219					✔		✔		✔		✔	
76. Oregon/*Sunset Bay State Park* 220	✔				✔		✔		✔			✔

Non-Motorized Boating Only	Fishing	Beach	Swimming	Waterskiing	Snorkeling & Diving	Picnic Areas	Trails	Horse Trails	Nature Programs	Bicycling	Golf	Tennis	Fitness Center	Playground	X-Country Skiing	Downhill Skiing	Snowmobiling	Gift Shop
	✓	✓		✓		✓	✓		✓					✓				
	✓		✓			✓	✓	✓	✓									
	✓			✓		✓	✓		✓						✓		✓	✓
	✓	✓		✓	✓	✓	✓		✓	✓				✓	✓		✓	
	✓	✓	✓		✓	✓	✓	✓	✓	✓	✓	✓	✓	✓	✓			✓
✓	✓		✓			✓	✓		✓			✓		✓	✓			✓
	✓	✓			✓	✓	✓	✓	✓		✓	✓	✓	✓				✓
	✓	✓		✓	✓	✓	✓		✓		✓	✓		✓				✓
	✓	✓	✓	✓	✓	✓	✓	✓	✓	✓	✓	✓		✓				✓
	✓	✓	✓	✓		✓	✓		✓		✓	✓		✓				✓
	✓	✓	✓				✓		✓	✓				✓				
	✓	✓	✓	✓	✓	✓	✓		✓	✓				✓				
	✓	✓	✓		✓	✓	✓							✓				

		Visitor Center	Lodge/Hotel	Restaurant	Cabins & Cottages	RV Camping	Primitive Camping	Tent Camping	Group Lodge Dormitories	Group Camping	Marina	Boating	Boat Launch
77.	Pennsylvania/*Ohiopyle State Park* 224					✔		✔					
78.	Pennsylvania/*Pymatuning State Park* 226			✔	✔	✔		✔		✔			✔
79.	Pennsylvania/*Ricketts Glen State Park* 228	✔			✔	✔		✔		✔			✔
80.	Rhode Island/*Goddard Memorial State Park* 231											✔	✔
81.	South Carolina/*Hunting Island State Park* 234	✔			✔	✔		✔		✔		✔	✔
82.	South Carolina/*Santee State Park* 236	✔		✔	✔	✔		✔		✔		✔	
83.	South Dakota/*Custer State Park* 239	✔	✔	✔	✔	✔		✔		✔		✔	✔
84.	South Dakota/*Lewis and Clark State Recreation Area* 243		✔	✔	✔	✔		✔		✔	✔	✔	✔
85.	Tennessee/*Fall Creek Falls State Resort Park* 246		✔	✔	✔	✔		✔	✔				
86.	Tennessee/*Paris Landing State Resort Park* 249		✔	✔		✔	✔	✔				✔	✔
87.	Texas/*Davis Mountains State Park* 252		✔	✔		✔	✔	✔					
88.	Texas/*Brazos Bend State Park* 254	✔				✔	✔	✔					

(handwritten annotations near entry 81: "Hunt. Beach St. Pk. S. Liv — Readers Choice"; near entry 85: "S. Liv Readers Choice")

Non-Motorized Boating Only	Fishing	Beach	Swimming	Waterskiing	Snorkeling & Diving	Picnic Areas	Trails	Horse Trails	Nature Programs	Bicycling	Golf	Tennis	Fitness Center	Playground	X-Country Skiing	Downhill Skiing	Snowmobiling	Gift Shop
✔	✔		✔			✔	✔		✔	✔				✔	✔		✔	✔
✔	✔	✔			✔	✔	✔		✔	✔				✔	✔		✔	
✔	✔	✔			✔	✔	✔	✔	✔						✔		✔	
	✔	✔				✔	✔	✔	✔						✔			
	✔	✔				✔	✔		✔					✔				
	✔	✔				✔	✔		✔	✔		✔		✔				
	✔	✔		✔		✔	✔	✔	✔	✔				✔	✔		✔	✔
	✔	✔		✔		✔	✔	✔	✔	✔				✔	✔		✔	
✔	✔		✔			✔	✔	✔	✔	✔	✔	✔	✔	✔				✔
	✔	✔	✔	✔	✔	✔	✔		✔		✔	✔		✔				✔
		✔				✔	✔		✔					✔				✔
						✔	✔		✔	✔				✔				✔

CONTENTS

	Visitor Center	Lodge/Hotel	Restaurant	Cabins & Cottages	RV Camping	Primitive Camping	Tent Camping	Group Lodge Dormitories	Group Camping	Marina	Boating	Boat Launch
89. Texas/*Palo Duro Canyon State Park* 256	✔				✔		✔					
90. Utah/*Wasatch Mountain State Park* 260					✔	✔	✔		✔			
91. Vermont/*Groton State Forest Parks* 264		✔			✔	✔	✔				✔	✔
92. Virginia/*Douthat State Park* 267	✔		✔	✔	✔		✔	✔	✔			✔
93. Virginia/*Seashore State Park and Natural Area* 269	✔			✔	✔		✔				✔	✔
94. Washington/*Deception Pass State Park* 272					✔	✔	✔				✔	✔
95. Washington/*Fort Canby State Park* 275	✔				✔	✔	✔	✔			✔	✔
96. West Virginia/*Canaan Valley Resort State Park* 279	✔	✔	✔	✔	✔		✔					
97. West Virginia/*Pipestem Resort State Park* 281	✔	✔	✔	✔	✔		✔					
98. Wisconsin/*Devil's Lake State Park* 285					✔		✔		✔			✔
99. Wisconsin/*Peninsula State Park* 287					✔		✔		✔		✔	✔
100. Wyoming/*Glendo State Park* 290		✔			✔		✔			✔	✔	✔

CONTENTS

Non-Motorized Boating Only	Fishing	Beach	Swimming	Waterskiing	Snorkeling & Diving	Picnic Areas	Trails	Horse Trails	Nature Programs	Bicycling	Golf	Tennis	Fitness Center	Playground	X-Country Skiing	Downhill Skiing	Snowmobiling	Gift Shop
						✓	✓	✓	✓									
							✓	✓	✓	✓	✓				✓		✓	
	✓	✓				✓	✓		✓					✓	✓		✓	
✓	✓	✓				✓	✓		✓	✓					✓			✓
	✓	✓				✓	✓		✓	✓								
	✓	✓				✓	✓		✓									
	✓					✓	✓		✓									
	✓		✓			✓	✓		✓	✓	✓	✓	✓	✓	✓	✓		✓
✓	✓		✓			✓	✓	✓	✓	✓	✓	✓	✓	✓	✓			✓
✓	✓	✓		✓		✓	✓		✓	✓					✓			
	✓	✓				✓	✓		✓	✓	✓	✓		✓	✓		✓	
	✓	✓		✓		✓	✓							✓				

List of Maps

ALASKA *Chugach State Park* 13

ARKANSAS *Petit Jean State Park* 23

CALIFORNIA *Anza-Borrego Desert State Park* 27

Humboldt Redwoods State Park 33

COLORADO *Golden Gate Canyon
State Park* 41

FLORIDA *Myakka River State Park* 58

HAWAII *Kauai's Northwest Coast Parks* 69

ILLINOIS *Shelbyville State Park* 81

INDIANA *Harrison-Crawford-
Wyandotte Complex* 85

KENTUCKY *Lake Cumberland State Resort
Park* 103

MAINE *Baxter State Park* 111

MARYLAND *Assateague State Park &
Chincoteague National
Wildlife Refuge* 116–117

NEBRASKA *Fort Robinson State Park* 151

NEVADA *Lake Tahoe–Nevada State Park* 157

NEW JERSEY *Wharton State Forest* 171

NEW YORK *Letchworth State Park* 180–181

NORTH CAROLINA *Morrow Mountain
State Park* 193

OREGON *Sunset Bay State Park* 221

SOUTH DAKOTA *Custer State Park* 241

TENNESSEE *Fall Creek Falls State
Resort Park* 247

TEXAS *Palo Duro Canyon State Park* 257

UTAH *Wasatch Mountain State Park* 261

WASHINGTON *Deception Pass State Park* 273

To Get the Most from This Guide

A general feeling prevails that our splendid national parks are becoming jammed with visitors and the strain is showing on both the parks and the visitors. The alternative? State parks! Largely unknown outside their own state—and sometimes even within—several thousand state parks offer a wide variety of opportunities for outdoor recreation, usually with elbow room that's hard to beat. What's more, state parks are often only a few steps from your own backyard. This book introduces you to 100 of America's best-loved state parks.

The Selection Process

How do you select America's 100 best-loved state parks from close to 4,000? With trepidation, awe, and a few criteria.

I asked each state to nominate up to five parks that: (1) are places of impressive natural beauty or possess unique features; (2) offer a wide variety of recreational facilities for both day use and overnight visitors; (3) are open all or most of the year and are generally accessible by good roads; and (4) have other attractions within an easy drive from the park that would enrich a trip to this area.

These criteria weren't set in concrete. They couldn't be because even what constitutes a state park varies widely. Some states include historic sites as state parks, others don't. Some include state forests, yet others exclude them. At times it did feel as if I were comparing apples and oranges. To simplify, I classified them all as enjoyable fruit—if the property was controlled by the state parks headquarters it was a state park.

Flexibility was the name of the selection process. Often a park that did not stack up too strongly on paper turned out to be a gem when I visited. As I've said, the states, themselves, made the initial nominations, but I made the final selection. If you disagree, I'm to blame. One note, however, some state parks—not in this guide—are already so popular that they are running close to capacity. Neither the states nor I wanted to add to the almost squeezed and huddled environment by including those parks. Which may account for why your favorite state park is not here. But then again, a few times a park proved to be so distinctive I couldn't leave it out—however crowded it may sometimes be.

Getting the Most from the Listings

THE STATE LISTINGS

Each state's listings starts with the number of state parks to give you an indication of the size of that state's park system.

The **Contacts** section gives you the address and phone of both the state's park headquarters and the state's tourism office. These go by a variety of names, but they are where you can write or call for additional information on both the parks and the state's other attractions for visitors.

The **General Information** section covers details common to all that state's parks.

General Fees are usually entrance or parking fees, but may include special fees common to all that state's parks. If the past is any guide, the odds are that some of these fees, plus all other fees, from camping to whatever, will have changed by the time you read this. And, again harkening to experience, the odds are they will be up rather than down. Most park systems are scrambling for operations and maintenance funds in a world of rising costs, so you may run into some creative new fees that didn't exist before. Also, fees I've quoted do not include state or local taxes, but expect to see them in your bill.

Use the fees listed strictly as a planning guide. Even if you run into higher fees, you'll find most of them are still nominal when compared to the prices of commercial tourist attractions—in fact, they compare favorably to a movie ticket. If you're concerned about the exact cost, call the appropriate listed state contact or the individual park for the latest prices.

Camping and Accommodations gives you the basic information you'll need to know about where and how you can overnight in that state's parks. It covers campsites, cabins, and resort-type accommodations.

Unless otherwise noted, campgrounds have the usual facilities: toilets, showers, picnic tables, etc. But, in the northern states, where winter can hit hard, the parks themselves may remain open while the facilities—especially bathhouses—may close for the winter.

When a park accepts reservations, it's a good idea to reserve as far ahead as you're permitted to, especially for summer and holiday weekends. A growing number of states accept major credit cards for reservations. When campsites are strictly on a first-come basis—in other words, no reservations—it's also a good idea to call ahead to ask whether a vacancy may be available when you expect to arrive. Don't expect guarantees—that'd be a reservation system—but a call will at least give you your odds of getting a site.

Camping often means the pleasure of an open fire. Of course, out-of-control campfires are a major hazard to parks, so learn the rules for fire safety and follow them.

The rules on gathering firewood vary. Cutting down park trees is universally a crime. Some parks allow you to pick up branches that are "dead and down," but in other parks this wood should be left on the ground to rot and replenish the soil. Find out whether you can pick up firewood from the forest's floor, or if you have to bring your own, or whether you can purchase it in the park or locally outside the park.

Pets. If I had to list one subject that park personnel in all states expressed strong feeling about it would be bringing pets to parks. All states have rules on this and these are the rules most often ignored by visitors.

Pets in this book means all pets, but most comments refer to dogs, which are the most common pets owners bring with them.

Your dog can be the joy of your life, so it may seem taking your dog to a state park would be the ideal thing to do. Give it a treat. Let it enjoy the great outdoors, too.

In reality, the opposite is usually true. Although many parks permit pets, almost without exception, park personnel strongly suggest they be left at home. Their experience is that most family pets do not enjoy this outdoor holiday, and for some it can be a nerve-racking, dangerous, even a deadly, experience.

A park's strange sights, sounds, and smells may make even the most well-behaved and affectionate dog nervous. Rarely can they roam free. In most parks you'll have to keep them on a leash and under your control at all times; no leaving them alone while you go off. At night, they must be kept in your tent, vehicle, or a cage. Being constantly on a leash or penned up can be upsetting to both the dog and you. You'll also be responsible for being a good neighbor and keeping it quiet, so it doesn't disturb other park visitors, and clean up after it. And be prepared to show proof of current rabies vaccination.

If that's not enough, there are often restrictions on where you can take them; buildings and swimming areas, for example, are almost always off-limits. If they are permitted to roam, there's a chance they'll run off and get lost in unfamiliar surroundings. And the wilderness environment of most parks is not hospitable to pets. They can get bitten by everything from snakes to wild, and sometimes rabid, animals, or attract ticks, fleas, or other bugs that can cause serious illness or even death.

For your pet's sake, give serious consideration to leaving it at home.

Fishing. With few exceptions, if you plan to fish, you'll need a state license and possibly an additional tag or stamp for going after certain species, like trout. Sometimes these can be purchased in the parks; however, in most states you'll have to buy them in nearby, or not-so-nearby, towns.

Alcoholic beverages. Here's another place where the rules can not only change from state to state, but from park to park. They range from prohibition to just enforcing the legal drinking age. If you don't want to spoil your vacation, find out these rules and obey them.

LAW AND ORDER

Most of the park personnel who deal with the public go by the title of ranger or something similar. No matter the title, as a group I found them friendly, helpful, and easy to get along with. This isn't just a job for them. They truly love their parks. Just as truly they are offended by visitors who will damage their park or cause trouble for other visitors. In many states, rangers are law enforcement officers. In others they have no police jurisdiction. But, in every case they have the authority to deal with those who break the rules. If you do, you may get a polite, but firm warning; you may be told to leave, or you may wind up in the local jail. Treat the park like your own home. No, even better, treat it like your boss's home. A good philosophy to live by is take only memories and leave only footprints.

NEARBY ATTRACTIONS

Finally, part of the fun and adventure of visiting a state park is using the park as a base for exploring the surrounding area. Places worth exploring are listed under **Nearby Attractions.**

An Invitation to the Reader

In researching this book, I discovered many wonderful parks and nearby attractions. I'm sure you'll find others. Please tell us about them, so we can share the information with your fellow travelers in upcoming editions. If you were disappointed with a recommendation, we'd love to know that, too. Please write to:

Robert Rafferty
Frommer's America's 100 Best-Loved State Parks
Macmillan Travel
15 Columbus Circle
New York, NY 10023

An Additional Note

Please be advised that travel information is subject to change at any time—and this is especially true of prices. We therefore suggest that you write or call ahead for confirmation when making your travel plans. The author, editors, and publisher cannot be held responsible for the experiences of readers while traveling. Your safety is important to us, however, so we encourage you to stay alert and be aware of your surroundings. Keep a close eye on cameras, purses, and wallets, all favorite targets of thieves and pickpockets.

Alabama

JOE WHEELER STATE PARK

DESOTO STATE PARK

GULF STATE PARK

Alabama has 24 state parks.

Contacts

- Division of State Parks, Alabama Department of Conservation and Natural Resources, 64 N. Union St., Montgomery, AL 36130. Information/reservations, call toll free 800/ALA-PARK or 334/242-3333. Central Reservations Center Monday to Friday 8am to 5pm (except holidays).
- Alabama Bureau of Tourism and Travel, 401 Adams Ave., Suite 126, Montgomery, AL 36104 (tel. toll free 800/ALABAMA).

General Information on Alabama State Parks

Alabama stretches from the end of the Appalachian foothills in the north to the Gulf of Mexico in the south, and the state has parks that preserve its natural beauty and provide recreational opportunities. For those who enjoy the outdoors but don't want to camp in tents, 11 parks have hotels, lodges, or cabins. Six of Alabama's state parks are classified as resort parks.

GENERAL FEES

Entrance (where charged) is 50¢ to $1 per person.

CAMPING AND ACCOMMODATIONS

Fees vary by park. Prices given are a range that includes all state parks; prices do not include sales tax, which may be added in some parks. Hotel/cabin/campsites reservations may be made by phoning the park directly or through the Central Reservation Center.

Resort hotel rates for double range from $43 to $91 per night. Modern **cabin** rates for up to four persons are $35 to $97. Rates are higher for cabins that sleep six to eight persons. Rustic cabin rates for up to four persons are $35 to $72. Most resort parks offer a variety of package plans.

Camping (improved sites). The base rate is $8 to $12 per night for four persons or less. Each additional person over 6 years old costs $1, to maximum of eight persons per campsite. Primitive camping is $3 to $8 per night.

Pets. Not allowed in some parks. Where allowed, a dog, cat, or other animal must be on a leash not longer than six feet or otherwise under physical restrictive control at all times. No animal of any type is allowed in any beach area in any state park. Pets are normally not permitted in any hotel or cabin rooms.

Alcoholic beverages. Park rules on public display and consumption of alcohol varies by county.

Discounts. Seniors, 62 and older, and disabled persons are eligible for an admission discount at parks that charge an entrance fee, as well as a 15% discount on camping and golf fees, except on holiday weekends.

Desoto State Park

Visitor Center · Lodge/Hotel · Restaurant · Cabins & Cottages · RV Camping · Tent Camping · Primitive Camping · Boating · Boat Launch · Fishing · Swimming

Picnic Areas · Tennis · Trails · Nature Programs · Bicycling · Playground · Gift Shop

Capsule Description: Natural park on a mountaintop with developed facilities.

Location: Northeastern Alabama on Lookout Mountain, about 60 miles south of Chattanooga, Tennessee. From I-59 take SH 35 (Fort Payne exit) to CR 89, then northeast to the park.

Address: Desoto State Park Headquarters, Route 1, Box 210, Fort Payne, AL 35967 (tel. 205/845-0051). Desoto State Park Lodge, Route 1, Box 205, Fort Payne, AL 35967 (tel. 205/845-5380).

Area Contacts: Fort Payne Chamber of Commerce, P.O. Box 125, Fort Payne, AL 35967 (tel. 205/845-2741).

Insider Tips: A special Bed-and-Breakfast package is usually available Sunday through Thursday nights from December through April. If you want to observe or photograph wildlife up close, ask to use the park's observation blind.

Although a final decision is still pending, there are plans to turn the park and the nearby wildlife management area into a national preserve operated jointly by the state and the federal government; the state would continue to operate the lodge and campgrounds.

Oak, hickory, poplar, and loblolly and Virginia pine populate the woods of Desoto State Park, which straddles 100-mile-long Lookout Mountain, just below its midpoint. Named for the Spanish explorer Hernando De Soto (c. 1500–42), who passed through here with his party, the park boasts 15 waterfalls. The highest is 100-foot-tall Desoto Falls; it splashes into a mountain lake, Desoto Lake, where you can swim, fish, or boat. Little River, the only river in the United States that forms atop a mountain and stays there, is found in this park. Its gorge is among the deepest east of the Rocky Mountains—averaging 400 feet and plunging to 600 feet at its deepest point. In May and June, the blooming of the Catawabe rhododendron and mountain laurel turn many areas of the park into a riot of colors.

Three scattered areas make up Desoto Park, which totals 5,067 acres. In the main section are the major park facilities including the information center, lodge, cabins, and campgrounds. The Desoto Falls area is located seven miles north of the information center. The Little River Canyon area is 10 miles south of the information center.

Activities

Desoto's nature program is seasonal; the Nature Center (tel. 205/845-5075) is open from May 1 to October 31. The park's naturalist arranges nature walks, wildflower programs, scenic hikes, and the use of a wildlife photo blind from which you can photograph deer, wild turkeys, and perhaps even a bobcat. The park has seven hiking trails; one is a self-guided nature path. The Rhododendron Trail on the west bank of the Little River meanders past many of the park's waterfalls (the rhododendrons are in peak bloom in May and June). Some of the hiking trails are intertwined so hikers can follow them to a maximum of about nine miles. Bikers can blaze down the main surfaced roads through the park. The Little River Wildlife Management Area adjoins the park and offers more foot and biking trails.

Fishermen can try for largemouth bass, Coosa bass, sunfish, and catfish in Little River and the lakes. At Desoto Lake, there's a small ramp to launch canoes and flat-bottom boats with trolling motors.

Swimmers can dip into Desoto Lake; the water is usually warm enough for swimming from the beginning of April to the end of October. From Memorial Day to Labor Day, an Olympic-sized pool with life guards is open at the lodge; it's free to lodge and cabin guests, and others are charged a small fee.

The waters of the Little River are calm above the dam, and powerboats are allowed here; a launchsite accommodates them. Below the dam, the river has Class IV and V rapids, putting it in the expert category for white-water runners.

The Little River Canyon has terrain for rock climbing and rappelling; the park requires permits for both of these activities.

Rimming the western rim of the canyon is the Little River Canyon Parkway (Highway 176), a 22-mile scenic drive.

Camping and Accommodations

The original stone walls of the **Lodge** were built by the Civilian Conservation Corps (CCC) in the 1930s. These, and the beamed ceiling and large fireplace, were retained when the building was modernized. The lodge now has 25 guest rooms, all with access to a country porch complete with rocking chairs for lounging. Each motel-style room has air conditioning/heat, TV, and a phone. The lodge also has a full-service dining room; however, this is a dry county, so no public display of alcoholic beverages is allowed. Two unlighted tennis courts are located near the lodge swimming pool. (Seasonal rates: double $43 to $49.)

The 11 modern, A-frame–type light house-keeping **cabins,** called mountain chalets, are fully equipped to sleep up to four persons. All are air-conditioned, heated, and have fireplaces, screened porches, and sun decks. On the grounds are 11 rustic cabins of native logs and stone also constructed by the CCC in the 1930s. All the original furniture was handmade by the men of the CCC. Today these cabins are fully equipped for up to six persons, with air conditioning, heat, and screened porches; most have fireplaces. Cabins have TV but no phones. (Modern cabins for one to four persons $64 to $68. Rustic cabins for one to two persons $47 to $52, for one to four persons $49 to $54, for one to six persons $62 to $66.)

The park has 78 multiuse **campsites,** all with water and electric hookups. Twenty of these also have sewer connections. In addition to groceries and other supplies, the country store in the campgrounds sells local crafts, and campers can rent some sports equipment. Primitive camping is permitted in the "wilderness area" but there are no designated sites. (Campsites $11.)

Nearby Attractions

Cloudmont Ski and Golf Resort (tel. 205/634-4344), the only ski resort in Alabama, is nearby. True, they make their own snow in winter and do grass skiing in summer and the slopes are mostly for beginners, but it's still downhill skiing. Three members of the well-known country and western group Alabama live on Lookout Mountain, and the Alabama **Fan Club** has a small museum and gift shop (tel. 205/845-1646) in Fort Payne. The nearby town of **Mentone** has a number of antiques and crafts shops. About an hour's drive to the west, on the TVA's 69,000-acre Lake Guntersville, is **Lake Guntersville State Park**

(tel. 205/571-5444), another resort park, offering a variety of water-based sports, a 100-unit lodge, 35 cabins, 322 campsites, and an 18-hole golf course. To the north, also about an hour away, is **Chattanooga**, Tennessee, with **Rock City Gardens** (tel. 706/820-2531), **Ruby Falls**, (tel. 615/821-2544), the **Incline Railroad** (tel. 615/821-4224), **Point Park** on Lookout Mountain (615/821-7786), and **Chattanooga and Chickamauga National Military Park** (tel. 706/866-9241).

Gulf State Park

Visitor Center | Lodge/Hotel | Restaurant | Cabins & Cottages | RV Camping | Tent Camping | Group Lodge Dormitories | Boating | Boat Launch | Fishing | Swimming | Beach

Picnic Areas | Golf | Tennis | Trails | Nature Programs | Bicycling | Playground | Gift Shop

Capsule Description: A saltwater resort park.
Location: Southern Alabama, about 60 miles south of Mobile and 40 miles west of Pensacola, Florida, on SH 182 east of the city of Gulf Shores, right on the Gulf of Mexico.
Address: Gulf State Park Headquarters, 20115 SH 135, Gulf Shores, AL 36542 (tel. 334/948-7275). Gulf State Park Resort Hotel, P.O. Box 437, Gulf Shores, AL 36547-0437 (tel. toll free 800/544-4853 or 334/948-4853). Open at all times.
Area Contacts: Alabama Gulf Coast Area Chamber of Commerce, P.O. Drawer 3869, Gulf Shores, AL 36547 (tel. 334/968-6904).
Insider Tips: The resort has earned a listing in *Better Homes and Gardens* magazine as one of America's 30 Favorite Family Vacation Resorts. Ask about the latest hotel package plans; these offer the best bargains.

On the barrier island of Pleasure Island in the Gulf of Mexico, Gulf State Park has two miles of beaches with sand that looks like powdered sugar. This resort park is heavily wooded with magnolia, slash pine, live oak, and Chinese tallow trees—a contrast to the tree-cleared lawns of the neighboring commercial resort communities. The park boasts the closest proximity of a freshwater lake to saltwater in the United States. Offered at reasonable prices are fishing, swimming, boating and water sports, golf, and tennis.

Habitating the park are white-tailed deer, bobcats, raccoons, marsh rabbits, and alligators—from babies to a 12-footer who keeps to himself in the nature preserve. Shorebirds abound, as do migratory birds in the winter season. The official birdlist, available free at the park, names close to 300 species such as scissortail flycatchers, bluejays, cardinals, sparrows, and toehees.

Activities

Extending 825-feet into the waters of the Gulf is a fishing pier. Anglers here catch king and Spanish mackerel, redfish, pompano, and flounder. Bait is sold and fishing equipment is rented at the pier. Anglers fishing off the pier are charged $4 per person, and a sightseeing stroll on the pier costs $1 per person. The park has three freshwater lakes that yield largemouth bass, bluegill, and catfish. Johnboats without motors can be rented. The state of Alabama requires fishing licenses for both salt-water and freshwater fishing; licenses may be purchased at the pier or at the park headquarters.

Swimmers can plunge into the waters of the Gulf or the lakes; the heated pool at the hotel is open year round.

Powerboats are permitted on those lakes that have launch sites. Surfboards, sailboards, Sunfish sailboats for two, and a 16-foot Hobie Cat are among the water craft for rent at the pier.

Awarded 3½ stars out of a possible 4 by *Golf Digest*, the park's 18-hole golf course has a par of 72. With sandy dune ridges, it's a pretty course and well-kept for a state park course.

The park has five easy trails through the woods; they range from about ¾ to 1½ miles long.

From Memorial Day to Labor Day, the Nature Center (tel. 334/948-7275) offers canoe trips in the fresh water lake preserve (which can only be visited on guided tours), beach walks, bike hikes (some outside the park), campfire programs, and summer programs for kids.

Camping and Accommodations

The **hotel** has 144 rooms (including four handicap-accessible) in 12 buildings lining the beach. Although the concrete buildings look stark from the outside, the rooms compare favorably to those in a good motel and have TV, phone, and air conditioning/heat. The highlight of each room is a private balcony overlooking the turquoise waters of the Gulf. The full-service restaurant offers a menu strong in fresh Gulf seafood as well as an inexpensive buffet most nights. The lounge is open every day but Sunday. A heated swimming pool is open all year, but lifeguards are on duty in the summer only. Hotel reservations are accepted at any time. (Seasonal rates: double $49 to $91, suite $95 to $175.)

Seventeen modern light-housekeeping **cabins** (two handicap-accessible) overlooking Lake Shelby, are mostly two–bedroom/one-bath. Fully equipped for four, each can sleep up to six. One larger cabin will sleep eight. Cabins have TVs but no phones. Five fishing piers jut out on the lake for guest use. Three rustic, one-room cabins, built as part of the original park by the Civilian Conservation Corps (CCC) in the late 1930s, are located in the woods near the lake. These sleep four; one larger rustic cabin sleeps eight. All cabins have air conditioning and heat. Cabin reservations for a week or more (seventh night free) accepted up to a year in advance; for less than a week, up to 30 days in advance. Only week-long reservations accepted for the months of June, July, and August. (Modern cabins for one to four persons $35 to $65, for one to six persons $50 to $85. Rustic cabins for one to two persons $30, for up to six persons $45.)

All 468 **campsites** have water and electric hookups and 220 of them also have sewer connections. Although the sites are close together, most are shaded and have good privacy buffers between them. Camp facilities include bathhouses, a laundry, store, activities center, nature center, tennis courts, and bicycle rentals. Two-day campsite reservations are accepted up to a year in advance. A three-day minimum stay over major holidays is required. (Campsites $11.)

In keeping with its resort status, the park offers a number of package plans, including a honeymoon package and a golf package, with rooms and some meals provided.

Nearby Attractions

Nearby, to the west, at the end of the peninsula forming the mouth of Mobile Bay, is the historic

Fort Morgan (tel. 334/540-7202 or 7125), one of the last Confederate forts to fall to Union forces in 1864.

Mobile, Alabama, and Pensacola, Florida, are only about an hour's drive away. Among the sights in **Mobile** are the historic districts and the **USS Alabama Battleship Memorial Park** (tel. 334/433-2703). During the azalea season (usually late March to early April), the 37-mile-long, self-guided **Azalea Trail** blazes with color through

the city. On the way to Mobile, on CR 59, is **the Bellingrath Gardens and Home** (tel. 334/973-2217). **Pensacola**, first settled by the Spanish in 1559, also has several historic districts. **Historic Pensacola Village** (tel. 904/444-8905) is a collection of museums, and the **National Museum of Naval Aviation** (tel. 904/452-3604), at the naval air station, ranks among the largest air and space museums in the world. **Gulf Islands National Seashore** is also there.

Joe Wheeler State Park

Lodge/ Hotel   Restaurant   Cabins & Cottages   RV Camping   Tent Camping   Primitive Camping   Group Lodge Dormitories   Marina   Boating   Boat Launch   Fishing   Swimming

Beach   Picnic Areas   Golf   Tennis   Trails   Nature Programs   Playground   Gift Shop

Capsule Description: A lakeside park with resort facilities.

Location: Northern Alabama, off U.S. 72 two miles west of Rogersville.

Address: Route 4, Box 369A, Rogersville, AL 35652. Park Headquarters (tel. 205/247-5466). Resort Lodge (tel. toll free 800/544-JOEW (800/544-5639) or 205/247-5461).

Area Contacts: The Chamber of Commerce of the Shoals, 104 S. Pine St., Florence, AL 35630 (tel. 205/764-4661).

Insider Tip: Fishing, golf, and other package plans offer great bargains.

This 2,600-acre park is split into three separate areas with the main section located on the shore of the 63,000-acre Wheeler Lake, the largest of the TVA's three stair-stepping Tennessee River lakes in northern Alabama. Another of the state's resort

parks, it offers visitors a comfortable lodge, cabins, campsites, restaurant, picnic areas, hiking trails, golf, tennis, and, of course, boating, fishing, and a full range of sports on the lake. There's even a full-service marina with 134 slips. Most of these are leased, but there are a number of open slips with full hookups for transient boaters, plus dock tie-offs in front of the lodge for boaters who just want to visit the park briefly or eat in the lodge dining room.

Activities

The lodge swimming pool is heated, but there is no lifeguard. Swimming is also permitted in the lakes. The 18-hole golf course features a clubhouse, pro shop, and practice driving, chipping, and putting areas. The four lighted tennis courts have all-weather surfaces. Five playgounds for children are scattered throughout the park.

Fishing is a major activity at Joe Wheeler with catches of largemouth, smallmouth, and spotted bass; crappie, channel catfish, and freshwater drum. March, April, and May are the best fishing months, with September and October running a close second. Fishing boats with motors, as well as pontoon boats and canoes, can be rented at the marina.

The park lodge offers golf, fishing, and other package plans.

The five easy hiking trails wind through woods of oak and longleaf pine. These woods are a bird-watcher's delight with a large number of species sighted all year long. Deer and wild turkey can also be spotted.

Camping and Accommodations

Each of the 75 **lodge** rooms (including three handicap-accessible) has a balcony with a panoramic view of the lake. All have air conditioning/heat, TV, and phones. The full-service restaurant is in the three-story redwood and stone main building. (Seasonal rates: double $58 to $63, executive room $70 to $73, suite $99 to $114.)

The 23 rustic **cabins** are the heart of the second park area, located on SH 101 on the south side of Wheeler Dam, 12 miles east and south from the main park. Most of these light-housekeeping cabins have two bedrooms that sleep four. Also available on the lake are several large three- and four-bedroom cabins, which can sleep up to eight. Originally these brick houses were built for senior TVA personnel when the dam was going up in the 1930s. Boat ramps here give access to both Wheeler Lake above the dam and Wilson Lake below it. One of the two group lodges in the park is also located here. This one has a capacity of 20. The other group lodge is in the third park section, on the Elk River off U.S. 72 west of Rogersville; it

sleeps up to 30. (Seasonal rates for cabins: up to four persons $35 to $40, up to six persons $43 to $49, up to eight persons $50 to $58.)

The 116 multiuse **campsites** are in the main park area. All have full hookups for electric, water, and sewage, and all are close to the water. The day-use public beach is nearby. A country store and Laundromat are located at the entrance to the campgrounds. A primitive camping area has room for up to 35 tents. (Campsites: RV $11, tent $10, primitive $6.)

The park is in a dry county; no alcoholic beverages in public areas.

Nearby Attractions

Popular local attractions include the two dams that form the lakes. Visitors can tour the nearby **Wheeler Dam powerhouse** (tel. 205/386-2444) and parts of **Wilson Dam** (tel. 205/386-2444) at Florence. Wilson Dam boasts one of the world's highest single-lift locks, capable of lifting boats up to 100 feet in a single operation. To fill the lock, it takes 50 million gallons of water; it's emptied in 12 minutes. The **home and museum of the famed blues composer W. C. Handy** (tel. 205/760-6434) is also in Florence.

Just south of Florence, in **Tuscumbia,** are the **birthplace of Helen Keller** (tel. 205/383-4066) and the **Alabama Music Hall of Fame** (tel. 205/381-4417), honoring more than 500 musicians from Handy to Tammy Wynette, Alabama, and Lionel Richie.

To the east is **Huntsville;** the city spans the ages from its historic districts filled with antebellum homes to the space-age exhibits at the **U.S. Space and Rocket Center** (tel. 205/837-3400) and tours of NASA's **Marshall Space Flight Center** (tel. 205/837-3400).

Alaska

CHENA RIVER STATE
RECREATIONAL AREA

CHUGACH STATE PARK

Alaska has 132 state park units.

Contacts

Alaska is not a place you just drop in on. A journey to this state takes planning. These contacts can help you get all the information you need in advance to make your plans work so you can reap all the rewards you expect of your travels.

- Division of Parks and Outdoor Recreation, Department of Natural Resources, P.O. Box 107001, Anchorage, AK 99510-7001 (tel. 907/762-2617).
- Alaska State Division of Tourism, P.O. Box 110801, Juneau, AK 99811-0801 (tel. 907/465-2010).
- Alaska Public Lands Information Centers (Provide information on national and state parks, recreational facilities, wildlife refuges, and national forests.)
  - 605 W. 4th Ave., Suite 105, Anchorage, AK 99501 (tel. 907/271-2737 or 907/258-7275 for recorded information).
  - 250 Cushman St., Suite 1A, Fairbanks, AK 99701 (tel. 907/456-0527).
  - Box 359, Tok, AK 99780 (tel. 907/883-5667).
- Alaska Marine Highway, P.O. Box 25535, Juneau, AK 99802-5535 (tel. toll free 800/642-0066). (This ferry system, which carries passengers and automobiles, connects 28 Alaska towns with British Columbia and Bellingham, Washington.)
- Alaska Railroad, P.O. Box 107500, Anchorage, AK 99510-7500 (tel. toll free 800/544-0552).

General Information on Alaska State Parks

Rugged beauty, vast wilderness, and abundant wildlife are among our largest state's greatest treasures. With 3.2 million acres, Alaska has the largest acreage of land devoted to state parks in the nation and holds nearly one-third of the nation's state park acreage. In fact, when national parks are added in, more than half our nation's parklands are found in Alaska. The state parks range in size from the half-acre Potter Section State Historic Site to the 1.6 million wild acres of Tikchik State Park. They offer a total of 75 campgrounds with more than 2,000 individual sites, plus 21 cabins. Many of the state parks are just as grand as the national parks, but are generally more accessible and often less expensive to visit.

Because the parks are well away from the glare of city lights, in fall and early spring you can usually count on seeing sensational aurora borealis or northern lights.

GENERAL FEES

Admission varies by park. Entrance is free to a number of parks while others charge a moderate fee.

CAMPING AND ACCOMMODATIONS

Fees for **camping** range from $6 to $12 per night, with most campgrounds charging $6 to $8. Camping is on a first-come basis; no reservations. Annual passes allowing unlimited camping in all state park campgrounds cost $75. Tent campers should note that Alaska's summers can be wet; you'll need a tent fly and ground cloth. All summer visitors will also need a good insect repellent to hold off the mosquitoes, which can grow to trophy size.

There are a dozen public use **cabins** at Nancy Lake State Recreation Area, four each at Shuyak Island and Chena River, and one at Olivers Inlet. They're rustic, sleep from three to ten persons, and are equipped with wooden sleeping platforms, wood stove, table, benches, and kitchen counter. Reservations may be made up to 180 days in advance. Maximum stay varies by site from three to seven days. Rates also vary from $15 to $25 per night for up to four people, $5 for each additional person. For information, contact the Division of Parks and Outdoor Recreation, listed above.

Pets. Must be on leashes at all developed facilities, such as campgrounds and picnic areas, and under control in all parks at all times to prevent conflict with wildlife.

Alcoholic beverages. Permitted in all parks.

Chena River State Recreational Area

Cabins & Cottages | RV Camping | Tent Camping | Primitive Camping | Group Camping | Non-Motorized Boating Only | Fishing | Picnic Areas | Trails | Horse Trails | X-Country Skiing | Snow-mobiling

Capsule Description: Wilderness park with limited developed facilities.

Location: Central Alaska, approximately 26 miles east of Fairbanks on Chena Hot Springs Road.

Address: 3700 Airport Way, Fairbanks, AK 99709 (tel. 907/451-2695).

Area Contacts: Alaska Public Lands Information Center, 250 Cushman St., Suite 1A, Fairbanks, AK 99701 (tel. 907/456-0527).

Fairbanks Convention and Visitors Bureau, 550-Q 1st Ave., Fairbanks, AK 99701 (tel. 907/456-5774).

Insider Tips: Hiking in the back country is best in winter, as the swamps are frozen over. The fall colors in the forest are at their most brilliant in early September.

The 254,000 acres of this park cover the upper Chena Valley from bottom to ridgetops—and beyond—along approximately 30 miles of the winding, clearwater Chena River. To give a small indication of the park's size, it runs from mile 25.5 to mile 50.5 on the Chena Hot Springs Road.

Wildlife abounds here. Moose are frequently seen in beaver ponds and sloughs along the Hot Springs Road from mid-June through August. Small mammals such as beavers and hares are regularly seen and you may occasionally catch a glimpse of weasels, mink, muskrat, porcupine, and marten. Waterfowl and shorebirds can be spotted along the river and black bears are usually visitors to the river corridor during salmon migrations and can be seen eating their fill in the berry patches on the hillsides in August and September. Backcountry hikers in the alpine areas may even encounter grizzly bears.

Activities

There are three short nature trails, a mile or less each, that are easy walks. The three major developed trails in the park, however, are truly for hikers only. No gentle strolls here. Even the shortest, the 3½-mile Angel Rocks Trail, goes from 1,000-foot elevation to a high point of 1,750 feet and portions of the trail are steep and rocky. The reward here is a spectacular view of the Alaska Range and other distant landmarks. The Granite Tors Trail is not as steep an ascent, but it's a lot longer—a 15-mile loop to alpine meadows and equally impressive views. The longest trail is the Chena Dome Trail, which makes a 29-mile loop circling the entire Angel Creek drainage. The entire trail is a good three-day trip for backpackers, but hiking portions of the trail offers scenic out-and-back day hikes.

Bikes are allowed on most trails and there are also designated trails for horses, and trails and areas for all-terrain vehicles, off-road vehicles, and snowmachines.

The main road parallels the Chena River, offering many entry and exit points for canoeing or floating in the lower reaches of the river.

The Chena River is also one of the most popular fishing spots for arctic grayling, which are most abundant in July and August. Five small lakes near the main road are also stocked. Most fisherman do catch and release. Salmon migrate up the river in July and August, but they can't be fished.

Winter activities include snowmachining, trapping, cross-country skiing, and dog mushing. Two major dog mushing races use portions of the old Chena Hot Springs Trail.

Camping and Cabins

There are two developed **campgrounds:** Rosehip campgrounds, which is closest to the park entrance, has 38 sites; Tors Trail campground has 23 sites. Most sites are multiuse and will accommodate RVs up to 35 feet in length.

(Campsites $6.) Informal camping is permitted in many areas including on gravel bars along the river.

The four rustic **cabins** are scattered throughout the park. Only the North Folk cabin is close enough to the main road to be driven to year-round. The other three are each about six miles from the road and, depending on the season, can only be reached by all-terrain vehicles, dog team, snowmachine, skies, on foot, or, since all are on creeks, sometimes by boat. Normal backcountry hazards exist in the areas around these cabins, so they are only for the adventurous and it's required that at least one person in the party be experienced in backcountry travel. All cabins sleep at least four people. Reservations may be made up to 180 days in advance, for up to 3 consecutive nights at $25 per night. For information and reservations, write: State Park Cabins, 3700 Airport Way, Fairbanks, AK 99709 (tel. 907/451-2695.)

Groups (and individuals) may also rent 12 primitive cabins and other group facilities (dining hall and rec hall) at Twin Bears Camp, located near milepost 30 on the Chena Hot Springs Road. This camp is operated by a nonprofit association under an agreement with the parks division. For information contact Twin Bears Outdoor Education Association, Inc., P.O. Box 82953, Fairbanks, AK 99708 (tel. 907/451-2753.)

Nearby Attractions

If you continue up Chena Hot Springs Road to the east, you'll come to a couple of resorts with cabins, restaurants, bars, snowmobile rentals, dog-sled and sleigh rides, and other facilities for summer and winter activities.

Going west on Chena Hot Springs Road takes you to **Fairbanks,** Alaska's second-largest city. Here you can pan for gold (for a fee) at several commercial gold camps. Other places to visit include the **University of Alaska Museum** (tel. 907/474-7505) at the campus of the **University of Alaska–Fairbanks** (tel.

907/474-7211); the **Dog Mushers Museum** (tel. 907/456-6874); and **Alaskaland** (tel. 907/459-1087), a touristy amusement park. The riverboat *Discovery* (tel. 907/479-6673) offers a four-hour trip down the Chena River from mid-May to mid-September.

Chugach State Park

Visitor Center | Cabins & Cottages | RV Camping | Tent Camping | Primitive Camping | Group Camping | Fishing | Picnic Areas | Trails | Horse Trails | Nature Programs | Bicycling

X-Country Skiing | Downhill Skiing | Snow-mobiling | Gift Shop

Capsule Description: A huge wilderness park with some developed facilities.

Location: Southcentral Alaska, east of Anchorage, Alaska's largest city. Park headquarters at Mile 115 on Alaska Highway 1, also known as the Seward Scenic Byway.

Address: HC 52, Box 8999, Indian, AK 99540 (tel. 907/345-5014 for headquarters, 907/694-6391 for recorded information). Eagle River Visitor Center (tel. 907/694-2108).

Area Contacts: Anchorage Convention and Visitors Bureau, 546 West 4th Ave., Anchorage, AK 99501 (tel. 907/274-3531).

Alaska Public Lands Information Center 605 W. 4th Ave., Anchorage, AK 99501 (tel. 907/271-2737 or 907/258-7275 for recorded information).

Insider Tips: Finding a parking spot can be a problem at all parking areas during the summer months. In winter the snowmobile corridor, by Upper Huffman Trailhead, often has severe parking problems. Early arrival is the best solution.

Check with the park staff or the bulletin boards scattered throughout the park for the times to see the tidal bore, then get to your viewing point at least a half hour before you expect the bore to arrive.

Anchorage is a big city with a population of around 240,000—almost half of Alaska's population—and having all the urban amenities. But you only have to go a little way past the city limits to realize that all but a minuscule portion of this huge state is still frontier country. Chugach State Park, on the outskirts of Anchorage, captures an easily accessible microcosm of this wilderness.

Chugach's 495,000 acres—making it one of America's largest state parks—offer breathtaking scenery that ranges from coastal forests and rushing streams to rugged mountains and high-alpine glaciers. One of the natural phenomena in the park is the bore tide in Turnagain Arm where a virtual wall of water, up to six feet high, races up the channel as the tide comes in.

Golden eagles, waterfowl, Dall sheep, and moose are frequently sighted. More elusive but still common to spot are mountain goats, wolves, and brown and grizzly bears. And from the shoreline, during salmon spawning season, it's not unusual to see whales.

Activities

A day-use fee of $2 is charged to enter the developed areas of the park. The park headquarters is found in the Potter Section House, a historic building that was once part of a railroad crew camp and now houses a railroad museum. The Eagle River Visitor Center, located at Mile 12, Eagle River Road, has interpretive displays on the park's history and natural history. Rangers give interpretive programs and conduct walks during the summer. Outside is the Rodak Nature Trail, a self-guided, ⅔-mile trail designed to be an easy walk and a nature trail for the handicapped.

Two other hiking trails start here. The Albert Loop Trail is a three-mile hike on easy grades that takes you through the forest to the Eagle River. For the heartier hiker, the historic Iditarod/Crow Pass trail (26 miles) heads into the backcountry and through the heart of the park on a historic transportation and mail route between the villages of Portage and Knik.

The Turnagain Arm Trail, the main trail from the Potter Section House, parallels the coastline and Seward Highway for a little over nine miles. An easy trail, it offers scenic overlooks of the Chugach and Kenai mountains. Beluga Point is about five miles out on this trail. In July and August, this is a favorite spot to watch for beluga whales when these small, shallow-water whales routinely come into Cook Inlet.

Beluga Point is also one of the better places to see the daily bore tides in Turnagain Arm. A bore tide is created when an inrush of water advances upstream through a narrow, shallow channel with a wave-like front. These occur when there is a wide range between high and low tides—in this case, more than 35 feet in Cook Inlet. Turnagain Arm and nearby (about 5 miles north) Knik Arm are the only locations in the United States where tidal bores occur on a regular basis. These are not huge bores—the world's biggest go as high as 26 feet and can reach speeds of 24 miles per hour—but even these comparatively small bores can be a sight to behold. Depending on tidal conditions—extreme tides are usually best during new- or full-moon periods—they range from just one-half foot up to six feet in height and travel at 10 to 15 m.p.h.

Five designated trails start near Eklutna Lake. Most are rated easy to moderate and range from about four miles up to about 14 miles. The longest one leads to the Eklutna Glacier.

A number of trails throughout the park are open for horseback riding and mountain bikes. Horses and mountain bikes can be rented in Anchorage, Eagle River, and Eklutna. Designated trails are open for all-terrain vehicles, but days and times are more restrictive.

Eklutna Lake is open to all watercraft; however, there are no boat ramps for trailers. Small boats, inflatable rafts, and kayaks and canoes are recommended. Rafters and kayakers can try the Class II white water on the Eagle River. Anglers will find both the lake and the river excellent places to put in a line. The main catches are salmon, trout, and verden.

Come winter, the park offers a number of places for both cross-country and downhill skiing, ski touring, snowshoeing, dog mushing, and snowmobiling. The main downhill ski area is at Arctic Valley where the Anchorage Ski Club leases land from the park. There are chair, poma, T-bar, and rope-tow lifts here. The club lodge provides food services, but no overnight accommodations.

Camping and Cabins

There are 125 **campsites** in the three developed campgrounds in the park: 50 sites each at Eklutna Lake and Eagle River campgrounds and 25 at Bird Creek. All are multiuse sites with water hookups. Site fees are $10 or $12 per night depending on campground. Each campground also has a different limit on the maximum number of consecutive nights you can stay. The most popular is the Eagle River campground, which has a four-night limit; Bird Creek is seven days, and Eklutna is 15.

At the time this guidebook went to press, there was one rustic **cabin** for rent in the backcountry near Eklutna Lake, but others were under construction. For information and reservations call 907/762-2261. Rent is $25 per night.

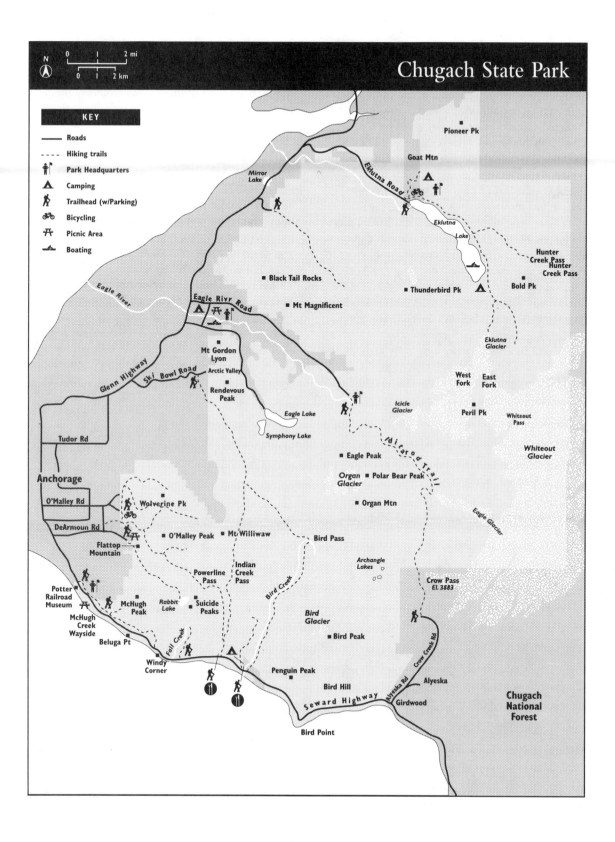

Chugach State Park

KEY

— Roads
- - - Hiking trails
Park Headquarters
Camping
Trailhead (w/Parking)
Bicycling
Picnic Area
Boating

0   1   2 mi
0   1   2 km

Pioneer Pk

Goat Mtn

Eklutna Road

Mirror Lake

Eklutna Lake

Hunter Creek Pass
Hunter Creek Pass

Black Tail Rocks

Thunderbird Pk

Bold Pk

Eagle River

Eagle Rivr Road

Mt Magnificent

Eklutna Glacier

Mt Gordon Lyon

Arctic Valley

West Fork   East Fork

Glenn Highway

Ski Bowl Road

Rendevous Peak

Eagle Lake

Icicle Glacier

Peril Pk

Whiteout Pass

Symphony Lake

Eagle Peak

Iditarod Trail

Whiteout Glacier

Tudor Rd

Organ Glacier   Polar Bear Peak

Anchorage

O'Malley Rd

Wolverine Pk

Organ Mtn

Eagle Glacier

DeArmoun Rd

O'Malley Peak   Mt Williwaw

Bird Pass

Flattop Mountain

Archangle Lakes

Crow Pass
El. 3883

Powerline Pass

Indian Creek Pass

Potter Railroad Museum

McHugh Peak

Rabbit Lake

Suicide Peaks

Bird Creek

Bird Glacier

McHugh Creek Wayside

Beluga Pt

Fall Creek

Bird Peak

Crow Creek Rd

Windy Corner

Penguin Peak

Alyeska Rd

Alyeska

Seward Highway

Bird Hill

Girdwood

Chugach National Forest

Bird Point

Nearby Attractions

Continuing east and south on the Seward Scenic Byway (Alaska Highway 1) will take you to nearby **Chugach National Forest** (tel. 907/271-2500) and the **Portage Glacier Recreation Area,** which gets its name from one of the five glaciers in Portage Valley. You can do it on your own, of course, but the easiest and best way to see the glaciers is on a guided tour offered at the Visitor Center (tel. 907/783-2326). Beautiful as these glaciers are, they are not the most impressive glaciers in Alaska. Still, because of their proximity to Anchorage and the fact that you can drive up to them on good roads, Portage Glacier and its sisters are often listed as Alaska's number-one tourist attraction.

Although most visitors are lured to the state by its natural beauty, **Anchorage** itself does pretty well in being a tourist attraction. Just down Highway 1 to the west of the park, it offers all the lures of a big city from restaurants to entertainment. Among its attractions are **Imaginarium** (tel. 907/276-3179), a hands-on science museum; the **Anchorage Museum of History and Art** (tel. 907/343-4326); and the **Alaska Zoo** (tel. 907/346-3242). There's nothing marvelous to see at **Earthquake Park**—just sunken land—but it does give you a sense of nature's dark side; it's a memorial to the disastrous big shake of 1964 that registered on the Richter scale as the strongest ever recorded in North America.

About five hours' drive north of Anchorage is **Denali National Park and Preserve** (tel. 907/683-2294). Reigning over this six-million-acre park is 20,320-foot Mt. McKinley, the highest mountain in North America.

Arizona

LAKE HAVASU AND
CATTAIL COVE STATE PARKS

Arizona has 25 state parks.

Contacts

- Arizona State Parks, 1300 W. Washington Ave., Suite 415, Phoenix, AZ 85007 (tel. 602/ 542-4174).
- Arizona Office of Tourism, 1100 W. Washington Ave., Phoenix, AZ 85007 (tel. 602/542-8687).

General Information on Arizona State Parks

Not many states have a prison as a state park, but Arizona does: Yuma Territorial Prison State Historic Park. Much of the Grand Canyon State is desert, so you would expect most of the parks to be desert parks. But Arizonians believe in making the most of their water resources, so the majority of the parks are built on lakes and reservoirs.

GENERAL FEES

Day-use admission to recreational parks is $5 April to September, $3 rest of year.

CAMPING

Camping in state-operated parks is on a first-come basis; no reservations. (Reservations are accepted by the concession operating the marina and RV park at Cattail Cove. See Lake Havasu State Park, below.) Base rate, depending on campsite, ranges from $5 to $12 for up to six persons and two vehicles.

Pets. Pets must be on a leash. They are not permitted in buildings, ramadas, or on developed swimming beaches.

Alcoholic beverages. Permitted in parks. No glass containers permitted on public beaches or swim areas.

Lake Havasu and Cattail Cove State Parks

Visitor Center   Restaurant   RV Camping   Tent Camping   Primitive Camping   Group Camping   Marina   Boating

Boat Launch   Fishing   Beach   Waterskiing   Picnic Areas   Trails

Capsule Description: A natural park on a lake with some developed facilities.

Location: Western Arizona, vicinity of Lake Havasu City on Arizona Highway 95 on the border with California. From I-40 take Arizona Highway 95 (Exit 9) south approximately 20 miles. From I-10, take Arizona Highway 95 (Exit 17) north approximately 85 miles.

Address: 1801 Hwy. 95, Lake Havasu City, AZ 86406 (tel. 602/855-7851). Cattail Cove P.O. Box 1990, Lake Havasu City, AZ 86405 (tel. 602/855-1223).

Area Contacts: Lake Havasu Area Visitor and Convention Bureau, 1930 Mesquite Ave., Suite 3, Lake Havasu City, AZ 86403 (tel. toll free 800/242-8278 or 602/453-3444).

Insider Tip: If you're looking for quiet camping, rent a boat in town and try one of the park's boat-in campsites.

Together, these two adjoining parks sit on more than 13,000 acres of parkland covering close to 15 shorefront miles of the 45-mile-long lake. However, only about 380 acres are developed.

On the northern end, near Lake Havasu City, Lake Havasu State Park has both a beach unit with campsites that can be reached by road and, farther down the lake, a number of campsites that can be reached only from the water.

About 15 miles south (from Highway 95, take Spur 95 at Milepost 168) is the 40-acre state park at Cattail Cove, which offer campsites, a swimming beach, boat launch, and a courtesy dock. A con-

cession operates additional campsites, a marina, and restaurant here.

Activities

In the undeveloped areas, including some of the boat-in campsites, you might expect to see both bighorn sheep and wild burros.

Aside from the camping, picnicking, and campfire programs in the winter season, the main activities in the developed areas of these parks are all tied to the lake. Swimming, boating, waterskiing, fishing—if it's a water sport you can probably do it here. And if you don't bring the essentials with you, you can rent just about everything you need in Lake Havasu City to make the most of these activities.

More than a million visitors come here each year, so the city is geared to tourism. An illustration of just how important tourism is to the area is the presence of London Bridge. When the British discovered that there was truth to the children's rhyme that "London Bridge is falling down," their government put the bridge up for sale. Robert McCulloch, founder of Lake Havasu City, decided this would be a unique attraction for his city, so he bought the bridge for $2,460,000. It was taken apart, each stone coded to indicate its position, shipped to Lake Havasu, and reassembled. Reconstruction was accomplished using a method traced back to the way the Egyptians built the pyramids. Sand mounds beneath each arch were formed to the profile of the original bridge arches, serving the same function as molds. When the work was completed, the sand was removed. A one-mile channel was dredged under the bridge and water was diverted from the lake to make an island for the bridge to serve.

There are five golf courses in the city, tennis and racquetball courts, restaurants, and a wide range of motels and resorts. A number of international tournaments and a variety of festivals are scheduled here, especially during the cooler desert months of September through May.

Camping

The **Windsor Beach unit** of Lake Havasu State Park, located north of London Bridge, is primarily a day-use area, but it does have 32 rustic multiuse **campsites** without hookups. Swimming is permitted (no lifeguards). A portion of the lakeside walking path is marked as a self-guided nature trail. Windsor Beach also features a Cactus Garden, two picnic areas, two boat-launching ramps with a total of 12 lanes, and a group campsite.

The rest of Lake Havasu's camping facilities are all boat-in; scattered along the shoreline are 225 that can be reached only by boat. Facilities vary, but most sites have vault toilets, shaded picnic tables, and fire pits.

Cattail Cove State Park has 40 multiuse campsites with electric and water hookups. There's a swimming beach (no lifeguards), a courtesy dock for boaters, and a boat launch. Part of

the park, operated as a concession, is the Sandpoint Marina and RV Park (tel. 602/855-0549), which offers additional and slightly more plush facilities at a higher rate. The 175 multiuse campsites with three-way hookups can be reserved ($22.50 per night). As the name states, this is also a full-service marina where you can rent everything from fishing boats to houseboats. It has boat slips, tackle shop, restaurant, and grocery store. The hiking trail in the park runs about three miles.

Nearby Attractions

Immediately to the north of the park is the 40,000-acre **Havasu National Wildlife Refuge** (tel. 619/326-3853). Huge flocks of snow geese and Canada geese join the tourists wintering here. Another unit of Havasu Refuge is south of Cattail Cove. To the east of the park, about an hour's drive on old U.S. Highway 66, is **Oatman** (tel. 602/754-4121), a resurrected ghost town. Just across the Colorado River from Bullhead City—an hour's drive—is **Laughlin, Nevada;** this glitter and glitz town has close to a dozen gambling casinos.

To the south of the park, forming the lake, is **Parker Dam** (tel. 602/667-4310), which can be visited on a self-guided tour. Near the dam is **Buckskin Mountain State Park** (tel. 602/667-3231) on the Colorado River. Water sports reign here, too. The two units of this park have a total of 116 multiuse campsites.

Arkansas

PETIT JEAN
STATE PARK

DEGRAY LAKE RESORT
STATE PARK

Arkansas has 48 state parks.

(By an 1881 General Assembly resolution, the state's name is officially pronounced *Ark*-an-saw.)

Contacts

- Arkansas Department of Parks & Tourism, One Capitol Mall, Little Rock, AR 72201. Division of State Parks (tel. 501/682-1191). Division of Tourism (tel. toll free 800/628-8725 or 501/682-7777).

General Information on Arkansas State Parks

The Arkansas parks offer a wide variety of choices: mountaintop hideaways with cloud-capped lodges, lakeshore cabins with cozy fireplaces, more than 1,600 campsites including some on the famed White River, an island retreat with resort amenities, a museum village re-creating life in frontier Arkansas, a diamond mine where you can keep the gems you find, a folk cultural complex in the Ozarks—all there for you to experience and enjoy.

GENERAL FEES

There is no extra entrance fee if you use park campsites, lodges, cabins, and golf facilities. For day use, however, 31 of the 48 parks have a fee of $2 to $4 per vehicle depending on vehicle size and number of passengers.

CAMPING AND ACCOMMODATIONS

Reservations are taken by individual parks. Reser-

vations for the period April through October are accepted beginning January 1 of the same year.

Lodge rates for a double range from $35 to $80 per night. Each additional person in the room is $5. Most resort parks offer package plans. **Cabin** rates range from $40 to $65 per night for two persons plus $5 a night for each additional person.

Most **campsites** are on a first-come basis; however, some are available by reservation from April through October by phone or visit to the park visitor center. Camping reservations for a site for two to six consecutive nights must be made within 30 days prior to scheduled arrival date. Reservations for seven to 14 consecutive nights will be accepted beginning January 15 of the same year. Base rate, depending on campsite facilities, ranges from $6.50 to $14.50 per night. Rates are cut in half in most parks in December, January, and February.

Lodge rooms, cabins, and campsites are all limited to one 14-day stay within a 30-day period.

Pets. Pets are welcome, but must be kept on a leash, caged, or otherwise restrained to both avoid disturbing visitors and protect the pets. Pets are *not permitted* in cabins or lodge rooms.

Alcoholic beverages. Park rules on public display and consumption vary by township.

Discounts. Camping discounts are available for U.S. citizens age 65 and over and U.S. citizens permanently and totally disabled.

DeGray Lake Resort State Park

Lodge/Hotel • Restaurant • RV Camping • Tent Camping • Marina • Boating • Boat Launch • Fishing • Swimming • Beach • Picnic Areas • Golf

Trails • Nature Programs • Bicycling • Gift Shop

Capsule Description: A resort park on a lake.

Location: Southwestern Arkansas. Take I-30 to Exit 78 (Caddo Valley/Arkadelphia), then Scenic Highway 7 north about six miles. From Hot Springs, take Scenic Highway 7 south approximately 21 miles.

Address: Route 3, Box 490, Bismarck, AR 71929-8194. Visitor Center and Camping (tel. 501/865-2801). Lodge (tel. toll free 800/737-8355 or 501/865-2851).

Area Contacts: Arkadelphia Chamber of Commerce, P.O. Box 38, Arkadelphia, AR 71923-0038 (tel. 501/246-5542).

Arkansas River Valley/Scenic Highway 7, c/o Dardanelle Chamber of Commerce, P.O. Box 208, Dardanelle, AR 72834 (tel. 501/229-3328).

City of Hope Chamber of Commerce, P.O. Box 667, Hope, AR 71802 (tel. 501/777-6701).

Hot Springs Convention and Visitors Bureau, P.O. Box K, Hot Springs, AR 71902 (tel. toll free 800/772-2489).

Insider Tips: The resort has earned a listing in *Better Homes and Gardens* magazine as one of America's 30 Favorite Family Vacation Resorts. Each January, the park offers a special three-day program on eagles.

On the north shore of DeGray Lake, Arkansas's premier resort park abounds with recreational opportunities at its lodge, which is surrounded by a forest of shortleaf pine, hickory, and oak. The park boasts an 18-hole championship golf course. De-Gray Lake Resort Park makes an excellent base for day trips to the famed city of Hot Springs and its national park as well as President Clinton's hometown of Hope.

Activities

Park interpreters provide nature programs all year long. On a guided walk, you may spot white-tailed deer, quail, snowy egrets, loons, and even an eagle—about three dozen bald eagles routinely winter here, arriving in late October and staying until early March.

Each January, the park offers a special three-day program called "Eagles Et Cetera," with educational programs about eagles featuring speakers and videos; owl prowls at night; boat trips on the lake to see eagles in flight, hunting, or sitting and preening; and other guided bird walks. The Bird Garden, behind the Visitors Center, is planted with holly and pyrocanthos and has feeders to attract cardinals, sparrows, wrens, and juncos.

The lodge has a swimming pool, and two swimming beaches are found on the lake. No lifeguards are posted at any swimming area.

The five trails in the park are all leisurely walking trails rather than hiking trails; they range from ¼ mile to a mile. Bikes may be rented at the lodge and ridden on all hard-surface roads, but there are no designated bike trails.

Year round park interpreters offer an array of barge trips on the lake from sunset tours to wild-flower tours in spring to a lake history trip. For romantics and others, a Full Moon Cruise is run on the appropriate night each month from April through October; reservations can be made at the marina 24 hours in advance (see below).

The full-service marina (tel. 501/865-2811) is the place to rent all types of boats including a fishing boat with motor, a 16-foot Hobie Cat or a Sunfish, a canoe, or a paddleboat. If those aren't big enough, there's also a houseboat that sleeps six and pontoon fishing party barges for 10 for rent. Smaller? How about jet skis or tube skis. There are no ski boats here, but they are available for rent at private marinas on the lake. If you bring your own boat, rental slips are available at the marina on a first-come basis.

Fishing gear can also be rented at the marina. The lake yields several species of bass including fighting hybrids, as well as bream, crappie, and channel, blue, and flathead catfish.

The terrain of the 6,900-yard championship golf course offers a variety of challenges as the front nine holes are in the open while the back nine wind through a pine and hardwood forest. Golfers can practice their shots at a driving range and putting green. A pro shop rents clubs. Golf package plans are available through the Lodge.

Camping and Accommodations

The **lodge** sits on an island in the lake and is reached by a causeway. Many of the 96 rooms in the three-story building face the lake. Each room is equipped with all the amenities of a modern hotel including TV and phone. No-smoking rooms are available as are two rooms for the handicapped. The full-service restaurant has a view of the lake and the wooded foothills of Ouachita Mountain. This is a dry area, so no public display of alcoholic beverages is allowed. The swimming pool is located lakeside near the lodge. (Lake-view rooms $70 double, woods-view rooms $60 double.)

There are 113 RV **campsites** with tables, grills, water and electric hookups. All are tree-shaded and many have a lake view. For golfers, there are also sites near the golf course. Sixty of these sites have pads that can be used for tent camping. Some sites may be reserved, for a minimum of two nights, but the majority are on a first-come basis. The park store, at the marina, carries the usual stock of camping supplies and firewood, and has a coin laundry. (Campsites $12.50 to $14.50.)

Nearby Attractions

The U.S. Army Corps of Engineers operates more than a dozen small parks around the lake offering camping and picnic sites. To the southeast of De-Gray Lake, **Arkadelphia,** the nearest city, is home of Henderson State University and Ouachita Baptist University—their campuses separated only by a street and a ravine.

Interested in a diamond in the rough? You may find one at **Crater of the Diamonds State Park** (tel. 501/285-3113). Southwest of DeGray Lake, near Murfreesboro, this is the only diamond site in North America where the public may prospect and keep the gems they find in a designated 35-acre field. Prospectors can bring their own tools, or these can be rented or bought at the gift shop. A small daily mining fee is charged. Diamonds were first discovered here in 1906, and since then more than 70,000 have been dug up (17,000 since Crater became a park in 1972). Amethyst, garnet, jasper, agate, quartz, and other precious and semiprecious stones are also found here. This park has 60 campsites with bathhouses and water and electric hookups.

President Bill Clinton's birthplace in **Hope,** a small city long famed for its huge watermelons, is also to the southwest of DeGray Lake, just off I-30.

Lake Catherine State Park (tel. 501/844-4176) to the northwest, and just a stone's throw from Hot Springs, offers 17 lakeside cabins and 70 campsites, and a marina with rental boats.

Probably the biggest attraction in the area is **Hot Springs National Park** (tel. 501/624-3383), America's only national park located in a city. The thermal waters of the springs were a traditional stopping place for several Indian tribes who bathed here and named the area "Valley of the Vapors." On **Bathhouse Row,** at the historic **Buckstaff Bathhouse** (tel. 501/623-2308), you can take a bath in thermal waters and get a massage. Accommodations in the city of Hot Springs range from grand old hotels to bed-and-breakfast inns. The city's attractions are just as varied, including: **Oaklawn Park** (tel. 501/623-4411), a Thoroughbred racetrack with a sea-son that runs from January through April; miles of scenic drives and hiking trails; the downtown area's **Mountain Tower** (501/623-6035), with an elevator that takes you to the top at 216 feet for a scenic view; **Magic Springs** (tel. 501/624-5411), a family theme park; and Arkansas's largest aquarium, the **National Park Aquarium** (tel. 501/624-3474).

Petit Jean State Park

Visitor Center — Lodge/Hotel — Restaurant — Cabins & Cottages — RV Camping — Tent Camping — Group Camping — Boating — Boat Launch — Fishing — Swimming — Picnic Areas

Tennis — Trails — Nature Programs — Playground — Gift Shop

Capsule Description: Nature park on mountaintop with developed facilities.

Location: Western Arkansas, about 60 miles north-west of Little Rock on Petit Jean Mountain. Coming from the east on I-40, take Exit 108 (Morrilton) to Highway 9. Go south 9 miles to Oppelo, then west 12 miles on Highway 154 to the park. Coming from the west, take Exit 81 (Russellville) to Scenic Highway 7. Go south on Highway 7 to Centerville, then east 16 miles on Highway 154 to the park.

Address: Route 3, Box 340, Morrilton, AR 72110. Park office (tel. 501/727-5441). Lodge and cabin reservations (tel. toll free 800/264-2462 or 501/727-5431).

Area Contacts: Little Rock Convention and Visitors Bureau, P.O. Box 3232, Little Rock, AR 72203 (tel. toll free 800/844-4781 or 501/376-4781).

Morrilton Chamber of Commerce, 118 N. Moose, Morrilton, AR 72110-0589 (tel. 501/354-2393).

Russellville Chamber of Commerce, 708 W. Main St., Russellville, AR 72801 (tel. 501/968-2530).

Insider Tips: The last few miles of Hwy. 154 leading to the park from both directions carry signs that the road is "crooked and steep." In this case, believe what you read, and use your car's climbing gear—especially on the road coming in from the west.

Three days in April and three in October are set aside for special programs for seniors.

In the 16th century, a young Parisienne girl disguised herself as a boy and called herself Jean so that she could sail with her fiancé, a nobleman named Chavet, and his exploring party to America. During the Atlantic voyage, Petit Jean served as a cabin boy. The party landed in this part of Arkansas and hunted and fished with the Native Americans. All the while, Petit Jean's identity was concealed—even from her beloved, who had forbidden her request to accompany him out of fear for her safety—until she became deathly ill with a fever. During her delirium, she confessed her deception to Chavet and asked for his forgiveness. The legend says that her final request was to be buried on the mountain that's now named for her, not far from the park, so that her grave would overlook the Arkansas River.

The beauty of Petit Jean Mountain inspired the people of Arkansas to set up a state parks system in 1923. At an elevation of 1,100 feet above the Arkansas River Valley, this 3,471-acre park was the state's first. It was built by the Civilian Conservation Corps in the 1930s; the CCC's handiwork has stood the years well and can can be seen in dozens of places around the park. Today much of the wooded acres remain unspoiled, probably looking much as they did when Petit Jean saw them 400 years ago. In the pine and hardwood forests, hikers may pass deer, wild turkeys, and gray fox. Occasionally, during winter, bald eagles are sighted; they usually winter in the nearby **Holla Bend National Wildlife Refuge** (tel. 501/229-4300).

Activities

With more than 20 miles of interconnected trails, this is a hiker's park. The shortest is the Cedar Creek Self-Guiding Trail, which is about 1½ miles long. Most of this trail is little more than a walk, but in a few places rock steps and some inclines make it a little more arduous. The other trails are for hikers who are in good physical condition. Along with Cedar Creek Trail, two others are designated as National Recreation Hiking Trails—Cedar Falls, a little over two miles, including a view of the waterfall that cascades more than 90 feet to the canyon floor; and Seven Hollows, which is about 3½ miles long. The longest is the Boy Scout Trail, which covers around 13 miles.

Lake Bailey (120 acres) and Lake Roosevelt (40 acres) are stocked annually, and fishermen can expect to catch largemouth and smallmouth bass, white and black crappie, bluegill bream, and catfish. The park operates a boat house on Lake Bailey from Memorial Day to Labor Day. Flat-bottomed John boats with electric trolling motors

and paddleboats can be rented. Boats on the lakes are limited to 10 horsepower.

Swimming is not permitted in the lakes, but a public pool near the camping area is open Memorial Day to Labor Day (a small admission is charged). Tennis buffs can play on two courts by the pool (no charge).

Camping and Accommodations

The CCC built the rustic log and stone **Mather Lodge** on a bluff that offers a panoramic view of the river valley. Its 24 rooms all have TV but no phones. The lodge complex includes a gift shop, swimming pool (open seasonally for lodge and cabin guests only), and a full-service restaurant that's open seven days March through November from 7am to 8pm. December to February it is only open Wednesday to Sunday from 11am to 6pm. This is a dry township so there's no public display of alcohol. (Double $35 to $40.)

In the woods nearby are 32 **cabins**. Twenty of these are housekeeping cabins with kitchens, heat, and air conditioning. Nine are rustic-style CCC cabins with huge stone fireplaces. The other 11 are modern duplex cabins. These also have fireplaces, although not as impressive, plus a screened porch. Each sleeps up to six persons. Four of these cabins are handicapped-accessible. There are also 12 cabins called "Overnighters" without kitchens, half with fireplaces. Each of these sleeps up to four persons. (Housekeeping cabins $70 to $95 double, Overnighters $45 double.)

There are 127 multiuse **campsites** (38 are pull-through) with water and electric hookups. Only 24 sites may be reserved from April through October. All others are on a first-come basis. There is also a 50-unit rally-style camping area available for camping clubs, and a group tent camping area that can be reserved from April through October. For those who don't own camping equipment, there's are two Rent-A-Camp packages available during the same period. Each of these includes a tent, cots, stove, and other essential camping gear.

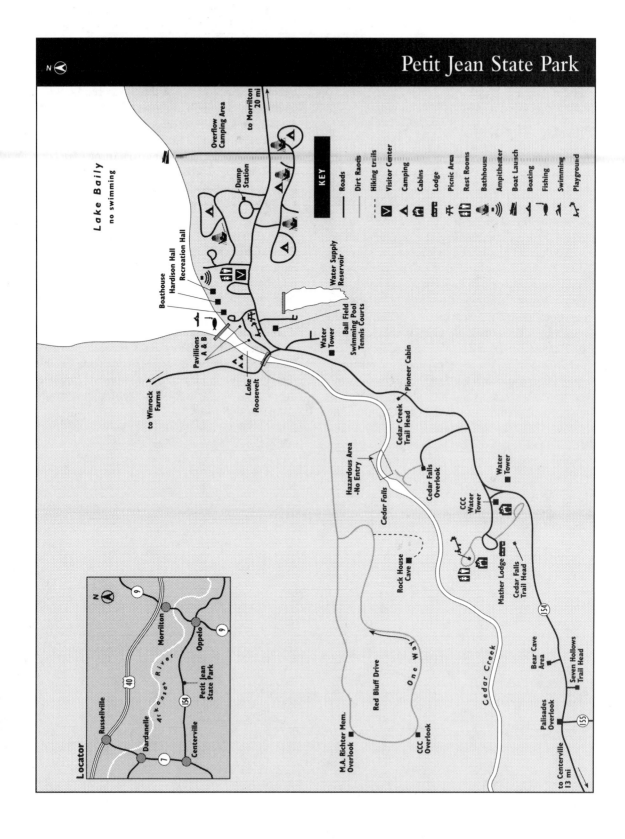

Petit Jean State Park

N

Lake Baily
no swimming

Overflow Camping Area

to Morrilton 20 mi

Dump Station

Boathouse
Hardison Hall
Recreation Hall

Pavillions A & B

Lake Roosevelt

to Winrock Farms

Water Supply Reservoir

Water Tower

Ball Field
Swimming Pool
Tennis Courts

Pioneer Cabin

Cedar Creek Trail Head

Cedar Falls Overlook

Hazardous Area -No Entry

Cedar Falls

CCC Water Tower

Water Tower

Rock House Cave

Mather Lodge

Cedar Falls Trail Head

Red Bluff Drive

One Way

M.A. Richter Mem. Overlook

CCC Overlook

Cedar Creek

Bear Cave Area

Seven Hollows Trail Head

Palisades Overlook

to Centerville 13 mi

154

155

KEY

Roads	
Dirt Roads	
Hiking trails	
V	Visitor Center
⛺	Camping
	Cabins
	Lodge
	Picnic Area
	Rest Rooms
	Bathhouse
	Ampitheater
	Boat Launch
	Boating
	Fishing
	Swimming
	Playground

Locator

N

Russellville

Dardanelle

Morrilton

Oppelo

Centerville

Arkansas River

Petit Jean State Park

40

7

9

9

154

154

(Campsites $12.50 to $14.50, Rent-A-Camp $25 per day plus deposit.)

Nearby Attractions

A half mile before the entrance to Petit Jean State Park on Highway 154 is the **Museum of Automobiles** (501/727-5427). Founded by Governor Winthrop Rockefeller, the museum displays President Clinton's 1967 acqua Ford Mustang and a 1914 Cretor's Popcorn Wagon along with other antique cars. The museum is one of the sponsors of an Annual Auto Fair on the third weekend in June. Six miles north of the park are the headquarters of **Winrock International** (501/727-5435), a nonprofit organization that helps third-world countries; it has a museum with a small section on the Rockefeller family.

Little Rock, the state capital, is a relatively short excursion down I-40 to the southeast from the park. Arkansas's Capitol building is a three-quarter-scale replica of the nation's Capitol. The **Territorial Restoration** (501/324-9351) offers a one-hour guided tour of three restored houses, a tavern, and a print shop from the period 1819 to 1860. The **Old State House** (501/324-9685) is a history museum with a Clinton exhibit that shows the Oval Office. The **Arkansas Museum of Science and History** (501/324-9231) is the birthplace of General Douglas MacArthur. The **Children's Museum of Arkansas** (501/753-8600) offers kids a bubble table, face painting, and a farmer's market where they can shop. **Wild River Country** (501/753-8600) is a water-theme park with slides. The **Little Rock Zoo** (501/666-2406) is noted for its "Great Ape Display" with silver-back gorillas, orangutans, and chimpanzees.

Northwest of the park in Russellville is the **Arkansas River Valley Arts Center** (tel. 501/968-2452) with two galleries of changing exhibits displaying the work of both nationally recognized artists and local artisans. The center also features community theater.

California

HUMBOLDT REDWOODS
STATE PARK

CALAVERAS BIG TREES
STATE PARK

PFEIFFER BIG SUR
STATE PARK

ANZA-BORREGO DESERT
STATE PARK

California has 275 state parks.

Contacts

• California Department of Parks & Recreation,
P.O. Box 942896, Sacramento, CA 94296-0001
(tel. 916/653-6995; toll free 800/444-PARK
[444-7275] for camping reservations).
• California Office of Tourism, P.O. Box 1499,
Dept. 02, Sacramento, CA 95812-1499 (tel. toll
free 800/862-2543).

General Information on California State Parks

What might be considered California's first "state
park" came into being in 1864 when Abraham
Lincoln approved the Yosemite Grant that gave
the land to California to preserve. It was the first
time in our history that the government set aside
land to be protected. Yosemite became a national
park in 1890; then a little more than 10 years
later, the state of California acquired 2,500 acres
near Santa Cruz and created Big Basin Redwoods
State Park, now the oldest existing state park in
the state.

GENERAL FEES
Day-use entrance fees vary from $2 to $6 depending on the facilities provided and level of service.
Annual passes covering entrance to most parks are
for sale.

Camping and Accommodations

The state park system has more than 14,000
campsites. Reservations are made through the
MISTIX reservation system—toll free 800/444-
PARK (444-7275) from 8am to 5pm PST daily
except Thanksgiving, Christmas, and New Year's
Day. Periods when campsites may be reserved vary
from park to park. In some parks, like Anza Borrego Desert State Park, campsites may be reserved
all year. Others only take reservations during the
peak summer season. During "nonreservation"
periods, campsites are on a first-come basis.

Camping reservations may be made up to eight
weeks (actually 56 days) in advance of your planned
arrival date. All reservations must be paid for in
advance. MISTIX will accept most major credit
cards for phone reservations. If you use a check or
money order, it must arrive at MISTIX within
seven days of your reservation call. Mail-in reservations may be sent to MISTIX, P.O. Box 85705, San
Diego, CA 92186-5707. Applications received up
to one week before the eight-week advance reservation period will be held and processed on the
56th day. However, an application received more
than nine weeks in advance will be returned to you.

Campsite fees range from $8 to $25 per night,
depending on location and season, with the average site costing about $14 to $16 in high season.
This usually covers up to eight persons and one
vehicle. An extra vehicle costs $5 to $6. There is

also a nonrefundable reservation fee of $6.75 per campsite.

Only one park has a **lodge**—The Big Sur Lodge at Pfeiffer Big Sur State Park. For details, see that park's listing that follows.

Pets. You may bring your pet to most parks, but it must be kept on a leash or in a vehicle. Pets are not allowed in most buildings, on trails, or most beaches. A $1 per night fee is charged for each dog, except guide dogs.

Alcoholic beverages. Permitted in parks.

Discounts. A Golden Bear Pass is available for anyone 62 years of age or older with a limited

income. A Limited Use Golden Bear Pass covering day-use entry to most parks in off-season is available to anyone aged 62 or older. Full passes are available for disabled veterans. Discount passes are available for permanently disabled persons. For details on these, contact the Office of Public Relations at the Department of Parks and Recreation.

A senior citizen, 62 or older, may also receive a $2 per night campsite fee discount, but only if requested when making a reservation on a campsite paid for and occupied by the senior citizen.

Anza-Borrego Desert State Park

| Visitor Center | RV Camping | Tent Camping | Primitive Camping | Group Camping | Picnic Areas | Horse Trails | Nature Programs | Bicycling | Gift Shop |

Capsule Description: A huge desert park with some developed facilities.

Location: Southern California. As its name states, this park is located in the desert about 90 miles northeast of San Diego or 150 miles southwest of Los Angeles between I-10 and I-8. From I-10, take California Highway 86 (near Coachella) south to S22 (just north of Salton City), then west to the Visitors Center. From I-8, take California Highway 86 (near El Centro) north to S22 then west to the Visitors Center or take S2 (near Ocotillo) north to S22, then east to the Visitors Center.

Address: Box 299, Borrego Springs, CA 92004 (tel. 619/767-5311).

Area Contacts: Borrego Springs Chamber of Commerce, P.O. Box 66, Borrego Springs, CA 92004 (tel. 619/767-5555).

California Desert Tourism Association, P.O. Box 364, Rancho Mirage, CA 92270 (tel. 619/328-9256).

Julian Chamber of Commerce, P.O. Box 413, Julian, CA 92036 (tel. 619/765-1857).

California's largest park, Anza-Borrego illustrates how much of Southern California looked before water was brought in by irrigation. The founding of this desert park in the early 1930s predates the better known Joshua Tree and Death Valley national monuments. Its grand landscapes vary from eroded badlands near sea-level elevation to a woodland mantle on 6,000-foot-high mountains. It lays claim to being the largest state park in the lower 48 states.

Captain Juan Bautista de Anza, a Spanish soldier, led an expedition through this area in 1775; hence the first part of park's name. "Borrego" refers to the rare species of bighorn sheep, *borrego cimarrón*. More commonly called the peninsular

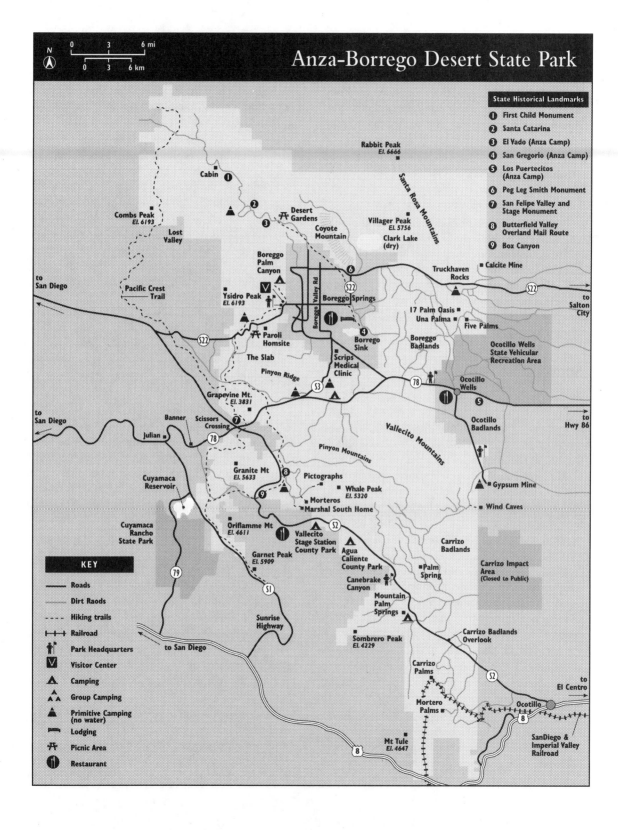

Anza-Borrego Desert State Park

N

0 3 6 mi
0 3 6 km

State Historical Landmarks

1 First Child Monument
2 Santa Catarina
3 El Vado (Anza Camp)
4 San Gregorio (Anza Camp)
5 Los Puertecitos (Anza Camp)
6 Peg Leg Smith Monument
7 San Felipe Valley and Stage Monument
8 Butterfield Valley Overland Mail Route
9 Box Canyon

Rabbit Peak
El. 6666

Cabin 1

Combs Peak
El. 6193

Lost Valley

Santa Rosa Mountains

Desert Gardens

Coyote Mountain

Villager Peak
El. 5756

Clark Lake (dry)

Calcite Mine

Truckhaven Rocks

to San Diego

Pacific Crest Trail

Boreggo Palm Canyon

Ysidro Peak
El. 6193

Boreggo Valley Rd

Boreggo Springs

S22

17 Palm Oasis
Una Palma

Five Palms

to Salton City

S22

S22

Paroli Homsite

The Slab

Pinyon Ridge

Borrego Sink

Boreggo Badlands

Ocotillo Wells State Vehicular Recreation Area

to San Diego

Grapevine Mt.
El. 3831

Banner

Scissors Crossing

Julian

Scrips Medical Clinic

S3

78

Ocotillo Wells

Vallecito Mountains

Ocotillo Badlands

to Hwy 86

78

Pinyon Mountains

Cuyamaca Reservoir

Granite Mt
El. 5633

Pictographs

Morteros

Marshal South Home

Whale Peak
El. 5320

Gypsum Mine

Wind Caves

Cuyamaca Rancho State Park

9

Oriflamme Mt
El. 4611

Vallecito Stage Station County Park

Agua Caliente County Park

Carrizo Badlands

Carrizo Impact Area (Closed to Public)

79

Garnet Peak
El. 5909

S2

Palm Spring

S1

Canebrake Canyon

Mountain Palm Springs

Carrizo Badlands Overlook

Sunrise Highway

Sombrero Peak
El. 4229

Carrizo Palms

to San Diego

Mortero Palms

S2

Ocotillo

to El Centro

8

Mt Tule
El. 4647

8

SanDiego & Imperial Valley Railroad

KEY

— Roads
— Dirt Raods
- - - Hiking trails
├┼┼ Railroad
Park Headquarters
Visitor Center
Camping
Group Camping
Primitive Camping (no water)
Lodging
Picnic Area
Restaurant

bighorns, 300 of the 500 remaining in the United States live on the rough, rocky terrain here. They have a reputation for being wary of man, but when mating season hits in fall and early winter, bighorns are often seen close to the campgrounds and park roadways—as rangers have noted, looking for a mate takes precedence over avoiding humans. During the summer, the bighorns often descend the mountains to seek water in the canyons.

In the spring of most years—depending on winter rainfall—a stunning display of colors come to the park as wildflowers carpet the desert floor and climb into the surrounding hills and mountains. It's estimated that half the park's visitors come during this season, and the park has a **Wildflower Hotline** (tel. 619/767-4684) to tell callers what's blooming.

Activities

At the Visitors Center (619/767-4205), you're introduced to the park and desert with a 15-minute slide show. Four-hundred slides are displayed on nine computer-controlled projectors. Exhibits at the center range from local geology to the history of the Native Americans who once lived here.

During high season, October through May, the park rangers and naturalists give frequent talks and lead walks and tours. Outdoor activities are normally scheduled in the morning and talks in the evening.

Hikers can choose from more than 100 miles of designated trails. About 35 miles are part of the Pacific Crest Trail that goes from Mexico to Canada. To help hikers find their way, detailed Geographic Survey maps are for sale at the Visitors Center. Hikers can register at the center and give an estimated time when they'll return from the back country. Should they not check back in, rangers will head out to look for them.

For walkers, the park offers a number of interesting short nature trails. The Borrego Palm Canyon Trail starts at the main campground and will take you to a grove of California fan palms, the largest palm species in North America, and a year-round stream—just one of the 25 oases in the park. Brochures are available at the visitor center for a number of these nature trails.

Along with the bighorn sheep, in the backcountry you'll probably see myriad smaller animals such as rabbits, opossum, and desert mice, and reptiles ranging from the desert iguana to the chuckwalla—the largest lizard in the park, which can grow more than 16 inches long. Although you probably won't see any snakes—unless you're careless and disturb them—you may come across the tracks of the sidewinder, well known for its unique method of locomotion. Perhaps you'll even spot coyotes, mule deer, and a bobcat or a mountain lion.

A number of horseback trails surround the park's Vernon Whitaker horse camp (see Camping, below). One trail ascends 12 miles to the top of the mountains. Riders may also use all the dirt roads in the park, but are not allowed on nature or hiking trails.

Bicycles and motorcycles (if they are street licensed) may be ridden on the more than 500 miles of roads in the park. Vehicles are not allowed to go off the roads in the park, but the Ocotillo Wells State Vehicular Recreation Area (tel. 619/767-5391) borders the park—here at this 42,000-acre site, it's wide open fun for dirt bikes, dune buggies, and four-wheel-drive vehicles.

Camping

Two developed campgrounds accommodate RV and tent campers. Borrego Palm Canyon campground has 52 full hookup and pull-through sites ($14 to $18) and 65 multiuse sites without hookups ($10 to $14). Another 27 multiuse nonhookup sites are situated at Tamarisk Grove ($10 to $14). All of the park's nonhookup sites have shade ramadas.

Five group campsites hold from 9 to 24 people at Borrego Palm Canyon. All five sites can be reserved en masse for 120 people.

You and your horse can stay at the park's Vernon Whitaker horse camp. All of the 10 campsites can hold up to eight people and have corrals for four horses. Reservations are made through MIS-TIX (tel. 619/767-4205). The horse camp is at the hub of many miles of riding trails.

It's recommended that you leave pets (like dogs) at home. If you must bring them, pets must be on a leash or under complete control at all times and confined to your vehicle or tent at night. Pets are not allowed in the Visitors Center, on foot trails, or in the backcountry. Much of this is for their own protection since coyotes, rattlesnakes, cactus, and soaring summer temperatures can harm them.

Bow Willow is a primitive camping site off S2. It has picnic tables and portable toilet facilities. Once you are out of the developed areas of the park, you can camp just about anywhere along its 500 miles of primitive roads. Only two restrictions apply. First, you must keep your vehicle within one car length of the dirt road so as not to damage the fragile plant life. Second, you mustn't camp near a watering hole or spring as it scares off the wildlife.

Nearby Attractions

The tiny town of **Borrego Springs,** just down the road from the Visitors Center, is set up for tourism. If you're not into camping, here you'll find several resorts and motels, all with swimming pools, and even some condos with rental units. The town also offers about a dozen restaurants, three public and one private golf course, tennis courts, and a variety of shops.

West of the park, on California Highway 78, is the former gold-mining town of **Julian** where you can tour an old gold mine. Julian is now famed for its apple and pear orchards.

To the northwest of the park (45 miles) is the **Palomar Observatory** (tel. 619/742-2119), the mountaintop home of one of the largest telescopes in the world. And farther to the north are a number of popular desert resort communities, such as **Palm Springs, Rancho Mirage,** and **Palm Desert.**

For birders, to the east of the park (50 miles) in El Centro is the **Salton Sea National Wildlife Refuge** (tel. 619/393-3059).

Calaveras Big Trees State Park

| Visitor Center | RV Camping | Tent Camping | Primitive Camping | Group Camping | Fishing | Swimming | Picnic Areas | Trails | X-Country Skiing |

Capsule Description: An almost mile-high park with developed facilities among the giant sequoias.

Location: East-central California on California Highway 4 about 20 miles east of Angel's Camp.

Address: P.O. Box 120, Arnold, CA 95223 (tel. 209/795-2334).

Area Contacts: Amador County Chamber of Commerce, P.O. Box 596, Jackson, CA 95642 (tel. toll free 800/649-4980 or 209/223-0350).

Calaveras County Visitors Center, P.O. Box 637, Angel's Camp, CA 95222 (tel. toll free 800/225-3764 or 209/736-0049).

Tuolumne County Visitors Bureau, P.O. Box 4020, Sonora, CA 95370 (tel. 209/533-4420; toll free 800/446-1333 in California only.)

Insider Tip: Ask to see the 20-minute slide show on the park at the Visitors Center.

Millions of years ago, when dinosaurs roamed, the giant sequoia and other redwoods dominated the cone-bearing forests of the entire northern hemisphere. Just three species of these tall trees, the oldest living things, survive: the dawn redwoods of central China; the coast redwoods of northern California (see Humboldt Redwoods State Park, below); and the Sierra redwoods or giant sequoias that grow in a scattered pattern along the western slopes of the Sierra Nevada and in the two groves at the heart of this park. While the coast redwoods lay claim to being the world's tallest living things, the Sierra redwoods are the largest. They can attain heights of 300 feet and grow to a diameter of 32 feet, and their weight can reach 6,000 tons. It's common for them to live 2,000 years.

Most visitors to Calaveras Big Trees Park come to gaze in awe before these giants of the North and South Groves. This species of redwoods does not grow in pure stands, you'll find them intermingled with ponderosa and sugar pine, cedar, white fir, and flowering dogwood.

Activities

The Visitors Center (tel. 209/795-3840) has exhibits on the big trees and free brochures; detailed interpretive guides to the major trails are also sold here. On most evenings from mid-June to Labor Day, campfire programs with cultural and natural history themes are offered here.

Of the park's two groves, the North Grove, by the entrance to the park and its campgrounds, is the more heavily visited. The self-guiding trail through this grove of 150 giants is a gentle, well-marked loop, about a mile long. With a guidebook in hand, you can easily stroll it in an hour. Daily mid-June to Labor Day, park rangers conduct guided walks through this grove. A special feature of this grove is the short, 600-foot-long "Three Senses Trail," designed to help visitors touch, smell, and hear the wonders of nature. Rangers conduct guided tours of this trail for children, and it has braille signs and a guiding rope for the blind.

The far larger South Grove—with a thousand tall trees—is remote and relatively untouched by man. It's a 9-mile drive south from the entrance of the park on the Walter W. Smith Parkway. Depending on the route you chose at the trail head, the trail runs from 3½ to 5 miles through rolling mountain terrain. It's not a difficult hike but large sections of the trail are a steady climb—200 feet in one mile. Halfway around the loop is a side trail that leads to the Agassiz tree, the largest tree in the park. Named after one of America's leading naturalists, it's 250 feet tall and 25 feet in diameter at 6 feet above the ground.

Three other maintained trails wander through the park. Perhaps the most challenging is the River trail; over the course of four miles, it descends 1,500 feet from the North Grove to the Stanislaus River. Most visitors find it advisable to have a car waiting for them at the river after their hike down. Usually, only those in peak physical condition attempt the ascent from the river to the grove.

Most people who swim at the park do so at Beaver Creek; beaches are found at the picnic grounds. The Stanislaus River has some small sandy beaches and rocky areas from which you can take a swim—perhaps in July and August when the water is warmer—but no lifeguards are posted. Since a power plant dam was constructed upriver in the early 1980s, the river has been colder and faster than in years past, the park staff reports. Six miles from the entrance of the park on the Walter W. Smith Parkway, a parking area has steps that lead down to the river and a small beach.

The Stanislaus River is stocked frequently in summer with Rainbows. Angling for native brown trout is also "okay" here, says one ranger.

In the virgin forest birding is good. Owls, turkey vultures, humming birds, quail, and juncos are sighted. Hikers can expect to see deer, raccoons, porcupines, and other small animals. Black bear, bobcats, coyotes, and mountain lions live in these woods, but the cover of the forest offers many hiding places for these man-shy animals, so sightings are rare.

During the winter, the park staff conducts cross-country ski and snowshoe hikes for groups with a minimum of 10 people. For reservations call 209/795-2334, two weeks in advance.

Commercial companies offer white-water rafting trips down the North Fork of the "Stan," a Class IV river with good rapids—not for first-timers. In spring with the runoff of melting snow the river has a higher flow. A major run starts above the park at the Sour Grass Ravine Campgrounds and has a take-out in Calaveras Park. Contact All Outdoors (tel. toll free 800/24RAFTS) and White Water Voyages (tel. toll free 800/488-7238) for more information.

Camping

There are 129 campsites in the park. Seventy-four are in the North Grove Campground, adjacent to the Visitors Center and the North Grove Big Trees Trail, and the rest in the Oak Hollow Campground to the east of that grove. All are multiuse sites with forest shade, but some are too small for the larger RVs. There are also a few primitive campsites for backpackers and group camping is available in the summer. All sites may be reserved through MISTIX (tel. toll free 800/444-PARKS) from mid-May to mid-September. The rest of the year they are on a first-come basis. (Campsites $12 to $14.)

Additional fees include the standard dollar a day for pets. If you're camping, bring plenty of change with you. You'll need 50¢ for three minutes of hot water in the showers.

There are no stores in the park, but supplies can be purchased in the nearby towns of Arnold and Dorrington.

Nearby Attractions

Held each May in the town of Angel's Camp is the **frog-jumping contest** made world famous by Mark Twain's short story. From Big Trees Park, take California Highway 4 east for 20 miles to Angel's Camp—it's about 3,000 feet lower in elevation. **Angel's Camp City Museum** (tel. 209/736-2963) has exhibits on the gold-rush days.

Surrounding Big Trees Park is the million acres of **Stanislaus National Forest** (tel. 209/962-7862) with Alpine Lake, Cherry Lake, and Pinecrest Lake for swimmers, boaters, anglers, and water-skiers.

In the town of Bear Valley on Highway 4, the **Bear Valley Ski Company** (tel. 209/753-2301) offers downhill skiing. Snowmobiles can be rented and ridden at **Bear Valley Snowmobiles** (tel. 209/753-2323).

Mercer Caverns (tel. 209/728-2101), near the town of Murphy's on Highway 4, offers a 45-minute guided tour of 10 rooms with limestone formations. A 45-minute family tour of **Moaning Caverns** (tel. 209/736-2708) takes you to the biggest room (165 feet tall) in California with calcite formations; it's near the town of Vallecito on Highway 4.

South of Angel's Camp, on California Highway 49, is the **Columbia State Historic Park** (tel. 209/532-4301), a reconstructed original mining town at Columbia; and at Jamestown is **Railtown** (tel. 209/984-3953), another state historic park with steam-train rides and an authentic roundhouse.

Not far to the south is **Yosemite National Park** (tel. 209/372-0200) and to the north is **Lake Tahoe.** (A shortcut to Tahoe is to go east on California 4 to connect with roads going north. But don't try this in winter or even early spring; the narrow road through Ebbet's Pass [8,314 feet] is steep at points, sometimes switchbacked, and almost always closed due to snow from November until late May.)

Humboldt Redwoods State Park

| Visitor Center | RV Camping | Tent Camping | Primitive Camping | Group Camping | Fishing | Swimming | Picnic Areas | Trails | Horse Trails | Nature Programs | Bicycling | Gift Shop |

Capsule Description: A large park with developed facilities among the coastal redwoods, the world's tallest trees.

Location: Northern California, on the Avenue of the Giants, adjacent to U.S. Highway 101, south of Weott and approximately 45 miles south of Eureka.

Address: P.O. Box 100, Weott, CA 95571 (tel. 707/946-2409).

Area Contacts: Avenue of the Giants Association, P.O. Box 219, Miranda, CA 95553 (tel. 707/923-2555).

Eureka/Humboldt County Convention & Visitors Bureau, 1034 Second St., Eureka, CA 95501 (tel. toll free 800/346-3482 or 707/443-5097).

Ferndale Chamber of Commerce, P.O. Box 325, Ferndale, CA 95536 (tel. 707/786-4477).

Garberville-Redway Chamber of Commerce, P.O. Box 445, Garberville, CA 95440 (tel. 707/923-2613).

Insider Tips: The complete Trail Guide booklet for sale at the Visitors Center is well worth the small price. To see the Giant Tree, the current Champion Coast Redwood, in the Rockefeller Forest, take the Mattole/Bull Creek Flats Road west to the Big Tree Area parking lot. From there walk over the foot bridge across Bull Creek and take the trail to the left. It's an easy five-minute walk.

Majestic. Impressive. Gigantic. These words are all accurate, but still too weak to do justice to a description of the perfectly named Avenue of the Giants, which winds its way more than 30 miles through the park. At the least, driving mile after mile between groves of coastal redwoods that soar upward to as high as 30 stories is awe-inspiring. For some, it may be overwhelming.

The magnificent coast redwood is the world's tallest known tree. Average mature trees, several hundred years old, stand up to 240 feet tall and have diameters of 10 to 15 feet. Some of these trees have measured up to 360 feet tall. Unlike the giant Sierra redwoods (see Calaveras Big Trees State Park) that always grow intermingled with other trees, the coast redwoods often form almost pure stands. A number of these pure-stand groves are in this park.

The present range of these giants is a narrow strip, about 40 miles wide and 450 miles long, along the Pacific Ocean from central California to southern Oregon. In this redwood belt, temperatures are moderate year-round and heavy winter rains and dense summer morning fog provide the trees with the water they need. This 51,000 acre park, the third largest in the state, sits close to the middle of this zone and includes some of the world's most impressive redwood groves. In fact, about 17,000 acres are old-growth redwoods—old growth is generally defined as trees over 200 years old. The oldest recorded coastal redwood tree was found in this park and was over 2,200 years old. The rest of the land is a combination of second-growth redwoods, mixed forest, and prairie.

Activities

This is another park where tree-watching is a major occupation for visitors.

An auto-tour flyer for the Avenue of the Giants is available at the Visitors Center. If you want to start your own auto tour on the way in, these flyers are normally available at either end of the avenue.

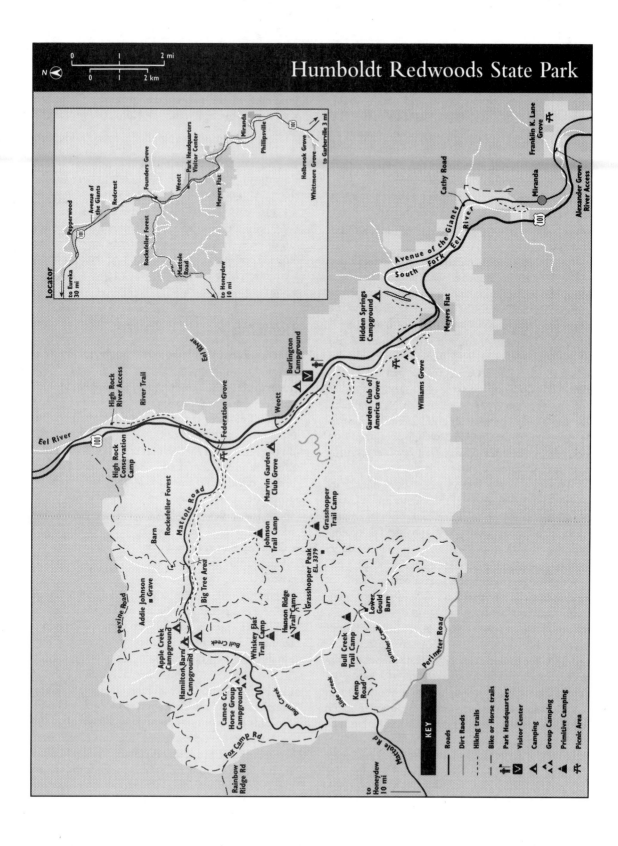

Humboldt Redwoods State Park

N

0   1   2 mi
0   1   2 km

Locator

to Eureka 30 mi

Pepperwood

Avenue of the Giants

Redcrest

Founders Grove

Rockefeller Forest

Weott

Park Headquarters
Visitor Center

Miranda

Phillipsville

Myers Flat

Mattole Road

Holbrook Grove

Whittmore Grove

to Honeydew 10 mi

to Garberville 3 mi

Franklin K. Lane Grove

Miranda

Cathy Road

Alexander Grove River Access

South Fork Eel River

Avenue of the Giants

Meyers Flat

Hidden Springs Campground

Williams Grove

Garden Club of America Grove

Burlington Campground

Weott

Federation Grove

River Trail

High Rock River Access

Eel River

High Rock Conservation Camp

Rockefeller Forest

Barn

Mattole Road

Eel River

Marvin Garden Club Grove

Grasshopper Trail Camp

Johnson Trail Camp

Grasshopper Peak EL 3379

Addie Johnson Grave

Big Tree Area

Peavine Road

Apple Creek Campground

Hamilton Barn Campground

Bull Creek

Whiskey Flat Trail Camp

Hanson Ridge Trail Camp

Lower Gould Barn

Bull Creek Trail Camp

Cameo Cr. Horse Group Campground

Panther Creek

Perimeter Road

Cuneo Creek

Slide Creek

Kemp Road

Burns Creek

Fox Camp Rd

Mattole Rd

Rainbow Ridge Rd

to Honeydew 10 mi

KEY

Roads	
Dirt Roads	
Hiking trails	
Bike or Horse trails	
Park Headquarters	
Visitor Center	
Camping	
Group Camping	
Primitive Camping	
Picnic Area	

Or you will probably find commercial flyers available in the small towns north and south of the park. These tout paid attractions, of course, but will usually include a sketch map of the Avenue of the Giants. There are a number of turnouts and parking areas along this route from which short loop trails reach into the forest.

With more than 100 miles of trails, the park is set up to serve both the leisurely stroller, the walker, and the serious hiker as well as bicyclists and riders.

For the leisurely stroll try the Founders Grove self-guided nature trail. It is only about a half mile long, but includes an excellent sampling of living giants plus the Dyerville Giant, a tree that held the title of the Champion Coast Redwood until it fell in 1991. (The new champion is off Mattole Road in the Rockefeller Forest.) Walking alongside this fallen tree is a good way to realize just how huge these redwoods are. The tree measures around 362 feet, that's about 200 feet taller than Niagara Falls. It's also 17 feet in diameter and 52 feet in circumference and is estimated to weigh over a million pounds. A Founders Grove trail booklet is available at the Visitors Center.

There are a number of other short trails scattered along the Avenue of the Giants and Mattole Road that range up to about two miles in length, and much longer hiking trails into the backcountry, like the 12-mile Grasshopper Peak Trail. A complete trail guide booklet is for sale at the park. On the longer hikes you'll have a better chance of seeing some of the park's wildlife. Deer are common and you may also see porcupines, skunks, raccoons, gray foxes, river otters, and coyotes. Even an occasional bear or mountain lion may be spotted. For birders, turkey vultures, hawks, California quail, the endangered spotted owls, warblers, juncos, and woodpeckers are often seen. Ospreys are often seen swooping down to catch salmon in season, and occasionally they are joined by bald eagles.

If you want to know more, the Visitors Center is the place to go. Here you will find a number of publications (free and pay), exhibits, and an audio-visual program. In summer, campfire programs are presented in the major campgrounds. There are also ranger-guided walks, and programs for children.

Anglers can expect to catch king and steelhead salmon, some trophy size, in the Eel River that runs through the park. Fishing here is best during the fall and winter, after the first rains in October up until early March. Summer fishing is considered poor because of the warm- and low-water conditions. If the water isn't too low, floating along the river on an air mattress or seeking out a swimming hole is a popular way to spend an afternoon.

Camping

This park has 249 multiuse campsites in three forested campgrounds. None of the sites have hookups. The Burlington campground has 56 sites near the park headquarters on the Avenue of the Giants. These are in a second-growth area and sites are close together. About five miles farther south on the Avenue of the Giants are 154 well separated sites in a mixed forest area at the Hidden Springs campground. The final 39 sites are in a second-growth forest at Albee Creek, on Mattole Road about five miles west of U.S. 101. Mattole Road passes through a redwood grove so extensive it's called the Rockefeller Forest. At 9,000 acres, it's reputed to be the largest grove of old-growth redwoods in the world.

Farther out on this road is the Cuneo Creek Horse Group Camp, which can accommodate up to 50 people with horses. This camp offers access to many miles of fire roads that riders can use to explore the backcountry.

The park's two environmental camps are also in the forest about 100 yards off this road. These camps were established to reintroduce an old idea: camping as a means of getting away from it all. For backpackers and bicyclists who want to get even farther away from it all, there are five trail camps that are two to four miles into the woods. Hikers and bikers who want to stay closer to civilization can use the Hike and Bike Campgrounds on the Avenue of the Giants about 1½ miles north of the park headquarters.

The group campgrounds on the Avenue of the Giants at Williams Grove will accommodate up to 100 people, or two smaller groups.

The family campgrounds at Burlington, the group camp, and the environmental camps may be reserved through MISTIX. The horse group camp may be reserved through the park headquarters. All others are on a first-come basis. However, of the major campgrounds, only Burlington is open all year. Hidden Springs and Albee Creek are closed October 1 until May (sometimes late May). (Campsites $12 to $14.)

Nearby Attractions

If you want to see how trees become lumber, head north of the park on U.S. 101 to **Scotia.** Here, in one of the last company-owned towns, the **Pacific Lumber Company** (tel. 707/764-2222) offers free self-guided tours of the world's largest red-wood mill and the **Historic Logging Museum.**

Eureka, less than an hour's drive north on U.S. 101, is the largest town on the northern California coast. Among the attractions here are more than 100 Victorian homes, a zoo, several museums, bay and harbor cruises, and, of course, theaters and restaurants.

On the way to Eureka is the town of **Ferndale** where Victorian architecture reigns. So much so they call it the "Victorian Village"; it's a state historical landmark.

In the southern part of the park, on the Avenue of the Giants, is the small town of **Garberville,** which has a nine-hole public golf course and public tennis courts. Two miles farther south, on U.S. 101, is **Benbow Lake State Recreation Area** (tel. 707/923-3238). Here the South Fork of the Eel River is dammed up each summer for canoeists and others with small watercraft, and fishermen.

About 25 miles to the west is what is called the **Lost Coast;** lost because the mountains, which rise from the shore, leave no room for good roads—only narrow, unimproved, and unmaintained dirt roads. The best way to get to the Lost Coast is to take U.S. 101 from Redway, north of Garberville, to Shelter Cove on the Pacific. The rugged area of the lost coast is a nature lover's paradise; parts of it encompass the **King Range National Conservation Area** (tel. 707/986-7731) and the **Sinkyone Wilderness State Park** (tel. 707/986-7711). Both parks have beaches where you might see migrating whales or other sea mammals.

Pfeiffer Big Sur State Park

Visitor Center | Lodge/Hotel | Restaurant | RV Camping | Tent Camping | Group Camping | Non-Motorized Boating Only | Fishing | Swimming | Picnic Areas | Trails | Nature Programs | Gift Shop

Capsule Description: A small park on one of the most beautiful stretches of California coast.

Location: On the central California coast. On California Highway 1, 28 miles south of Carmel.

Address: Big Sur Station #1, Big Sur, CA 93920 (tel. 408/667-2315. Lodge (tel. 408/667-2171).

Area Contacts: Big Sur Chamber of Commerce, Box 87, Big Sur, CA 93920 (tel. 408/667-2100).
Monterey Peninsula Visitors and Convention

Bureau, P.O. Box 1770, Monterey, CA 93942-1770
(tel. 408/649-1770).

San Simeon Chamber of Commerce, P.O. Box
1, San Simeon, CA 93452 (tel. toll free 800/342-5613
or 805/927-3500).

Santa Cruz County Convention and Visitors Bureau, 701 Front St., Santa Cruz, CA 95060 (tel. toll
free 800/833-3494 or 408/425-1234).

Insider Tips: The most spectacular panoramas are at
the end of the Valley View and the Buzzard's Roost
hiking trails. During the summer, traffic can crawl
along Hwy 1. When driving to or leaving the park,
allow yourself plenty of traveling time and consider periodic stops at the highway turnouts,
where you can relax and enjoy the view.

The Big Sur refers to a 90 miles of rugged California coastline between Carmel on the north and
San Simeon (the site of the Hearst Castle) on the
south. California Highway 1, known worldwide as
one of the most spectacular scenic drives in our
country, winds its way along this coast with the
cliffs and foothills of the Santa Lucia Mountains on
one side looking as if they are plunging into the
Pacific Ocean surf on the other. Although relatively small, this 810-acre park enhances this image
of natural grandeur for those who take the time to
stop.

Here are some of the last groves of the giant
coast redwoods that march hundreds of miles
along the Pacific from Oregon to mid-California.
Perhaps because this is near the southern limit of
this redwood species range, these trees do not
attain the heights of the trees to the north, but they
are still impressive. In this setting, the park offers
campgrounds, a lodge, nature and hiking trails,
fishing and other activities. It is also an ideal
jumping-off place for visits to both the natural
splendors and the man-made attractions along this
engaging coast.

Admission to the park is $6 per car, but you can
bike in or walk in free.

Activities

The six marked trails in the park range from a self-
guiding nature trail, that shouldn't take you more

than a half hour to stroll through, to the Buzzard's
Roost Trail that involves a rugged two-hour hike.
This longer trail takes you to the top of Pfeiffer
Ridge where you'll be rewarded for your efforts
with a magnificent panoramic view of the Pacific
Ocean and the Santa Lucia Mountain Range. One
of the more popular trails is the stroll through the
redwood groves along Pfeiffer-Redwood Creek.
This usually takes about an hour and ends at a
scenic delight—a 60-foot waterfall.

The park borders on the 167,000-acre Ventana
National Wilderness, which straddles the Santa
Lucia Mountains and is part of the Los Padres
National Forest, so wildlife is abundant in the area.
Abundant, but hard to see. True, even in the
campground area you'll occasionally see deer and
other wildlife, and chances of seeing wildlife in-
creases on the trails. But a combination of dense
vegetation to hide in and a natural shyness toward
man let most of animals remain unseen. Birders
will have an easier time spotting their quarry. A
birdlist is available at the park's entrance station.

During the season, rangers conduct frequent
nature walks and campfire programs.

You can swim or wade in the Big Sur River, but
there are no designated swimming areas and no
lifeguards. Kayaks and rafts are also permitted on
the river, but no motor craft are allowed.

Anglers can go after steelhead rainbow trout in
the river. However, the season is severely limited as
is the catch. Check with the rangers for details.

Camping and Accommodations

The **Big Sur Lodge,** the only lodge in the state
park system, is located near the entrance to the
park. Rather than one building, there are 61 garden court cottages with decks, many with fireplaces and some with kitchens. The maximum
number of persons per room is six. Amenities
include a heated swimming pool in the summer
season, restaurant, gift shop, and convenience
store. Rates are seasonal and range from a low of
about $70 for a standard room in winter to $169
for a kitchen suite with fireplace in summer and on

holidays. These rates include admission to the park and except during the summer/holiday high seasons, they also include a breakfast for two. Reservations may be made directly with the lodge. Weekend reservations require a minimum two-day stay, holidays require a minimum of three days.

The 218 multiuse **campsites** are located along the Big Sur River, which runs through the park, in redwood groves, oak woodlands, and grassy meadow areas. There are no hookups, but restrooms and hot showers (25¢ for three minutes of hot water) are located throughout the campgrounds within easy walking distance of every site. In summer there is a camp store and coin laundry. Peak camping season is early April through late October, but reservations for sites may be made through MISTIX all year. (Campsites $14 to $16.)

There is a small bike-in camp; however, bicyclists are permitted to ride on paved roads only. They are not allowed on trails. For groups there are two hike-in group camps. These are open Memorial Day through September and can accommodate up to 50 campers each.

Nearby Attractions

The journey into the mountains to the east is not easy. Hiking is the only way is to get to them. The park's Oak Grove Trail leads to the Mt. Manuel Trail in the **Ventana Wilderness.** That, in turn, leads backpackers to more than 200 miles of trails and 55 designated camps.

Pfeiffer Big Sur Park has no direct access to the beaches to the west, but about a mile south of the park entrance there's a road that leads to Pfeiffer Beach, where the ocean has carved imposing holes and arches through the huge boulders in the sea. Another way to get to the beach is through **Andrew Molera Park** (tel. 408/667-2315), a few miles to the north. Here it's a flat, easy walk from the parking area on Highway 1 to the beach. Don't look for a visitor center here; there's none as this is one of several small parks in the area administered through Pfeiffer Big Sur. Ocean fishing is permitted year-round at the beach.

Molera Point, at the end of the Headland Trail in this park, is a good place for spotting sea otters, harbor seals, and California sea lions. From mid-December through February, Molera Point is a popular place for whale-watching. January is the best time for viewing.

Continuing north from Andrew Molera Park another couple of miles on Highway 1 brings you to the **Point Sur Light Station,** which served the coast for almost 100 years and is now a state historic park. Guided tours—not leisurely—are given every Saturday and Sunday, weather permitting. Getting around involves a steep half-mile hike each way and a 300 foot climb in elevation. For details, check at Pfeiffer Big Sur or call 408/625-4419 for recorded tour information.

Another 15 miles up Highway 1 brings you to **Point Lobos State Reserve** (tel. 408/624-4909), a mosaic of bold headlands, gigantic wave-eroded rock formations, irregular coves, and rolling meadows. From the cliffside trails here you can see sea otters, sea lions, and harbor seals. In spring and summer, Bird Island is home to a large colony of cormorants. December to February—and sometimes as late as May—the California gray whales pass close to shore here on their annual migration to warmer waters. They can also be seen on their return trip north in spring, but are usually farther offshore and harder to see.

More than half of Point Lobos Reserve is underwater. Divers have listed it as among the best cold water diving in the world because the warmer southern and colder northern California currents meet here making a rich underwater environment with ecosystems from both. To preserve it, only 15 diving teams of 2 to 3 divers are permitted to dive here each day. Reservations for certified diving teams may be made through MISTIX. The reserve is open 9am to 5pm in winter and 9am to 7pm in summer.

Admission to Point Lobos is $6 per car, but you could park on the road and walk in free.

Three miles farther north is the city of **Carmel.** Once an artists' and writers' retreat, it's now more tourist-oriented but still an enjoyable place to visit. Carmel is usually considered the northern end of Big Sur, and it's a jump-off point for the **17-mile drive** (tel. 408/624-6669, admission is $6.50 per car) around the **Monterey peninsula** and on to **Pacific Grove,** famed for the monarch butterflies that winter here from November to March; the ultradeluxe lifestyle of the community of **Pebble Beach** with its well-known golf course; and finally on to **Monterey** with its famed **Fisherman's Wharf, Cannery Row,** and **Presidio.**

An easy drive around Monterey Bay brings you to **Santa Cruz,** a seaside city with a population of close to a quarter of a million people and the Santa Cruz Beach Boardwalk, California's only beach amusement park.

If you've ventured this far up Highway 1, you might as well go another 25 miles north and visit the unique **Año Nuevo State Reserve** (tel. 415/879-0227). Perhaps the most compelling attraction here is the large colony of northern elephant seals that come ashore here at various times of the year to molt, mate, and give birth. During the breeding season, December to April, access is restricted to guided tours for which reservations are required ten days in advance through MISTIX (tel. toll free 800/444-PARK). For information

on the seal population at the time of your visit, other tours, and access, call 415/879-0227 or write the reserve at Pescadero, CA 94060.

Going south on Highway 1 from Pfeiffer Big Sur, two places are worth a visit. The first, about 12 miles away, is **Julia Pfeiffer Burns State Park** (tel. 408/667-2315). This 3,580-acre park is on the coastline and about half of it is an underwater reserve. The most popular trail in the park goes from the entrance station back under Highway 1 to a bluff that overlooks a waterfall that drops some 80 feet onto an ocean beach.

The second southern daytrip from the park is to take the slow, scenic drive about 65 miles down Highway 1 to the **Hearst San Simeon State Historical Monument.** Better known as Hearst Castle, it crowns a hilltop and has 130 rooms in the main house and 35 more in guesthouses—furnished with Spanish and Italian antiques and art. It's set in 127 acres of gardens, with terraces, pools, and walkways. Several different tours are conducted daily, except for Thanksgiving, Christmas, and New Year's Day. Daytime tours cost $14 for adults; the evening tour, which is not conducted all year, costs $25. Reservations may be made by calling MISTIX at 800/444-4445.

Colorado

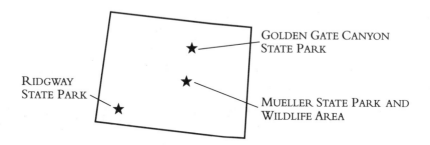

GOLDEN GATE CANYON
STATE PARK

RIDGWAY
STATE PARK

MUELLER STATE PARK AND
WILDLIFE AREA

Colorado has 37 state parks.

Contacts

- Colorado Division of Parks and Outdoor Recreation, 1313 Sherman St., room 618, Denver, CO 80203 (tel. 303/866-3437). Campground reservations only (tel. toll free 800/678-CAMP [800/678-2267]).
- Denver Tourism Board, 225 W. Colfax, Denver, CO 80202 (tel. toll free 800/433-2656).

General Information on Colorado State Parks

Whether your idea of fun is a beach on a hot summer day, a secluded alpine lake in a mountain wilderness, or miles and miles of open water for boating, waterskiing, windsurfing, and fishing, or enjoying winter sports like ice skating or cross-country skiing, you'll find there's a Colorado park to meet your desires.

GENERAL FEES

A valid parks pass is required on every vehicle entering a state park. A daily pass is $3. An annual pass—good for the entire calendar year at all state parks and recreation areas—is $30. Passes are available at all state park entrances, the parks division's four regional offices, and various licensed agents such as grocery and sporting goods outlets.

CAMPING AND ACCOMMODATIONS

The Campground Reservation Service is open Monday to Friday from 8am to 5pm from April 1 through September 15. Call toll free 800/678-2267. (In the Denver metro area, call 470-1144.) Campground reservations are taken by phone only—no mail or walk-in reservations accepted. The reservation fee is a one-time charge of $6.75 per site. The rest of the year, if the campgrounds are open, campsites are available on a first-come basis. Weather permitting, most parks attempt to keep at least some campsites open during the fall and winter months.

Reservations can be made a maximum of 60 days and a minimum of 3 days in advance. You may reserve up to six sites per call. Camping fees range from $6 to $10 per campsite per night, depending on services offered.

For group camping reservations, contact the park directly.

The only other accommodations in the parks are seven rustic cabins in the Colorado State Forest State Park. These may be reserved year-round a maximum of 120 days and a minimum of 10 days in advance. (When Campground Reservation

Service is closed, call the park at 303/723-8366.) Cabin capacity varies from six to 15. Depending on size, location, and day of week, they rent from $15 to $40 per night.

Pets. Pets are welcome in most parks but must be on a leash no longer than six feet at all times. They are not permitted on swimming beaches or in cabins.

Alcoholic beverages. Only 3.2% alcohol content beer is permitted. Some parks restrict this to cans or kegs, no bottles.

Discounts. Colorado residents age 62 and older can purchase an annual Aspen Leaf Pass at a discount. Vehicles of Colorado disabled veterans displaying a Colorado Disabled Veteran license plate are admitted without a pass.

Golden Gate Canyon State Park

Visitor Center · RV Camping · Tent Camping · Group Camping · Fishing · Picnic Areas · Trails · Horse Trails · Nature Programs · Bicycling · Playground

Capsule Description: Natural mountain park with developed facilities.

Location: North-central Colorado, about 30 miles west of downtown Denver. From Denver, take I-70 west to Colorado Highway 58 exit. Continue west on Highway 58 to Highway 93. Go north approximately one mile on Highway 93 to Golden Gate Canyon Road (which becomes Highway 46). Go west on Golden Gate Canyon Road approximately 15 miles to the Visitors Center.

Address: 3873 Hwy. 46, Golden, CO 80403 (tel. 303/592-1502).

Area Contacts: Golden Area Chamber of Commerce, 507 14th St., Golden, CO 80401 (tel. 303/279-3113).

Greater Denver Chamber of Commerce, 1445 Market St., Denver, CO 80202 (tel. 303/534-8500).

Metro Denver Convention and Visitors Bureau, 225 W. Colfax Ave., Denver, CO 80202 (tel. 303/892-1112).

Morrison Town Hall, P.O. Box 95, Morrison, CO 80465 (tel. 303/697-8749).

If you visit this park during the fall leaf-turning season, you might think its name came from the golden colors of the aspen foliage. Actually, it refers to real gold. No gold was found in the area now occupied by the park, but in the late 1850s a bonanza was struck six miles to the south. Two gold camps, Black Hawk and Central City exploded with growth. To reach them, settlers built a road through the canyon and called it Golden Gate Road. In the first few weeks more than 5,000 prospectors used the road. But a few years later another shorter route was cut through another canyon and the present park area was turned back to ranching, farming, logging, and a little quartz mining.

The elevation in this 10,500-acre park ranges from 7,600 to 10,400 feet. More than 60 miles of trails wander through the spectacular mountain landscape of forested hillsides, open meadows, and rocky outcrops. To preserve the backcountry integrity, development is concentrated on the perimeter; however, picnic areas, campgrounds, observation decks, and even most fishing spots are easily accessible from the park's roads.

From Panorama Point, on the north end of the park, you can see over 50 miles of snowcapped peaks along the Continental Divide.

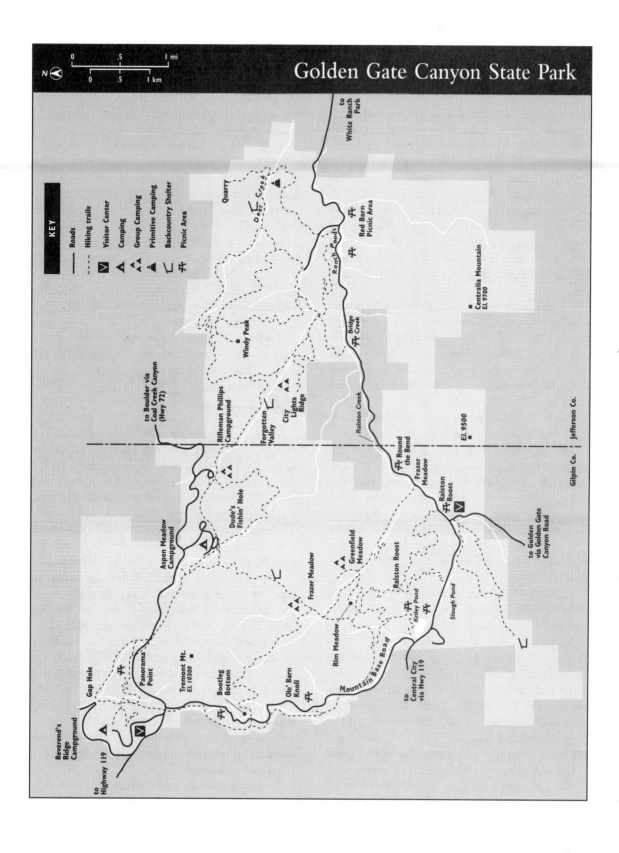

Golden Gate Canyon State Park

N

0   .5   1 mi
0   .5   1 km

KEY

- Roads
- Hiking trails
- V Visitor Center
- △ Camping
- △△ Group Camping
- ◣ Primitive Camping
- ⌐ Backcountry Shelter
- ⟠ Picnic Area

to White Ranch Park

Quarry

Deer Creek

Red Barn Picnic Area

Ranch Ponds

Centralia Mountain EL 9700

Windy Peak

Bridge Creek

to Boulder via Coal Creek Canyon (Hwy 72)

Rifleman Phillips Campground

City Lights Ridge

Forgotten Valley

Ralston Creek

EL 9500

Round the Bend

Aspen Meadow Campground

Dude's Fishin' Hole

Frazer Meadow

Greenfield Meadow

Ralston Roost

Frazer Meadow

Ralston Roost

V

to Golden Gate via Golden Gate Canyon Road

Gilpin Co. | Jefferson Co.

Reverend's Ridge Campground

Gap Hole

Panorama Point

Tremont Mt. EL 10300

Bootleg Bottom

Ole' Barn Knoll

Rim Meadow

Frazer Meadow

Mountain Base Road

Kriley Pond

Slough Pond

to Central City via Hwy 119

to Highway 119

Activities

Campfire programs, moonlight hikes, and other activities are scheduled at the amphitheater in the Reverend's Ridge campground most weekends from Memorial Day through Labor Day.

The 60 miles of trails are broken into 14 trails that range in length from around two miles up to six miles. Each trail is named for an animal native to the area and marked with signs showing the animal's footprint. The background shape and color of the signs indicates the degree of difficulty of the trail ranging from easy to moderate to difficult.

So you don't miss the forest for the trees, you can borrow a trail adventure pack at the Visitors Center. This includes a magnifying glass to observe plants up close, litmus paper to check the acidity of a stream or pond, and other gadgets and nature books making up a do-it-yourself nature study kit.

On these trails there's a fair chance you'll catch a glimpse of some of the park's wildlife that includes elk, mule deer, porcupine, beavers, the great horned owl, and red-tailed hawk. Although normally too elusive to be seen, you may run across tracks or other evidence of coyotes, bears, mountain lions, and bobcats. And for wildlife of a different kind, you might also come across the sites of one of the numerous moonshine stills that brewed white lighting here during the Prohibition era.

Mountain bikes are permitted on about 20 miles of trails. Some are easy, but several involve challenging climbs and hair-raising descents.

Especially popular at sunset is the 2½-mile Raccoon Trail, rated moderate in difficulty, that forms a loop from Reverend's Ridge to Panorama Point and back. At the Point is a large wooden observation deck which overlooks 50 miles of mountaintops that make up the Continental Divide. You might also find you're overlooking a wedding, since this grand overlook is frequently scheduled (not reserved) for that occasion.

For a leisurely stroll there are self-guided nature trails near the Visitors Center and the Reverend's Ridge Campground office. In the Visitors Center are ecological and historical displays, exhibits, and a topographical scale map of the park.

Outside the Visitors Center is a Show Pond where four- to eight-pound rainbow trout can be seen cruising the shallows. You can feed them, but, sorry, no fishing here. Fishing is permitted in every other stream and pond in the park. In the summer, Ralston Creek, a major creek in the park, and several of the ponds are periodically stocked with rainbow trout and, occasionally, with brown trout. This includes Dude's Fishing Hole, which is an easy 15-minute hike from the Aspen Meadows campground. When winter comes, ice fishing becomes a popular sport here.

Other winter sports you can take part in are cross-country skiing, ice skating, snowshoeing, and sledding and tubing.

Camping

The two campgrounds are both in the northern sections of the park and offer a total of 141 campsites. The 106 campsites at Reverend's Ridge Campground are located in a lodgepole pine forest at 9,200 feet elevation. Sites are multiuse, accommodating both RVs and tents, without hookups. This campground is normally open seasonally. Depending on snow conditions that's approximately May through October. (Campsites $7.)

Aspen Meadow campgrounds is located in an aspen and pine forest with rocky outcrops. It has 35 campsites for tents only. (Campsites $6.) It's open all year, but road conditions may make a four-wheel-drive vehicle a necessity to get there in winter. Organized groups can reserve the Rifleman Phillips Group Camp Area, just east of Aspen Meadow, for up to 75 persons by calling the park. There are also some camping sites and parking designed for horseback campers at this campground. Horse campers may also ride to the remote and primitive campsite at Deer Creek in the northeast backcountry.

In addition to 23 backcountry tent sites ($2),

there are also four shelters set in large scenic meadows surrounded by 10,000-foot peaks. These are three-sided structures, with a roof and wooden floor, built in the Appalachian trail-hut tradition, and can sleep up to six people with no need of a tent. These sites are available year-round. (Shelters $10.)

All backcountry camping, including horse camping, requires a permit from the Visitors Center.

Nearby Attractions

Just about six miles south on Colorado Highway 119 are the old mining towns of **Black Hawk,** the site of Colorado's richest gold strike, and **Central City,** which lays claim to "the richest square mile on earth." The **Black Hawk and Central City Narrow-Gauge Railroad** offers a 30-minute ride through the early-day goldfields. Each city also has a mine tour. The **Peak-to-Peak Highway,** one of Colorado's eight Scenic and Historic Byways, covers about 55 miles on Highways 7 and 72, going through the **Arapaho and Roosevelt**

national forests between Central City and Estes Park, the gateway to **Rocky Mountain National Park** (tel. 303/627-3471).

In the city of **Golden,** to the east, you can take a tour of the **Adolph Coors Brewery** (tel. 303/279-6565), visit **Buffalo Bill's Grave,** and the **National Earthquake Center** (tel. 303/273-8500).

To the south, at **Morrison,** are the tiny and the huge: **Tiny Town** (tel. 303/697-6829), a miniature handcrafted village; and **Red Rocks Amphitheater,** a natural 8,000-seat concert amphitheater. Here you can also see dinosaur footprints and dinosaur bones still embedded in the rock of a quarry dating from 1877.

Denver is less than an hour's drive away. The city's more than a dozen museums run the gamut from the **Children's Museum** (tel. 303/433-7433) to the **Denver Art Museum** (tel. 303/640-2793) to the **Arabian Horse Center** (tel. 303/254-7800). Restaurants, theaters, amusement parks, a zoo, and professional sports—they're all waiting for you in Colorado's mile-high capital city.

Mueller State Park and Wildlife Area

| RV Camping | Tent Camping | Group Camping | Fishing | Picnic Areas | Trails | Horse Trails | Nature Programs | Bicycling | X-Country Skiing |

Capsule Description: Natural mountain park with limited developed facilities.

Location: Central Colorado, about 27 miles west of Colorado Springs and 3½ miles south of Divide. From Colorado Springs, go west on U.S. Highway 24 to Divide, then south on Colorado Highway 67.

Address: P.O. Box 49, Divide, CO 80814 (tel. 719/687-2366).

Area Contacts: Colorado Springs Convention and Visitors Bureau, 104 S. Cascade, Suite 104, Colorado Springs, CO 80903 (tel. toll free 800/368-4748 (800/DO-VISIT) or 719/635-7506).

Cripple Creek Chamber of Commerce, P.O. Box 650, Cripple Creek, CO 80813 (tel. 719/689-2169).

Divide Chamber of Commerce, P.O. Box 101, Divide, CO 80814 (tel. 719/687-6011).

Manitou Springs Chamber of Commerce, 354 Manitou Ave., Manitou Springs, CO 80829 (tel. toll free 800/642-2567 or 719/685-5089 or 719/685-1963 (fax)).

Insider Tips: It should be noted that even if a trail is rated easy or moderate in difficulty, it may prove strenuous to some hikers not used to the high elevation. Take it easy until you are acclimated to the altitude. The trails that go through elk and bighorn sheep habitats are closed mid-May through mid-June because this is their calving and lambing season.

"The scenery is such to bankrupt the English language." That's how Teddy Roosevelt summed up his impression of the original Mueller Ranch area when he passed through here in 1901. A little over 90 years later, Colorado opened more than 12,000 acres of this beautiful area as one of its newest state parks.

At elevations ranging from 8,500 to 9,800 feet, this mountain park offers the visitor close to 90 miles of trails through spring-fed meadows, and forested ridges, plus massive rock formations and spectacular views. Partly because of the park's proximity to population centers and the development of the mountains, wildlife is more concentrated in this park than might be expected. Here the habitat is shared by elk, bighorn sheep, mule deer, eagles, hawks, and a wide variety of small mammals and songbirds. In the remote areas, bears, bobcats, and mountain lions roam. Stands of spruce, fir pine, juniper, and aspen flourish here, as does myriad wildflowers including the rare calypso orchids.

Among the several overlooks offering spectacular views, the overlook at the summit of Grouse Mountain—at 9,843 feet, the park's highest point—offers a panorama that includes Pikes Peak and the Sangre de Cristo Mountains.

To preserve this pristine wilderness, with the exception of the roads, all park development is concentrated in just 350 acres confined to the northern half.

Activities

An excellent way to begin your visit to this park is to take the Wapiti Nature Trail. This self-guided trail of less than a mile winds through several captivating ecosystems containing a variety of plant and animal life plus some fascinating geological features. Numbered points on the trail are matched up with descriptions in a brochure available at the trailhead. Most of this trail is an easy walk, but some uphill slopes are involved. At one point near the end of the trail, there's a good view of Pikes Peak.

This is just one of more than 40 marked and numbered trails in the park that range in length from about a mile to up to nine miles. They form an interconnecting network running off 13 trailheads so you can hike as long and as far as you want—close to 100 miles if you did them all. A park trail map is available at the entrance or the headquarters.

One of the more popular shorter trails goes a little less than two miles to several spectacular overlooks on Outlook Ridge. A more challenging hike is the Dome Rock Trail. This goes about 8½ miles and takes you to its namesake, Dome Rock, a geological feature that rises 800 feet above the valley floor. Be prepared to get your feet wet; this trail crosses a bridgeless creek eight times before you reach Dome Rock.

For those who don't want to hike, one overlook, Big View, is accessible by car. It offers a view of Pikes Peak and at least three surrounding mountain ranges.

In addition to hiking, in winter all trails are open for snowshoeing and cross-country skiing. Equipment may be rented in nearby communities. Trails are rated for beginning, intermediate, and advanced skiers. Other winter sports include sledding and tubing. Snowmobiles are not allowed.

Mountain bikers can use about 28 miles of trails with a difficulty rating of moderate, and there are 70 miles of horseback riding trails rated easy to moderate.

In summer there are campfire programs in the amphitheater at the campgrounds on weekends and a variety of hikes lead by rangers.

Several of the small ponds in the park are stocked with cutthroat, rainbow, and brook trout. All the ponds are hike-in only with walks ranging from 1½ to 3 miles. Fishing is also permitted in the one major creek.

This is a new park and development is still going on. For example, there are plans to put up a Visitors Center and one of the ponds is being set up for ice skating. Maybe these will be in place by the time you visit.

Camping

There are 78 multiuse campsites with electric hookups, plus 12 walk-in tent sites, located about 300 yards from a road, with no hookups. (Multiuse sites $10, walk-in $7.) Campers are limited to one camping unit and a maximum of six persons per site. Eleven of the multiuse sites are available for group camping.

Nearby Attractions

Nicknamed the "$300-million cow pasture," **Cripple Creek** is a historic mining town; in 1900 it had 500 goldmines. It's south of the park on Highway 67. You can descend 1,000 feet into the **Mollie Kathleen Gold Mine** (tel. 719/689-2465) for a tour of the inner workings of a mine from late May to October. This one produced that precious metal from the 1890s until the 1960s. For a broader view of gold mining go to the **Cripple Creek District Museum and Assay Office** (tel. 719/689-2634). The **Cripple Creek–Victor Railroad** offers a steam-train ride on narrow-gauge tracks to another nearby old mining town, **Victor,** where the streets were once paved with gold—albeit of a poor grade ore not fit for milling. During the summer at Cripple Creek, you can sneer and cheer at the longest-running classic melodrama in the U.S. performed at the theater in the **Imperial Hotel** (719/689-2922).

To the northwest, off U.S. Highway 24, is **Florissant Fossil Beds National Monument** (tel. 719/748-3204); here along with the fossils is a petrified sequoia stump, 11 foot high and 10 feet in diameter.

Going southeast on U.S. 24 toward Pikes Peak and Colorado Springs, you can stop in **Manitou Springs.** This town thrives on tourism. The **Manitou and Pikes Peak Cog Railway** (tel. 719/685-5401), known as the highest railroad in the U.S., climbs from a starting elevation of 6,571 feet to 14,110 feet at the summit. Displayed at the **Pikes Peak Hill Climb Museum** (tel. 719/685-4400) are race cars that entered the annual Pikes Peak Climb.

Also on U.S. 24 is **Santa's Workshop** (tel. 719/684-9432) at the North Pole, where it's Christmas every day of the year.

Among the many attractions in **Colorado Springs** is the **U.S. Air Force Academy** (tel. 719/472-1818); the **Garden of the Gods** (tel. 719/578-6939), a National Natural Landmark renowned for its unusual giant red sandstone formations; the **Cheyenne Mountain Zoo** (tel. 719/636-2544); and the **Old Colorado City historic district**. Among the city's museums are the **Pro Rodeo Hall of Fame** (tel. 719/528-4764), and the **World Figure Skating Hall of Fame and Museum** (tel. 719/635-5200). The **U.S. Olympic Training Center** (tel. 719/632-5551) is also found here.

Ridgway State Park

Visitor Center   RV Camping   Tent Camping   Marina   Boating   Boat Launch   Fishing   Beach   Waterskiing   Snorkeling & Diving

Trails   Horse Trails   Nature Programs   Bicycling   Playground   X-Country Skiing

Capsule Description: Natural mountain park on a lake with developed facilities.

Location: Southwest Colorado. From Montrose, on Highway 50, take Highway 550 south about 20 miles.

Address: 28555 Hwy. 550, Ridgway, CO 81432 (tel. 303/626-5822).

Area Contacts: Montrose Chamber of Commerce, 1519 E. Main St., Montrose, CO 81401 (tel. toll free 800/873-0244).

    Ouray County Chamber of Commerce, P.O. Box 145, Ouray, CO 81427 (tel. toll free 800/228-1876 or 303/325-4746).

    Silverton Chamber of Commerce, P.O. Box 565, Silverton, CO 81433 (tel. toll free 800/752-4494 or 303/387-5654).

    Telluride Chamber Resort Association, P.O. Box 653, Telluride, CO 81435 (tel. 303/728-3041).

This 2,000-acre park is built on the shore of a 1,000-acre, 5-mile-long lake and two stretches of river in the midst of snowcapped mountains just north of an area known as "The Switzerland of America." With a sandy beach, beach house, and full-service marina, the lake park offers boating, fishing, swimming, scuba diving, waterskiing, and windsurfing. Although situated at an elevation of 6,870 feet, the water in the lake approaches 70 degrees by June.

The focus here is on summer recreation, but the winter brings cross-country skiing and other winter sports.

A feather in the cap of the designers of this park is that they made more than 80% of the campsites and all major facilities accessible to disabled people.

Activities

Water sports on the crystalline waters of the lake are king here in summer. Waterskiing, jet skiing, sailboarding, and swimming (no lifeguards) are just a few ways to use the lake. All types of boating from motor to sail are permitted on the lake and the full-service marina rents equipment including pontoon, skiing, fishing, and paddle boats. During peak runoff, you can raft on one stretch of the Uncompahgre River, and a second portion of the river is being improved to support trophy fishing. The lake is stocked with rainbow trout annually and both rainbow, brown, and cutthroat trout can be caught in the river. Another catch is kokanee salmon. Tackle can be rented at the marina.

Information about other activities is available at the Visitor Center. Campfire programs and ranger-guided nature hikes are given from Memorial Day through Labor Day.

In addition to some planned activities for children, there are six modern-design playgrounds scattered around the park.

Four miles of developed hiking and biking trails wind through the park offering a chance to enjoy the scenery of the rugged, mountainous terrain. One trail leads to a scenic overlook of the nearby

Cimarron Mountain Range. These trails range from a moderate walk to a challenging hike. Horseback riding is also permitted on some of the trails. The trails offer the best chance of seeing mule deer and elk, as well as smaller animals like porcupines and raccoons. But anywhere around the lake you can expect to see waterfowl, golden eagles, hawks, and osprey. Winter is the best time for wildlife-watching.

Winter also brings a chance for cross-country skiing, sledding, tubing, and ice skating. No snowmobiles are allowed.

Camping

There are 177 multiuse camp sites with electric hookups in two campgrounds, plus 10 walk-in sites for tents only. Some of these have shade shelters. Dakota Terrace campground is within walking distance of the lake and the swim beach, while Elk Ridge campground is located in a piñon-juniper forest with panoramic views of the nearby San Juan Mountains. But the park is still growing and by the time you read this there may be an additional 81 multiuse sites and 10 more sites for tents only. (Campsites $10, sometimes discounted in winter when some facilities are closed.) There are also plans to add some boat-in campsites.

There is no designated group camping area, but groups may reserve campsites together anywhere in the campgrounds.

Nearby Attractions

A number of national forests surround the park. The major ones are the one-million-acre **Uncompahgre National Forest** and the **Gunnison National Forest** with more than a million and a half acres.

Northeast of the park, via Highways 550, 50, and 347, is the **Black Canyon** of the **Gunnison National Monument** containing one of the deepest, narrowest gorges in the world.

About a mile south of Montrose, on Highway 550, is the **Ute Indian Museum** (tel. 303/ 249-3098), where the memorable history of this tribe is on display.

For mountain bikers, the **Tabeguache Trail,** part of the Colorado Plateau Mountain Bike Trail System, starts in Montrose and goes northwest to Grand Junction.

South of the park is the town of **Ouray,** which has been called the "Jeep Capital of the World" because the area offers hundreds of miles of off-highway driving. You can rent a four-wheel-drive vehicle here or take a guided tour. Ouray also offers a walking tour of its national historic district, a waterfall right at the edge of town, and a bathhouse featuring natural hot springs.

The **Alpine Loop Byway** connects Ouray with Lake City and Silverton. This is one of the eight designated scenic and historic roads in the state.

About an hour's drive south from Ridgway will take you to the hills and ski resorts of the winter playground of **Telluride.** This small mining town, a National Historic Landmark, is a popular destination even without snow. For one thing, you can take a chair-lift ride to view the alpine scenery. Summer is also the time of a film festival. Colorado's highest waterfall, **Bridal Veil Falls** (450 feet) is about two miles east of town.

Another mining town to the south of the park that's also a National Historic Landmark is **Silverton.** Producing gold since 1874, the Sunnyside is still mining on a small scale. Consider taking the **Durango and Silverton Narrow-Gauge Railroad,** in operation since 1882. During the summer only, this steam train makes a 90-mile, 3½-hour trip through breathtaking mountain scenery between Silverton and Durango.

Connecticut

ROCKY NECK
STATE PARK

Connecticut has 52 state parks.

Contacts

- Department of Environmental Protection, State Parks Division, 79 Elm Street, 6th Floor, Hartford, CT 06106 (tel. 203/566-2305).
- Department of Economic Development, 865 Brook St., Rocky Hill, CT 06067-3405 (tel. toll free 800/282-6863 [800/CT-BOUND] or 203/258-4290).

General Information on Connecticut State Parks

With a 250 miles of shoreline on Long Island Sound, it's not surprising that Connecticut, in 1776, was the birthplace of the first submarine. It also was a leader in bringing the Industrial Revolution to America. You can find evidence of this trend toward high-tech in some of its historic parks, but most of the state parks are given over to providing a respite from the modern world for the nature lover. Here is the beauty of dense woodlands, rocky points jutting into the Sound, bathing beaches, rolling hills, gushing trout streams and, in winter, powdery ski trails.

GENERAL FEES

Entrance or parking fees vary by park. Some are free, some charge on weekends and holidays, and others charge every day. Where there is a fee it normally runs about $5 for state residents on weekdays and $7 on weekends to $7 for out-of-state visitors on weekdays and $12 on weekends and holidays. Connecticut residents may buy a special season pass for a nominal fee. There is also a free pass available for residents age 60 and over.

CAMPING

Eleven of the state's parks have campgrounds with a total of more than 1,400 sites. Most campgrounds are open only for the summer season from mid-April to the end of September; however, a limited number of campsites are open as late as the end of December. Contact the Parks Division for information on off-season camping. All campgrounds are closed from January 1 through mid-April.

Most campsites may be reserved from Memorial Day through Labor Day. Reservations are by *mail only* directly to the park. You must write for a camping permit application first. Applications for any time in the year will be accepted beginning January 15. Any application postmarked prior to January 14 will be returned. Applications must be received at least 10 days in advance of the intended reservation period. The minimum reservation is two nights. Most campsites cost $12 a night with that fee covering four persons, including children. The maximum number of persons per campsite is six. Each extra person will be charged $2 per night.

As a safety measure for out-of-state travelers, some Connecticut state parks located on or near major highways offer an emergency overnight stopping plan for motorists with suitable camping equipment, who find themselves unable to obtain lodging or gain access to a regular camping area late at night. Temporary space may be assigned in an open field or parking lot at participating parks. The fee is $9 and campers in this emergency stop-over program must leave the park by 8am the following morning.

Pets. Pets are normally permitted in picnic areas and on hiking trails. They are prohibited in campgrounds and on beaches. Where they are permitted they must be under control and on a leash not to exceed seven feet in length. Dogs must have rabies vaccinations and owners may be required to show proof.

Alcoholic beverages. Beer in containers larger than one (1) liter is prohibited.

Discounts. Charter Oak Passes—available to Connecticut senior citizens age 60 and over—allow free parking and admission to state parks.

Rocky Neck State Park

| RV Camping | Tent Camping | Boating | Boat Launch | Fishing | Beach | Snorkeling & Diving | Picnic Areas | Trails | Nature Programs | X-Country Skiing |

Capsule Description: A saltwater beach park.

Location: On Long Island Sound, west of New London. Take Exit 72 off I-95. Follow the turnpike connector south to Connecticut Route 156 and take this east to the park.

Address: P.O. Box 676, Niantic, CT 06357-0676 (tel. 203/739-5471).

Area Contacts: East Lyme Chamber of Commerce, P.O. Box 535, Niantic, CT 06357 (tel. 203/739-0208). Southeastern Connecticut Tourism District, 27 Masonic St., P.O. Box 89, New London, CT 06320 (tel. toll free 800/TO-ENJOY outside Connecticut or 203/444-2206).

Insider Tip: A wildlife observation deck and scenic overlook is found at the marsh on Four Mile River.

A half mile of beach frontage on Long Island Sound puts this 710-acre park in the running for one of Connecticut's finest saltwater bathing beaches.

Bounded on the west by a tidal river and on the east by a broad salt marsh, Rocky Neck is a place of abundant fish and wildlife. High spring tides allow schools of herring to swim into Bride Brook toward inland spawning grounds. The osprey, or fish hawk, is a frequent early summer visitor and in the fall, herons and mute swans wade among the cattails and rose mallow.

Activities

Going down to the sea is the big thing here.

Clear waters, the stone-free beach, and a wide expanse of white sand make this an refreshing place for swimmers. Lifeguards are on duty from 10am to 6pm from Memorial Day to Labor Day. Scuba divers can go in west of the rock jetty. No alcoholic beverages or pets are allowed on the beach.

Anglers have a choice of saltwater or freshwater fishing. Fishing from the beach is permitted from sunset to 6:30am from Memorial Day through the end of September. There's also a stone jetty, although it's difficult to walk out on. Depending on the season, the catch might include bluefish, mackerel, striped bass, and flounder. One nice thing is saltwater fishing does not require a license. Freshwater fishing is permitted at all times in Bride Brook and Four Mile River, but here you need a license. There's also a designated area for crabbing and a fishing spot for disabled anglers.

In season, the staff puts on campfire and other interpretive programs and conducts guided nature walks.

There are about five miles of easy trails for hikers. One of these trails is the park's half-mile, self-guiding nature trail. The trail starts at a man-made object, the curved masonry pavilion built in 1935. (Ninety percent of the materials in this building were obtained from the state's parks and forests. The flagstone for the walks and terraces was taken from Devil's Hopyard in East Haddan. The field stones used in the walls and terraces were quarried at Rocky Neck. Each of the 42 wooden pillars inside was taken from a different Connecticut forest.) A brochure is available for this walk. Among the flowers you'll see on this walk is the mountain laurel, the Connecticut state flower.

In the winter, the trails are used for cross-country skiing.

Camping

The 165 campsites are made up of 141 multiuse and 24 for tent camping only. Some sites are in the woods and others in open areas. None of the sites has hookups. Each camping permit allows for a maximum of two vehicles. Campsites are provided without fireplaces. Fires are permitted if the campers supply their own fire container, which must be at least 12 inches above the ground so the fire won't destroy the grass. (Campsites $12.)

From the campground to the beach is an easy walk.

This park has an emergency stopover area (see above) for out-of-state visitors caught in a lurch.

There is no separate group camping area, but organized youth groups can reserve sites together at a reduced rate.

Nearby Attractions

A few miles east of the park on Route 156 is the **Millstone Information and Science Center** (tel. 203/691-4670) on Main Street in **Niantic.** Along with exhibits on nuclear energy and the nearby nuclear power station, the center offers computer energy games, interactive video displays, and multimedia shows. It's free. If you want to fish the Sound, both party fishing boats and charter boats operate out of Niantic.

Continuing east on Route 156 (or you can go back up to I-95 and head east) will bring you to **New London.** Nature lovers won't want to miss the 425 acres of native trees and shrubs, ponds, wildflowers, and hiking trails in the **Connecticut College Arboretum** (tel. 203/439-2140); no admission. Another major attraction, and another freebie here, is the **U.S. Coast Guard Academy** (tel. 203/444-8444). The smallest of the service academies, it still has a lot to offer visitors who take the self-guided tour.

From New London ferries whisk passengers and cars to **Block Island,** Rhode Island; **Fishers Island,** New York; and **Orient Point** on Long Island, New York.

Just across the Thames River is **Groton,** home port of our Atlantic submarine fleet. The naval base is closed to visitors except for Armed Forces Day (some time in May) and Navy Birthday (some time in October). but you'll probably see some subs on the river. Commercial boat companies offer tours of the Thames. Off the base, the USS *Nautilus Memorial* (tel. 203/449-3174) can be visited daily 9am to 4pm except on Tuesday. Now decommissioned, the *Nautilus* was the world's first nuclear-powered submarine and the first sub to go under the ice to the North Pole.

Another short drive east and you'll be in **Mystic.** The biggest attraction here is **Mystic Seaport** (tel. 203/572-0711), a living-museum village that re-creates a 19th-century maritime port.

Delaware

CAPE HENLOPEN
STATE PARK

Delaware has 12 state parks.

Contacts

- Delaware Division of Parks and Recreation, P.O. Box 1401, 89 King's Highway, Dover, DE 19903 (tel. 302/739-4702).
- Delaware Tourism Office, P.O. Box 1401, Dover, DE 19903 (tel. toll free 800/282-8667 in Delaware, 800/441-8846 out of state).

General Information on Delaware State Parks

Although Delaware and has only a dozen state parks, our second-smallest state offers a variety of facilities. You can canoe the bald cypress trail, enjoy surf fishing, swimming, or just a stroll along 14 miles of ocean beaches, spend a lazy afternoon rowing on one of the many pristine ponds, hike on more than 80 miles of scenic trails in eight of the parks, camp, and enjoy a wide range of other outdoor activities.

GENERAL FEES

An entrance fee is charged at all parks every day from Memorial Day weekend through Labor Day as well as Saturdays, Sundays, and holidays in May, September, and October. The fee is $2.50 for vehicles registered in Delaware, $5 for out-of-state vehicles. Six-permit booklets sell for $12.50. (Out-of-state vehicles must use two permits per visit.) Annual permits cost $20 for Delaware-registered vehicles, $40 for out-of-state.

CAMPING

All campsites are on a first-come basis; no reservations. Camping season is normally from April through October. Sites vary by park from three-way hookups ($18 per night) to no hookups ($9 to $12 per night). As many as 10 people may use one campsite, but there is an additional charge of $2 per person for all over the total of four.

Pets. Pets are permitted, but must on leash and be attended at all times. Each park has its own rules; however, pets are normally not allowed on beaches during the summer season, in buildings, on nature trails, or in bird-nesting areas.

Alcoholic beverages. There are different rules in different parks; in general, however, alcoholic beverages in cans and bottles are permitted in all parks.

Discounts. Senior Citizens, age 62 and older, may purchase annual permits at one-half the regular rate.

Cape Henlopen State Park

Visitor Center

RV Camping

Tent Camping

Group Lodge Dormitories

Fishing

Beach

Picnic Areas

Tennis

Trails

Nature Programs

Bicycling

Capsule Description: A saltwater beach park.

Location: On a sandy peninsula known as the "hook," which marks the south end of Delaware Bay and the beginning of the Atlantic Ocean. Take the Coastal Highway, Delaware Route 1, to Lewes. Follow the signs east to the Cape May-Lewes Ferry Terminal. Continue on about half a mile to the park.

Address: 42 Cape Henlopen Dr., Lewes, DE 19958 (tel. 302/645-8983 for the office, 302/645-2103 for the campgrounds).

Area Contacts: Lewes Chamber of Commerce and Visitors Bureau, P.O. Box 1, Lewes, DE 19958 (tel. 302/645-8073).

Prime Hook National Wildlife Refuge, RD #3, Box 195, Milton, DE 19968 (tel. 302/684-8419).

Rehoboth Beach-Dewey Beach Chamber of Commerce, P.O. Box 216, 501 Rehoboth Ave., Rehoboth Beach, DE 19971 (tel. toll free 800/441-1329 or 302/227-2233).

Insider Tip: From mid-May through June, Delaware Bay becomes the second-largest staging area for shorebirds in North America. The reason: the Bay is also the principal breeding ground for horseshoe crabs on the east coast. The eggs of the horseshoe are a major lure for birds, and these six weeks are the peak of the crab's mating season. It's estimated the crabs lay an estimated 320 tons of eggs, so the birds find an abundance to gorge on. Only the vast Copper River Delta in Alaska hosts more shorebirds each spring.

In 1682, the duke of York gave William Penn the lands below the southern boundary of Penn's Province of Pennsylvania. When granting a request to use land at Cape Henlopen, Penn stipulated that the cape and all its natural resources were to be for the common usage of the people of Lewes and Sussex County. In principle, he gave the land to the people.

Today, the main lure for visitors to this park is four miles of Atlantic coast beach. This 3,020-acre park is also home of one of the highest sand dunes between Cape Hatteras and Cape Cod. Known as the Great Dune, it rises 80 feet above the shore. Here too are the "walking dunes." Park programs are heavily into nature with a year-round nature center, trails, and a number of programs for visitors.

During World War II, Fort Miles was located on what's now parkland. Heavy guns were put in bunkers to protect against attacks, especially submarine attacks, from the sea. The dunes and other natural features were used to mask these fortifications. The guns are gone, but some of the bunkers and observation and aiming towers remain.

Activities

The primary drawing card is the Atlantic surf. Lifeguards patrol the two swimming beaches in season. Beach umbrellas and chairs, boogie boards, and rafts can be rented at concessions on the beach.

Fishing in the surf or from the quarter-mile-long pier can yield catches of bluefish, flounder, sea trout, and sand sharks. In season, a golf cart is available to take disabled fishermen out on the pier. Crabbing is also excellent in park waters.

If you want to see live fish up close, visit the aquarium in the Seaside Nature Center where a flotilla of ocean fish are on display in five large tanks. This center, one of only two all-year nature centers in Delaware parks, is also the site of exhibits, films, nature demonstrations, and the start point for nature interpretive walks.

There are two nature trails in the park: the Seaside Interpretive Trail, a little over half a mile long; and the Pinelands Nature Trail, a little over a mile long. One trail in the park is the easternmost point on the American Discovery Trail, which goes across the country from Delaware to California.

For an overall view of the park, weather permitting, one of the old coast artillery towers is open for those who want to make the long climb to the top. There's also an overlook platform for a fine view of the ocean where you can sometimes see dolphins swimming near the shore.

Bikes are permitted on some of the trails, and, although there are no designated horse trails, some horseback riding is permitted on the beaches.

Tennis courts, basketball courts, softball and field hockey fields, and a nine-hole disc golf course (played with Frisbees) add to the park's recreation facilities.

For birders, migratory, sea, and shore birds abound most of the year. Among the more common birds are varieties of loons, cormorants, snowy egrets, geese, ospreys, gulls, wrens, and starlings. During the summer the park is a nesting area for the tiny piping plover, a small, stocky bird protected by the Endangered Species Act.

Camping

About 90% of the 159 multiuse campsites have water hookups. (Campsites $13 in season, $12 after Labor Day.) Campground open April 1 to October 31.

Youth groups may reserve space in 18 dormitories. Sixteen of these hold up to 15 people and the other two have a capacity of 25. There is a also a primitive camping area for youth groups.

Nearby Attractions

A mile west, on Route 1, is **Lewes** (pronounced Lewis) on Delaware Bay. The town traces its history back to when the Dutch settled here in 1631, making it the oldest settlement in Delaware. (Actually the Dutch set up a whaling station here in 1609, but the Native Americans quickly put an end to that venture by massacring all the whalers.)

During the War of 1812, a British frigate bombarded the town. A building on Front Street struck by a cannonball is now a small marine museum, appropriately called the **Cannonball House.** The **Zwaanendael Museum** (tel. 302/645-9418) features the history of the Dutch settlement and the growth of the Lewes. In Shipcarpenter Square are several restored 18th- and 19th-century homes and next to it the **Lewes Historical Society Complex** (tel. 302/645-7670) of buildings dating back as far as 1780.

A 79-foot topsail schooner offers two- or three-hour sailing excursions, and fishing party boats and charter boats operate out of the port. For a longer day's excursion, take a round-trip on the ferry over to **Cape May, New Jersey.** From there **Atlantic City** is less than an hour's drive.

About six miles south is the popular touristy seashore areas of **Rehoboth Beach** and **Dewey Beach.**

To the north about 10 miles is the 8,817-acre **Prime Hook National Wildlife Refuge** (tel. 302/684-8419), which is open to visitors.

Florida

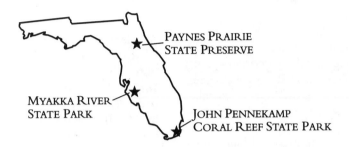

PAYNES PRAIRIE
STATE PRESERVE

MYAKKA RIVER
STATE PARK

JOHN PENNEKAMP
CORAL REEF STATE PARK

Florida has 110 state parks.

Contacts

• Division of Recreation and Parks, Department of Natural Resources, 3900 Commonwealth Blvd., Tallahassee, FL 32399-3000 (tel. 904/488-9872 or 904/488-2850).
• Division of Tourism, Department of Commerce, 107 W. Gaines St., Tallahassee, FL 32399-2000 (tel. 904/488-7300).

General Information on Florida State Parks

The management objective for the Florida parks is to treat the parks as natural systems; that is as representative examples of native landscape conditions and biological communities. This is the reason that 85,000 acres of the 415,000 acres of parkland are actually submerged lands. In fact, one of the parks included in this *100 Best-Loved* is John Pennekamp Coral Reef State Park, which has only 2,350 acres of upland while 53,661 acres are under water.

General Fees

Park entrance fees vary from park to park and range from about $2 to about $3.50 for a vehicle with a maximum of eight people. Children under 6 admitted free. An annual entrance permit for a family is available for about $60, plus tax. These are available through individual park offices.

Camping and Accommodations

Reservations may be made for 50% of the campsites in 26 of the 43 parks with campgrounds. The other 50% and all the campsites in the other 17 parks are on a first-come basis. Reservations may also be made for the vacation cabins located in six parks, primitive sleeping cabins in two additional parks, and group campsites in three parks. Reservations should be made directly to the park of your choice by phone or in person only; no mail reservations.

Camping. Reservations are accepted between 8am and 5pm daily, no more than 60 days in advance. Four persons are allowed per campsite for the basic camping fee. Each additional person is $1. There's also an extra fee of $2 for a waterfront site and $2 if you use an electrical hookup. Stays in a camping area are limited to two weeks. Camping fees range from about $8 to about $20 depending on location, facilities, and season—winter is high season here. Most sites are in the $8 to $14 range even in high season.

Cabins. Cabin reservations may be made up to six months in advance. Fees range from about $40 to $110, with most in the $50 to $85 range; once again depending on location, facilities, and season. The primitive sleeping cabins go for about $20 all year.

Pets. Pets are *not* allowed in camping areas, on bathing beaches, and in most buildings. Where pets are permitted, they must be on a leash no longer than six feet and under control at all times.

Alcoholic beverages. Intoxicants are *not* permitted in any state park.

Discounts. Senior Citizens and disabled citizens of Florida are entitled to a discount of one-half the base fee for camping.

John Pennekamp Coral Reef State Park

 Visitor Center
 RV Camping
 Tent Camping
 Group Camping
 Marina
 Boating
 Boat Launch
 Fishing

 Beach
 Swimming
 Snorkeling & Diving
 Picnic Areas
 Trails
 Nature Programs
Gift Shop

Capsule Description: An underwater park with land-based facilities.

Location: The Florida Keys, about 60 miles south of Miami on U.S. Highway 1 at Key Largo. Numbered mile markers are posted on Highway 1. They start at 127, south of Florida City, and end at zero in Key West. The park is at mile marker 102.5.

Address: P.O. Box 487, Key Largo, FL 33037 (tel. 305/451-1202).

Area Contacts: Islamorada Chamber of Commerce, P.O. Box 915, Islamorada, FL 33036 (tel. toll free 800/322-5397 or 305/664-4503).

Key Largo Chamber of Commerce, 105950 Overseas Hwy., Key Largo, FL 33037 (tel. toll free 800/822-1088 or 305/451-1414).

Tropical Everglades Visitor Association, 160 U.S. Hwy. 1, Florida City, FL 33034 (tel. toll free 800/388-9669 or 305/245-9180).

This was the first underwater park in the world and is still the only underwater state park in the United States. It was developed to protect an exquisite coral reef—the only living coral reef in United States continental waters. Coral reefs are earth's largest formations made by living organisms, small marine animals called polyps. Although coral appears to be rock-hard, it's actually extremely fragile. Even slight contact by a foot or a swim fin, or just about anything else, can weaken and lead to the disintegration of a piece of coral that may have taken a century to grow.

When founded in 1960, the park went almost eight miles out to sea. But in the mid-1970s, the federal government took control of U.S. underwater areas beyond three miles to a depth of 300 feet. So, today, the state park boundary ends at three miles from shore and includes what's known as the inner reefs. The Key Largo National Marine Sanctuary takes over from there and contains the outer reefs. Boundaries are hard to see in the water, however, so most residents still refer to the whole area—178 nautical square miles of coral reefs, sea-grass beds, and mangrove swamp—as Pennekamp.

Activities

Of the 56,000 acres in this park, all but about 2,300 acres are under water. Even those upland acres are mostly waterlogged. Only about 70 acres are truly land; the rest is mangrove swamp.

Before venturing out on or into the water, the best way to get a quick understanding of this park is at the Visitors Center with its "reef you can walk through." Here, in a 30,000-gallon saltwater tank, you can watch some of the 650 varieties of tropical fish found in the reef. There's also a display that shows how a coral reef grows, and several smaller aquariums containing other sea creatures, like the spiny lobster.

Video and slide shows in the center theater present nature programs all day. Some programs are on the park; others include shows on alligators, manatees, and the nearby Everglades. During the winter season—November through March—there are guided nature walks, campfire programs, and guided canoe programs.

In addition to picnicking, other land activities include two short hiking trails, a self-guided nature trail, an observation tower, and saltwater swimming at three small beaches (no lifeguards).

Sixty-seven threatened or endangered species of birds, mammals, and reptiles have been recorded in the park; that's more than in some states. A number of rare and endangered plants also grow here.

Of the million or so visitors who come to this park every year, about half come in boats. Mooring is available at the marina, but there's no fuel for private boaters. If you don't have your own boat, rental boats (motor, sail, and canoe), as well as a variety of windsurfing boards, are available at the marina.

You can also rent snorkel or scuba equipment at the dive shop. Boats make three trips a day carrying snorkelers out to the reef. The charge of $22 includes rented gear. Scuba boats make two trips a day. The price of about $33 does not include equipment. Scuba divers must be certified. There are courses offered for those seeking certification.

Fishing is permitted and the main catches are usually snapper, barracuda, and grouper. If you rent a boat, you can also rent fishing equipment.

Want to experience the beauty of the reef without getting wet? Glass-bottom-boat tours are run three times a day. The boat hovers over the reef as a guide explains what you're looking at. For the best view, wear polarized sunglasses.

Reservations are strongly recommended for all tours. You can call ahead (tel. 305/451-1621).

Camping

There are 47 multiuse campsites with water and electric hookups. Most are shaded, but there's not much separation between sites. Campsites are $19 per night plus a $2.50 county fee. (The county also tacks on a 50¢-a-head charge on the state's regular entrance fee.) A primitive tent camping area is available for organized groups.

Nearby Attractions

Just about anything you can arrange to do in the park can also be arranged in **Key Largo:** glass-bottom boat tours, fishing, and diving—but it'll probably cost more. And, of course, there are restaurants and resorts with all the trimmings. South of Key Largo is another resort area at **Islamorada.** Well named as **Overseas Highway,** Highway 1 can be driven down the necklace of keys for 100 miles to Mile Marker Zero at **Key West.**

On the peninsula to the northwest about 70 miles from Pennekamp lies **Everglades National Park** (tel. 305/242-7700). This is the largest remaining subtropical wilderness in the contiguous United States. The park entrance is on Highway 9336. A lodge and campgrounds are available here. The park is interlaced with hiking trails. Guided tram tours and boat tours run through the everglades from the Flamingo Marina. Canoes, skiffs, and bikes can be rented at this marina, too.

Myakka River State Park

Visitor Center | Cabins & Cottages | RV Camping | Tent Camping | Primitive Camping | Group Camping | Boating | Boat Launch | Fishing | Picnic Areas

Trails | Horse Trails | Nature Programs | Bicycling | Playground | Gift Shop

---

Capsule Description: A large wilderness park with some developed facilities.

Location: Southwest Florida, about 12 miles east of Sarasota on Florida Highway 72. Take Exit 37 off I-75 and go nine miles east on Highway 72.

Address: 13207 SR 72, Sarasota, FL 34241-9542 (tel. 813/361-6511).

Area Contacts: Sarasota Convention and Visitors Bureau, 655 N. Tamiami Trail, Sarasota, FL 34236 (tel. toll free 800/522-9799 or 813/957-1877).

Venice Area Chamber of Commerce, 257 N. Tamiami Trail, Venice, FL 34285-1534 (tel. 813/488-2236).

Twelve miles of the Myakka River, a state-designated wild and scenic river, flow through this 28,875-acre park, the largest state park in Florida, giving it its name. The river gives visitors access to a variety of distinct biological communities. The main park drive winds through oak and palm hammocks that open to give a view of grassy marshes, sloughs, and the 850-acre Upper Myakka Lake. Deer, raccoon, and many species of birds are easily viewed along this drive. An especially good view of wading and shorebirds can be seen from a 330-foot-long bird-viewing boardwalk on the lake. Hikers who venture off the main drive can traverse large, open expanses of dry prairie, pine woods, and numerous small wetlands. Deer, rabbits, bobcats, hawks, and other wildlife are commonly seen in this area of the park. Another resident commonly seen in marshes, swamps, and lakes is the American alligator.

One of the purposes of the Florida park system is, where possible, to keep the native systems in the original state that would have been encountered by the first Europeans who came here in the 16th century. In keeping with this, 7,500 acres of the park, undisturbed by development, have been designated a wilderness preserve. Open daily from 8am to sunset, entrance to the preserve by foot or boat is by permit only, and only a limited number of people are allowed to visit this wilderness area each day.

Activities

The slide program and exhibits in the interpretive center offer you a chance to get a grip on the details of this large park before venturing out to explore it.

Another good way to get the big picture is to take one of the boat or tram tours. The boat tour is in a 70-passenger enclosed airboat—touted as "the world's largest airboat." It makes a scenic cruise of the lake and the airboat configuration lets it get into shallow grassy places, not possible with a conventional prop, for a better view of shoreline water birds and other wildlife. The tram tour gets off the paved road into remote areas of subtropical forests and marshlands. Each tour costs $6 for adults. No reservations. For schedule and other information call 813/365-0100.

Once you know your way around, foot or boat

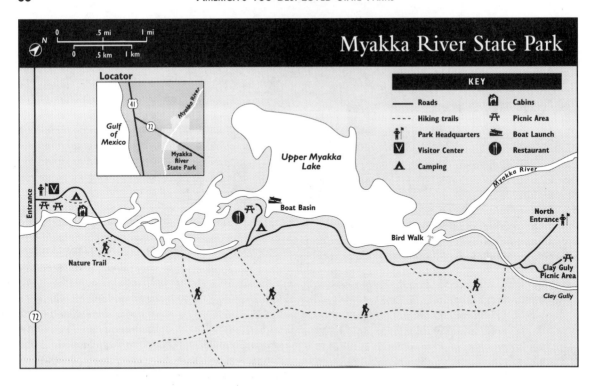

are the best ways to explore the land, and see the birds and the abundant wildlife. In addition to a ¾-mile, self-guided nature trail, for hikers, there are 39 miles of trails. The prairie trails are blanketed with brilliantly colored wildflowers from August through October. Boaters, of course, have the river and the lake. (There's a no-wake law on both.) Boats and canoes may be rented at the boat basin on the lake. Bicycles, too.

There's no horse camping, but there are three designated riding trails adding up to a total of 12 miles. More than 68 miles of service roads are also normally open for horses.

Birdwatching programs for beginners are usually offered during the winter. And there are always plenty for birders to watch, from wading birds and waterfowl to red-shouldered hawks and wild turkey. On a recent Christmas Day bird count, more than 9,000 birds of 108 species were recorded.

Fishing is permitted, with bass, bream, and catfish abundant in the past; however, the park waters have been invaded by hydrilla, an exotic weed, and this has made fishing unpredictable. There is also some saltwater fishing in one end of the park. If you go for both fresh- and saltwater catches, you'll need separate licenses.

One word of caution: Alligators are abundant in the park. They are interesting to observe and may appear docile, but they are dangerous since they are opportunistic carnivores that will eat almost anything. They should not be approached, teased, frightened, or fed. Feeding is a violation of state law and makes these creatures lose their fear of people, making them doubly dangerous. It also conditions them to associate people with food and go looking for people. They are also surprisingly agile, even on land, so give them the respect and distance they deserve.

Camping and Accommodations

Five rustic **log cabins** with fireplaces are available for rent. Built of palm logs and tar by men of the

Civilian Conservation Corps (CCC) in the 1930s, they've been maintained in excellent condition and upgraded with air conditioners, electric stoves and refrigerators, and hot-water showers, but no TV or phones. Each may be reserved up to a year in advance for from two days to two weeks. One-night reservations are accepted up to 30 days in advance for Sunday through Thursday nights (except holidays). Each cabin costs $50 per night for up to four people. They sleep up to six, but it's $5 extra for each extra person. (No extra charge for children under 6 years old.) One cabin is equipped for the handicapped. No pets are allowed.

The 76 multiuse **campsites** are in two sections. In one, all 24 sites have water and electric hookups. In the second section 24 of the sites have water and electric hookups and the rest have only water. All campsites are shaded, but they are close together and there's not much privacy buffer between sites. In high season (December 1 to April 30) sites cost $14. The rest of the year it's $10. The park concession store carries a stock of most items required by campers as well as day-use visitors.

Primitive camping is available for youth groups and hikers.

Nearby Attractions

In the early 1900s, circus magnate John Ringling decided that the Sarasota area on the Gulf Coast would be an ideal place of retreat from his life on the road. He and his circus family have had an impact on the area, which you can enjoy on a day's visit as **Sarasota** is just a short drive west from the park. Housed in an Italian Renaissance–style villa, the **John and Mable Ringling Museum of Art** (tel. 813/355-5101) has one of the nation's outstanding collections of baroque art; true to its heritage, the museum also has a **Circus Gallery** and the **Circus Ring of Fame.** At Sarasota's **Asolo Center for the Performing Arts** (tel. 813/351-9010), you can enjoy everything from opera to ballet to jazz. Drama is produced at the **Asolo State Theater** (813/351-9010), whose professional company is considered one of the nation's leading regional troupes. The **Sarasota Jungle Gardens** (tel. 813/355-1112) is home to exotic animals and has jungle trails to walk. A colorful collection of orchids and other tropical plants is found at **Selby Gardens** (tel. 813/366-5730). A little to the south of Sarasota is **Venice,** the off-season home of the Ringling Bros. and Barnum & Bailey Circus.

Paynes Prairie State Preserve

| Visitor Center | RV Camping | Tent Camping | Boat Launch | Non-Motorized Boating Only | Fishing | Picnic Areas | Trails | Horse Trails | Nature Programs | Bicycling | Playground |

Capsule Description: A large prairieland park with some developed facilities.

Location: Northeast Florida, 10 miles south of Gainesville and about 3 miles east of the Micanopy exit (Exit 73) off I-75 on U.S. Highway 441.

Address: Route 2, Box 41, Micanopy, FL 32667-9702 (tel. 904/466-3397).

Area Contacts: Alachua County Convention and Visitors Bureau, 30 E. University Ave., Gainesville, FL 32601 (tel. 904/374-5231).

Gainesville Area Chamber of Commerce, P.O.

Box 1187, Gainesville, FL 32602-1187 (tel. 904/334-7100).

A vast prairie, buffalo, wild horses, and a park named after a Native American chief; this is Florida?

Yes, it is. However, the prairie is wet, and the buffalo and wild horses, although definitely here, roam in small herds and the shy animals are rarely seen in the vastness of this 19,000-acre preserve. Native American artifacts dating back 10,000 years have been found in the area, but the park is named after a chief from more recent times—King Payne of the Seminoles who inhabited this area about 200 years ago. In the early 1800s, the U.S. Army was ordered to deport the Seminoles to reservations on the plains west of the Mississippi. The Seminoles decided not to go. The result was the Seminole Wars. Most of the battles were fought farther south, but there were several Seminole raids and skirmishes fought in this area.

Within the park are 20 distinct biological communities, such as the wet prairie, pine flatwoods, hammocks, swamp, and ponds. This variety also leads to a rich variety of animal life ranging from eagles to alligators.

Activities

You can get a bird's-eye view of the prairie from an observation tower near the Visitor Center. From the top level of the three-level, 50-foot-tower (54 steps) you can look out over a sea of grass and observe wildlife. In spring and fall you'll see a sea of color as the wildflowers bloom on the prairie.

The interpretative exhibits in the Visitor Center explain the natural and cultural history of the preserve. In season (October to March) there are a number of ranger-led walks and hikes, usually on weekends. And the last weekend of each month there's a backpacking trip with an overnight in a primitive campsite. The walks and hikes are free, but there's a moderate fee for the overnight.

Want to go on your own? There are about 30 miles of trails you can try. Some easy, some moderate, some will give you strenuous exercise. Several miles of the 17-mile Gainesville-Hawthorne State

Trail pass through the park. This trail, like some of the park trails, is designed for walking, cycling, and horseback riding. A rule on these trails is that pedestrians yield to cyclists who, in turn, yield to horses.

In addition to the small herds of buffalo and wild horses, wildlife in the park includes otters, bobcats, and a wide variety of waterfowl, hawks, and wading birds.

The preserve is a major wintering ground for around 2,000 sandhill cranes that migrate here from their breeding grounds in Michigan and Wisconsin in mid-October to late November. The mating dance of the cranes is a sight to see. Facing each other, they leap into the air with wings extended and feet thrown forward. Then they bow to each other and repeat the performance, uttering loud croaking calls. Pair bonding is usually long term.

The significant alligator population means no swimming in Lake Wauberg, but boating and fishing are permitted. Boats can be paddle, sail, or powered by electric motors only; no gasoline power. The lake is regularly stocked with sunshine bass. Other catches may include largemouth bass, speckled perch, crappie, and catfish.

Remember that the alligators, buffalo, and wild horses may appear tame, but they are wild and unpredictable, therefore dangerous. Observe only. Don't try to approach or feed them.

Camping

There are 37 multiuse campsites, all with water and electric hookups. Sites are all shaded and, although close together, most have an adequate privacy buffer. There are also 15 tent campsites. These also have water and electric hookups, but require a walk in from the parking lot. All sites are on a first-come basis; no reservations. Sites go for $8 to $10 depending on the season.

Nearby Attractions

The northern boundary of this park is so close to **Gainesville** that you could take a short jog on one of the park's trails and find yourself on that city's SE 15th Street. A 63-block area in the northwest section of Gainesville is a historic district listed in the National Register of Historic Places. Among the several museums in the city is the **Fred Bear Museum** (tel. 904/376-2411, ext. 5), which displays trophy animals collected from around the world by expert bowhunter Fred Bear; also displayed is a collection of archery artifacts dating back to the Stone Age. Gainesville is also the home of the University of Florida. On campus is the **Florida Museum of Natural History** (tel. 904/392-1721); it's rated among the 10 most comprehensive natural history museums in the nation.

Georgia

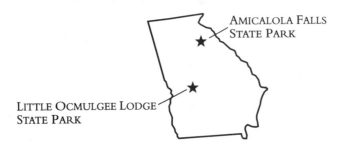

AMICALOLA FALLS
STATE PARK

LITTLE OCMULGEE LODGE
STATE PARK

Georgia has 58 state parks.

Contacts

- Georgia State Parks and Historic Sites, Georgia Department of Natural Resources, 205 Butler St., Suite 1352, Atlanta, GA 30334 (tel. toll free 800/869-8420 or 404/656-2770).
- Georgia Department of Industry, Trade and Tourism, P.O. Box 1776, Atlanta, GA 30301-1776 (tel. toll free 800/847-4842 or 404/656-3590).

General Information on Georgia State Parks

As an Atlantic coast state and the largest state east of the Mississippi, Georgia's parks go from the mountain beauty of the Blue Ridge in the north to the lush wetlands of the Okefenokee Swamp and to its colonial coast. One of its parks contains the highest waterfall east of the Mississippi.

GENERAL FEES

A $2 daily parking fee is charged in all state parks. Overnight guests pay one $2 fee for the duration of their stay. An annual Georgia ParkPass cost $25.

CAMPING AND ACCOMMODATIONS

The 39 parks with **campgrounds** offer a total of more than 2,500 multiuse campsites with electric and water hookups. Most campsites are on a first-come basis. A limited number of sites can be re-

served for a period of two-days; reservations can be made in person or by telephoning the park up to three months in advance. Campsites go for $10 to $15 per night, with the higher rate usually for lakefront or high-season sites.

Walk-in tent campsites and primitive campsites, group camps and dormitory-style group lodges are also available in a number of parks.

Five parks have **lodges:** Amicalola Falls, George T. Bagby, Little Ocmulgee, Red Top Mountain, and Unicoi. Lodges vary in size from 30 to 100 rooms, all with TV, phone, and individual climate controls. The special features offered varies by lodge and may include sleeping lofts for children, suites with separate bedrooms, and private porches. All have handicapped-equipped and no-smoking rooms. Children under 12 stay free when accompanied by an adult in the same room. Maximum occupancy is four in a double room and six in a double room with a loft. Reservations are accepted up to 11 months in advance. For information and reservations call the lodges directly. Depending on season and location, a double runs from $40 to $65 in high season. Suites run about $70 to $110.

Cottages are available in 24 of the parks. Most are two-bedroom, but some parks also have one- and three-bedroom cottages. All have kitchens, heat, and most have air conditioning. Many have porches or decks and wood-burning fireplaces or stoves. Rates range from a low of $30 for a one-bedroom on a weekday to $80 for a three-bedroom on a weekend. The exception is Unicoi State Park where a one-bedroom goes for $70 and a three-bedroom for $90 every night in that park's high-season month of October. Reservations are accepted by the individual parks up to 11 months in advance.

Pets. Pets are not permitted in lodges or cabins and, where permitted in other areas, must be on a leash and under control at all times.

Alcoholic beverages. It's against the law for any person to use or consume alcoholic beverages or intoxicants in any public use area.

Discounts. Senior Citizens, 62 and older, can purchase an annual Georgia ParkPass at a discount. They also receive 20% off campsite rates year round and 20% off individual cottage and lodge room rates, Sunday through Thursday, December 1 through March 31. Ask about other discounts, including golf fees. Discounts apply only when the vehicle is registered to the senior.

Georgia residents who are disabled veterans are eligible to apply for a Certificate for Eligibility for Reduced Fees at State Parks (VSO Form 22) which discounts most park fees by 25%.

Amicalola Falls State Park

| Visitor Center | Lodge/ Hotel | Restaurant | Cabins & Cottages | RV Camping | Tent Camping | Primitive Camping | Fishing | Picnic Areas | Trails | Nature Programs | Playground |

Capsule Description: A developed mountain park with the highest waterfall east of the Mississippi River.

Location: In the mountains of northeastern Georgia, 15 miles northwest of Dawsonville and about 54 miles north of Atlanta's perimeter I-285. From Dawsonville, take Georgia Highway 183 approximately 13 miles to Georgia Highway 52. Go east on Highway 52 about two miles to the park entrance on the right.

Address: Star Route, Box 215, Dawsonville, GA 30534 (tel. 706/265-8888).

Area Contacts: Alpine Helen/White County Convention and Visitors Bureau, P.O. Box 730, Helen, GA 30545 (tel. 706/878-2181).

Atlanta Convention and Visitors Bureau, 233 Peachtree St., Suite 2000, Atlanta, GA 30303 (tel. 404/521-6600).

Dahlonega-Lumpkin County Chamber of Commerce, 101 S. Park St., Dahlonega, GA 30533 (tel. 706/864-3711).

Dalton Convention and Visitors Bureau, P.O. Box 2046, Dalton, GA 30722-2046 (tel. 706/272-7676).

Dawson County Chamber of Commerce, P.O. Box 299, Dawsonville, GA 30534 (tel. 706/265-6278).

Insider Tips: Special packages are offered through the park for golf, goldmining, and rafting. All these activities are outside the park, about a 20- or 30-minute drive.

Amicacola is a Cherokee Indian word meaning "tumbling waters." The waters here "tumble" 729 feet letting Amicacola lay claim to being the highest falls east of the Mississippi (some say east of the Rocky Mountains). The water falls in a series of seven cascades, not a straight drop but still a long way down. And with a 23% grade on the road, it can also be a long way up.

Activities

Falls viewing is high on the list of activities here. The Reflection Pool at the base of the falls and a nearby viewing platform are both prime viewing spots for seeing the falls come tumbling down toward you. For a stunning top-down view, there's another platform at the top.

Hikers can roam the seven short hiking and nature trails in the park. One interpretive trail is handicapped-accessible. In spite of the park development, this is basically a wilderness area, and it adjoins the Chattahoochee National Forest, so a wide variety of wildlife common to the Appalachian Mountains may be seen in the hardwood forest. These include white-tailed deer, raccoons, opossum, and a number of birds like wild turkeys and cardinals. Two species you may not see much of are the gray bat and mountain rabbit. They both live here, but are on the endangered list.

If you are really bent on taking a long hike, the 8½-mile Approach Trail goes out of the park into the neighboring national forest to link up with the southern terminus of the 2,160-mile Appalachian Trail, which will take you all the way to Maine.

Anglers can put a line into the creek that flows through the park and forms the falls and may catch one of the stocked rainbow or brown trout that go up to 16 inches in length. Poles can be rented at the Visitor Center. You'll need both a fishing license and a trout stamp.

The park staff put on a number of nature and campfire programs, guided nature walks, and holiday programs throughout the year.

Camping and Accommodations

The **lodge** is located at the top of the falls where the panoramic view adds a free frill to your stay. Most of its 57 units are doubles, but there are several loft suites as well as junior suites with private porches. There's one handicapped-equipped room. Rates depend on size and season and range from $55 for a

double to $100 for the one executive suite from December through March. The rest of the year it's $65 to $110. Children under 12 stay free in the room when accompanied by an adult. There is a full-service restaurant in the lodge. A swimming pool is in the advanced planning stage.

The 14 **cottages** are also located by the falls. The five at the base are one- and two-bedroom. The other nine are on the mountain at the top of the falls. These are two- and three-bedroom. All have heat and air conditioning and other essentials, but no TV or phones. The cottages at the top of the falls also have fireplaces and porches. On weekdays, the cottages go for $50 to $70 depending on size. Weekends they are $60 to $80. And in October, when the leaves turn, the rates do, too, with the weekend rates in effect every day.

With only 17 multiuse **campsites** in the 1,340-acre park, camping is not a major activity. All have electric and water hookups, but due to the steep (23%) incline, trailers are limited to 17 feet. Three of the sites may be reserved; the others are strictly first-come. Sites are $15 in October and $12 the rest of the year.

A primitive campground is located about a quarter-mile walk from the Visitor Center. Reservations may be made up to 11 months in advance. It's $1 a person with a $12 deposit.

There are plans in the works to construct a unique Walk-In Lodge, possibly in 1996–97. This will be a rustic building that will accommodate up to 40 people—families or groups. The term "Walk-In" is accurate—a five-mile hiking trail will be the only way in. It will be powered by wind and solar energy.

Nearby Attractions

A main attraction in nearby **Dawsonville** is a small museum dedicated to local NASCAR racing hero Bill Elliott. If you are here in the fall, you may want to pick a pumpkin at one of the pumpkin farms in the area.

To the east is **Dahlonega,** a town that holds a place in history as the site of America's first gold rush in the 1830s. You can still be a part-time prospector and pan for gold at commercial mines here. There's also a Gold Museum and mine tours.

Farther east is **Helen,** called Alpine Helen because of the Bavarian Alpine architecture that dominates the town. You can pan for gold here, too. And nearby is **Unicoi State Park** (tel. 706/878-2201), another mountain gem with swimming, fishing, boating, campsites, cottages, and a 100-room lodge.

For something different, especially if you're in a big-time-shopping mood, or even if you're not, you might make a trip to the west to **Dalton.** This city touts itself as the "Carpet Capital of the World." Over 200 carpet mills and more than 100 carpet outlet stores are located here.

And, of course, **Atlanta** is in striking distance, although you might not want to try that on just a daytrip.

Little Ocmulgee Lodge State Park

Visitor Center | Lodge/Hotel | Restaurant | Cabins & Cottages | RV Camping | Tent Camping | Primitive Camping | Group Camping | Boating | Boat Launch | Fishing

Swimming | Waterskiing | Picnic Areas | Trails | Golf | Tennis | Playground | Gift Shop

Capsule Description: A lakeside park with well-developed facilities.

Location: Southcentral Georgia, two miles north of McRae on U.S. Highways 319/441.

Address: P.O. Box 149, McRae, GA 31055 (tel. 912/868-2832; 921/868-7474 for lodge and cottage information and reservations).

Area Contacts: Dublin–Laurens County Chamber of Commerce, P.O. Box 818, Dublin, GA 31040 (tel. 912/272-5546).

Hawkinsville–Pulaski County Chamber of Commerce, P.O. Box 447, Hawkinsville, GA 31036 (tel. 912/783-1717).

Statesboro Convention and Visitors Bureau, P.O. Box 1516, Statesboro, GA 30458 (tel. 912/489-1869).

Insider Tips: Light planes, including small jets, can fly into the Telfair-Wheeler County Airport, which is right across the highway from the park. The lodge restaurant usually closes Sunday after lunch.

This is another park that owes its origin to the depression-era Civilian Conservation Corps. The men of the CCC spent close to five years building the park, which opened in 1940. There have been many additions and improvements to the 1,397-acre park since then, including the lodge and the golf course, but much of the CCC handiwork can still be seen and admired.

Activities

Most of the action is around the lake—boating, fishing, swimming—and the golf course. An 11-minute video on the park is available for viewing at the Visitor Center.

Powerboats, including waterski boats, are permitted on the lake, but there are horsepower limits imposed after 6pm and all boats must be off the lake at sunset. Fishing boats and canoes can be rented. Plans are in the works to build a public beach.

Brim, largemouth bass, catfish, and panfish are the normal catches in the lake or off the fishing dock near the Visitor Center.

In addition to the 18-hole golf course, there's a miniature golf course open in season, and four lighted tennis courts.

Real hikers won't find much in the way of trails here, but for walkers there are two self-guided nature trails—one a little under two miles long and the other a little over two. Even though the park is busy, you might catch a glimpse of white-tailed deer or wild turkeys. The observation boardwalk at the lake is an excellent spot for common birds, like wood ducks and blue herring, and also for spotting the occasional alligator. (The new beach will be alligator-proof.)

Also lakeside is a small museum explaining the CCC's role in building the park.

Camping and Accommodations

The **lodge** has 29 rooms and one suite. One room is set up for the handicapped. All have TV, phones, and other normal motel amenities, and there is a full-service restaurant open for all meals except Sunday dinner. A double costs $53 year-round, and the suite goes for $76. The nearby pool is for lodge and cottage guests.

The 10 **cottages** are on the 265-acre lake. Four are one-bedroom and go for $45 on weekdays and $55 on weekends; the other six are two-bedroom and go for $55 on weekdays and $65 on weekends. All have heat and air conditioning and, by the time you read this the plan to put TV, phones, and microwave ovens in the cottages may have been accomplished. One cottage has wheelchair access.

All 58 multiuse **campsites** are on a first-come basis; no reservations. Sites have electric and water hookups and are shaded, but they are packed in a little tight. (Campsites $10.)

There are also primitive camping areas and groups can reserve the group camp, which has six screened buildings holding six persons each, plus a kitchen and dining area.

Nearby Attractions

South of the park, the nearest town is **McRae,** where you can see a half-size **replica of the Statue of Liberty,** built to honor that New York Harbor lady's 100th birthday, and a **replica of the Liberty Bell.**

To the west is **Hawkinsville** and the **Hawkinsville Harness Horse Training Facility** (tel. 912/892-9463). The town itself is called the Harness Capital of Georgia, and horses are brought down from the north for training here from fall until early April.

To the north is the town of **Dublin.** Naturally, there's a St. Patrick's Day Festival here, but the rest of the year you can visit the historic downtown area, take a farm tour or a historic driving tour of the county.

On a long daytrip, head east to **Statesboro,** where you can visit **Georgia Southern University** (tel. 912/681-5611), the **Georgia Southern Botanical Gardens** (tel. 912/871-1114), and several historic districts. On the way there you'll pass through **Vidalia,** the farm town that gave the Vidalia onion its name.

Hawaii

KAUAI'S NORTHWEST
COAST PARKS

Hawaii has 58 state parks.

Contacts

- Division of State Parks, Department of Land and Natural Resources, P.O. Box 621, Honolulu, HI 96809 (tel. 808/587-0300).
- Hawaii Visitors Bureau, 2270 Kalakaua Ave., Suite 801, Honolulu, HI 96815 (tel. 808/923-1811).

General Information on Hawaii State Parks

The very name "Hawaii" brings visions of tropical beauty to mind. To preserve this beauty, as well as the heritage of the Hawaiian people, there are parks on five of the six main islands that make up the Hawaiian chain. They range from the formal landscaped grounds of the Iolani Palace State Monument in downtown Honolulu, the only royal palace existing in the United States, to the wild and scenic cliffs of the Na Pali Coast State Park on Kauai.

A number of these are drop-in parks that you should include in any visit to the tourist centers on the various islands. Others, however, like those below, are away from the routine tourist routes. It takes some planning to visit them, but the planning will pay off in experiences that cannot be duplicated in the parks of any other state. Here is where your most exquisite visions of unspoiled old Hawaii come to life.

GENERAL FEES
There are no entrance, parking, picnicking, or camping fees.

CAMPING AND ACCOMMODATIONS
Permits are required for both camping and lodging. These may be obtained by mail from the division headquarters in Honolulu, or by phone or in person at the district headquarters on Hawaii, Maui, Oahu, and Kauai. Permit applications are accepted up to a year in advance, but must be received at least seven days in advance. The exception is Oahu camping application permits, which will be accepted no sooner than 30 days before the first day of camping. Campgrounds are open every day on the neighboring islands, but only Friday through Tuesday on Oahu.

The maximum length of stay under each permit for both camping and lodging at any one park is usually five consecutive nights.

Developed campgrounds are available at two state parks on Kauai, one state park and three state recreation areas on Oahu, one state park on Molokai, and one state park and one recreation area on Maui.

Housekeeping cabins are available at Kokee State Park on Kauai, Malaekahana State Recreation Area on Oahu, Polipoli Springs State Recreation Area and Waianapanapa State Park on Maui, and Kilauea and Mauna Kea State Recreation Areas on the island of Hawaii. Cabin size ranges from one to three bedrooms with a capacity of up to seven persons. Rates are per person per night on a sliding scale that runs from $10 for the first adult to $5 for the seventh. Children under 12 are at half the adult rate. Some cabins are operated by a concessionaire and reservations must be made through that concessionaire.

Pets. Pets and other animals must be crated, caged, on a six-foot or shorter leash, or otherwise under physical restrictive control at all times. They are not permitted in restaurants, pavilions, swimming areas, campgrounds, lodges, on beaches, or wherever posted.

Alcoholic beverages. The use or possession of alcoholic beverages in any state park is prohibited.

Kauai's Northwest Coast Parks

| Restaurant | Cabins & Cottages | Tent Camping | Primitive Camping | Fishing | Beach | Picnic Areas | Trails |

Capsule Description: A string of four wilderness parks with a minimum of developed facilities covering most of the northwest section of Kauai. Some of these parks touch and some are separated from other parks; however, they are so linked in concept that we consider them as one.

Location: Haena State Park is at the end of Highway 56, the Kuhio Highway.

Na Pali Coast State Park is accessible by the Kalalau Trail, which has a trailhead in Haena State Park.

Kokee State Park is 15 miles north of Kekaha on Highway 550, Kokee Road.

Waimea Canyon State Park is about 11 miles north of Kekaha on Highway 550, Kokee Road, adjoining Kokee State Park.

Address: District Office, Division of State Parks, 3060 Eiwa St., Room 306, Lihue, HI 96766-1875 (tel. 808/241-3444).

Area Contact: Kauai Chapter Office, Hawaii Visitors Bureau, Lihue Plaza Building, Suite 207, 3016 Umi St., Lihue, HI 96766 (tel. 808/245-3971).

Insider Tips: Often called Hawaii's most beautiful island, Kauai is attracting more and more tourists. This influx, compounded by narrow roads, can create serious traffic problems. Allow yourself plenty of time to get from place to place. Dirt roadways leading into the forests require 4-wheel-drive vehicles during the rainy season. Do the rugged cliffs of the Na Pali coast look familiar? If so you may have seen them in several films, including *Raiders of the Lost Ark.*

Called the Garden Island, Kauai radiates in all directions from Mt. Waialeale, the wettest spot on earth. The nearly 500 inches of rain that fall here annually flow down to water the lush vegetation in almost every part of the island.

Activities

Lovers of wild and unsullied nature will find these parks close to paradise.

Haena State Park is the northern gateway to this tropical wonderland. Only about 66 acres, it's the smallest of the four. A main attraction here is Kee Beach offering swimming, shore fishing, and views of ancient sea caves and the spectacular wind and wave-worn Na Pali palisades interspersed with long fingers of green that run down from the cliffs to the ocean.

Here, too, is the trailhead for the Kalalau Trail in the 6,175-acre Na Pali State Park. This engaging trail is the only land access to this part of the rugged coast. It hugs the coastline going from the scenic panoramas of high sea cliffs (*pali* in Hawaiian) down past waterfalls in narrow, lush, stream valleys and back up again ending at Kalalau Beach where it is blocked by a sheer, fluted cliff. It's 11 miles one-way, and parts of it are arduous, so only well-conditioned hikers should plan to do it all the way. Although it can be done in a full day, it's best to plan on overnighting, which means you'll need a permit for the limited primitive campsites along the trail. In fact, if you go past the first two miles on the trail you'll need a permit even if you don't camp.

But day hikers aren't ruled out. They can delight in the short two-mile hike to Hanakapiai Valley and Beach. The sand beach here is a scenic joy; however, swimming and even wading are not recommended because of treacherous rip currents and powerful surf.

You can drive to the other two adjoining state parks in this area. The 4,345-acre Kokee State Park is the more developed of the two. But its tropical wilderness is still its main attraction, with more than a dozen trails, ranging from less than a mile up to several miles, adding up to a total of 45 miles. Anglers can also try for rainbow trout, which may be taken during the annual open season in August and September, in the 15 miles of fishable streams and ditches and a 15-acre reservoir.

Also here is the Kokee Museum with its displays explaining the natural history and the life of the people of the island. It's free, but donations are accepted. The staff also leads periodic nature hikes.

Next in line is Waimea Canyon State Park, which includes one of the state's scenic treasures—the deep, colorful gorge of the canyon it's named after; a miniature version of the Grand Canyon set in the tropics. Overlooks not only give views of the canyon, but also of Niihau, the Forbidden Island, 17 miles away.

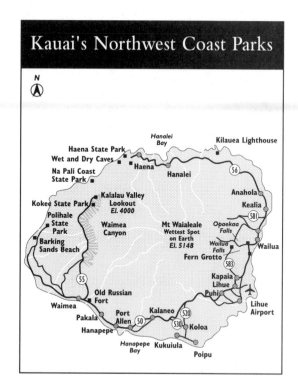

Camping and Accommodations

With the exception of the primitive campgrounds along the Kalalau Trail in Na Pali Coast State Park, all the overnight facilities are in Kokee State Park.

Kokee Lodge, located at 3,600 feet where the mountain air is cool and crisp, consists of an office and restaurant surrounded by a dozen housekeeping cabins. The units vary in size from one large room, which sleeps three, to two-bedroom cabins that accommodate seven. Rates are $35 and $45 per cabin. Breakfast and lunch are served daily at the lodge, but dinner is only available Friday and Saturday evenings.

The **campgrounds** at Kokee are limited to tents and a total of 75 campers. There's no fee, but permits are required.

Nearby Attractions

Everything is relatively nearby on this island that's only 33 miles long and 25 miles wide. You can walk the **Na Pali coastline,** but you can also see it by boat or helicopter; contact **Captain Zodiac Raft Expeditions** (tel. toll free 800/422-7824), the **Chopper Shop and Island Activities** (tel. toll free 800/829-5999), and **Ohana Helicopter Tours** (tel. 800/222-6989). **Kauai Downhill** (tel. toll free 800/234-1774) offers mountain bike tours of the Kokee and Waimea Canyon areas.

Kamokila is an authentically restored Hawaiian village, and the **Grove Farm Homestead** (tel. 808/245-3202) is a plantation-life museum. A profusion of beautiful beaches dot the island, such as **Poipu Beach, Lumahai Beach,** and those in **the Haena region. The National Tropical Botanical Garden** (tel. 808/941-6650) can be visited in Lawai.

Idaho

FARRAGUT
STATE PARK

BRUNEAU DUNES
STATE PARK

Idaho has 23 state parks.

Contacts

- Idaho Department of Parks and Recreation, Statehouse Mall, Boise, ID 83720-8000 (tel. 208/334-4199).
- Idaho Travel Council, Idaho Department of Commerce, P.O. Box 83720, Boise, ID 83720 (tel. toll free 800/635-7820).

General Information on Idaho State Parks

Idaho is a state of spectacular scenery and vast, relatively undeveloped wilderness areas. The state's parks system didn't get started until 1965, so it is fairly new. But it wasn't until the Idaho Centennial in 1990 that the system was given both focus and impetus. Now it is on track and growing.

GENERAL FEES
The entrance fee is $2 per vehicle for noncamping visits. There's no fee if you walk or bike in. An Annual Park Passport sells for $25–$15 if purchased before February 1.

CAMPING AND ACCOMMODATIONS
Fifteen parks have **campgrounds**. Most sites are without hookups, but some do have two- and three-way hookups. Campsite reservations are accepted at only four parks: Farragut, Ponderosa, Hells Gate, and Priest Lake. All others are on a first-come basis. Although some parks are open all year for camping, the season is normally April 1 through the beginning of November. Reservations are accepted by mail *only* from the first working day of January through March 31. Telephone and walk-in reservations are accepted after March 31 or whenever each park's visitor center opens for its season. Campsite fees range from $5 to $8 plus an additional $1 to $3 for hookups where available. There is also a one-time reservation fee of $5 to $6. Stays are limited to 15 days in any 30-day period.

A few **cottages** are available for rent at Heyburn State Park. These start at $55 and go up.

Pets. Although pets are permitted in most parks, you are encouraged to leave them at home for their own protection. If you bring a pet it must be on a leash no longer than six feet and under control at all times. They are not permitted on beaches.

Alcoholic beverages. Permitted as long as you abide by the state's laws related to drinking.

Discounts. Idaho residents 65 or over, or disabled residents may receive a discount up to $3 per day on campsites.

Bruneau Dunes State Park

Visitor
Center

RV
Camping

Tent
Camping

Primitive
Camping

Group
Camping

Non-
Motorized
Boating
Only

Fishing

Beach

Picnic
Areas

Trails

Horse
Trails

Nature
Programs

Capsule Description: An unusual desert oasis park.

Location: Southeast of Boise in the southwest corner of the state. Going west on I-84, take the Hammett/Idaho Highway 78 exit and continue west about 15 miles. Going east on I-84, take Exit 95/Mountain Home and follow signs to Idaho Highway 51. Follow Highway 51 to Snake River, then turn left on Highway 78 and go two miles to the park.

Address: HC85, Box 41, Mountain Home, ID 83647 (tel. 208/366-7919).

Area Contacts: Mountain Home Chamber of Commerce, P.O. Box 3, 110 N. 3rd East, Mountain Home, ID 83647 (tel. 208/587-4334).

Southwest Idaho Travel Association, P.O. Box 2106, Boise, ID 83701 (tel. toll free 800/635-5240).

Insider Tip: If the desert heat starts to get to you, head for the Visitor Center where you can see displays on desert life in air-conditioned comfort.

A desert in Idaho? Yes, this area receives less than 10 inches of precipitation a year. Bruneau has the tallest and largest, single-structured sand dune in the nation. Below the dunes—one of which towers to the record 470 feet—is an oasis with several small lakes.

The Bruneau Dunes are unique in the western hemisphere. Other dunes in the Americas form at the edge of a natural basin; these form near the center. The two prominent dunes cover about 600 acres of the 4,800-acre park. Unlike many dunes, these do not drift far because the two prevailing winds blow from the southeast 28% of the time and from the northwest 32% of the time, keeping the dunes fairly stable.

Activities

Most people think of the desert as dead land where nothing grows. Desert parks like this soon dispel that impression. The desert is alive to those who will take the time to look and observe.

An array of mammals, reptiles, and birds make this their homes. These include the black-tailed jackrabbit, mountain cottontail rabbit, coyote, muskrat, badger, and occasionally, mule deer. In the sky and near the lakes, there's a fair chance you'll see both the golden and the bald eagles, hawks, the great horned owl, and in fall and winter, Canada geese, blue herons, and other migrating waterfowl. The most common reptiles are lizards and snakes.

In summer, the temperature can climb to over 100 degrees. To survive, the desert creatures hide from the heat (as you probably will, too). The best time to see them is early morning and late afternoon. And the best places to see them is on the trails. A favorite of the several trails in the park is the Sand Dunes Hiking Trail, which follows markers through desert terrain for five miles. A high point here is climbing the big sand dune to its 470-foot crest. Other trails include a half-mile self-guided nature trail through the dunes, and an equestrian trail with alternative routes that go up to nine miles.

The lakes are a recent, but natural addition to the park. The theory is that they are a result of a higher water table in the area due to reservoirs on the nearby Snake River and irrigation projects on the desert near the dunes. The two main lakes total about 200 acres. And where there's water there's swimming and fishing. Swimming is at a small beach (most of the park is just one big beach). There are no lifeguards. Sportfishing is permitted from nonmotorized boats (electric motors permitted) including canoes and rubber rafts. According to reports, these little lakes are excellent for bass and bluegill.

Other popular sports are hang gliding and sand blasting—riding down the dunes on snowboards or even skis.

Camping

Bruneau Dunes has the longest camping season in Idaho's park system. Campers start coming in early March and continue until late into October. Of the 48 camp sites, 32 are multiuse with water and electric hookups ($11) and the other 16 are tent sites with no hookups ($8). All sites are on a first-come basis.

There is a primitive camping area that is also used for equestrian campers, and a group camp for up to 100.

Nearby Attractions

To the south (25 miles) lies the **Bruneau Canyon** (tel. 208/384-3300), a hidden canyon with a stellar overlook.

The nearest large town with amenities for visitors is **Mountain Home,** a short drive west on I-84. Beyond that, less than an hour's drive, is **Boise.** On the way, you'll pass the **Snake River Birds of Prey Natural Area** (tel. 208/384-3300), which encompasses about 482,000 acres. This is home to the densest population of nesting raptors in the world. Eagles, hawks, and falcons can be seen gliding gracefully on the updrafts. It's a rough drive into this area, but guided boat tours are available from area outfitters, such as **Birds of Prey Expeditions** (tel. 208/922-5285) or **MacKay Bar** (tel. 208/344-1881). You can also get a close look at a number of raptors on a two-hour tour of the **Peregrine Fund World Center for Birds of Prey** (tel. 208/362-8687) in Boise or at the **Boise Zoo** (tel. 208/384-4125), which features the largest birds of prey display in the Northwest.

Among the other sights in the capital city are the **state capitol building;** the **Old Idaho Penitentiary** (tel. 208/368-6080); the **botanical gardens** (tel. 208/343-8649); the **Morrison-Knudsen Nature Center** (tel. 208/386-5000), a cross between an aquarium and a wildlife park; several museums; and, especially for children, **The Discovery Center of Idaho** (tel. 208/343-9895).

To the east of Bruneau Dunes and worth a daytrip is **Island Crossing** (tel. 208/366-2394). At this small park on the Snake River is a herd of American bison and longhorn cattle.

Farragut State Park

Visitor Center　RV Camping　Tent Camping　Primitive Camping　Group Camping　Boating　Boat Launch　Fishing　Beach　Waterskiing

Picnic Areas　Trails　Horse Trails　Nature Programs　Bicycling　Playground　X-Country Skiing

Capsule Description: A wooded, lakeside park with developed facilities.

Location: Northern Idaho, 20 miles north of Coeur d'Alene. Take U.S. Highway 95 north from Coeur d'Alene to the Athol/Idaho Highway 54 exit. Go east on Highway 54 four miles to park entrance.

Address: 13400 E. Ranger Rd., Athol, ID 83801 (tel. 208/683-2425).

Area Contacts: Coeur d'Alene Convention and Visitors Bureau, P.O. Box 1088, Coeur d'Alene, ID 83816. (tel. 208/664-0587).

North Idaho Travel Committee, P.O. Box 928, Sandpoint, ID 83864 (tel. toll free 800/800-2106).

Insider Tip: One of the games visitors often play at Farragut is "Spot the Mountain Goat." The elusive white goats are rarely seen in the park, but can be viewed with binoculars on the mountains across the lake.

In World War II the navy set up a training center here and Pres. Franklin D. Roosevelt named it after the first admiral in the U.S. Navy, Adm. David Farragut. That name went into the history books and legend when, in the battle to take New Orleans in 1864, Farragut ordered his ship past another Union warship sunk by a torpedo, shouting "Damn the torpedoes! Full speed ahead!"

That navy tradition was taught to more than 300,000 sailors on this site during World War II when it was the navy's second-largest training center. That center is long gone, but since Lake Pend Oreille (pronounced Pond Uh-ray), the largest lake in Idaho, has a depth of 1,150 feet it is still used by the navy for specialized submarine research. Because of its size (4,000 acres) and variety of available activities, Farragut played host to tens of thousands of Boy Scouts and Girl Scouts for both national and world gatherings in the 1960s and 1970s.

Activities

As in most parks, the Visitor Center is a good place to get a handle on what to do and where to do it. The center also has displays on the World War II naval training center and scouting memorabilia.

The scenic forested setting includes ponderosa pines, which can grow to 150 feet tall, other pines, Douglas fir, and poplar. The forests are home to white-tailed deer, badgers, black bears, coyotes, bobcats, and elk. Most of these avoid man, but you may see deer or elk on the miles of hiking trails. Common birds include wild turkeys, owls, hummingbirds, hawks, woodpeckers, bald eagles, waterfowl, and Idaho's state bird, the mountain bluebird.

In addition to the 20 miles of hiking trails, there's an easy, one-mile self-guided nature trail.

For bicyclists, there's a marked nine-mile route along park roads and some of the hiking trails are open to them. For horseback riders, riding is permitted on trails north of Highway 54 and there are some campsites for riders in one of the group camp areas.

The lake is the major attraction. Encircled by mountains, it is more than 43 miles long and a thousand feet deep. In the park, you can swim from the small beach under the watchful eyes of lifeguards, or go out on the lake for sailing, boating, waterskiing, or fishing. If you don't have your own boat, there are paddleboats for rent. More than 14 species of game fish have been caught here ranging from a variety of trout to bass to kokanee salmon. After hard fights, a world-record 37-pound kamloop and a state-record 32-pound Dolly Varden were caught here.

Other facilities include an amphitheater, where the staff puts on nature programs in summer; a rifle range, open to organized groups; and a large field for flying radio-controlled model airplanes.

Although the main campgrounds close in winter, the park is open all year—primitive camping is allowed—and, during the short snow season, offers places for sledding and more than nine miles of groomed trails for cross-country skiing.

Camping

The campgrounds are open from April 1 through early November. The 135 individual multiuse campsites are in two campgrounds, both in forest settings. Of the 45 sites in Snowberry Campground, 29 are pull-throughs, and all have water and electric hookups and go for $12 per night. The other 90 sites are in the Whitetail Campground. There are no hookups here, so sites cost $8. All sites can be reserved.

Naturally, a park that has hosted Boy Scout Jamborees of up to 20,000 would have group camps, and this one does—in fact, it has several group camps that can hold from 30 to 500 people.

Nearby Attractions

The Sandpoint (tel. 208/263-4598), a stern-wheeler, makes regular excursions on the lake from the **Scenic Bay Marina** in Bayview, just north of the park. Also near the park, on Highway 95, is **Silverwood** (tel. 208/683-3400), a turn-of-the-century theme park with carnival rides and entertainment.

Going north on Highway 95 takes you to **Sandpoint,** which features the **Vintage Wheel Museum** (tel. 208/263-7173), a collection of antique cars, and a market place on a bridge. Nearby is the **Schweitzer Ski Resort** (tel. 800/831-8810), where you can do downhill in winter or take a chair-lift ride for an unsurpassed mountain view when there's no snow.

Coeur d'Alene lies south on Highway 95. *National Geographic* magazine called the lake here "one of the five most beautiful in the world." Lake Coeur d'Alene is also the home of the largest population of osprey in the western U.S. A cousin of the bald eagle, the fish-eating osprey is a spectacular diver and aerial acrobat. The **Spokane River Queen** (tel. 208/773-1611) and **Lake Coeur d'Alene Cruises** (tel. 208/765-4000) run boat trips on the lake. Other sights in the city include the **Museum of North Idaho** (tel. 208/664-3448) and the **Fort Sherman Museum** (tel. 208/664-3448).

Just a few miles west of Coeur d'Alene, off I-90 at the Idaho-Washington border, is a year-round **Coeur d'Alene Greyhound Racetrack.**

Illinois

PERE MARQUETTE
STATE PARK

SHELBYVILLE
STATE PARK

Illinois has 266 state parks and recreation sites.

Contacts

- Office of Public Information, Department of Conservation, 524 S. Second St., Room 500, Springfield, IL 62701-1787 (tel. 217/782-7454; 312/814-2071 in the Chicago area).
- James R. Thompson Center, Illinois Bureau of Tourism, 100 W. Randolph St., Suite 3-400, Chicago, IL 60601 (tel. toll free 800/ABE-0121 [800/223-0121]).

General Information on Illinois State Parks

When the glaciers came through what is now Illinois, they did a good job of leveling the land of the "Prairie State"; its highest point is just a little more than 1200 feet. Some craggy areas in the southern part of the state and miles of rolling grasslands and hills, too, add variety to the state's level—but not flat—terrain. Illinois is also called the the "Land of Lincoln," and the Department of Conservation—while developing excellent recreational facilities—works to keep much of the half-million acres of parkland in the same natural condition it was when Lincoln walked the land.

Most parks are open all year, closing only for Christmas and New Year's Day.

General Fees

There are no entrance fees to the parks; however, some park beaches charge a day-use fee.

Camping and Accommodations

Lodges, inns, and **cabins** are available in eight parks: Cave-in-Rock, Eagle Creek, Giant City, Illinois Beach, Pere Marquette, Rend Lake, Starved Rock, and White Pines. Rates depend on the park, the facilities, and the season and range widely from less than $50 per night for a one-room pioneer cabin to about $135 for a deluxe double room in a lodge at high season and up to $160 for a suite. Each additional person is usually $10 with children under 17 staying free in the room with adults. All accept reservations.

There are **campgrounds** in about 60 parks. Individual sites vary from Class A sites with showers, electricity, and vehicular access, to Class D, which are tent camping or primitive sites. Class A sites go for about $11 while Class D cost $6, with B and C site fees scaled between those. Most campsites are on a first-come basis; however, about 15 parks accept reservations for an additional fee. A number of parks also offer primitive camping for youth groups.

Pets. Must be under control at all times—on a leash no longer than 10 feet in length or in a vehicle. Not allowed in lodges, cabins, or most other buildings, or on beaches.

Alcoholic beverages. Generally legal in all parks; however, some parks have specific restrictions on containers and areas.

Discounts. Illinois residents who are 62 or older or have a Class 2 disability ID card from the office of the Secretary of State will be charged half the regular fee for campsites with access to electricity and showers Monday through Thursday. For campsites without access to electricity or showers, no fee is charged of seniors Monday through Thursday and no fee any day for residents with a Class 2 disability. Resident disabled veterans and former Prisoners of War may camp free any day of the week.

Pere Marquette State Park

 Visitor Center
 Lodge/Hotel
 Restaurant
 Cabins & Cottages
 RV Camping
 Tent Camping
 Group Camping
 Group Lodge Dormitories
 Marina
 Boating
 Boat Launch
 Fishing

 Swimming
 Picnic Areas
 Trails
 Horse Trails
 Nature Programs
 Bicycling
 Tennis
 Playground
 Gift Shop

Capsule Description: A large natural park on the Mississippi with well-developed facilities.

Location: Southwestern Illinois on the border with Missouri, about 30 miles north of St. Louis, Missouri, at the confluence of the Illinois and Mississippi rivers. From I-270 at the Mississippi River, take Illinois Highway 3 north to 143 at Alton, then 143/100, the Great River Road, northwest about 25 miles to the park.

Address: P.O. Box 158, Grafton, IL 62037 Office (tel. 618/786-3323). Visitor Center (tel. 618/786-2204). Lodge (tel. 618/462-2331).

Area Contacts: Department of Conservation, Region 4 Office, 4521 Alton Commerce Pkwy., Alton, IL 62002 (tel. 618/462-1181).

Collinsville Convention and Visitors Bureau, 1 Gateway Dr., Collinsville, IL 62234 (tel. 618/345-4999).

Greater Alton/Twin River Convention and Visitors Bureau, 200 Piasa, Alton, IL 62002 (tel. toll free 800/258-6645 or 618/465-6676).

St. Louis Convention and Visitors Bureau, 10 S. Broadway, Suite 1000, St. Louis, MO 63102 (tel. toll free 800/325-7962 outside Missouri or 314/421-1023).

Insider Tips: October is usually the month with the highest number of visitors.

Père, the French word for "father," refers to Père Jacques Marquette, the missionary who accompanied the French explorer Louis Joliet on his explorations of this area in 1673. They were the first Europeans to visit what is now Illinois. A large white cross marking the spot where their party camped is located just east of the entrance to this park, which bears the father's name. At close to 8,000 acres, this is the largest state park in Illinois.

The park also includes the McAdams Peak Hill Prairie, a 54–acre natural area.

Activities

A large color-coded map outside the Visitor Center shows the 15 miles of trails that go through the forests and along the towering bluffs. Almost all the main trails are a mile or less in length, but the Fern Hollow Trail is a little over two miles. Most are rated as easy to moderate. One of the mile trails is also set up as a 15-station exercise trail. On the trails you are likely to see deer and turkey and a wide variety of birds. In season, migratory waterfowl stop over and in winter, bald eagles nest here from about December through February. In spring, the wildflowers that paint the park attract many visitors, as do the autumn colors of the hardwood forest. Hikers may also explore the 54-acre McAdams Peak Natural Area located in the southwest corner of the park. The peak offers one of the best overlooks of the twin rivers in the park.

The Visitor Center is open all year, but the days vary by season. The park interpreter and naturalist staff offer frequent guided hikes and other programs, especially during the summer.

If you bring your own horse, the park has about 12 miles of horse trails and a parking area for trailers. (Plans are in the works for an equestrian campground.) However, you have to notify the park staff (tel. 618/786-2156) you're coming so they can unlock the gate going into the area. If you don't have your own horse, you can rent one from the park riding stable. It's open all year, weather permitting, but you'll need reservations from April 15 through October 31 for the guided trail rides. Rides last around an hour and cost about $10. Children ride free doubled with parent.

In addition to a bike trail inside the park, there is another trail starting from the park that follows the Great River Road for about 14 miles southeast toward Alton.

The rivers are open for all river sports. For boaters, the park's marina is open from April until November where you can dock or launch boats. Among the river fish anglers can go after are bluegill, carp, catfish, crappie, drum, and several varieties of bass.

Camping and Accommodations

The most prominent feature of the rustic Great Room in the **Lodge** is the 700-ton stone fireplace that dominates one end. The lodge itself offers 50 rooms and there are 22 rooms in nearby natural-stone cabins. Each room has all the amenities including TV and phone, and some have views of the river. Other guest amenities include an indoor swimming pool, sauna, whirlpool, exercise room, tennis courts, restaurant, cocktail lounge, and gift shop. A double in the lodge or cabins goes for about $66. Each additional person is $10. Children under 17 stay free in a room with adults.

There are 80 multiuse **campsites** with electricity at each site. Water is available at some sites. Reservations may be made for 28 of these sites from May 1 through October 31. Otherwise they are on a first-come basis. Sites cost $11 and the reservation fee is $5. The maximum stay in one month's time is 14 days. The park also offers the Rent-A-Tent program for those who want to camp but don't have the equipment.

There are two types of group-camping areas. First is a tent-camping area with a capacity of up to 500 people. The other type consists of three group camps with sleeping cabins and a mess hall. The minimum number for these is 25 and the maximum is 145.

Nearby Attractions

Day tripping is easy from this park. You can start right at the entrance going southeast between the river and the limestone cliffs and the apple orchards on the Great River Road. In the nearby town of **Grafton,** from mid-May through October, you can take a 90-minute scenic cruise on the Mississippi or splash in the wave pool at a water park. A little farther on is a road leading to the village of **Elsah,** an entire community listed in the National Register of Historic Places.

Alton, the nearest large town, has three distinct neighborhoods listed in that national register. The Lincoln-Douglas Square in Alton marks the site where Abraham Lincoln and Stephen Douglas held the last of their 1858 debates in the Senate race, which Douglas won. Riverboat gambling is available here on boats that cruise the Mississippi. The Alton Belle Casino (tel. 800/336-7568) and the Casino Queen (tel. 800/777-0777) both run such boats.

Farther south, near Collinsville, is the **Chaokia Mounds State Historic Site** (618/346-5160). The central section of the largest prehistoric In-dian city north of Mexico is preserved here; it's been designated a United Nations World Heritage Site, ranking it in the same class as other World Heritage sites like the Pyramids and the Taj Mahal. A small museum is on the premises, as are hiking trails. Entrance to the site is free.

Also an easy daytrip from the park is **St. Louis,** where you'll find museums, riverboats, theater, amusement parks, professional sports, and all the other attractions of a major city.

Shelbyville State Park: Eagle Creek and Wolf Creek

 Lodge/ Hotel
 Restaurant
 RV Camping
 Tent Camping
 Primitive Camping
 Group Camping
 Boating
 Boat Launch
 Fishing
 Beach
 Picnic Areas
 Trails

 Horse Trails
 Nature Programs
 Golf
 Tennis
 Playground
 X-Country Skiing
 Snow-mobiling
 Gift Shop

Capsule Description: Two developed park units facing each other across the central portion of an 11,000-acre lake.

Location: East-central Illinois. Two units, Eagle Creek and Wolf Creek, on opposite shores of Lake Shelbyville. From I-57, take Exit 190/Mattoon, go west on Illinois Highway 16. To go to Wolf Creek, turn north on Highway 32 to Wolf Creek Park Road, then west to park. To go to Eagle Creek, continue west on Highway 16 to Highway 128, then north to Eagle Creek Park Road, then east to the park.

Address: P.O. Box 16, Findlay, IL 62534 (tel. 217/756-8260). Inn at Eagle Creek reservations only (tel. toll free 800/876-3245).

Area Contacts: Central Illinois Tourism Council, 629 E. Washington, Springfield, IL 62701 (tel. toll free 800/262-CITC or 217/525-7980).

Champaign/Urbana Convention and Visitors Bureau, 40 E. University Ave. P.O. Box 1607, Champaign, IL 61824 (tel. toll free 800/369-6151 or 217/351-4133).

Decatur Area Convention and Visitors Bureau, 202 E. North St., Decatur, IL 62523 (tel. toll free 800/331-4479 or 217/423-7000).

Springfield Convention and Visitors Bureau, 109 N. 7th St., Springfield, IL 62701 (tel. toll free 800/545-7300 or 217/789-2360).

Insider Tip: The Inn at Eagle Creek has been cited by *Better Homes and Gardens* magazines as one of America's 30 Favorite Family Vacation Resorts. From November to January, the Inn also serves as the base and information center for the annual **Lake Shelbyville Festival of Lights,** a three-mile route lined with about 400 displays and more than 600,000 lights arranged in six themed areas, beginning with a tunnel of lights and ending in toyland.

Add up the facilities at these two units and you'll find a little bit of everything you'd want in a state park. The 2,200-acre Eagle Creek unit is a little more developed and lives up to the resort image with an inn, indoor pool, tennis courts, and golf course. But it still provides ample opportunity for getting back to nature with its campgrounds, hiking and cross-country skiing trails, and a wildlife management area. On the other shore, the 1,900-acre Wolf Creek unit offers more camping and more extensive trails for hiking, riding, and snowmobiling. Both, of course, offer the chance for boating, fishing, and other water sports on the lake.

Activities

Eagle Creek offers four easy trails ranging from ½ to 1½ miles long. For the heartier hiker, there's the Chief Illini Trail, more difficult and 12 miles long. In the winter, five miles of the trails are open for cross-country skiing. A popular spot in Eagle Creek is an area known as Pansy Hill, where wild pansies take over the landscape in spring. The six hiking trails at Wolf Creek are all rated easy and run from ½ to 2½ miles. This unit also has a 16-mile horseback trail and a snowmobile trail the same distance. Wolf Creek also has a half-mile trail for the handicapped as well as a wildlife observation deck and scenic overlooks. In both units you can expect to see deer—more often at Wolf Creek—turkey, pheasant, raccoons, and a wide variety of birds, including an occasional bald eagle.

Although there is no designated bike trail, biking is allowed on the roads.

Both parks have launching ramps going down to the lake. The park does not offer boat rentals, but boats are available for rent at several private marinas on the lake. Waterskiing and windsurfing are both popular here. The miles of flood brush, timber, and rock riprap shorelines and the hundreds of tributary streams emptying into the lake make it a prime fishing area. Catches include black and white crappie, largemouth bass, walleye, catfish, bluegill, muskie, and carp.

Wolf Creek has a swimming beach (no lifeguards) open from May to the middle of September. There's no entrance fee to either park, but there is a $1 per person fee to use the beach.

And, for the golf enthusiast, there's an 18-hole, 6,908-yard course at Eagle Creek.

Interpretive programs are offered in the summer at both parks and there is a year-round activity director for those staying at the Inn at Eagle Creek.

Camping and Accommodations

The 128 rooms in the lakeside **Inn at Eagle Creek** have balconies, some furnishings by local Amish craftspeople, TV, phones, and all the amenities you'd expect in a resort. The 10 executive suites have all of the above plus fireplaces. Handicapped-equipped and no-smoking rooms are available. The inn also offers two restaurants, a cocktail lounge, sauna, hot tub, indoor pool, exercise room, boat dock, four tennis courts and the golf course, and, a hard-to-find extra, day care. A double room goes for $115 to $135 in high season and $75 in low season. Suites go for $150 to $160 year-round. Each additional person in a room is $10.

There are 131 multiuse campsites with electricity and 66 without electricity in the campgrounds at Eagle Creek. Some of these campsites may be reserved. Wolf Creek offers 304 with electric hookups, 106 without hookups. Camping fees at both parks range from $6 to $11 depending on facilities. If you don't have camping equipment, there's a Rent-A-Camp program for an additional $8 per night. In addition, there are primitive campsites and camping areas for organized groups at both parks, and an equestrian campground with 35 sites at Wolf Creek.

Nearby Attractions

Want to know more about this large lake? The **Lake Shelbyville Visitor Center** (tel. 800/874-3529)—at the east end of the dam, a mile east of Shelbyville, off Route 16—has exhibits, audiovisual programs, and occasional dam tours.

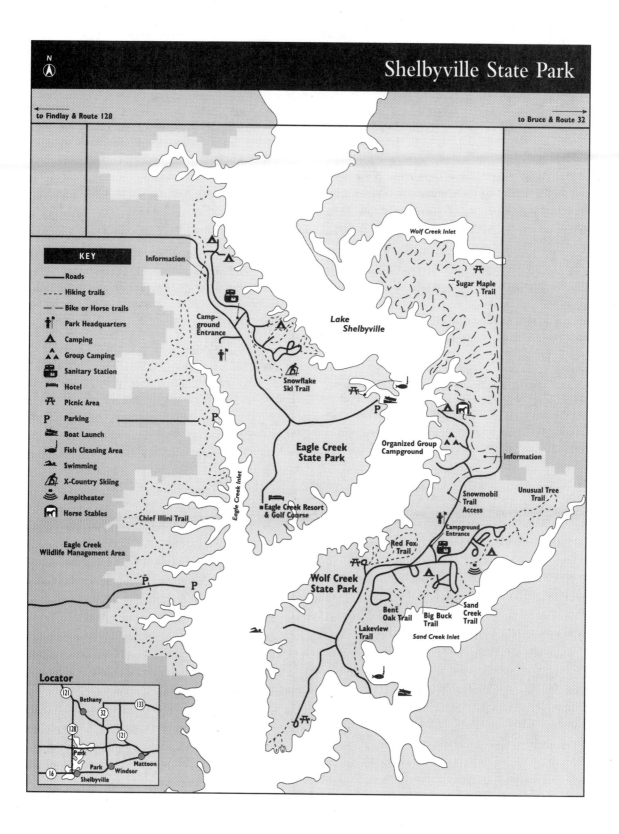

Shelbyville State Park

to Findlay & Route 128

to Bruce & Route 32

KEY

- —— Roads
- ---- Hiking trails
- — Bike or Horse trails
- ⛑ Park Headquarters
- △ Camping
- △△ Group Camping
- 🚽 Sanitary Station
- 🛏 Hotel
- ⛺ Picnic Area
- P Parking
- 🚤 Boat Launch
- 🐟 Fish Cleaning Area
- 🏊 Swimming
- ⛷ X-Country Skiing
- 🎭 Ampitheater
- 🐴 Horse Stables

Information

Wolf Creek Inlet

Sugar Maple Trail

Lake Shelbyville

Campground Entrance

Snowflake Ski Trail

Eagle Creek State Park

Eagle Creek Inlet

Organized Group Campground

Information

Snowmobil Trail Access

Unusual Tree Trail

Chief Illini Trail

Eagle Creek Resort & Golf Course

Campground Entrance

Red Fox Trail

Eagle Creek Wildlife Management Area

Wolf Creek State Park

Bent Oak Trail

Big Buck Trail

Sand Creek Trail

Lakeview Trail

Sand Creek Inlet

Locator

Bethany

121

32

133

128

121

Park

16

Park Windsor

Mattoon

Shelbyville

A number of interesting daytrips can be made from the park.

To the northeast, in Amish country, near the town of **Arcola,** is the **Rockome Gardens** (tel. 217/268-4216), featuring 12 acres of flower and rock gardens and a re-created frontier village.

Continuing northeast will take you to the twin cities of **Champaign/Urbana.** It would be easy to spend the day here just visiting the nine museums at the **University of Illinois** (tel. 217/333-1000). And, of course, if you hit at the right time, the university has Big Ten basketball and NCAA football and a performing arts complex of theaters and concert halls that offer programs.

If you're a railroad buff, from Champaign, go west on I-72 to the turn-off for **Monticello.** Here you'll find a restored depot, two railroad museums, and a train you can ride.

Decatur is the next large city on I-72 going west (north from the park if you go direct). Eighty

acres of buildings in this city are listed in the National Register of Historic Places, and the convention and visitors bureau (tel. 217/423-7000) offers walking-tour maps. Other places worth a visit include the **Homestead Prairie Farm** (tel. 217/423-4913), a living history farm; a children's museum; and a children's zoo.

Springfield, the state capital, is located northwest of the park. It proclaims itself the "City Lincoln Loved," and boasts an abundance of Lincoln-related places to back up that claim. The **Lincoln Home** (tel. 217/789-2357), the **Lincoln Memorial Garden,** his **tomb,** his law offices, and even his church pew, are among them. Springfield holds plenty of other attractions with merits of their own: the zoo, the Illinois State Museum, two Civil War museums, a botanical garden, and both the present and Old State Capitol buildings.

New Salem, a restored village where Lincoln once lived and worked, is about a half-hour drive from Springfield, close to Petersburg.

Indiana

Spring Mill State Park

Harrison-Crawford-Wyandotte Complex

Indiana has 59 state parks.

Contacts

- Division of State Parks, Department of Natural Resources, 402 W. Washington St., Room W256, Indianapolis, IN 46204 (tel. 317/232-4020).
- Division of Tourism, Indiana Department of Commerce, 1 N. Capitol Ave., Indianapolis, IN 46204 (tel. toll free 800/289-6646 or 317/232-8860).

General Information on Indiana State Parks

The Hoosier State is one of those states where it's hard to come up with an exact count of the number of state parks because there are four land-holding divisions that operate recreation-type properties. The count above is a compromise that includes those properties normally listed as state parks in other states.

As you travel through the state, look for brown signs with a drawing of binoculars on them. These alert you to nearby wildlife viewing areas.

General Fees

Some Department of Natural Resources properties charge an entrance fee. Where one is charged, it is $2 per day for noncommercial vehicles with an Indiana license plate and $5 per day for all others.

If you bring a horse, the daily horse permit costs $1.50. Walk, bike, or ride in and the fee is 50¢.

An annual entrance permit costs $18.

Camping and Accommodations

Six state parks have **inns** with a total of 550 rooms: Brown County, Clifty Falls, McCormick's Creek, Pokagon, Spring Mill, and Turkey Run. Reservations may be made directly with the inns up to two years in advance. Rates per night range from $39 to $72 on weekdays and $40 to $78 on weekends and holidays.

Family housekeeping **cabins** are available at eight parks: Brown County, Chain O'Lakes, Harmonie, Lincoln, McCormick Creek, Potato Creek, Shakamak, and Whitewater Memorial. All the cabins have heat—some with wood stoves or fireplaces—but only a few have air conditioning. Most have a capacity of six to eight persons. Depending upon location and whether linens and other items are provided, rates range from $25 to $78 a night. Reservations may be made directly with the park up to two years in advance; however, there are minimum-stay periods during the peak seasons that range from two nights to two weeks.

The rules by which **campsites** may be reserved vary from park to park. The general rule is that first-come gets the site through May 6. From May 7 through Labor Day, 50% of all campsites may be reserved for up to 14 days. However, there are a number of exceptions, so contact the Division of State Parks for the details. Ask for the parks *Recreation Guide* that spells it all out. One solid rule is that phone reservations are never accepted—mail or walk-in only. Site fees range from $7 to $13 a night. A few parks have a Rent-A-Tent program—bring your own gear. These can be reserved from May 1 through October 30 for $15 a night. Six parks have group camps.

Pets. Pets must be attended at all times and on a leash six feet or less in length. Pets are not permitted in inns, cabins, or most other buildings.

Alcoholic beverages. Except for Indiana Dunes State Park and all youth camps, alcoholic beverages are permitted.

Discounts. Indiana residents 60 or older or residents eligible for Social Security disability payments may purchase an annual **Golden Hoosier Passport** for $5. This pass admits the bearer and all passengers in a noncommercial vehicle free to all Department of Natural Resources properties.

Harrison-Crawford-Wyandotte Complex

| RV Camping | Tent Camping | Primitive Camping | Group Camping | Boating | Boat Launch | Fishing | Swimming | Picnic Areas | Trails | Horse Trails | Nature Programs |

Capsule Description: A large forested park with a developed recreation area.

Location: Southeastern Indiana. From I-64 East take Exit 105 (Corydon) to Indiana Highway 135, then south to Highway 62, then west to the park. From I-64 West, take Exit 92 (Leavenworth) to Indiana Highway 66, then south to Highway 62 and east to the park. Located in the Harrison-Crawford State Forest are the Wyandotte Woods State Recreation Area and the Wyandotte Caves.

Address: Wyandotte Woods State Recreation Area, 7240 Old Forest Rd., Corydon, IN 47112 (tel. 812/738-8232). Wyandotte Caves, RR #1, Box 85, Leavenworth, IN 47137 (tel. 812/738-2782).

Area Contacts: Harrison County Chamber of Commerce, 310 N. Elm St., Corydon, IN 47112 (tel. 812/738-2137).

Southern Indiana Convention and Visitors Bureau, 540 Marriott Dr., Clarksville, IN 47129 (tel. 812/282-6654).

At Harrison-Crawford State Forest, logging operations—planting, thinning, and harvesting—work in harmony alongside the recreational components of the park. One of the nation's largest state parks, Harrison-Crawford has more than 24,000 acres. The Wyandotte Woods State Recreation Area (SRA) offers camping, swimming, fishing, picnicking, and hiking and equestrian trails through its hardwood forests. Two caves can be toured at the Wyandotte Cave Area. The Big Cave has well-preserved helictites, which are rare, twisted formations.

Activities

More than 100 miles of trails wind through the forest. The 27-mile Adventure Trail was designed so that it can be covered in pieces on one-day hikes, which are rated moderate to rugged. Eight shorter trails can be followed through the SRA, as

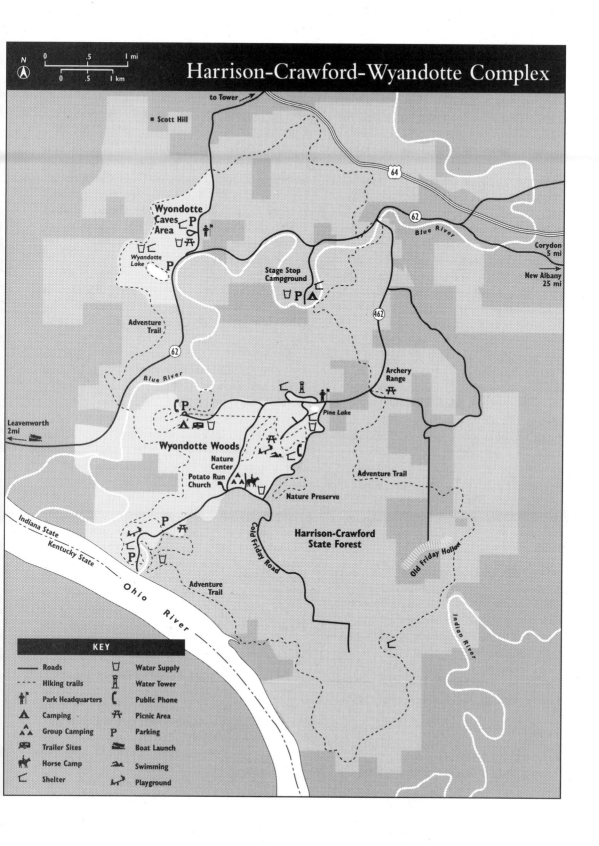

Harrison-Crawford-Wyandotte Complex

N

0 .5 1 mi

0 .5 1 km

to Tower

Scott Hill

Wyondotte Caves Area

Wyandotte Lake

Stage Stop Campground

64

62

Blue River

Corydon 5 mi

New Albany 25 mi

462

Adventure Trail

62

Blue River

Archery Range

Pine Lake

Leavenworth 2 mi

Wyondotte Woods

Nature Center

Potato Run Church

Nature Preserve

Adventure Trail

Harrison-Crawford State Forest

Indiana State

Kentucky State

Ohio River

Cold Friday Road

Old Friday Hollow

Indian River

Adventure Trail

KEY

——	Roads	🚰	Water Supply
- - -	Hiking trails	🗼	Water Tower
⛟	Park Headquarters	C	Public Phone
▲	Camping	⛩	Picnic Area
▲▲	Group Camping	P	Parking
🚐	Trailer Sites	⛵	Boat Launch
🐎	Horse Camp	🏊	Swimming
C	Shelter	🤸	Playground

well as a self-guided nature trail. Hikers may sight deer, raccoons, and wild turkey. On your forest wanderings, you may come across some logging operations.

Horses are permitted on most of the forest trails; but, sorry, no bikes.

A full-time naturalist is on duty at the nature center. Nature hikes and other programs are offered year round.

The Blue River, which flows through the complex, is popular with fishermen going after smallmouth bass and crappie, and with canoeists who can enter it from any of three access points in the SRA. You can also fish and boat on the Ohio River, which runs along the southern edge of the forest and forms the border between Indiana and Kentucky.

For swimming, the SRA has an Olympic size pool open from Memorial Day to mid- or late August. Admission is $1.50.

The tours of Wyandotte Caves range in length, degree of difficulty, and price. The shortest and easiest one is of the Little Cave; the tour takes less than an hour and goes about half a mile inside this surface cave. You can take in the Big Cave on a one-hour tour, but serious spelunkers will opt for the eight-hour tour. The longer tours all follow some rocky paths and include steep climbs that may be too strenuous for some people.

Camping

The modern campgrounds are open from April through November. Primitive camping is offered all year. The 281 modern sites are all multiuse and come with electric hookups. Modern sites go for $11 per night and primitive camping for $5. Reservations may be made by mail only.

There are no stables in the park, but equestrian campgrounds are available. In addition to the charge for the campsite, there's a fee for each horse.

Nearby Attractions

A number of attractions are just a short drive from the park; most are on or near Highway I-64. To the east is Corydon, which served as the state capital from 1816 to 1825. Walking-tour maps of the historic district are available from the Chamber of Commerce (tel. 812/738-2137). **Squire Boone Caverns** (tel. 812/732-4381), a cave discovered by Daniel Boone and his brother Squire, is about 12 miles south of Corydon on Highway 135; cave tours are offered. The nearby touristy Squire Boone Village displays Indian relics, offers hayrides, and sells souvenirs, of course. Squire Boone is buried by a waterfall, just a mile away.

Continuing east on I-64 takes you to Jeffersonville, where you can see baseball's famous Louisville Slugger bats being made at the **Hillerich Bradsby Company** (tel. 402/585-5226).

Just across the Ohio River, reached by I-65, is the city of **Louisville,** Kentucky. Its famed **Churchill Downs** is home of the Kentucky Derby. This river city has the internationally acclaimed Actor's Theatre, a zoo, a motor speedway, a museum dedicated to coffee, and the Zachary Taylor National Cemetery, where our 12th president is buried. The *Belle of Louisville,* the oldest operating steamboat on the Mississippi River system, offers cruises on the Ohio River.

Two famous names are in the titles of the better known attractions west of the park— Lincoln and Santa Claus. The farm where Abe Lincoln lived for a number of years is now the **Lincoln Boyhood National Memorial** (tel. 812/937-4541), on Indiana Highway 162 just south of Lincoln City. In nearby **Lincoln State Park** (tel. 812/937-4710), they put on the outdoor musical drama *Young Abe Lincoln* during the summer.

And back east just a bit, on Highway 245, is the town of **Santa Claus.** Besides being famous for the postmark it puts on Christmas mail, this town has a **small amusement park** (tel. toll free 800-GO-SANTA [800-467-2682]) built around the holidays of Christmas, the Fourth of July, and Halloween.

Spring Mill State Park

Visitor Center   Lodge/Hotel   Restaurant   RV Camping   Tent Camping   Group Camping   Boat Launch   Non-Motorized Boating Only   Fishing   Swimming

Picnic Areas   Trails   Horse Trails   Nature Programs   Playground   Gift Shop

Capsule Description: A well-developed, compact park with a historic village.

Location: Southern Indiana, about 35 miles south of Bloomington. Take Indiana Highway 37 to Mitchell, then east on Highway 60 just over three miles to the park.

Address: Box 376, Mitchell, IN 47446 (tel. 812/849-4129).

Area Contacts: Bloomington/Monroe County Convention and Visitors Bureau, 2855 N. Walnut, Bloomington, IN 47404 (tel. 812/334-8900).

Insider Tips: Cave exploring on your own is prohibited. On guided cave tours, wear shoes with thick treads as the footing may be muddy.

The village of Spring Mill prospered in the mid-1800s when its massive water-powered gristmill operated day and night. The mill was so busy customers often had to wait nine or ten days to get their corn and wheat ground into meal.

The mill is still here, as a centerpiece of a reconstructed pioneer village, and it still grinds corn. You won't have to wait so long for your corn meal, though. Three-pound bags are for sale in the village daily from spring through fall.

The pioneer village is just one of the many draws of this park. You can hike, swim, boat, fish, take a trail ride, take cave tours, and go to the theater. You can even jump from the 19th century to the space age at the memorial to "Gus" Grissom. He was one of the seven original astronauts to make suborbital flights as part of the Mercury space program, which preceded the Apollo flight to the moon.

This is also one of the six Indiana parks with an inn.

Activities

A good place to get to know the lay of the land of this 1,300-acre park is the Virgil I. Grissom Memorial Visitor Center. Here you can learn about the park and also see displays on Grissom, the astronaut who made the first suborbital flight in 1961. He was killed in 1966 while preparing to command an Apollo flight to the moon.

You can visit the three-story gristmill, which was built of limestone in the early 1800s and operated commercially until 1892. Surrounding it in the Pioneer Village are a number of restored buildings including a blacksmith shop, carpenter shop, sawmill, spring house, distillery, tavern, and several houses.

On the other side of the park is a feature just as old and perhaps more precious—the Donaldson Woods Preserve, 67 acres of virgin forest. It is one of the few tracts of old-growth hardwoods—mostly white oak and tulip—left in the state.

There are also caves to visit in the park. Boat rides that go about 500 feet into Twin Caves run from April through October. The ride costs a dollar and is so popular that during peak times they start a waiting list each morning at 9 am. Naturalist-guided walking tours into other caves are also offered.

The water from the cave systems drains into Spring Mill Lake, a 30-acre lake that is used for fishing and boating. Bass, bluegill, trout, and other small game fish are caught here. Boats are restricted to electric trolling motors. You can also rent canoes, paddleboats, and rowboats.

There's no swimming in the lake, but the park's Olympic-size pool is open from around Memorial Day to Labor Day. Admission is $1.50.

The two-story nature center includes a stained-glass history wall and a large wildlife observation window, plus displays and multimedia presentations on the park. Hikers on any of the five trails can expect to see deer and a variety of small animals. The trails range in length from a ½ mile, rated moderate, to a 2½ mile, rated rugged. No designated equestrian trails exist, but trail rides are offered at the Saddle Barn (tel. 812/849-4279). Price depends on the length of the ride with the longest running about $10. For old farm country entertainment, hayrides are available in the evenings from April through October.

Camping and Accommodations

The limestone **Spring Mill Inn** (tel. 812/849-4081), which is more than 50 years old, has 75 rooms including more than two dozen designated no-smoking and four for the handicapped. There is a full-service restaurant and an indoor/outdoor swimming pool. Rooms rent for $43 to $47 on weekdays and $46 to $52 on weekends and holidays. Reservations are accepted, but only by mail or walk-in.

Of the 224 **campsites,** 188 have electric hookups. Most will accommodate trailers. These cost $11 per night. The other 36 go for $7 per night. Some may be reserved by mail or in person.

Nearby Attractions

A pleasant and fairly fast drive north on Highway 37 leads to **Lake Monroe,** the largest lake in Indiana. Six state recreation areas surround this 10,750-acre lake.

From there it's just a short drive farther north to **Bloomington.** A prime place to visit in this city is the campus of **Indiana University** (tel. 812/855-4826). Here you'll find a mini-forest and a number of museums. A standout is the university art museum (tel. 812/855-4826), which has a permanent collection that includes works of Matisse, Monet, Picasso, Rodin, and Warhol.

Indiana limestone is a quality building material that has been used in major buildings all over the country. If you want to see it in the rough, some of the many quarries and stone mills in the area permit visitors and tours.

Iowa

BACKBONE
STATE PARK

LAKE MACBRIDE
STATE PARK

Iowa has 76 state parks.

Contacts

- Iowa Department of Natural Resources, Wallace State Office Building, East 9th Street and Grand Street, Des Moines, IA 50319-0034 (tel. 515/281-5145).
- Division of Tourism, Iowa Department of Economic Development, 200 E. Grand Ave., Des Moines, IA 50309 (tel. toll free 800/345-4692 or 515/242-4705).

General Information on Iowa State Parks

If you have the impression that Iowa is all just flat farm country, it's probably because you haven't ventured off the interstate highways. Get off them and you'll find that the fertile land that produces world-famous corn and other crops also produces lush meadows, rolling hills, and cool forests. The state has wisely snatched up a number of pieces of this countryside for parks.

State parks, forests, and recreation areas are open year-round; however, when the temperature drops below freezing, water facilities are generally not available. In some cases electricity is also cut off. So if you're planning a late fall or early spring visit, especially if you plan to camp, it might be a good idea to call ahead to find out what's available.

GENERAL FEES
Admission to parks is free.

CAMPING AND ACCOMMODATIONS
There are 58 **campgrounds** with a total of 5,700 campsites. All sites are available on a first-come basis; no reservations are accepted. Fees vary according to the season and the campground's facilities. They range from $4 per night off-season in a nonmodern area without showers, flush toilets, and electric hook-ups to $12 per night peak season in a modern area with all of these facilities.

Cabins may be rented in eight parks: Backbone, Dolliver, Lacey-Keosauqua, Lake of Three Fires, Lake Wapello, Palisades-Kepler, Springbrook, and Wilson Island. The one-bedroom cabins sleep four comfortably with a maximum limit of six. Two-bedrooms sleep six comfortably with a maximum limit of eight. During the summer season—May 1 through Labor Day weekend—only full-week reservations are accepted (Saturday to Saturday). The rest of the year, reservations may be made for a minimum of two nights. All reservations must be made directly with the park. Only mail reservations are accepted.

They may be sent in during December, but are accepted for the year starting the second business day after January 1. One-bedrooms rent for about $150 a week or $25 per night, two-bedrooms for $225 a week or $40 a night.

Pets. Permitted in most parks, but must be under control and on a leash not longer than six feet.

Alcoholic beverages. Beer and wine are permitted, but other intoxicating beverages are not allowed.

Backbone State Park

| Cabins & Cottages | RV Camping | Tent Camping | Boat Launch | Non-Motorized Boating Only | Fishing | Beach | Picnic Areas | Trails | Horse Trails | Playground | X-Country Skiing | Snow-mobiling |

Capsule Description: A developed lakeside park.

Location: Northeastern Iowa, approximately 50 miles west of Dubuque. From Iowa Highway 3, just south of Strawberry Point, take Highway 410 south to the park's north gate.

Address: Rural Route #1, Dundee, IA 52038 (tel. 319/924-2527).

Area Contacts: Dubuque Chamber of Commerce, P.O. Box 705, Dubuque, IA 52004-0705 (tel. toll free 800/798-4748 or 319/557-9200).

Dyersville Area Chamber of Commerce, 1410 9th Street SE, P.O. Box 187, Dyersville, IA 52040 (tel. 319/875-2311).

Waterloo Convention and Visitors Bureau, P.O. Box 1587, Waterloo, IA 50704 (tel. toll free 800/728-8431 or 319/233-8350).

Insider Tips: On one of the hills adjacent to the Backbone are pine trees that are more than two centuries old. Some of these have diameters of 3½ feet thick. A privately operated golf course, open to the public, is just north of the park.

Dedicated in 1919, Backbone was Iowa's first state park. The 1,750-acre park takes its name from the "Devil's Backbone," a rugged ridge of rocks, surrounded on three sides by the Maquoketa River, that resembles a backbone.

The park is listed in the National Register of Historic Places, partly because many of the park buildings that are still in use were constructed by the Civilian Conservation Corps (CCC) in the 1930s. That Depression-era organization also dug the 85-acre Backbone Lake. In fact, the CCC did so much work on this and other Iowa parks that a museum dedicated to telling the history of the CCC in Iowa was opened here in 1990.

Activities

The importance of the lake and the river to this park is well illustrated by the fact that most of the major facilities are on either one or the other. The river is a fun place for floating and wading. For swimming, there's a beach on the lake (no lifeguards) and paddleboats, canoes, and rowboats can be rented here. Boats can use electric trolling motors only.

Fishing at the lake can yield catches of bass, crappie, bluegill, and bullhead. Anglers can also fish in a clear, cold stream at the north end of the park that is stocked with trout twice a week from April to November.

For hikers, there are six trails which add up to about 10 miles. These range in difficulty from easy to rugged and rocky. One of the trails goes up a rough, rocky staircase to the top of the Devil's

Backbone. There's also a small cave to explore. If you're looking for something more strenuous—and you're qualified—rock climbing and rappelling on the limestone bluffs are popular sports.

Equestrian trails run through the forest in the northern part of the park, and horses may be ridden on forest fire lanes. No designated bike trails exist, but bikes can be used on all the roads.

In the winter, most of the trails are open for cross-country skiing and snowmobiling.

The park abounds with wildlife and you'll have a good chance of seeing deer, wild turkeys, raccoons, and eagles. Birders will find plenty to spot since most of the park is forested and serves as a wildlife refuge.

And if you want to learn more about the Civilian Conservation Corps, don't forget to visit the museum. Although the displays here concentrate on the work of the CCC in Iowa, keep in mind that the CCC was responsible for building parks all over the United States. The work of the young men of the corps laid a solid foundation for the park systems in dozens of states.

Camping and Accommodations

There are 20 one- and two-bedroom **cabins** by the lake. The one-bedrooms are rustic without heat or air conditioning and rented only from mid-May through the first weekend in October. The log-style two-bedrooms have central heat and air conditioning and are available all year. You provide bedding and all other little accessories. You also have to provide your own contact with the outside world—no clock, radio, phone, or TV provided. Fees are listed under general information, above, but there is also a $50 security deposit required when you make reservations.

The 160 multiuse campsites are in two campgrounds. The main campground, near the lake, has 32 sites with electric hookups. The rest are in the nonmodern campground near the park's west gate. Some of these have electrical hookups. All are

available on a first-come basis; no reservations are accepted. Depending on location, facilities, and season, sites rent for $4 to $12 per night.

Nearby Attractions

At the **Wilder Memorial Museum** (tel. 319/933-2501) in Strawberry Point, just north of the park, you can see a collection of more than 800 dolls, with some dating back to 1750. You can better this number by going east to Dyersville where the **Dyer-Botsford Doll Museum** (tel. 319/875-2414) has about 900 dolls on display. Keeping along the toy line, the **National Farm Toy Museum** (tel. 319/875-2727) is also here. And Dyersville is where the movie *Field of Dreams* was filmed. ("If you build it, they will come.") You can see the photogenic field here.

Farther east—but still an easy daytrip since it's about an hour's drive from the park—is the city of **Dubuque** on the Mississippi. Attractions here include the **Crystal Lake Cave** (tel. 319/556-6451), the **Dubuque Arboretum and Botanical Gardens** (tel. 319/556-2100), the **Dubuque Greyhound Park** (tel. toll free 800/373-3647), and the **Mississippi Riverboat Museum** (tel. 319/557-9545). Gambling and non-gambling riverboat cruises on the Mississippi are offered by the **Diamond Jo Casino** (tel. toll free 800/582-5956) and the **Silver Eagle Casino** (tel. toll free 800/745-8371). For another view of the mighty Mississippi and three states, take a short ride on what's known as the **Fenelon Place Elevator** (tel. 319/557-9545), listed as the world's shortest, steepest scenic railway. Erected in 1882, it elevates passengers 189 feet from Fourth Street to the viewpoint on Fenelon Place.

If you're still in the toy mood, go just south of the park to the **Red Barn Model Railroad Museum** (tel. 319/924-2482) in Dundee.

About an hour's drive to the west are the adjoining cities of **Waterloo** and **Cedar Falls** where the attractions include several more museums and another greyhound racetrack.

Lake Macbride State Park

RV Camping | Tent Camping | Primitive Camping | Group Camping | Boating | Boat Launch | Fishing | Beach

Picnic Areas | Trails | Bicycling | X-Country Skiing | Snow-mobiling

Capsule Description: A lakeside park with developed facilities.

Location: Southeastern Iowa, between Iowa City and Cedar Rapids. From I-80 on the east side of Iowa City, take Exit 246/Iowa Highway 1. Go north on Highway 1 to Solon. For the northern unit, take Highway 382 west four miles to the park. For the southern unit take Fifth Street (County Road F-28) in Solon and go three miles west.

Address: 3525 Hwy. 382 NE, Solon, IA 52333 (tel. 319/644-2200).

Area Contacts: Amana Colonies Convention and Visitors Bureau, P.O. Box 303, Amana, IA 52203 (tel. toll free 800/245-5465 or 319/622-7622).

Cedar Rapids Area Convention and Visitors Bureau, 119 First Ave. SE, Cedar Rapids, IA 52401 (tel. 319/398-5009).

Coralville Convention and Visitors Bureau, 408 First Ave., Coralville, IA 52241 (tel. toll free 800/283-6592 or 319/337-6592).

Insider Tip: For a scenic view of both the park lake and the Coralville Reservoir, take a stroll to the overlook at the dam and spillway. While there, go to see the working model of the dam in the Visitor Center.

The 2,150-acre park has two units on the 812-acre lake. The northern unit has modern campgrounds, a beach, boat ramps and boat rentals, picnic areas, and the park office. The southern unit offers a non-modern campground, boat ramps, picnic areas, a Frisbee golf course, and a native prairie.

This is another park that owes much of its construction to the labor of the Civilian Conservation Corps.

Activities

Lake Macbride State Park is one of the largest in the Iowa state park system with close to 20 miles of shoreline. It is fed by two creeks and spills over into the Coralville Reservoir. During the summer, lifeguards are on duty at the beach, which is one of the busiest in the state.

There are six boat ramps on the lake. An additional ramp allows boats to enter the Coralville Reservoir. A 10-horsepower limit is in effect from late May to early September. Horsepower is unrestricted the rest of the year, but there's a no-wake rule, so no waterskiing is permitted. Pontoon and fishing boats, motors, canoes, sailboats, and paddleboats can be rented. Sailing and windsurfing are especially popular.

In addition to boat fishing, anglers can also try their luck from the seven fishing piers, one of which is handicapped-accessible, or throw a line in along the miles of shoreline. Bass, crappie, and catfish are common catches and the lake is stocked annually with walleyed muskies and catfish. Lake Macbride is also the only lake in Iowa where you might catch a Kentucky spotted bass.

About 15 miles of multiuse trails wind around the lake. Most are easy hiking. There's also a short, self-guided nature trail. A five-mile bike trail follows the north arm of the lake, beginning at the park entrance and ending in Solon.

Water draws wildlife, so there's a good chance you'll see white-tailed deer and wild turkey among other land creatures. In fall and spring there's an abundance of waterfowl, including cormorants and blue heron. And there's always a wide variety of hawks. The best time to see the flowers is in the spring when trillium, May apple, jack-in-the-pulpit, and others color the trails. But fall has its attractions, too, when the rich amber and brown foliage steals the scene.

Winter brings cross-country skiing on the hiking trails and snowmobiling on marked trails. The lake offers the chance for ice skating and ice fishing.

Camping

The modern campground has 40 sites with electric hookups and 20 more without hookup. In high season these go for $12 with the hookup and $9 without. The other campground also has 60 sites, but it's classified as nonmodern, which in this case means pit latrines. But it is a little closer to the lake and has a Frisbee golf course nearby. These cost $6 in high season and $4 the rest of the year.

Three group campsites are available for organized youth groups only.

Nearby Attractions

One of the major craft and folk art centers in Iowa, the **Amana Colonies** (tel. 319/622-7616) is just about 30 miles west of the park. Iowa's only operating woolen mill is found here as are several small museums and a variety of craft shops. One of the state's 19 welcome centers is also located at the Colonies.

To the south, on the campus of the University of Iowa in **Iowa City,** you can tour the **Old Capitol** (tel. 319/335-0548). In West Branch, ten miles east of the city, is the birthplace and boyhood home of our 31st president, Herbert Hoover (tel. 319/643-5301).

To the north is **Cedar Rapids,** where history is also alive and well. A major draw here is **Brucemore** (tel. 319/362-7375), a 26-acre estate with a historic home featuring 14 fireplaces and five chimneys. Another place to take a step back in time is **Usher's Ferry Pioneer Village** (tel. 319/398-5104), a turn-of-the-century Iowa town.

Kansas

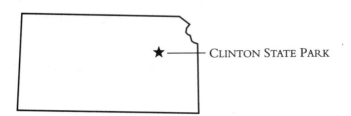

★———— CLINTON STATE PARK

Kansas has 24 state parks.

Contacts

- Kansas Department of Wildlife and Parks, 512 SE 25th Ave., Pratt, KS 67124 (tel. 316/672-5911).
- Travel and Tourism Development Division, Department of Commerce, 700 SW Harrison St., Suite 1300, Topeka, KS 66603-3712 (tel. toll free 800/252-6727 [800/2-KANSAS] or 913/296-2009).

General Information on Kansas State Parks

From the Flint Hills and timbered Cherokee Lowlands in the east to the rugged Cimaroon Grasslands and Smoky Hills in the west, The Sunflower State is rich in frontier history and pioneer spirit. Its state parks reflect this with outdoor recreation that can bring you into contact with species of wildlife that roamed the prairies long ago.

GENERAL FEES

Vehicles are charged $3 for a one-day permit. An annual permit, for the calendar year, costs $20.50.

CAMPING

There are more than 2,500 campsites available in 21 of the state's parks and their camping fees are among the lowest in the nation. At the time this book went to press, the fees ranged from $3 to $6 per night. The highest fee includes three-way hookups. Unfortunately, only seven parks offer these. An annual camping permit is available at each park and costs $35.

In most parks, 10% to 30% of the sites may be reserved. The rest are taken on a first-come basis. Reservations are made directly with the park by phone or mail, or in person. Reserved campsites are offered from April 15 through mid-October and requests may be made after January 1. There is a $5 reservation fee. A two-day minimum stay is required for weekends and the limit for a stay in any one campground is 14 consecutive days.

Some parks also offer Rent-a-Camp, which provides a reserved campsite, tent, and the basics, for $15 per night.

Pets. Pets are allowed, but must be controlled at all times. This means the pet must be on a hand-held leash or a chain tether not more than 10 feet long, or it must be in a pen or other confined area. Pets are not allowed on swimming beaches or in buildings.

Alcoholic beverages. In most parks only 3.2% proof beer is allowed. No other alcoholic intoxicants are permitted.

Clinton State Park

RV Camping · Tent Camping · Primitive Camping · Group Camping · Marina · Boating · Boat Launch · Fishing · Beach

Waterskiing · Picnic Areas · Trails · Nature Programs · Bicycling · X-Country Skiing

Capsule Description: A lakeside park with a marina, campsites, and primitive camping.

Location: Northeast Kansas. From Lawrence, go four miles west on U.S. Highway 40 to Douglas County Road 13, then three miles south to the park entrance.

Address: 798 N. 1415 Rd., Lawrence, KS 66049 (tel. 913/842-8562).

Area Contacts: Lawrence Convention and Visitors Bureau, P.O. Box 586, Lawrence, KS 66044 (tel. 913/865-4411).

Kansas City Convention and Visitors Bureau, 727 Minnesota Ave., Kansas City, KS 66101 (tel. 913/321-5800).

Topeka Convention and Visitors Bureau, 1275 SW Topeka Blvd., Topeka, KS 66612 (tel. toll free 800/235-1030 or 913/234-1030).

Insider Tip: If you don't have your own camping gear, this park has a Rent-a-Camp program.

This 1,500-acre park is located on the northern shore of Clinton Lake, a 7,000-acre Corps of Engineers reservoir. The lake is rimmed by about 85 miles of shoreline, with high bluffs and woods surrounding much of the clear water. The park is less than 20 years old, but archeological sites indicate that hunting groups began to use this area as early as 8000 B.C.

Activities

Naturally, the lake is the center of park activities, offering swimming, boating, fishing, and other water sports.

A swimming beach is located near the main camping area. An admission fee is charged, and no lifeguards are on duty.

For boaters, there's a full-service marina with rental slips and rental boats plus eight courtesy docks. The four boat ramps are capable of launching 16 boats at any one time. Windsurfers and jet skiers have separate launching areas. There are no horsepower restrictions on the lake, so waterskiing is popular.

Both boat fishing and fishing from the shoreline are rated excellent for catching bass, carp, crappie, and channel catfish. Other catches may include bluegill, drum, and walleye.

Deer, beaver, muskrat, raccoon, and other small animals are common sights on the 12 miles of hiking trails in the rolling, wooded terrain along the lakeshore. The two major trails are also open for mountain bikes, offering both novice and expert sections. In fact, these are the only trails anywhere at Clinton Lake that are open to bicyclists. In high season, the staff conducts interpretive programs and nature walks.

Birders can expect to see scissor-tailed flycatchers, Canada geese, and bluebirds. The park is in a Bluebird Restoration Area. Its Bluebird Trail has 75 houses for this bird, which is making a comeback in the area. In spring, there's a good chance you'll see bald eagles since some have been nesting here since 1989.

In the winter, five miles of the trails are set up for cross-country skiing, and ice-fishing can be enjoyed on the lake.

Camping

Of the 500 multiuse sites in the two campgrounds, half have water and electric hookups. The rest have no hookups. Only 15 sites can be reserved. There is also a primitive pack-in campground for tent camping only.

Nearby Attractions

Many day-trip destinations can be reached within an hour-long drive.

In the immediate area, if you want to see the lake from the other shore, you can boat over or take the short drive around to the Corps of Engineers parks where you can stop and picnic.

Lawrence, just four miles east, is the "Home of the Jayhawks" the 1,000-acre campus of the University of Kansas (tel. 913/864-2700), the largest university in the state, with an enrollment of more than 25,000. The university's **Dyche Museum of Natural History** features many fascinating displays, including Comanche, the horse that was the only cavalry survivor of the Battle of Little Bighorn. The art museum, the anthropology museum, and the Memorial Campanile are other popular places to visit. Among the historic buildings in downtown Lawrence is Liberty Hall (tel. 913/749-1972), the first movie theater west of the Mississippi.

Continuing east on I-70 for about 50 minutes brings you to the **Kansas City Metro Area,** which includes the city of that name in both Kansas and Missouri. Among the many things you can enjoy here are cruises on the Missouri River, a children's museum, a children's theater, or the zoo (tel. 816/871-5701), a steamboat museum, the ballet, symphony, opera, or opry. You can also cheer watching professional baseball, football, hockey, soccer, horse or greyhound racing; or learn more about President "Give 'em Hell" Harry at the **Harry S. Truman Library and Museum** (tel. 816/833-1225).

To the west of the park, on I-70, is the state capitol, **Topeka.** You can tour the **capitol building** and if you're there on a Friday afternoon, the **governor's mansion** (tel. 913/246-3232). Among the museums here is the **Combat Air Museum** (tel. 913/862-3303) with displays of aircraft used in armed conflict. Another place worth a visit is **Gage Park** (tel. 913/272-6150), which features one of the most extensive rose gardens in the country and a zoo.

Kentucky

Lake Barkley State Resort Park

Lake Cumberland State Resort Park

Barren River Lake State Resort Park

Kentucky has 44 state parks.

Contacts

- Kentucky State Parks, 500 Mero St., Frankfort, KY 40601-1974 (tel. toll free 800/255-PARK [800/255-7275] or 502/546-2172).
- Kentucky Division of Travel Development, P.O. Box 2011, Frankfort, KY 40602 (tel. toll free 800/225-TRIP [800/225-8747].

General Information About Kentucky State Parks

If you love parks, but don't like camping, Kentucky may be the state for you.

Kentucky brags that its parks are the "nation's finest," and overall, even if they are not "the finest," they are right up at the top of the list. The wise Kentuckians who started the park system chose parkland that was beautiful, but located mostly in remote and economically depressed areas with few if any commercial tourist facilities. This meant only campers and local residents could enjoy the parks. Also, most Kentuckians couldn't afford to go to high-priced resorts. So, the state built reasonably priced resorts and other overnight facilities in the expansive parks, thereby making the wonders of the outdoors accessible while providing comfortable and affordable retreats.

Today, Kentucky has 15 state resort parks with a variety of resort-type facilities centered around lodges. Thirteen of these resort parks and two other parks also offer fully equipped housekeeping cottages. And, not to neglect the campers, 26 parks have campgrounds.

Note: All parks are closed for a week around Christmas. Exact dates vary by year.

General Fees

There is no admission fee to any state park.

Camping and Accommodations

Reservations for rooms in the 15 park **lodges** may be made up to a year in advance. Each lodge has its own 800 number. All rooms have phones, TV, heat and air conditioning, and daily maid service. Rates are seasonal with a double room going for about $41 to $52 in the winter low season to $56 to $66 in the summer high season. The lodges at Lake Barkley and Cumberland Falls also offer suites at a higher rate. All resort lodges feature a dining room and gift shop. Children 16 and under can stay free in a room with adult family members. All lodge facilities and some of the rooms are equipped for the handicapped.

There are nine different types of **cottages** ranging from efficiencies to three-bedroom executives. All have phones, TV, and heat and air conditioning. Rates for an efficiency range from $52 to $65 depending on the season. At the other end of the scale, seasonal rates for a three-bedroom go from about $90 up to $150. These may be reserved the same way as lodge rooms.

There are more than 3,500 **campsites** available in 26 parks. Some campgrounds are open all year and others are seasonal. Most sites are multiuse and have some utility hookups. All are strictly on a first-come basis; no reservations are accepted. The rate is $10.50 for two persons.

Pets. Pets are allowed. They must be on a leash and under control at all times. They are not permitted in lodges, cabins, or most other buildings.

Alcoholic beverages. Regulations depend on the county in which the park is located. Most parks are in dry counties where there is no public display or consumption of alcoholic beverages.

Discounts. Lodging and camping discounts are available for Senior Citizens, 62 and over, and disabled adults.

Barren River Lake State Resort Park

Visitor Center | Lodge/Hotel | Restaurant | Cabins & Cottages | RV Camping | Tent Camping | Marina | Boating | Boat Launch | Fishing | Swimming | Beach

Waterskiing | Picnic Areas | Trails | Horse Trails | Nature Programs | Bicycling | Golf | Tennis | Playground | Gift Shop

Capsule Description: A developed resort park on a lake.

Location: South-central Kentucky. From I-65, take the Cumberland Parkway southeast to U.S. Highway 31E; take this southwest to the park.

Address: 1149 State Park Rd., Lucas, KY 42156-9709 (tel. 502/646-2151; toll free 800/325-0057 for reservations only).

Area Contacts: Bowling Green/Warren County Tourist/Convention Commission, 352 Three Springs Road, Bowling Green, KY 42104 (tel. 502/782-0800).
Cave Country, P.O. Box 1040-D, Bowling Green, KY 42012 (tel. 502/782-0800).

Insider Tips: Lower lodge rates and special package plans are available during the off-season. Airport transfers to and from the Glaskow airport, 13 miles away, can be arranged in advance.

Don't let the name of this 2,200-acre park fool you: "Barren" it's not. At least not now, but it was once. Long before the white settlers arrived, the Shawnee Indians repeatedly burned the forest to leave a treeless, grassy prairie—excellent for grazing—that attracted the buffalo, elk, and deer they hunted. The forests of oaks, maples, and pine have now recovered, and a 10,000-acre man-made lake sits in the midst of rolling hills covered with thick clusters of trees.

This resort park is located just a short drive from Kentucky's famous cave area, which includes Mammoth Cave National Park with the longest cave system in the world.

Activities

Normally, you go to a park to enjoy the wonders of nature not to be pampered or entertained, but you can have both here.

This is definitely not a wilderness park, but, for starters, there are three nature trails ranging from half a mile to two miles in length and in difficulty from easy walks to difficult hikes. On these trails there's a fair chance you'll catch glimpses of some of the park's wildlife, such as white-tailed deer, groundhogs, woodchucks, opossums, raccoons, and many species of birds, including cardinals, the state bird.

The park's stable has horses for rent and offers guided trail rides during the summer.

Out for some exercise? From March through October you can rent bikes and ride the 2½-mile, paved loop bike trail. The first mile of this trail is also an exercise trail with stations. For golfers there's an 18-hole regulation course open year-round. Two lighted tennis courts, a lighted basketball court, and volleyball courts are also provided.

But, always, the lake beckons. The full-service marina has rental fishing boats, pontoon boats, and houseboats that sleep up to 12. There are no power limits on the lake so waterskiing is popular, as are windsurfing and scuba diving. Fishing from the pier or a boat is good for largemouth, smallmouth, and white bass, as well as crappie, bluegill, walleye, and channel catfish.

Lodge and cottage guests can swim in the heated pool near the lodge, while campers and other visitors have use of the beach and bathhouse complex on the lake. Lifeguards oversee both in season.

You can do it all on your own or take advantage of the fact that this is a resort and join the many activities and special events—from nature programs to evening entertainment—put on year-round under the direction of a trained recreation director.

Camping and Accommodations

Each of the 51 rooms in the **lodge** provides a view of the lake. Rates range on a sliding seasonal scale from a low of $43 for a double from November through March, to $60 from late May through early September.

The 22 **cottages** are all two-bedroom, two-bath executive types, which sleep up to six. Rates go from a November to March low of $100 to a high summer rate of $150. Eleven of the cottages have fireplaces and two are equipped for the handicapped.

The 99 **campsites** are all multiuse with electric and water hookups. Most are in open areas without shade and there is not much separation between sites. Rates are $10.50 for two people. All are on a first-come basis; no reservations are taken.

Nearby Attractions

It's a short drive, about 30 miles, to **Mammoth Cave National Park** (tel. 502/758-2328). This cave, which contains the world's longest network of cavern corridors—more than 300 miles in length—is a must-see. You have your pick of tours that include a quarter-mile tour that takes a little over an hour, several two-hour tours, and the four-mile half-day tour. A guided tour for the disabled is also offered.

Nearby **Cave City** is tourist-oriented and has two amusement parks—the **Guntown Mountain Amusement Park** (tel. 502/773-3530) and the **Kentucky Action Park** (tel. 502/773-2636).

The largest city in the area is **Bowling Green,** about an hour's drive to the west. Here you can take walking tours of the six historic areas listed on the National Register of Historic Places. Coming back to the present, you can visit Bowling Green's **GM plant** (tel. 502/745-8000) and watch Corvettes being made. Tours are given twice a day on most weekdays.

Lake Barkley State Resort Park

Visitor Center | Lodge/Hotel | Restaurant | Cabins & Cottages | RV Camping | Tent Camping | Marina | Boating | Boat Launch | Fishing | Swimming | Beach

Waterskiing | Picnic Areas | Trails | Horse Trails | Nature Programs | Tennis | Fitness Center | Playground | Gift Shop

Capsule Description: A developed resort park on an extensive lake system.

Location: Southwestern Kentucky. From I-24, take the Cadiz/U.S. 68 exit. Go west on U.S. 68 through Cadiz to the park entrance.

Address: P.O. Box 790, Cadiz, KY 42211 (tel. 502/924-1131; toll free 800/325-1708 for reservations only).

Area Contacts: Hopkinsville/Christian County Tourism Commission, P.O. Box 1382, Hopkinsville, KY 42241 (tel. toll free 800/842-9959).

Land Between the Lakes, 100 Van Morgan Dr., Golden Pond, KY 42211-9001 (tel. 502/924-5602).

Paducah/McCracken County Tourist Commission, P.O. Box 90, Paducah, KY 42002-0090 (tel. toll free 800/359-4775).

Insider Tips: In winter, both golden and bald eagles soar in the park. A nominal fee is charged to use the Fitness Center.

As its name states, this 3,600-acre resort park sits on the banks of Lake Barkley, named after the late senator and vice-president from Kentucky, Alben W. Barkley. Lake Barkley is Kentucky's second-largest lake, extending 118 miles with over 1,000 miles of shoreline. At its northern end, a free-flowing canal connects it to the state's largest lake, Kentucky Lake, which is 184 miles long with 2,380 miles of shoreline. The lakes lie parallel to each other and, with the canal connection making them a continuous body of water in the shape of an upside-down U, together they form the world's largest man-made lake.

Activities

Although the lake is the big attraction here, there's a lot to do for the visitor who wants to stay land-based.

First, there are nine miles of trails. Most of these are relatively short and rated for easy to medium hiking. One is a self-guided loop nature trail. In the summer you can rent a horse at the park stables and ride the trails. However, with the exception of birds—golden and bald eagles can be spotted in winter—you probably won't see too much in the way of wildlife in this highly developed park.

For golfers there's an 18-hole course with a pro shop and all the typical facilities. The only supervised trapshooting range in a Kentucky park is found here, as is one of the few year-round park fitness centers with Nautilus equipment, racquetball courts, aerobics instruction, sauna, steam room, and whirlpool. Of the four tennis courts, two are lighted for night play.

In the resort mode, there's a full-time recreation director who offers a variety of programs all year long.

Lodge and cottage guests have a swimming pool at the lodge and other visitors can use the beach on the lake. Both are usually open from early June to early September and lifeguards are on duty.

In addition to swimming, the 57,920 acres of lake beckon for other sports. Want to waterski? At the full-service marina you can rent a runabout ski boat. They also rent fishing boats, pontoon boats, and paddleboats. Throw out a line and you might pull in a largemouth, smallmouth, Kentucky bass, bluegill, channel and other catfish, crappie, and sauger.

Camping and Accommodations

There are two **lodges** here. The rustic-looking semicircular main lodge is built to follow the contour of the shore so every one of the 120 rooms and four suites have a lake view from a private balcony. The Little River Lodge, nearby, has 10 rooms and one suite. Its rooms can be rented individually or as one unit by a group. Rates in high season, from the middle of May to early September, are $66 for a double. The same room goes for $45 in the low season, November through March. The suites, which sleep up to six, go for $140 April through October and $120 the rest of the year. Handicapped-equipped rooms are available.

There are nine two-bedroom, two-bath executive **cottages** and four two-bedroom, one-bath log cabins with fireplaces. All have TV, phones, and other standard conveniences. Both of these also sleep up to six and rent for $120 from April through October and $100 the rest of the year.

The 80 multiuse **campsites** all have electric and water hookups and, like all Kentucky campsites, are on a first-come basis; no reservations are accepted. Rates are $10.50 for two people.

Nearby Attractions

Cadiz, the nearest town just outside the park, made the listing in the National Register of Historic Places for its historic downtown. It also boasts that it is the "Country Ham Capital" of Kentucky.

The biggest attraction in this area is the **Land Between the Lakes,** a 40-mile long wooded peninsula to the west between Lake Barkley and Kentucky Lake. It has been developed by the Tennessee Valley Authority (TVA) as a national recreation area. To get the lay of the land, you can start with a 60-mile scenic lakes driving tour. The shoreline is undeveloped and no commercial facilities exist on the peninsula. The place does include, however, the Golden Pond Planetarium (tel. 502/924-1325) a living history 1850s farm, the Homeplace–1850, a nature station, where you can see eagles, deer, red wolves, owls, snakes, and other exhibits. If you didn't find enough trails at the resort to stretch your hiker's legs, there are 200 miles here to try, including the challenging 60-mile North-South Trail.

The closest cities to the park are Hopkinsville to the east and Paducah to the northwest. **Hopkinsville** has the **Pennyroyal Area Museum** (tel. 502/887-4270), and 15 miles south of it is **Fort Campbell** (tel. 502/798-2151), home of the Army's "Screaming Eagles" Division, the 101st Airborne. Among the more unusual sights in **Paducah** is the **Museum of the American Quilter's Society** (tel. 502/442-8856), where up to 200 quilts are on display. You can also watch Arabian and quarter horse racing here at **Bluegrass Downs** (tel. 502/444-7117).

Lake Cumberland State Resort Park

Visitor Center   Lodge/Hotel   Restaurant   Cabins & Cottages   RV Camping   Tent Camping   Primitive Camping   Marina   Boating   Boat Launch   Fishing   Swimming

Waterskiing   Picnic Areas   Trails   Nature Programs   Golf   Tennis   Playground   Gift Shop

Capsule Description: A large, developed resort park on a lake.

Location: South-central Kentucky. From Exit 62 at Russell Springs on the Cumberland Parkway, take U.S. 127 south to the park.

Address: 5465 State Park Rd., Jamestown, KY 42629-7801 (tel. 502/343-3111; toll free 800/325-1709 for reservations only).

Area Contacts: McCreary County Tourism Commission, P.O. Box 368, Stearns, KY 42647 (tel. 606/376-3008). (For information on Big South Fork National River and Recreation Area.)

Russell County Tourist Commission, P.O. Box 64, Russell Springs, KY 42642 (tel. 502/866-4333).

Insider Tips: On the five-mile drive entering the park, some deer may run across the road; others, more used to the traffic, may just saunter across. The park is just west of the line marking the beginning of the Central Time Zone.

The Wolf Creek Dam controls the flow of the Cumberland River, backing it up 101 miles to form Lake Cumberland—which has more than 50,000 acres of surface, an average depth of 90 feet, and 1,225 miles of shoreline. This state resort park (3,117 acres) sits on a peninsula on the western end of Lake Cumberland, just three miles north of the dam.

Activities

The lake is such a lure they even named the park's main lodge Lure Lodge.

For boaters there's a full-service marina that offers 100 open slips and rents fishing boats, pontoon boats, and ski boats. There's even a shuttle-bus service from the lodge to the state dock. But the prize here is that they also rent eight models of houseboats. The houseboats, which are normally available from May through September, range in size from a 46-foot-long model that sleeps eight to a 64-footer that sleeps 12. The rates also run the gamut depending on whether you rent midweek or on the weekend, and whether it's premium season or what's known as the super-saver season. Weekend rates, for example, range from about $450 super saver to $600 premium for the smallest, to $1,200 to $1,700 for the largest. For information and reservations on these boats, call toll free 800/234-3625.

In addition to boating and waterskiing, the lake calls to anglers with an abundance of smallmouth, white, and Kentucky bass; bluegill; crappie; rockfish; and walleye. According to the local experts, fishing for rainbow trout is best below Wolf Creek Dam.

Lodge and cottage guests have a year-round indoor pool available and there's an Olympic-size public pool with lifeguards, open from Memorial Day to Labor Day.

Serious hikers will not find much of a challenge here, but there is a four-mile self-guided nature trail for walkers. Since the trail is on a peninsula on which animals have been protected from predators

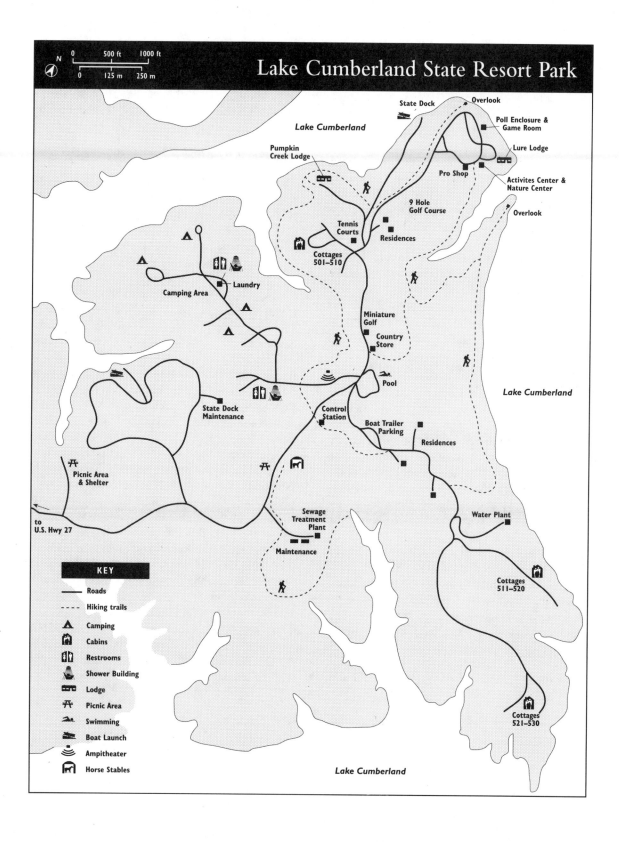

Lake Cumberland State Resort Park

N

| 0 | 500 ft | 1000 ft |
| 0 | 125 m | 250 m |

Lake Cumberland

State Dock
Overlook
Poll Enclosure & Game Room
Lure Lodge
Pumpkin Creek Lodge
Pro Shop
Activites Center & Nature Center
9 Hole Golf Course
Overlook
Tennis Courts
Residences
Cottages 501–510
Camping Area
Laundry
Miniature Golf
Country Store
Pool
State Dock Maintenance
Control Station
Boat Trailer Parking
Residences
Picnic Area & Shelter
to U.S. Hwy 27
Water Plant
Sewage Treatment Plant
Maintenance
Cottages 511–520
Cottages 521–530
Lake Cumberland
Lake Cumberland

KEY

- —— Roads
- ---- Hiking trails
- ▲ Camping
- Cabins
- Restrooms
- Shower Building
- Lodge
- Picnic Area
- Swimming
- Boat Launch
- Ampitheater
- Horse Stables

for years, deer, raccoons, and other small animals and birds populate it heavily. (If you're a confirmed hiker, you might want to enjoy other pleasures of this resort park and get in your hiking later with a day-trip to the nearby Big South Fork National River and Recreation Area.)

On-shore activities include golf on a nine-hole par-three course or "putting around" on the 18-hole miniature golf course; picnicking, tennis on two lighted courts, or a guided trail ride from the riding stable. Also available are a nature and an activities center, exercise room, year-round interpretive programs, and daily recreational programs in the summer.

You can also do rappelling in the park, but that requires a permit from the Department of Parks in Frankfort.

Camping and Accommodations

The 63 rooms in **Lure Lodge** all have a balcony with a lake view, air conditioning and heat, and TV. Some rooms are equipped for the handicapped. **Pumpkin Creek Lodge** has 10 rooms and three suites with the same amenities, plus some rooms have wet bars. Depending on the season, rates for a double range from about $43 to $60 with an additional charge of about $6 for rooms in the Lure Lodge pool area or a room with a wet bar in Pumpkin Creek.

The 30 **cottages** are one- and two-bedroom. The one-bedrooms rent for $65 to $73. The two-bedrooms come in two models: the standard two-bedroom, which rents for $75 to $83, and the Wildwood Cottages, which go for $80 to $88. Both hold up to four adults, but the 10 Wildwood units are contemporary chalet-style with upstairs bedrooms and fireplaces.

Of the 147 sites in the **campground,** 117 have electric and water hookups. The campground is open from April 1 to November 30, costs $10.50 for two people, and is on a first-come basis; no reservations are taken.

Nearby Attractions

The dam that made Lake Cumberland is just three miles south of the park entrance. At **Wolf Creek National Fish Hatchery** (tel. 502/343-3797), near the dam, trout is raised for Kentucky waters.

A little north of the park, although you have to go through **Jamestown** and back to get to it, you can take a lake cruise on *The Jamestown Queen,* (tel. 502/343-5253) a small sternwheeler. If you have a boat, you can follow the lake some 40-odd nautical miles to **General Burnside State Park** (tel. 606/561-4192). A marina and an 18-hole golf course are located there. This park is named after the Civil War general who went down in history not for his military exploits, but for his beard and mustache worn with a clean-shaven chin, called a "burnsider," now known as sideburns.

For hikers and those who want to experience wilder country, a daytrip to **Big South Fork National River and Recreation Area** (tel. 606/376-5073) will give you ample opportunity to get in touch with nature. Located to the south-east of the park, this 104,000-acre wilderness area stretches across the Kentucky border into Tennessee. The Blue Heron area, near the town of Stearns, features the sweeping vistas of the Devil's Jump overlooks. It is also the site of an old coal mining community that flourished here in the 1930s and 40s that's now a living museum. A fun way to get to this community is on a six-mile ride on the **Big South Fork Scenic Railway** from Stearns (tel. 606/376-5330).

Louisiana

Bayou Segnette
State Park

Louisiana has 14 state parks.

Contacts

- Office of State Parks, Department of Culture, Recreation and Tourism, P.O. Box 44426, Baton Rouge, LA 70804-9361 (tel. 504/342-8111).
- Louisiana Office of Tourism, P.O. Box 94291, Baton Rouge, LA 70804-9291 (tel. toll free 800/33GUMBO [800/334-8626] or tel. 504/342-8119).

General Information on Louisiana State Parks

The Louisiana park system fell on hard times in the mid-1980s when the petroleum industry and the state's considerable oil and gas resources fell victim to fluctuations in the world oil market. Up to that time, all park user fees went into the state's general fund. With the general funds down, the parks took a beating. To meet the crisis, the legislature approved a measure in 1989 to assign the revenues from user fees to a fund dedicated to the parks. Since then, the parks have shown steady improvement and the future appears bright.

General Fees

Entrance fee of $2 per car with up to four passengers plus 50¢ for each additional person. Walk-ins are 50¢. An annual day-use permit is available for $30.

Camping and Accommodations

Seven state parks contain a total of 96 vacation **cabins.** These can sleep four to six with a maximum capacity of two persons over the bedding accommodation number. Cabins have heat and air conditioning and some have fireplaces but no TVs or phones. The rate for the cabins runs from $35 to $50 depending on the size and the park. They may be reserved through the individual park. Usually reservations are accepted beginning January 2 for the period April 1 through September 30 and beginning July 1 for the period October 1 to March 31.

There are **campgrounds** in 13 of the 14 parks (only Cypremort Point has no camping) with more than 1,000 improved multiuse sites providing water and electric hookups, and another 190 unimproved sites with no hookups. The improved sites are $12 per night and the unimproved $10. Site reservations may be made directly with nine of the 13 parks. There is a $3 reservation fee. The maximum occupancy of any site is six persons and from April through September the maximum stay is 14 days within any 30-day period.

There are dormitory- or cabin-style group camps in six parks and family lodges that sleep 10 to 12 in two parks.

Pets. All pets must be leashed, caged, or crated and are not permitted in buildings or in designated swimming areas.

Alcoholic beverages. In general alcoholic beverages are permitted in all parks; however, there are certain area restrictions within some parks, such as no drinking in parking lots or at swimming pools.

Discounts. Senior Citizens, 62 and over, are entitled to free admission to all parks. In addition, they may purchase **Golden Pelican Discount Permits.** Some discounts are available without the permit.

Bayou Segnette State Park

| Visitor Center | Cabins & Cottages | RV Camping | Tent Camping | Group Lodge Dormitories | Boating | Boat Launch | Fishing | Swimming | Picnic Areas | Playground |

Capsule Description: A developed small park on the outskirts of New Orleans.

Location: Westwego, southwest on downtown New Orleans across the Mississippi. From I-10 west of downtown, take the U.S. 90/Clearview parkway exit and go south across the Huey P. Long Bridge, then east on Business 90/West Bank Expressway to the park entrance.

Address: 7777 West Bank Exp., Westwego, LA 70094 (tel. 504/736-7140).

Area Contacts: Greater New Orleans Tourist and Convention Commission, 1520 Sugar Bowl Dr., New Orleans, LA 70112 (tel. 504/566-5011.

Insider Tip: The park gates are locked from 10pm to 7am, April 1 to September 30; and 7pm to 8am, October 1 to March 31. You must check in before those times. When you check in, you'll be given the combination to the lock on the rear entrance gate, which you can use to exit or enter during the closed hours.

Location. Location! LOCATION! This is an instance where that real-estate cliché serves to boost an excellent small park into one of the *100 Best-Loved.* Cabins, campgrounds, boating, fishing, a wave pool . . . all just across the bridge from New Orleans.

Activities

Opened in 1986, this 580-acre park is relatively new. And one of its main attractions, the wave-pool complex, is even newer, having opened in 1993. The complex includes a Visitor Center, the 385,000-gallon wave pool that can hold up to 500 tubers, surfers, and swimmers, a kiddy pool, and a small sand beach. It's open from Memorial Day to Labor Day weekend. There is an entrance fee, which includes rental of a tube float.

Water plays an important part in other park activities, in addition to the pool. The boat launch is a popular spot to enter the bayou that gives the park its name. That bayou is a scenic avenue to Lake Catouatche, which lies south of the park, and to numerous areas not readily accessible by land routes.

Boat docks by the launch are available for those who want to leave their boats and enjoy the other facilities of the park, and fishing piers for those who want to try their luck in the waters of the bayou. Catches in the park include both fresh- and saltwater fish—like largemouth bass, crappie, and redfish—fresh in the pond in the picnic area, and saltwater in the bayou. (If you want to try for both, you'll need both a fresh and saltwater license.)

Wildlife-watching is mostly for small animals, like armadillos and rabbits, waterfowl and hawks. But there's a good chance you'll also see a prime resident of the brackish marsh waters, the alligator.

Camping and Accommodations

The 20 **cabins** that are perched on the bank of the bayou are clustered in pairs with a dock/fishing pier for each pair. Each cabin sleeps six providing a bedroom with a double bed downstairs and two sets of bunk beds in a loft. All have heat and air conditioning and come with a large screen porch looking out over the marsh, but no TV or phones. Four of the cabins are equipped for wheelchair access. Cabins cost about $50 per night and may be reserved up to six months in advance.

The 100 multiuse **campsites** all have water and electric hookups. Most are shaded, but the camp-grounds are tight and there's not much separation between sites. They cost $12. Reservations are accepted up to a year in advance, and the camp-grounds are always booked early for Mardi Gras, which is usually in late February, and for Jazzfest, usually at the end of April.

The park also has a three dormitory group camp with a capacity of 120 persons.

Nearby Attractions

Want to see the swamps close up? A number of commercial companies in the Westwego area offer tours.

There are no designated hiking trails at Bayou Segnette, but if you want to hike along natural trails, go to the Barataria unit of the **Jean Lafitte National Historical Park and Preserve** (tel. 504/589-3882), about 10 miles south; it's a short drive on a good road. It's also a good place for canoeing. The main unit of this park, closer in at Chalmette, was the site of the Battle of New Orleans, the last major battle of the War of 1812.

Prefer the open waters? It's an easy day-trip to the southwest, though you have to wend your way around the lakes, to **Grand Isle** on the Gulf.

And to the north, just across the bridge, lies **New Orleans** with its famed restaurants, French Quarter, museums, theater, riverboat tours, an aquarium, a zoo, professional sports, and all the other attractions of a major city.

Maine

BAXTER
STATE PARK

Maine has 31 state parks.

Contacts

- Bureau of Parks and Recreation, Maine Department of Conservation, State House Station no. 22, Augusta, ME 04333 (tel. 207/287-3821).
- The Maine Publicity Bureau, P.O. Box 2300, Hallowell, ME 04347 (tel. toll free 800/533-9595).

General Information on Maine State Parks

Unspoiled is an apt way to describe most of Maine, a state that is just about as big as the other five New England states combined. With 17 million acres of forestland, which makes it the most heavily forested state in the nation, a mile-high mountain, 3,000 lakes, and 3,500 miles of coastline, it offers an abundance of opportunities for outdoor recreation. Designed to harmonize with mountain, lake, and seashore, Maine's state parks are as diverse as its landscape.

GENERAL FEES

Most parks have an entrance or parking fee of $1 to $2 per person. An annual family pass is available for $30.

CAMPING AND ACCOMMODATIONS

Baxter State Park is the only one with cabins (see below).

About a dozen parks have campgrounds; however, most are only open from early or mid-May through the fall. Sites cost from $9 to $10 for residents and up to $13 for nonresidents. Most sites may be reserved for June 15 through Labor Day. There's a $2 per night reservation fee. Call 207/287-3824 (or in Maine toll free 800/332-1501) for all parks except Baxter (see below). The minimum stay for reservations is two nights at all parks except Sebago Lake, which has a four-night minimum. Maximum stay is 14 nights.

Pets. Pets are allowed in all parks except Baxter. They are not allowed on any beaches, and in Sebago Lake State Park they are not allowed in the campgrounds. Where allowed, they must be on a leash not exceeding four feet in length and under control at all times.

Alcoholic beverages. Intoxicating beverages of any type are not permitted.

Discounts. Seniors, 65 and older, are admitted free to most parks.

Baxter State Park

Cabins & Cottages RV Camping Tent Camping Primitive Camping Group Camping Group Lodge Dormitories Non-Motorized Boating Only Fishing Swimming Trails X-Country Skiing Snow-mobiling

Capsule Description: A huge wilderness park with a minimum of developed facilities.

Location: North-central Maine. From Millinocket, take Maine Highway 157 and park roads 18 miles northwest.

Address: 64 Balsam Dr., Millinocket, ME 04462 (tel. 207/723-5140).

Area Contacts: Millinocket Chamber of Commerce, P.O. Box 5, Millinocket, ME 04462 (tel. 207/723-4443).

Moosehead Lake Region Chamber of Commerce, P.O. Box 581, Greenville, ME 04441 (tel. 207/695-2702).

Northern Katahdin Valley Regional Chamber of Commerce, P.O. Box 14D, Patten, ME 04765 (tel. 207/528-2215).

Insider Tip: Although it's a state park, Baxter is administered and operated as a separate entity under the Baxter State Park Authority. This includes the setting of fees which may or may not be in agreement with those in other parks. The non-resident vehicle entrance fee, for example, is $8 per vehicle.

"Put your money where your mouth is," was not just a cliché for Percival P. Baxter, who loved the North Woods region around Katahdin Mountain, the highest mountain in Maine. As early as 1917, while a state legislator, he tried unsuccessfully to convince the state to set up a wilderness preserve there. Later, as governor from 1921 to 1925, he continued to strive valiantly to pass legislation that would make this a state park. After he left office, Baxter remained determined and undeterred; he decided to buy the land himself and turn it over to

the state. He raised the money and, piece by piece, bought the land and deeded it to the people of Maine. His first gift, made in 1931, included Katahdin Mountain. His last, in 1962, brought the park to its present size of 201,018 acres. He also set up two trust funds which, supplemented only by user fees, pay for park operations and maintenance.

His only proviso was that the park was to be "forever left in its natural, wild state."

There are four seasons in the park. May 15 to October 15 is open for general use and camping. October 15 to December 1, the park is open for day use only until the park director determines if weather or road conditions warrant closure of the gates to vehicles. December 1 to April 1, it's open for winter use; roads are not plowed or maintained during this period. April 1 to May 15, it's open for day use only, with roads opened or closed at the park director's discretion.

Since most of the roads are narrow, no private vehicle over 9 feet high, 7 feet wide, and 22 feet long is allowed in the park.

Activities

This is definitely an outdoorsman's park. For hikers and backpackers there are about 175 miles of trails. These include several self-guided nature trails. Here also is the northern terminus of the 2,050-mile Appalachian Trail that runs down to Georgia. Climbers can try their skill on the park's 46 mountain peaks and ridges, 18 of which exceed 3,000 feet, the highest being Katahdin, now called Baxter Peak, which is almost a mile high. Considering the huge expanse of wilderness, for safety sake, hikers and climbers are urged to check in with park officers to pick up detailed maps before starting out on their journeys.

The most common large game animals in the park are moose, black bear, and white-tailed deer. Moose and deer are plentiful and you'll have a good chance of seeing them, not only on the trails but near the campgrounds. The park has a well-established bear population of between 160 to 200, so, here again, there's a good chance of seeing one during your visit. Bears may appear harmless, but they are not, so review park rules about them. You may also spot smaller animals such as beaver, porcupine, raccoon, mink, and otters. Birds commonly flying park skies include the bald eagle, great blue heron, Canada goose, osprey, the great horned owl, and more than a hundred other species.

Brook trout is the main catch in two dozen lakes and ponds. Several of these lakes are restricted to fly fishing only. Only nonpowered boats are allowed.

Experienced canoeists and white-water rafters have two rivers and a major stream to run that are rated Class II to IV. Canoes can be rented in the park.

In winter, hiking, snowshoeing, technical climbing, ice and snow climbing, snowmobiling, cross-country skiing, and alpine skiing above the timberline are all popular. However, once again, for safety's sake, you'll have to get a permit for winter camping, mountain hiking, or climbing. This lets the park staff determine that you are adequately equipped and capable of taking care of yourself in the wilderness if harsh weather hits. Most other winter-sports activities do not require special permission, but it's still recommended that you check in.

Camping and Accommodations

There are 22 **cabins,** five bunkhouses, and 84 lean-tos in the park, all of which may be reserved. Cabins range in capacity from two to four. The summer season rates are $17 per person per night with a minimum of $30 for a two-bed cabin, $40 for a three-bed, and $50 for a four-bed. Children 1 to 6 stay free; ages 7 to 16 are $10 each. The bunkhouses sleep 6 to 13 at $7 per person. Reservations are made by the bunk, so if you're not with a group you can still share the bunkhouse. Lean-tos have a capacity of two to six, with most holding four. They cost $6 per person with a minimum of $12 per lean-to. In winter cabins are $30 per person per night, the bunkhouses are $15 to $25 per person, lean-tos are $12 per person. Many of the lean-to sites are accessible by backpacking only.

Campgrounds are open from mid-May to mid-September or October and hold about 100 tent sites. Most are situated at roadside on narrow roads, but a number are hike-in. Tents may also be pitched at some lean-to sites. There are no hookups. All sites may be reserved and reservations are required if you want a backcountry site. In summer, tent sites cost $6 per person per night with a minimum of $12. In winter, if sites are open, the fee is $12 per person per night.

Reservations may be made at park headquarters in writing or in person (no phone) after January 1.

Nearby Attractions

Not much change can be found in the landscape or in outdoor activities outside the park, just more comfortable accommodations, restaurants, and the other trappings of civilization in a scattering of towns. The area is developed in places where fishermen will find salmon as well as trout, and power boaters will find lakes big enough to accommodate them. There's more white water for rafters and canoeists to explore and almost limitless trails for serious hikers. In winter, hundreds of miles of groomed trails beckon snowmobilers and cross-country skiers.

To the east, in the town of **Patten,** is the **Lumberman's Museum,** (tel. 207/528-2650) a complex of nine buildings containing working models of a sawmill and a blacksmith shop, along with

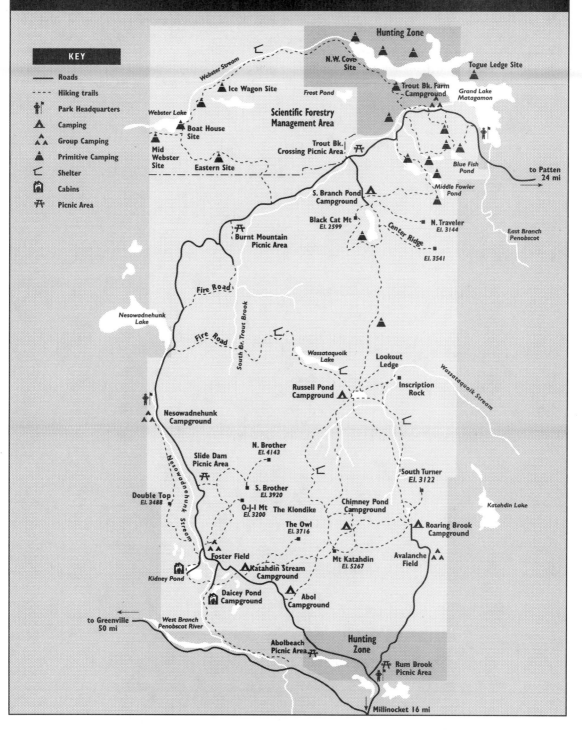

Baxter State Park

KEY

- —— Roads
- ---- Hiking trails
- Park Headquarters
- △ Camping
- △△ Group Camping
- ▲ Primitive Camping
- Շ Shelter
- 🏠 Cabins
- 🏕 Picnic Area

N
0 1 2 mi
0 1 2 km

Hunting Zone

N.W. Cove Site

Togue Ledge Site

Webster Stream

Ice Wagon Site

Frost Pond

Trout Bk. Farm Campground

Grand Lake Matagamon

Webster Lake

Boat House Site

Scientific Forestry Management Area

Mid Webster Site

Eastern Site

Trout Bk. Crossing Picnic Area

Blue Fish Pond

to Patten 24 mi

S. Branch Pond Campground

Middle Fowler Pond

Black Cat Mt El. 2599

N. Traveler El. 3144

East Branch Penobscot

Burnt Mountain Picnic Area

Center Ridge

El. 3541

Fire Road

Nesowadnehunk Lake

Fire Road

South Br. Trout Brook

Wassataquoik Lake

Lookout Ledge

Wassataquoik Stream

Russell Pond Campground

Inscription Rock

Nesowadnehunk Campground

N. Brother El. 4143

Slide Dam Picnic Area

South Turner El. 3122

Katahdin Lake

Double Top El. 3488

S. Brother El. 3920

O-J-I Mt El. 3200

The Klondike

Chimney Pond Campground

The Owl El. 3716

Roaring Brook Campground

Foster Field

Avalanche Field

Kidney Pond

Katahdin Stream Campground

Mt Katahdin El. 5267

Daicey Pond Campground

Abol Campground

to Greenville 50 mi

West Branch Penobscot River

Abolbeach Picnic Area

Hunting Zone

Rum Brook Picnic Area

Millinocket 16 mi

3,000 artifacts of the lumbermen who worked these North Woods.

A longer day-trip that's worth making is a visit to **Greenville,** about 45 miles southwest of the park. This recreation center, located on the southern tip of Moosehead Lake, Maine's largest lake, features the **Moosehead Marine Museum** (tel. 207/695-2716) on board the restored 1914 lake steamship *Karahdin,* which also offers scenic cruises. And you can take a chair-lift ride in summer to the top of nearby Big Squaw Mountain, or ski down that mountain in winter.

Maryland

DEEP CREEK LAKE
STATE PARK

ASSATEAGUE
STATE PARK

Maryland has 47 state parks.

Contacts

- State Forest and Park Service, Maryland Department of Natural Resources, Tawes State Office Building–E3, Annapolis, MD 21401 (tel. 410/974-3771; 410/461-0052 for campground information).
- Maryland Division of Tourism and Promotion, 217 E. Redwood St., 9th floor, Baltimore, MD 21202 (tel. toll free 800/445-4558; 800/543-1036 for Travel Kit).

General Information on Maryland State Parks

From Chesapeake Bay and the Atlantic Ocean on the Eastern Shore to the rising mountains in the west, Maryland parks and forests offer recreational diversity. Unfortunately, some parks are closed during the winter due to budget cuts. It's best to call the State Forest and Park Service before making an off-season trip to any park.

GENERAL FEES
Admission to the parks ranges from free to $4 per person or more, depending on both the park and the season. To be safe, expect a fee from Memorial Day through Labor Day. Entrance fees, when charged are usually $2 to $4 per person.

CAMPING AND ACCOMMODATIONS
Cabins may be rented at Herrington Manor (20 cabins), New Germany (11 cabins), Elk Neck (9 cabins), Janes Island (4 cabins), and Martinak (1 cabin). They are available on a weekly basis from the first Saturday in June through the first Saturday in September. The rest of the year there is a two-night minimum. Cabin capacity ranges from two to eight persons. The weekly rates go from a low of about $105 for a four-person cabin at Elk Neck to more than $400 a week for an eight-person cabin at New Germany. Reservations up to one year in advance may be made by contacting the park directly. Reservations are usually taken starting the first week of February.

Seventeen parks have **campgrounds** and boast a grand total of more than 2,300 improved sites, but only a small number of these have hookups. Another three parks have a few dozen unimproved sites. Most improved sites go for $15 a night, $18 with electric hookups. Most are on a first-come basis, but some may be reserved for a $5 fee.

Pets. The majority of the parks do not allow pets. Where they are permitted they must be under the control of their owners and are not allowed on swimming beaches, in picnic areas, cabin areas, or other developed day-use areas. Proof of current vaccination is required. Call the park you plan to visit for details.

Alcoholic beverages. Permitted in most parks; however, even when permitted there may be designated areas where use is restricted.

Discounts. Vehicles driven by senior citizens are admitted free to most parks. Sunday through Thursday, seniors, 62 and older, receive discounts on campsites.

Assateague State Park

Visitor Center | RV Camping | Primitive Camping | Group Camping | Boat Launch | Non-Motorized Boating Only | Fishing | Swimming | Beach | Trails | Nature Programs | Bicycling

Capsule Description: An Atlantic Ocean, barrier island beach park.

Location: Assateague Island. From U.S. Highway 50 going east toward Ocean City, take Maryland Highway 611 to the park.

Address: 7307 Stephen Decatur Hwy., Berlin, MD 21811 (tel. 410/641-2120).

Area Contacts: Ocean City Convention and Visitors Bureau, 4001 Coastal Highway, Ocean City, MD 21842 (tel. 410/289-8181).

Assateague Island National Seashore, 7206 National Seashore Lane, Berlin, MD 21811 (tel. 410/641-1443).

Worchester County Tourism, 105 Pearl Street, Snow Hill, MD 21863 (tel. 410/632-3617).

Insider Tips: If you're interested in catching your dinner of clams, mussels, or crabs, stop by the Barrier Island Visitor Center on Hwy. 611 for a free ''Shell-fishing in Maryland'' pamphlet on how and where to do it. Pony Penning, the annual auction sale of excess Chincoteague ponies from the Virginia herd, is held in Chincoteague the last Wednesday and Thursday in July.

This is a place wild horses might drag you to. Well, not horses but wild ponies. Assateague is a barrier island. The 770-acre state park, of which only 90 acres are on the mainland, is the gateway to the island. It leads, in turn, to the Assateague National Seashore run by the National Park Service and, beyond that, the U.S. Fish and Wildlife Service's Chincoteague National Wildlife Refuge. In addition to these organizational divisions, the 36-mile island is also split near its southern end by the border between Maryland and Virginia. The ponies are often referred to, in general, as the Chincoteague ponies, but this isn't strictly correct since only the Virginia herd has that name. Those ponies are actually owned by the Chincoteague Volunteer Fire Department and graze in the wildlife refuge by special permit.

There are about 300 wild ponies on the island, divided into two herds by a fence at the Maryland-Virginia border. The herds are kept below 150 ponies each to lessen the impact on the island's ecology. They are easiest to see on the Maryland side—in fact, in the park they are hard to miss since they roam everywhere.

Activities

The entire island is devoted to state and national parks, and so it's well-protected from the ravages of development. The beaches are of pristine white sand, the a surf is rarely dangerous, and the bottom slopes gently—two miles of beachfront ideal for all levels of swimmers. You can swim anywhere on the beach, except in the surfing area. Lifeguards are on duty from Memorial Day through the Labor Day. Concessions on the beach rent chairs, umbrellas, and boogie boards.

A 500-foot stretch of beach is set aside for surfers and users of boogie boards with fins. With steady ocean breezes and wide, relatively shallow water, windsurfing is also popular in the waters off the beach.

Fisherman can surf fish anywhere except within the three guarded areas and the surfing area. Among the more frequent catches are bluefish, drum, sea trout, flounder, and kingfish. Non-motorized boats may be launched from the beach at certain times, and there's a boat launch for motorized boats on the mainland park grounds at Sinepuxent Bay. There's also a crabbing pier near this boat launch. A bait and tackle shop is open during the summer.

For bicyclists, there's a bike trail that traverses the whole park.

During the summer season, guided interpretive walks and campfire programs are given by the ranger staff. If you get tired of the beach, you can explore the bayside areas. The bay waters are especially good for canoeing.

Among the large variety of birds that birders might spot here are the piping plover, a small, stocky, sandy-colored bird that's protected by the Endangered Species Act as a threatened species. Depending on the season, other common birds are loons, herons, cormorants, swans, geese, osprey and other hawks, and, of course, gulls.

In addition to the wild ponies, there are also a large number of sika deer that roam the park. These are often called Japanese elk because they make a sound like an elk. The basic rules regarding the ponies and the deer—strongly enforced by the rangers—are don't feed, don't touch, don't tease, don't frighten, don't even intentionally disturb. Part of this is for your protection. They may look tame, but they are wild and the ponies have kicked and bitten park visitors. Because these animals do roam free, no pets are allowed in the park.

Camping and Accommodations

The 311 campsites are set up just behind the beach dunes. The eight loops comprising the camping area have blacktop access roads and individual camping pads. Each loop has a bathhouse, but there are no campsite hookups. Maximum occupancy is six persons and two vehicles per campsite. More than half the sites may be reserved from mid-June through Labor Day. Reservations must be received at least two weeks prior to arrival. Otherwise, camping is on a first-come basis. Campsites are $20. During the summer, a camp store and small snack bar are open.

A group camping area for youth groups is available.

Nearby Attractions

The national seashore, bordering the park on the south, offers more beaches for swimming and fishing. Just south of the state park is the national seashore's **North Ocean Beach,** which is one of two with lifeguards in the summer. The other is at **Tom's Cove,** near the south end of the island, by the wildlife refuge. The rest of the miles and miles of beach are unguarded.

For hikers there are several trails, including one that goes north from the state park to the Ocean City Inlet. There are also campgrounds at the national seashore, but they are all primitive sites.

Both the national seashore and the wildlife refuge offer daily naturalist programs in the summer and weekend programs in the fall and spring.

For a better idea of what the national seashore is all about, stop at the **Barrier Island Visitor Center** on Highway 611, on the mainland before crossing the bay to the state park. There is another seashore visitor center at Tom's Cove, at the southern end of the island, by the wildlife refuge. And the refuge has a visitor center that offers wildlife land and boat tours. Both of these can be reached by driving down the island or coming in from the mainland on Virginia Highway 175.

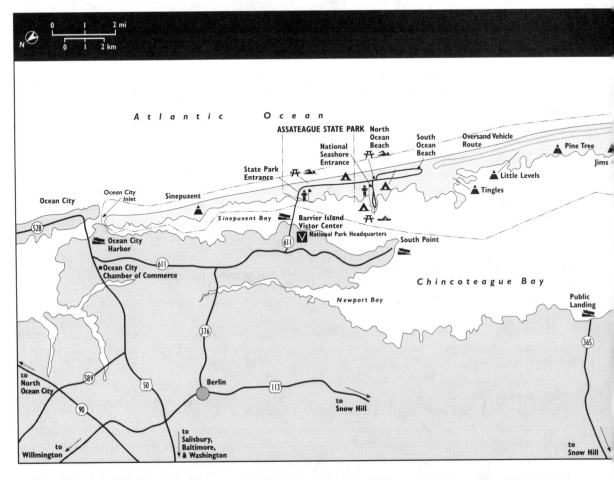

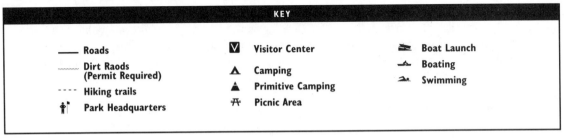

KEY

——— Roads	Visitor Center
········· Dirt Raods (Permit Required)	Camping
- - - - Hiking trails	Primitive Camping
Park Headquarters	Picnic Area

Boat Launch

Boating

Swimming

Assateague State Park & Chincoteague National Wildlife Refuge

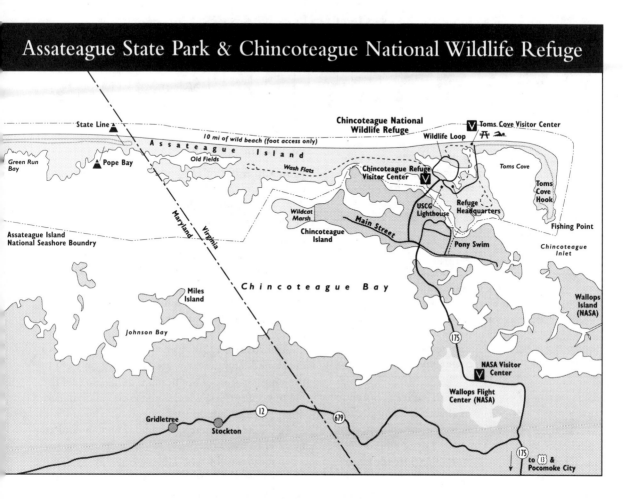

Also on Highway 175, in Virginia, opposite the southern end of the island, is the visitor center for **NASA's Wallops Island Flight Center.**

To the north lies **Ocean City,** the state's sole Atlantic coast resort city. As such, it has a three-mile boardwalk, restaurants, entertainment that includes harness racing, and all the water activities you'd expect in a city so appropriately named.

For longer day-trips—or perhaps overnight trips—the western shore of Chesapeake Bay is lined with interesting cities like **Annapolis, Washington, D.C.,** and, to the south, **Norfolk.**

Deep Creek Lake State Park

RV Camping　Tent Camping　Boating　Boat Launch　Fishing　Beach　Picnic Areas　Trails　Nature Programs　Bicycling　Playground　X-Country Skiing　Snow-mobiling

Capsule Description: A lakeside park with developed facilities on Maryland's largest lake.

Location: Western Maryland. From I-68, take U.S. 219 south to signs marking entrance to the park.

Address: Route 2, Box 69C, Swanton, MD 21561 (tel. 301/387-5563).

Area Contacts: Allegheny County Tourism and Public Relations, Western Maryland Station Center, Cumberland, MD 21502 (tel. 301/777-5905).

Deep Creek Lake-Garrett County Promotion Council, Garrett County Courthouse, 200 South 3rd Street, Oakland, MD 21550 (tel. 301/334-1948).

Insider Tip: A number of commercial tourist facilities dot the lake's 65 miles of shoreline.

The 1,900-acre park includes a mile of shoreline along the 3,900-acre lake that it is named after. The lake has about 65 miles of shoreline, most of it developed. In 1992, the state park united with the Deep Creek Lake Natural Resource Management Area and the Youghiogheny River Management Area to become part of what is now known as the Deep Creek Lake Recreation Area, combining recreational facilities and activities development planning for a large area around the park.

Activities

About 10 miles of trails wend through the park, most in the hardwood forest of oak and maple. The five major trails include a half-mile self-guided nature trail. Nature walks and evening campfire programs are scheduled throughout the year. Hikers have a good chance of seeing white-tailed deer, wild turkeys, and even an occasional black bear, although they are elusive. Bikes are allowed on most of the hiking trails, and in the winter some of them are also open for snowmobiling.

Approximately 700 feet of the park's beach have developed facilities, and lifeguards are on duty in the summer. Part of the beach is designated for the use of windsurfers. Waterskiing and skin diving are other popular lake sports.

For boaters, there's a launch area, a limited number of free boat docks for campers' boats, and a few rowboats for rent. Boats are also available for rent at several of the commercial marinas on the lake. Fishing is good from both the two park piers as well as from boats. Catches include largemouth and smallmouth bass, walleye, pike, pickerel, and rainbow and brown trout, both of which are re-stocked annually.

In addition to snowmobiling, winter also brings the chance for cross-country skiing and ice fishing.

Camping

The 112 campsites are all multiuse, on stabilized gravel pads, without hookups. They may be reserved up to the maximum length of stay of two weeks. No pets are allowed. Campsites go for $15 per night. The campgrounds are closed from November to April.

Nearby Attractions

Lake boating too tame for you? Go north about 10 miles and you can try your skill at white water sports on the Upper Yough River, one of Maryland's Scenic and Wild Rivers. (It's wild in a geographic sense, too—the river runs north, but the water that flows through it eventually ends up south in the Gulf of Mexico.) The river contains 20 Class IV and V rapids that challenge the skills of the most experienced white-water enthusiasts. If you aren't that skilled, but want to try it anyway, there are several commercial white-water rafting outfitters in the area who can give you a thrilling river experience. As part of the state forest and park service program of Outdoor Adventures, the **Deep Creek Lake Recreation Area** (tel. 301/387-5563), which you can contact through the park, also occasionally sponsors river trips for novice paddlers.

A little to the north, on U.S. 219, is the **Wisp Ski Area** (tel. 301/387-4911) where winter means downhill skiing. Nothing elaborate, but one run goes two miles.

Other state parks in the area include **Herrington Manor,** a small park with housekeeping cabins in the 6,800-acre Garrett State Forest (tel. 301/334-2038) and **Swallow Falls,** a mountain park that has the scenic and wild Youghiogheny River as one of its boundaries.

The nearest fair-sized city with all the amenities is **Cumberland,** to the east on I-68. It sits in the narrow strip of Maryland between a finger of West Virginia from the south and the straight border of Pennsylvania just a few miles to the north. Some of the historic sights here date back to the pre-Revolutionary era. This is, in fact, where George Washington had his first military headquarters in 1755, while still in the British militia. **The Chesapeake and Ohio Canal National Historical Park** (tel. 301/722-8226) Visitors Center is also here and from the center you can take a 17-mile scenic excursion train ride.

Massachusetts

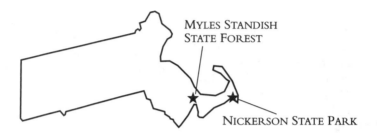

MYLES STANDISH
STATE FOREST

NICKERSON STATE PARK

Massachusetts has 100 state parks.

Contacts

- Department of Environmental Management, Division of Forests and Parks, 100 Cambridge St., 19th floor, Boston, MA 02202 (tel. 617/727-3180).
- Office of Travel and Tourism, 100 Cambridge St., 13th floor, Boston, MA 02202 (tel. 617/727-3201). For Massachusetts Vacation Kit only, call toll free 800/447-6277.

General Information on Massachusetts State Parks

Among U.S. states, Massachusetts ranks only 45th in size. But the area it devotes to state forest and parklands places it in the top 10 in the nation. From the beaches of Cape Cod on the coast to the forested hills of the Berkshires in the west, there are more than 270,000 acres of parklands waiting to be explored and enjoyed. The parks vary in size and diversity from the two-acre Lake Lorraine State Park and the nine-acre Pilgrim Memorial State Park, the site of Plymouth Rock, to the 16,000-acre October Mountain State Forest. And if that's not enough variety, the state also operates more than a dozen stand-alone skating rinks and 19 swimming pools.

GENERAL FEES

Although there's no entrance fee, a number of parks have a day-use fee if you want to use the recreational facilities. This is usually $5 per car. A season sticker for your car is for sale at all parks for $30.

CAMPING AND ACCOMMODATIONS

The only **lodge** in a state park is Bascom Lodge operated by the Appalachian Mountain Club in Mount Graylock State Reservation in the Berkshires. The rustic stone building on a mountaintop, originally built by the Civilian Conservation Corps (CCC), has four private double rooms, four dormitory-style bunkrooms that have a total capacity of 28, and a restaurant. The double rooms go for about $65 per night. (Reservations: call 413/743-1591.) There are also a few log **cabins** available at two parks: Savoy Mountain State Forest (three) and Mohawk Trail State Forest (five). These vary from one- to three-room units. Fees are about $20 per night and reservations are recommended.

Twenty-six parks have standard **campgrounds,** with a total of more than 3,400 campsites. An additional five parks have a limited number of wilderness campsites available. Most of these are on a first-come basis; however, some parks now permit reservations for a limited number of the sites and the reservation system is being expanded. You'll have to call to check. For a 7- to

14-day stay, reservations will be accepted 120 days in advance; for a 2- to 6-day stay, 60 days in advance. Reservations are required for all 29 wilderness campsites at the small Boston Harbor Islands State Park. Reservations will also be accepted in any park if a member of the camping party is physically challenged.

Campsite fees are based on facilities. Wilderness campsites—where you should be prepared to do some hiking—go for $5. Developed campsites with unimproved toilets are $8, with flush toilets $10, with flush toilets and showers $12. Few campsites have hookups. Where they are available, the fee goes up $2 for water, $2 for sewer, and $4 for electric. With the exception of a few wildlife camps and some self-contained RV campsites that remain open year-round, all campgrounds are closed in the winter.

Pets. In general, pets are allowed in all parks as long as they are on a leash no longer than 10 feet and attended and under control at all times. Most parks do have some pet restrictions; for example, they are not allowed on swimming beaches.

Alcoholic beverages. Alcohol is generally permitted in picnic areas and campsites. It is prohibited in swimming areas and other designated areas on a park-by-park basis.

Discounts. Some parks waive the day-use fee for Senior Citizens. Parking fees at all day-use areas is waived for vehicles bearing Handicapped or Disabled Veteran license plates or official placards issued by any state or Canada.

Myles Standish State Forest

| RV Camping | Tent Camping | Group Camping | Non-Motorized Boating Only | Fishing | Swimming | Picnic Areas | Trails | Horse Trails | Nature Programs | Bicycling | X-Country Skiing | Snow-mobiling |

Capsule Description: A large, forested park with some developed facilities.

Location: Southeastern Massachusetts. From I-495, take Exit 2 and follow signs. From Route 3 (Pilgrims Highway): going south, take Exit 5 and follow signs; going north, take Exit 3 and follow signs.

Address: P.O. Box 66, South Carver, MA 02366 (tel. 508/866-2526).

Area Contacts: Plymouth County Development Council, P.O. Box 1620, Pembroke, MA 02359 (tel. toll free 800/231-1620 or 617/826-3136).

Although not the largest park in the system, at 14,635 acres it is near the top in size and is one of the more fully developed forest parks. It was originally part of the Indian village of Patuxet, an area which English settlers acquired from Massasoit, Chief Sachem of the Wampanoag, in 1621. The settlers renamed it Plymouth. Cranberry bogs in the area have been harvested since the 19th century. Before that, in the 18th century, the area was mined for bog iron for use in industrial furnaces, and peat from the bogs was made into charcoal to fuel those furnaces.

In the 1930s, the Civilian Conservation Corps (CCC) built roads and trails, planted trees, and did other work that laid the foundation for this forest park today.

Activities

Interpretive programs are run at the height of the season, in July and August. These include pond shore walks to see the rare plants that grow there, cranberry bog explorations, and tours of the park's fire tower. Otherwise you're pretty much on your own to wander and enjoy the forest.

Hikers, and even walkers, can try the two major trails, which are three miles and eight miles long and rated easy to moderate in difficulty. The three-mile route is also a self-guided nature trail. Both go through the forest of red, white, and pitch pine and scrub oak. The park also has what's known as the Pine Barrens, one of the largest contiguous pitch pine/scrub oak communities in New England. This forest type can survive in sandy soil and has the ability to not only adapt to frequent fires but evolve from them.

Bicyclists have a choice of three trails, ranging from easy to difficult, adding up to 15 miles. There are also 20 miles of equestrian trails (but no equestrian camping), 40 miles of hills, sand, and curves for motorcross, and a 14-mile trail for ATVs. In winter, the bike trails are used for cross-country skiing and the 100 miles of dirt roads in the park are open for snowmobiling once they are covered with a minimum of four inches of hard-packed snow.

Thirty-five glacial "kettle ponds," adding up to about 300 acres are in the park. These were formed when the last glaciers receded about 15,000 years ago leaving behind large blocks of buried ice. When the ice melted depressions formed that were filled with groundwater, creating round-shaped ponds. Seasonal water levels fluctuate widely, but some of these ponds are open for nonmotorized boating (no inflatables),

fishing, and swimming. College Pond and Fearings Pond swimming areas are normally staffed from Memorial Day to Labor Day. Trout are stocked in Fearing Pond several times a year. There is also some stocking of bass, perch, and pickerel. Ice skating is permitted in winter at your own risk.

Camping

When operating at full capacity, the park offers about 430 **campsites.** All are multiuse without hookups. Some campgrounds have showers and others do not. Site fees are $10 without showers, $12 with, and $2 extra for a waterfront site. At the time this book went to press, all sites were on a first-come basis. However, there are plans for a reservation system for some of the sites, so call and check. Campgrounds are open from mid-April through Columbus Day.

Group campsites are available for nonprofit youth groups but these must be reserved.

Nearby Attractions

The early history of our nation is rich in this area, and many historical sites are within easy day-trip excursions. Head out in almost any direction and you'll stumble into places of both historical and modern-day interest.

For example, to the southeast, you can visit the reproduction of the first trading post in America at **Bourne,** or see the marine exhibits at the **Thayer Museum complex,** or take a whale watcher cruise at **Barnstable.** If you have the time you can continue heading east to visit **Cape Cod,** or take a passenger boat from Falmouth to the island of **Martha's Vineyard.**

Southwest trips can include visits to the battleship *Massachusetts,* one of five World War II warships at Battleship Cove in **Fall River;** or the Whaling Museum and the Children's Museum at **New Bedford.**

Just a short drive northeast brings you to **Plymouth.** In addition to Plymouth Rock— worth a visit for its historical significance, but really not sensational to look at—you can go to **Plimoth Plantation,** a living history museum portraying Pilgrim life in the colonies; see a reproduction of the *Mayflower;* visit **Pilgrim Hall Museum,** one of the oldest museums in the country; or learn everything you've ever wanted to know about cranberries on a short self-guided industrial tour of **Cranberry World.** One of the state park skating rinks is also in Plymouth.

Finally, if all this doesn't satisfy your curiosity, it's not too far to head north to **Boston.** But you should plan an overnight trip for that, at least.

Nickerson State Park

RV Camping / Tent Camping / Group Camping / Boating / Boat Launch / Fishing / Beach

Waterskiing / Snorkeling & Diving / Picnic Areas / Trails / Horse Trails / Nature Programs / Bicycling / X-Country Skiing

Capsule Description: A woodland park with developed facilities and beach access on Cape Cod.

Location: Southeastern Massachusetts, on Cape Cod. Take Massachusetts Route 6A east of Brewster to the park entrance.

Address: 3488 Main St., Brewster, MA 02631 (tel. 508/896-3491; 508/896-4615 for reservations only).

Area Contacts: Cape Cod Chamber of Commerce, Junction of Rts. 6 & 132, Hyannis, MA 02601 (tel. 508/362-3225).

Cape Cod National Seashore, P.O. Box 250 South Wellfleet, MA 02663 (tel. 508/349-3785).

Situated at the neck of Cape Cod, in an area known for its sand dunes, salt marshes, and beaches, this park stands out for its contrary terrain. It is heavily wooded, with pines and oak, and slopes down to five major "kettle ponds." These freshwater ponds, formed by the retreating glaciers at the end of the last Ice Age, add up to more than 300 of the park's 1,955 acres. And if you want saltwater, approximately 90 acres of the park are located on Cape Cod Bay, providing access to the saltwater beaches.

The land for the park was donated in 1934 by Addie Nickerson, widow of Roland Nickerson, the man the park is named after. Soon after, the Civilian Conservation Corps (CCC) moved in and laid the basis for the present park by planting 88,000 trees and building roads, campsites, and other basic facilities.

Activities

Four of the kettle ponds are large enough to offer a variety of water activities that include waterskiing, tubing, swimming, snorkeling and scuba diving, windsurfing, boating, and fishing.

All the ponds have gently sloping bottoms, are generally weed-free, and go to a depth varying from 35 to 80 feet. The rules generally depend on the pond size. You can have a ski boat or other gas-powered boat on the 200-acre Cliff Pond, for example, while no gas engines are permitted on the smaller Flax Pond. But you can rent canoes, paddleboats, and sailboats at that small pond. About the only smaller watercraft prohibited overall are jet skis and other personal type.

There are two beaches at Cliff Pond and one at Flax Pond, plus 3,000 feet of sandy tidal beach on Cape Cod Bay. No lifeguards at any beach.

Fisherman can try for saltwater fish in the bay or freshwater in the ponds. Brown and brook trout are stocked in three of the ponds in spring and fall and there are also occasional stockings of smallmouth bass and Atlantic landlocked salmon. The trout fishing is generally catch-and-release. Other catches include panfish, bluefish, and the record American eel came out of Cliff Pond. If the ponds ice over in winter, you can try ice fishing.

In addition to the wide variety of woodland birds who make a home in the park, the ponds are a regular stop on the migratory routes of a number of nonresidents, especially waterfowl.

The parks three hiking trails are more for walkers than serious hikers. They go around the ponds, are from one to three miles in length, and generally rated easy with only a few short hills. If you are into hiking, the Cape Cod Rail Trail goes through the park. This is thought of as more a bike trail than a hike trail, but it's open to walkers, runners, and even horseback riders. With a few breaks while going through towns, the rail trail lives up to its name by following a former railroad right-of-way most of its 19 miles from near Brewster to within a stone's throw of the headquarters of the Cape Cod National Seashore.

Within the park, there is an eight-mile bike trail. Mountain bikes are allowed on paved trails, woods roads, and unmarked single-track trails throughout the park. There is one two-mile marked equestrian trail, but riders are also allowed on woods roads and single-track trails as well as the Cape Cod Rail Trail (one side is gravel for horses).

If there is snow—and it's good to call ahead on this—cross-country skiers can use the ungroomed bike and hiking trails. Sledding is also permitted, but snowmobiles are not.

In high season the staff puts on a variety of tours, talks, and campfire programs. There is also a small nature center with exhibits that give you the natural history of the park area.

Camping

The regular campgrounds season here is from mid-April to mid-October; however, some sites are open for self-contained RVs all year. The 418 multiuse sites are all without hookups. About 150 of the sites may be reserved. For a 7- to 14-day stay (14 days is maximum stay from early June to Labor Day) you can call in up to 120 days in advance; for 2 to 6 days, up to 60 days in advance. There's a $5 reservation fee. All other campsites are on a firstcome basis, and there's usually a 1- to 3-day wait in high season. Sites go for $12 for a regular site and $14 for a waterfront site. Although there are no designated equestrian camping sites, some regular sites may be made available.

Group camp areas are available for nonprofit groups.

Nearby Attractions

This is Cape Cod, a mecca for tourists. So there is a lot to see and do within easy daytrips from the park.

Close by, in **Brewster,** for example you can visit the New England Fire and History Museum, the Cape Cod Museum of Natural History, or the Cape Cod Aquarium.

To the south, **Hyannis** offers not only the John F. Kennedy Memorial, but, on a lighter side, a marine show park, and cruises and an auto ferry to the islands of Nantucket and Martha's Vineyard.

Continuing east out on the Cape, there's the national seashore, a 40-mile stretch of ocean beaches, recreational facilities, and a smattering of historic buildings. All leading to **Provincetown,** the resort town at the tip of the Cape where the Pilgrims first landed, and where you can take a whale-watcher cruise from April through October.

Michigan

PORCUPINE MOUNTAINS
WILDERNESS STATE PARK

HARTWICK PINES
STATE PARK

Michigan has 100 state parks.

Contacts

- Information Services Center, Department of Natural Resources, P.O. Box 30028, Lansing, MI 48909 (tel. 517/373-2329).
- Michigan Travel Bureau, P.O. Box 30226, Lansing, MI 48909 (tel. toll free 800/543-2937 for recorded information only).
- Michigan Hotel, Motel & Resort Association, 6105 W. St. Joseph Hwy., Suite 204, Lansing, MI 48917 (tel. 517/323-1818).

General Information on Michigan State Parks

Although it's a thousand miles from the nearest ocean, Michigan claims to be the home of the largest pleasure boat fleet in any state, the largest freshwater dunes in the world, a thousand miles of public beaches, and a shoreline longer than the entire Atlantic seaboard of our country. Oh, and it also claims salmon fishing that exceeds that available in the Pacific Northwest.

Michigan? Yes! How come? Because it is touched by four of the five Great Lakes that give it 3,200 miles of coastline, plus it has 11,000 inland lakes. That's fine for summer, but what about the long winters? Then the deep snows that blanket the highest hills between the Alle-

ghenies and the Black Hills bring joy to winter-sports enthusiasts.

The Parks Division has taken full advantage of nature's blessings with more than 260,000 acres of choice recreational lands that include 120 miles of prime Great Lakes frontage, 200 miles of scenic lakes, rivers, and streams, and park winter sports areas.

GENERAL FEES

Vehicle entrance permit for most parks is $4 per car per day. An annual permit sells for $18. A few parks have additional user fees.

CAMPING AND ACCOMMODATIONS

There are more than 85 **cabins** available for rent in 16 parks. These are really for getting away from it all. They're rustic and minimally equipped with single beds or bunks, table, chairs, wood stoves, and outside vault toilets. Some have outside water pumps. At others you are merely given the location of the nearest water source. Almost all are hike-in. Some that are on lakes are provided with rowboats. The cabins may be reserved up to a year in advance and go for from $25 to $50 per night.

There are more than 14,000 **campsites** in the state park system. A majority are multiuse with electric hookups and bathhouses with modern toilets and showers nearby. Most campgrounds are open all year, but from mid-October to mid-May the water systems may not be in service.

Reservations may be made by mail, phone, or in person directly to the individual park. Reservations are accepted for one night in all Upper Peninsula parks, but all other parks require a two-night minimum on reservations. Maximum stay is 15 consecutive days in any one park. Sites are $8 to $14 depending on park and facilities available. Reservation fee is $4.

Pets. Pets must be attended at all times and kept under immediate control on a leash not longer than six feet. This is true even in the backcountry. They are not allowed in buildings or on bathing beaches.

Alcoholic beverages. The rules vary by park. Some allow it, others have seasons or places where it is prohibited. Check with the park.

Discounts. The annual vehicle entrance permit is available at a discount to Michigan residents who are 65 years and older.

Hartwick Pines State Park

Visitor Center — Cabins & Cottages — RV Camping — Tent Camping — Group Camping — Boat Launch — Non-Motorized Boating Only — Fishing

Picnic Areas — Trails — Nature Programs — Bicycling — Playground — X-Country Skiing — Snowmobiling

Capsule Description: A large, forested park with developed facilities.

Location: North-central section of the Lower Peninsula, about eight miles north of Grayling. Take Exit 259 off I-75 and go east two miles on Michigan 93.

Address: Route 3, Box 3840, Grayling, MI 49738 (tel. 517/348-7068).

Area Contacts: Grayling Regional Chamber of Commerce, P.O. Box 406, Grayling, MI 49738 (tel. 517/348-2921).

Traverse City Convention and Visitors Bureau, 415 Munson Ave., Suite 200, Traverse City, MI 49686 (tel. toll free 800/872-8377 or 616/947-1120).

Sleeping Bear Dunes National Lakeshore, 9922 Front St., Empire, MI 49630 (tel. 616/326-5134).

Insider Tips: After you've learned all about forest management at the Logging Museum, you can test your knowledge on an interactive computer terminal in the exhibit hall.

One of the highlights in this 9,672-acre park is man-made and another is nature at it finest. The Logging Museum offers exhibits interpreting Michigan's history as our nation's greatest lumber producer from 1869 to almost 1900. Altogether, 160 million board feet of pine were cut in Michigan by 1897, a quantity sufficient to build 10 million six-room houses or to floor the entire land area of Michigan with one-inch pine boards with enough remaining to cover the state of Rhode Island. On the other hand, there is 49-acre virgin forest of white and Norway pine that escaped the lumberman's ax. Crowning this forest—one of the last virgin white pine stands in the Midwest—is a pine 155 feet tall that's estimated to be 300 years old.

Activities

A vivid picture of the lumber industry in the last half of the 19th century, as well as current forest management, is painted by the exhibits and slide programs at the logging museum, which is open from April through October. In the Interpretive Center, you'll learn the natural history of forest growth and the creatures that live in the woods. You'll also learn about the millionaire lumber barons as well as the "shanty boys" who cut the trees, rode the logs down the rivers, and worked the sawmills. Then, a walk back through the virgin pines will bring you to the logging camp exhibits featuring large pieces of logging equipment, a steam-operated sawmill (that's run during special events), and typical buildings where the loggers lived and worked.

To see the forests firsthand, there are three self-guiding nature trails. The Virgin Pines Trail, which winds through that white pine stand, is about a mile long. It also takes you to the Chapel in the Pines, a log chapel constructed with hand tools and wood pegs. The AuSable River Trail, about three miles long, takes you past that river that is famed for its trout fishing. The Mertz Grade Nature Trail takes you two miles through a mixed forest that is typical of that which covered nearly half the land area in this state before man started to cut and burn. In summer the staff conducts nature walks and evening campfire programs.

For hikers there are three other trails that are 3, 5½, and 7 miles in length. Paralleling these are three mountain bike trails of the same length.

In winter, the trails are groomed, packed, and tracked for cross-country skiing. There is also a snowmobile trail that's over eight miles long and ties in with other trails that provide an additional 50 miles.

Want to see the forest without expending much energy? Try the eight-mile scenic auto trail that goes through a portion of the park. Prominent signs point out various natural features.

Along any of these trails, you're liable to see white-tailed deer, grouse, raccoons, wild turkeys, and cottontail rabbits. You may even catch signs or a glimpse of a black bear or red fox.

When it comes to trout fishing, the AuSable River is famed in the state and beyond for both brook and rainbow trout. (Fishing license and trout stamp required.) In addition to the three miles of that river that runs through the park, the two lakes in the park are stocked annually with both trout and smallmouth bass. Both lakes have handicapped-accessible piers and boat-launching ramps, but are really too little (less than eight acres each) for anything but a small fishing boat.

Camping and Accommodations

The one rustic log **cabin** in the park sleeps six, has a handpump for water, woodstove for heat, and a vault toilet. It can be reserved and costs about $30 per night.

Of the 100 multiuse **campsites,** 30 have electric hookups. They go from about $12 to $14 per night and can be reserved.

There's also a group camp area with preference given to youth groups.

Nearby Attractions

The AuSable River is also popular with canoeists. You can rent a canoe in a number of places in **Grayling** and other river towns. If you are really into paddling a canoe, you might want to enter the World Championship AuSable River Marathon, a 240-mile canoe race held every July that starts in Grayling.

There's also a challenge for hikers and bikers near Grayling. That town is about midpoint on the 240-mile Michigan Riding and Hiking Trail that goes between Lake Michigan and Lake Huron.

For downhill skiing, try the ski area south of Grayling. It's not as challenging as the other outdoor sports—the longest run is only about half a mile long—but it's still downhill.

A good daytrip excursion from the park is the trip to **Sleeping Bear Dunes National Lakeshore.** Take Michigan 72 west from the park to the Visitor Center near Empire on Lake Michigan. This park offers a diverse landscape ranging from towering dunes to forests and meadows and a variety of recreational facilities along close to 40 miles of shoreline.

Also to the west, on the way to Sleeping Bear Dunes, is **Traverse City,** which lays claim to being the "Cherry Capital of the World." In addition to orchard tours, there are also winery and vine-

yard tours, and a museum and zoo to visit. Southwest about 15 miles, off U.S. Highway 31, is the world-renowned **Interlochen Center for the Arts** where you can hear internationally known musicians perform in the summer.

Porcupine Mountains Wilderness State Park

Visitor Center · Cabins & Cottages · RV Camping · Tent Camping · Primitive Camping · Group Camping · Boating · Boat Launch · Fishing · Beach · Picnic Areas · Trails · Nature Programs · Bicycling · Playground · X-Country Skiing · Downhill Skiing · Snowmobiling · Gift Shop

Capsule Description: A huge wilderness park with developed facilities that include a ski area.

Location: Upper Peninsula on Lake Superior near the border with Wisconsin. From Ontonagon, go west on Michigan Highway 64 to Silver City, then west on Highway 107 to the park.

Address: 412 S. Boundary Rd., Ontonagon, MI 49953 (tel. 906/885-5275).

Area Contacts: Gogebic Area Convention and Visitors Bureau, P.O. Box 706, East U.S. 2, Ironwood, MI 49938-0706 (tel. 906/932-4850).

Ontonagon County Chamber of Commerce, P.O. Box 266, Ontonagon, MI 49953 (tel. 906/884-4735).

Upper Peninsula Travel and Recreation Association, P.O. Box 400, Iron Mountain, MI 49801 (tel. 906/774-5480; toll free 800/562-7134 in Illinois, Michigan, Minnesota, and Wisconsin only).

The "wilderness" in the name of this park is appropriate since most of the 60,000 acres fit that description. The park's more than 90 square miles

includes 35,000 acres of uncut virgin forest, secluded lakes, miles of wild rivers and streams, and 22 miles of shorefront on Lake Superior. It is one of the few remaining wilderness areas in the Midwest.

Another unusual point to note about the park is that it straddles the border of two time zones, eastern and central.

According to local legend, the "Porkies" were named by the Chippewa Indians who thought the mountains resembled a crouching porcupine.

Activities

You can get acquainted with the park at the Visitor Center's exhibits and multi-image slide program. There are also two one-mile loop self-guided nature trails to introduce you to various plants and trees and other natural features found in the park as well as tell the story of early copper mining activity in the region. Interpretive programs and occasional guided walks are given during July and August.

In the summer, hiking is the name of the game here. Twenty-one designated trails total up to about 90 miles.

The shortest is the half-mile Summit Peak Tower Trail that takes you to the park's highest point, at 1,958 feet, where there's a 40-foot observation tower. On a clear day you can see Wisconsin, Minnesota, and the Apostle Islands. On the way up to the summit, a viewing deck provides a panoramic view that ranks as one of the most scenic in the park.

The longest trail is the Lake Superior Trail. This 16-mile trail follows the rocky shore of that lake, affording many outstanding views. Remote and rugged, it's among the park's most challenging trails.

The East West River Trails lead to the three Presque Isle waterfalls—the highest of which is 25 feet—this area is boardwalked and has stairs to viewing areas.

Other trails take you to natural springs and through the magnificent stands of predominantly old-growth maple and hemlock. Some of Porcupine Mountains' trails connect with the North Country Scenic Trail, which goes well outside the park.

Bicycling is permitted on all paved roads in the park, but mountain bikes can only be ridden on a separate cross-country trail system that is about 24 miles in length.

Wildlife is abundant in this wilderness and includes white-tailed deer, beaver, porcupine, black bear, and the more elusive moose and gray wolf. Bald eagles, broadwing hawks, pileated woodpeckers, and even peregrine falcons are among the many birds that nest here.

The two main lakes in the park are the Lake of the Clouds and Mirror Lake, but the best boating is on Lake Superior. The park's only boat launch, at Union Bay, is limited by the lake level and boats over 20 feet may have trouble launching. The only river in the park suitable for white-water canoeists and kayakers is the challenging lower Presque Isle River.

The three most sought-after fish in the area are lake trout, brook trout, and salmon. Approximately 10,000 brown and rainbow trout are stocked annually at Union Bay. The only suitable swimming beach is also at Union Bay. There are no developed facilities here and no lifeguards.

Winter comes early and stays late in the Porkies with annual snowfall averaging more than 175 inches. With the snow comes skiing and other winter sports at the Porcupine Mountains Ski Area. There are 14 groomed alpine ski runs covering 11 miles of slope—with a low-cost lift system capable of handling 3,600 skiers per hour—and a wide variety of Nordic ski trails including 26 miles of groomed double-tracked cross-country trails. The spacious Ski Chalet offers a ski shop; cafeteria; ski, snowboard, and snowshoe rentals; and three large fireplaces to provide a cozy setting while picture windows provide an excellent view of skiers schussing down the slopes. For snowmobiling, there are 32 miles of groomed trails.

Camping and Accommodations

There are 16 rustic **cabins** available from April through November. These require a hike in of one to four miles, have a maximum capacity of from two to eight persons, and go for $30 a night. There are also three eight-bunk cabins that can be rented from December through March. Cabins on Mirror Lake, Lily Pond, and Lake of the Clouds are provided with rowboats.

Of the 204 **campsites,** 101 are modern with electric hookups and hot showers in the campground. These go for $10 per night. For $8 you can get one of the 89 sites with hot showers in the campgrounds, but no hookups. The other 14 lower-fee sites are rustic—a nice way of saying pit toilets in the campground and no other facilities.

Cabins and campsites may be reserved.

Backpackers may camp most anywhere off the trails for a fee of $6 per night for a group of four. There are also three no-fee Adirondack shelters on the trails that are on a first-come basis. A youth group campground is also available.

Nearby Attractions

It's only a short daytrip to see what's billed as the World's Tallest Indian. Head south to **Ironwood** and the 52-foot-high statue of Hiawatha. At nearby **Cooper Peak Ski-Flying Hill,** skiers race down a slide to reach a speed of 60 m.p.h. and then "fly" 500 feet or more. Winter and summer, you can take a chair lift to an observation platform with a panoramic view of three states.

Outside the park, marinas dot Lake Superior, and you can rent boats or arrange for a "deep lake" fishing trip.

Minnesota

ITASCA STATE PARK —★   ★—ST. CROIX STATE PARK

Minnesota has 66 state parks.

Contacts

- Department of Natural Resources Information Center, 500 Lafayette Rd., St. Paul, MN 55155 (tel. 612/296-6157; toll free 800/766-6000 in Minnesota only, 800/246-2267 for State Park reservations only).
- Minnesota Department of Tourism, 100 Metro Sq., 121 7th Place East, St. Paul, MN 55101 (tel. toll free 800/657-3700).

General Information on Minnesota State Parks

This is water country—close to 12,000 lakes 10 acres and larger, and 25,000 miles of rivers and streams that include 600 miles of national and state wild and scenic rivers. Plus it has a long frontage on Lake Superior—the ocean of the Midwest—and is the start point for the mighty Mississippi. The parks share in this water wonderland.

It's also iron country—boasting the world's largest open-pit mine—and timber country, symbolized by the folk tale legends of lumberjack Paul Bunyan and his giant blue ox "Babe".

In the parks, there are close to 800 miles of trails winding through pine forests, prairies, colorful hardwoods, marshes, and bog. Biking is permitted on park roads and designated trails that include surfaced bike trails in a dozen parks. And, although summers are short, 33 parks offers swimming in lakes or sand-bottom swimming pools.

Come the snows, you can just about name your choice of winter sports.

GENERAL FEES

A daily vehicle permit costs $4 per car. An annual permit is available for $18. A cross-country ski pass costs $1 a day or $5 annually.

CAMPING AND ACCOMMODATIONS

Itasca State Park has a small **lodge** (see below) and both Itasca and Tettegouche have **cabins**—some hike-in or ski-in. Cabins rent for $55 to $110.

There are more than 4,000 **campsites** in the park system. Most are multiuse, but there are also some hike-in, some bike-in, and even some canoe-in sites. In high season (usually May through October), multiuse campsites go for $10 to $12 plus $2.50 if there is an electric hookup. Off-season the sites are $8 per night. Backpack or canoe-in sites are $7. Campsite occupancy is limited to no more than six people. Stays are limited to 14 days in succession in the same park.

For reservations for cabins, the lodge, and campsites call The Connection® at toll free 800/246-2267. The reservation fee is $5.50. Cabin and lodge reservations may be made from three days to one year in advance. Campsite reservations will be taken from three days to 90 days in advance. Up to 70% of the campsites in each park can be reserved. The remaining 30% of campsites remain on a first-come basis.

There are also a number of group camps including houses for small groups or large families, group centers with buildings, and rustic camps. Some parks offer group camps for horseback riders.

Pets. Pets are permitted but they must be personally attended at all times and effectively restrained by a portable enclosure or a leash not exceeding six feet in length. They are not per-

mitted in buildings, on beaches, or on ski trails during the winter ski season.

Alcoholic beverages. Only 3.2% beer in kegs is allowed, and written permission from the park manager is required for this. It's unlawful for any person in a state park to consume intoxicating liquors or to display in public intoxicating-liquor containers.

Discounts. A special annual motor vehicle permit is available at a discount to Minnesota residents 65 or older and handicapped residents. Seniors and handicapped are also eligible for half-priced camping Sunday through Thursday.

Itasca State Park

Lodge/Hotel   Restaurant   Cabins & Cottages   RV Camping   Tent Camping   Primitive Camping   Group Camping   Group Lodge Dormitories

Boating   Boat Launch   Fishing   Beach   Picnic Areas   Trails   Nature Programs   Bicycling   Playground   X-Country Skiing   Snow-mobiling   Gift Shop

Capsule Description: A large natural park with developed facilities.

Location: North-central Minnesota. From Park Rapids, take U.S. Highway 71 north about 21 miles to the park.

Address: HCO5 Box 4, Lake Itasca, MN 56460-9701 (tel. 218/266-2114).

Area Contacts: Bemidji Chamber of Commerce, P.O. Box 850, Bemidji, MN 56601 (tel. toll free 800/458-2223).

Park Rapids Chamber of Commerce, P.O. Box 249, Park Rapids, MN 56470 (tel. 800/247-0054).

Insider Tips: You can compare the advantages and disadvantages of a managed forest with an unmanaged forest at the Forestry Demonstration Area along the Wilderness Drive.

Want to walk across the Mississippi River in just about 15 steps? You can do it in this park. Here, in the midst of 32,000 acres of forests of pines, aspen, and birch, and more than 100 pristine lakes, is where the mighty Ol' Man River begins its 2,500-mile journey to the Gulf of Mexico as a little stream. The park also contains a 2,000-acre natural area that is a registered National Natural Landmark.

Itasca has the distinction of being the first state park in Minnesota. Established in 1891, it was the beginning of a park system that has grown steadily over the past century.

In the summer, the University of Minnesota operates a Biological Station here where you can see exhibits of almost every plant and animal that inhabits the state—including 27 kinds of orchids.

Activities

There are two Visitor Centers open during the summer season, usually from mid-May to late September—one at the headwaters of the Mississippi and the other at the southern end of Lake Itasca. Either is a good place to start learning about the park and what you can enjoy in it. Both offer interpretive programs and tours and both have gift shops. In addition, you can take a 1½-hour narrated boat tour to explore Lake Itasca and the headwaters of the Mississippi from the South Itasca Center. Boat tours are normally given two or three times a day from about Memorial Day to Labor Day.

The 24 marked hiking trails vary in length and difficulty. Some are short, like the ⅓-mile Landmark Interpretive Trail located near the north boundary of the Itasca Wilderness Sanctuary, while others go deep through woodland corridors and can take most of a day. All together, including about 3½ miles of self-guided nature trails, the hiking trails add up to about 33 miles. Bicyclists have about 17 miles of trails marked for them. You can also rent bikes.

Come winter snows, 31 miles of trails are opened for cross-country skiing and an almost equal mileage for snowmobiling.

Among the sights worth hiking to are the state's largest red pine—120 feet tall, 9 feet in diameter, and more than 250 years old—and the largest white pine, which is more than 350 years old. There's an old Indian cemetery and Indian mounds, a restored old-time sawmill, and a lookout tower where you can get a bird's-eye view of the park.

And, of course, hikers have the best chance of seeing wildlife, which includes everything from bears to deer to porcupines and bluebirds to eagles to trumpeter swans.

If you don't want to hike, you can still see the wonders of nature from your car on the Wilderness Drive. This 11-mile drive is mainly on a narrow one-way road that takes you on a loop through much of the park. Tour books and cassette tour tapes are available for sale or rent at the two gift shops.

The lakes and streams mean boating, fishing, and swimming. Fishing can yield catches of bass, crappie, and pike, among others. You can bring your own boat or rent canoes, rowboats, pontoon boats, and motorboats in the park. In fact, the park operates a sports rental where you can rent a variety of items including rods, reels, depth finders, and trolling motors. There are some restrictions on speed on the lakes, and no waterskiing. For swimmers, there's a sand beach.

Camping and Accommodations

Douglas Lodge, built in 1905, and the nearby **Nicollet Court Motel** offer a total of 28 suites and guest rooms. Rents depend on facilities and run from $36 to $44 for a double with a charge of $8 for each additional person. There are 22 **cabins** ranging from one- to three-bedrooms and rustic to motel style. They go for $55 to $110. The lodge and cabins are usually open from Memorial Day weekend until mid- or late September.

The **Mississippi Headwaters HI/AYH Hostel** in the park offers both barracks-style bunk beds and a few private bedrooms for families. Rates are about $13 a person (tel. 218/266-3415).

There are two campgrounds. One hundred of the 198 multiuse **campsites** have electric hookups. About 20 sites are available all year, the rest are closed in the winter. There are also 11 hike-in sites available year-round.

Accommodations for groups include a 10-room clubhouse, a semimodern tent camping group center with dining hall, and a primitive camp.

Nearby Attractions

If you want to pose for a picture with Paul Bunyan, take a short daytrip northeast on U.S. Highway 71 to **Bemidji,** where there are huge statues of the mythical lumberjack and his blue ox, Babe. At the Bemidji Chamber of Commerce (tel. 218/751-3541), you can also see the **Fireplace of the States** built with stones from every one of the 48 contiguous states and some from Canadian provinces. The town's **Paul Bunyan Playhouse** (tel. 218/751-0752) has a summer-stock company

and offers community theater and concerts in winter.

A quick daytrip south on U.S. 71 takes you to **Park Rapids.** Attractions here include **Deer Town,** where you can see tame deer and take a stagecoach ride, and the authentic **Rapid River Logging Camp** (tel. 218/732-3444).

St. Croix State Park

Visitor Center　RV Camping　Tent Camping　Primitive Camping　Group Camping　Group Lodge Dormitories

Non-Motorized Boating Only　Fishing　Beach　Picnic Areas　Trails　Horse Trails　Nature Programs　Bicycling　X-Country Skiing　Snow-mobiling

Capsule Description: A large wilderness park with developed facilities.

Location: East-central Minnesota on the border with Wisconsin, midway between Duluth and the twin cities of Minneapolis–St. Paul. From I-35 take the Hinckley Exit (no. 183). Go east 15 miles on Minnesota Highway 48 to County Road 22, then south five miles to the park.

Address: Route 3, Box 450, Hinckley, MN 55037 (tel. 612/384-6591).

Area Contacts: Duluth Area Convention and Visitors Bureau, 100 Lake Place Dr., Duluth, MN 55802 (tel. toll free 800/4-DULUTH or 218/722-4011).

　　Greater Minneapolis Convention and Visitors Bureau, 4000 Multi-Foods Tower, 33 S. 6th St., Minneapolis, MN 55402 (tel. toll free 800/445-7412 or 612/348-4313).

　　Tourist Information Center, Mora Area Chamber of Commerce, P.O. Box 175, 20 N. Union, Mora, MN 55051 (tel. 612/679-5792).

The largest state park in Minnesota, St. Croix contains 34,000 acres of woodlands, marshes, and rivers. It is the rivers that help make this park special. Once the highways for Indians, explorers, and fur trappers, the two rivers in the park are now prime recreational waterways. The St. Croix River, which forms the border between the park and Wisconsin, was one of the original eight nationwide to be designated as a National Wild and Scenic River. The Kettle River, which runs through the western section of the park and flows into the St. Croix, was the first Minnesota State Wild and Scenic River.

Established as a National Recreational Demonstration Area in the mid-1930s, it was made into a state park in 1943. During those few years that it was under the direction of the National Park Service, the Civilian Conservation Corps (CCC) moved in and developed the basics of the park. Several of the structures they built are still standing and listed in the National Register of Historic Places.

Activities

Although most of the trails are relatively easy, there are 127 miles of trails making this a bonanza for hikers. Most of these trails radiate out from the All Seasons Trail Center. Two of these are self-guiding nature trails. The Footprints in Time Trail goes for about a mile along the banks of the St. Croix River. There are two long flights of stairs that must be used on this trail. The other nature trail is the 1½-mile Sun Dance Trail, which emphasizes the role of the sun in supporting natural life.

For the serious hiker, the Willard Munger State Trail goes through the park. This is a multiple-use trail, still being developed, that runs from St. Paul to Duluth. Actually it is not just one trail, but a complex system of interconnecting trails not only for hikers, but also for bicyclists, horseback riders, and, when the snow falls, snowmobilers.

Within the park there are also 75 miles of equestrian trails, and a 5½-mile, hard-surfaced bike trail, with rental bikes available.

In winter 80 miles of trails are groomed for snowmobiles, and 21 miles are set up for cross-country skiing.

Wildlife in the park includes white-tailed deer, beavers, raccoons, and black bears. Grouse are often seen along the roads and bald eagles and ospreys are commonly sighted along the St. Croix River. The eastern timber wolf is also known to inhabit the park, but is rarely seen.

Canoes and small boats are used on both major rivers and other rivers and streams in the park. Although the St. Croix and Kettle earn their titles as Wild Rivers, here they are more scenic with limited, and generally mild, white water. If you want to see white water, visit Banning State Park, north of Hinckley. The annual Champion International Kayaking Race takes place on the white-water of the Kettle River rapids that rush through this park.

The rivers and creeks are all popular with anglers. The St. Croix is widely known for bass, the Kettle for walleye, smallmouth bass, and sauger; and Hay Creek is considered a good trout stream. Canoes and tackle can be rented at the concessionaire Adventures Store (tel. 612/384-7806) and shuttle service is available.

Swimmers can use Lake Clayton Beach in season; no lifeguards.

In summer, the Interpretive Center is open and features displays on the park's natural, cultural, and historic features. A variety of interpretive programs are scheduled weekends during the summer season, and occasionally during the rest of the year. For a bird's-eye view of various sections of the park, there are several overlooks and an old Fire Tower now used as an observation point.

Camping and Accommodations

Forty-two of the 213 multiuse **campsites** have electrical hookups. Scattered over three campgrounds, the sites go for $12 from May through October and $8 the rest of the year. The electric hookups are $2.50 per night extra.

For equestrians, there's a 100-horse-capacity camping area that cost $8 per night per unit. If you want to backpack there are two rustic sites with Adirondack shelters holding a maximum of 12 people each. They go for $1 a person with a minimum of $7. Canoeists can paddle in to about a dozen primitive campsites.

For groups, there are two group centers with sleeping cabins and dining halls. There is also a guesthouse with six bedrooms that can accommodate up to 15 people.

Nearby Attractions

In the nearby town of Hinckley, the **Hinckley Fire Museum** (tel. 612/384-7338) tells the story of the disastrous forest fire that destroyed the town in 1894. At **Pine City** is a reconstructed fur trading outpost. Farther to the west, in **Onamia,** you can visit the **Mille Lacs Indian Museum and Trading Post** (tel. 612/532-3632), **Fort Mille Lacs Village,** and a gambling casino.

Using the park as a base, you can also go north to visit Duluth or south to the Twin Cities. You'll probably enjoy your visits more as an overnight because the distances are long; however, both are on I-35, so you could drive to either in less than two hours.

Highlights of **Minneapolis–St. Paul** include the state capitol; two zoos; a number of museums, including a children's museum and those on the campus of the **University of Minnesota** (tel. 612/625-5000); **Historic Fort Snelling** (tel. 612/725-2413); the **Guthrie Theater** (tel. 612/377-2224), one of the most famous regional theaters in the country; and a variety of professional sports events. **Duluth** is Minnesota's gateway to the sea. Among its lures are cruises on Lake Superior, a tour of an old Great Lakes ore carrier, a renovated 1892 railroad depot museum, and a 27-mile scenic drive on Skyline Parkway.

Mississippi

PAUL B. JOHNSON
STATE PARK

Mississippi has 27 state parks.

Contacts

- Office of Public Information, Department of Wildlife, Fisheries, and Parks, P.O. Box 451, Jackson, MS 39205 (tel. toll free 800/GO-PARKS [800/467-2757] or 601/364-2123).
- Division of Tourism Development, P.O. Box 1705, Ocean Springs, MS 39566-1705 (tel. toll free 800/WARMEST [800/927-6378]).

General Information on Mississippi State Parks

Those unfamiliar with the state often think of Mississippi as a place of flat delta land. That description is apt along the coast, but inland the terrain is diverse with rolling hills, forests, and pristine streams. The state parks reflect this diversity. Although small in number, the more than 16,000 acres of state parks offer visitors a wide variety of landscapes from saltwater beaches to unspoiled wildernesses. Park activities and accommodations are equally diverse. With the exception of some historic parks, most are built around water—from creeks and lakes to the Gulf of Mexico—so water sports rate high on the list of park activities. But hiking, tennis, even miniature golf are among the other activities available in a number of parks.

GENERAL FEES

There is an entrance fee of $2 per car with up to four persons and 50¢ for each additional person. In parks with a swimming pool, there is usually a fee for its use.

CAMPING AND ACCOMMODATIONS

Close to 200 rental **cabins** and **motel rooms** are available in 16 of the parks. These are classified as deluxe, standard, and rustic ranging from the newest and most modern to those originally constructed by the Civilian Conservation Corps (CCC) during the Depression. No matter when built, however, all cabins have heat and air conditioning. Reservations are not required, but are highly recommended, especially during the spring/summer season when the minimum length of stay for a reservation is three nights. Reservations are made to the individual park and are ranked in priority order by in-person, telephone, and mail requests. Reservations for the following January and February may be made starting the first Monday in October. For two weeks starting the first Monday in December, reservations are accepted for the rest of the year, but only for 7- to 14-day stays. Those cabins not reserved for the year during that period become available for shorter-time reservations starting January 2. Cabins range in capacity from 4 to 12 persons with most holding 4 to 6. Depending on size and facilities, rates go about $29 to $62 a night.

The parks offer a total of about 1,500 developed **campsites,** most with two- or three-way hookups, and a number of additional primitive sites. A limited number of sites may be reserved, but most are on a first-come basis. Reservations are accepted year-round. Developed sites go for $10 to $12 per night while primitive are $6 to $8.

Some parks offer group camping with dormitories or small group cabins year-round as well as authorizing group reservations for 10 or more units in regular campgrounds in the off-season.

Pets. Pets are permitted in day-use and campground areas only. They must be restrained on a leash no longer than six feet at all times. They are not permitted in or around the cabins or in other buildings.

Alcoholic beverages. Public display or consumption of alcoholic beverages in parks is illegal.

Discounts. Camping discounts are available for persons 62 years or older and for families whose head of household is permanently disabled.

Paul B. Johnson State Park

 Visitor Center
 Cabins & Cottages
 RV Camping
 Tent Camping
 Group Lodge Dormitories
 Boating
 Boat Launch
Fishing

 Beach
 Swimming
 Waterskiing
 Picnic Areas
 Trails
 Playground
  Gift Shop

Capsule Description: A small, developed lakeside park.

Location: Southeastern Mississippi, on U.S. Highway 49 approximately 15 miles south of Hattiesburg.

Address: 319 Geiger Lake Rd., Hattiesburg, MS 39401 (tel. 601/582-7721).

Area Contacts: Hattiesburg Convention and Visitors Bureau, P.O. Box 16122, Hattiesburg, MS 39404 (tel. toll free 800/638-6877 or 601/268-3220).

Mississippi Beach Convention and Visitors Bureau, P.O. Box 6128, Gulfport, MS 39506-6128 (tel. toll free 800/237-9493 or 601/896-6699).

This 800-acre park, on the shore of a 300-acre spring-fed lake, is located in the heart of the state's pine belt region where it is almost surrounded by forests of longleaf and loblolly pines, delicate dogwoods, and ancient oaks. The lake itself was built in 1943–44 by German POWs held at nearby Camp Shelby. Entrance to the park is across a spillway.

Activities

The park is located on one end of Geiger Lake, which offers ample opportunity for swimming, boating, fishing, and waterskiing.

For swimmers, there are two beaches, one on each side of the lake. (No lifeguards.) If you don't bring your own boat, you can rent a canoe or rowboat year-round or a paddleboat during the summer season. Waterskiing is permitted on the lake so there are no limits on motor power, except jet-propelled craft aren't allowed.

Anglers who don't want to boat fish can do it off the pier by the beach near the Visitors Center.

The lake is stocked periodically with bass, crappie, catfish, and bream.

The Trail of the Southern Pines, a 1½-mile self-guided nature trail, provides a look at Mississippi plant, bird, and animal life. This well-marked trail features two lookout towers providing a bird's-eye view of the wilderness. A trail brochure is available at the park office. On this trail you have the best chance of seeing deer, turkey, raccoons, or other inhabitants of the park.

The Visitors Center includes a game room featuring video games and pool tables. On permanent display here are all of the state flags of the United States. A brochure describing each flag and its place in our history is available at the reception desk. A sun deck at the center overlooks the lake.

Camping and Accommodations

All of the 16 **cabins** in the park are on the lake. All are modern cabins in the deluxe category with central air and heat, but no TV or phones. Twelve cabins are two-bedroom accommodating six persons and four are one-bedroom with a capacity of five. Most have screened porches and the one-bedrooms feature fireplaces. Cabins cost $43 to $45 per night.

There are 108 RV **campsites** on a scenic hilltop shaded by pines. Of these 88 have water and electric hookups and the other 20 sites have three-way hookups. Sites run about $10 to $12. There are 25 more sites without hookups for tent campers in a separate and secluded pastoral setting on the lake.

A group camp is available with facilities that can accommodate up to 100 in two dormitories.

Nearby Attractions

Paul B. Johnson State Park doesn't offer much in the way of hiking trails, but the **Black Creek Trail** in nearby **DeSoto National Forest** (tel. 601/928-4422) runs about 41 miles.

Just north of the park is the **Camp Shelby National Guard Military Base** (tel. 601/558-2000), the largest state-owned and -operated field training site in the country. The Armed Forces Museum here has more than 2,000 items of military memorabilia on display. It's open every day but Monday.

A little farther on to the north is **Hattiesburg.** The convention and visitors bureau here has free brochures on walking and motor tours of the city's historic neighborhoods. If you're here in late spring and early summer, when the roses bloom, a prime place to visit is the **All-American Rose Garden** on the campus of the **University of Southern Mississippi** (tel. 601/266-7011). For kids, there's a zoo in the city's Kamper Park.

If you get bored with freshwater activities, the saltwater tourist-oriented cities of **Gulfport** and **Biloxi** on the Gulf of Mexico are a fast daytrip away south on U.S. 49. Here you can visit an aquarium and an oceanarium, the last home of Jefferson Davis, president of the Confederacy, and the Seafood Industry Museum. Boat tours, shellfish expeditions, and even gambling are offered, too.

Missouri

THOUSAND HILLS STATE PARK

SAM A. BAKER STATE PARK

Missouri has 47 state parks.

Contacts

- Division of State Parks, Missouri Department of Natural Resources, P.O. Box 176, Jefferson City, MO 65102-0176 (tel. toll free 800/334-6946 or 314/751-2479).
- Missouri Division of Tourism, P.O. Box 1055, Jefferson City, MO 65102-1055 (tel. toll free 800/877-1234 for travel packet only or 314/751-4133).

General Information on Missouri State Parks

It was 1899 when a noted orator from Missouri used the expression, "I'm from Missouri, you've got to show me." Now the "Show Me" state turns the tables and does a good job of showing visitors Missouri's original natural features through its park system. That system is in the midst of a long-term campaign to restore parklands to the way they looked before man developed the state. Restoration projects are underway at more than 30 parks; projects that will not only bring back distinctive native landscapes, but also reintroduce native animals such as the elk and the American bison, which were once abundant here.

The parks offer more than 460 miles of trails for hikers, bicyclists, horseback riders, and off-road-vehicle users. Some parks also give access to the Katy Trail, which will be more than 200 miles long when fully developed, and the Ozark Trail, which will someday run more than 500 miles.

Ten of the parks have dining lodges ranging from modern restaurants to rustic dining rooms.

GENERAL FEES

There is no entrance fee, but some parks do charge a swimming fee.

CAMPING AND ACCOMMODATIONS

Eleven state parks have lodging facilities that include **cabins** and **motel units.** Most of these are open from about mid-April until the end of October. A few have longer seasons; for example, motel rooms at Big Lake State Park are available until the end of November, and to accommodate winter visitors, some housekeeping cabins and motel rooms at Montauk State Park remain open all year. Rates go from about $40 to $100 depending on location, facilities, and number of guests. Reservations are made directly with the parks. During the period from Memorial Day weekend to Labor Day weekend, reservations must be made for a minimum of two nights.

There are almost 4,000 **campsites** in the parks. The campgrounds are open all year, but, in most parks, water and showers are available only from April through October. The majority of the sites come without hookups, but there are some improved sites with a variety of hookup arrangements from electric to three-way. Only 11 parks accept reservations. All others are on a first-come basis. Reservations may be made by phone up to 14 days before arrival. Reservations are made directly with the park office; however, these parks can be reached through the parks division 800 number during normal operating hours. There is a reservation fee.

Many parks have youth camp areas for non-profit youth groups and seven parks have group camps with cabins and dining facilities.

Pets. Pets must be kept on leashes at all times and are not allowed in any buildings.

Alcoholic beverages. Alcoholic beverages are permitted in the parks, but are prohibited on beaches, parking lots, and off-road-vehicle areas.

Discounts. Citizens who are 65 years of age or older and persons who are disabled are entitled to a reduced camping fee.

Sam A. Baker State Park

Visitor Center · Restaurant · Cabins & Cottages · RV Camping · Tent Camping · Primitive Camping · Non-Motorized Boating Only · Fishing · Swimming

Picnic Areas · Trails · Horse Trails · Nature Programs · Playground

Capsule Description: A large, mountain wilderness park with developed facilities.
Location: Southeastern Missouri. From U.S. Highway 67, take Missouri Highway 34 west four miles to Highway 143, then north four miles to the park entrance.
Address: Route 1, P.O. Box 114, Patterson, MO 63956 (tel. 314/856-4411 for the office, 314/856-4223 for the park concessionaire).
Area Contacts: Cape Girardeau Chamber of Commerce, P.O. Box 99, Cape Girardeau, MO 63702-0098 (tel. 314/335-3312).

Cape Girardeau Convention and Visitors Bureau, 1707 Mt. Auburn Rd., Cape Girardeau, MO 63701 (tel. toll free 800/777-0068 or 314/335-1631).

Greater Piedmont Area Chamber of Commerce, P.O. Box 101, Piedmont, MO 63957 (tel. 314/223-4046).

Poplar Bluff Chamber of Commerce, P.O. Box 3986, Poplar Bluff, MO 63902 (tel. 314/785-7761).

One of the oldest state parks in Missouri, its 5,164 acres are set in the rounded hills and domes of igneous rock that make up the St. Francis Mountains—mountains that geologists say are one and a half billion years old. It features an expansive designated wilderness area of 4,420 acres that surrounds Mudlick Mountain, one of the largest of the rock domes. Big Creek and the St. Francis River border the park. The entire park is designated as a National Historic District because of the large number of intact buildings constructed by the Civilian Conservation Corps (CCC).

Activities

Nearly 20 miles of trails go through the designated park wilderness and natural areas, through forests of oak, hickory, black gum, sycamore, and shortleaf pine. The longest is Mudlick Trail, which provides a chance to visit one of the oldest mountain regions in North America. It's a moderately strenuous 12-mile trail climbing from 415 feet above sea level to almost 1,300 feet at the top of Mudlick Mountain. It's open for hikers and horseback riders. This trail is a National Recreation Trail, a designation that qualifies it for public recognition through the U.S. Department of the Interior publications. Backpackers are permitted to camp along the trail. Three stone shelters along the trail are open for overnight use by hikers from October 1 through May 15. This trail is the best place to catch sight of the park's population of deer and turkeys as well as the wide variety of birds. Bald eagles are often seen in the park during the winter.

The Shut-Ins Trail is a shorter trail leading to scenic bluffs along Big Creek. "Shut-ins" are a geologic feature consisting of masses of hard, erosion-resistant igneous rocks that remained after softer sedimentary rock was washed away. The result is a canyonlike gorge with solid rock ledges and huge smoothed and polished boulders along the bottom.

For a better understanding of the park's biodiversity, visit the hands-on exhibits in the nature center in the office complex. Other places to visit are the several buildings in the park built in the 1930s by the CCC.

You can swim or tube in the cool waters of Big Creek and the St. Francis River. Tubes can be rented at the park store. You can also arrange two-hour or all-day float trips on both waterways through the park concessionaire. The creek and river are also open for boating and fishing. Boats should be small and shallow draft because there are shallow spots. Canoes are available for rent. The main catches are bass, bluegill, and catfish.

Other activities include a variety of programs scheduled on a regular basis throughout the summer and on weekends in spring and fall. A popular sponsored event is the Annual Bluegrass Music Festival held in the park the fourth weekend in July.

Camping and Accommodations

Of the 19 **cabins** available, 18 are housekeeping cabins and the other is just a sleeping cabin. Three

are handicapped-accessible. Cabins sleep from 2 to 14 persons. No TV or phones. Reservations are made through the park concessionaire (tel. 314/856-4223).

There are 193 multiuse **campsites.** Ninety-four of these are basic sites renting for $6 per night. The other 99 have electric hookups and rent for $10. Most campsites are on a first-come basis, but a limited number may be reserved through the park office. Campsites are available year-round.

There are also two camps for backpackers, one about four miles from the nearest parking and the other about nine miles. No facilities, no reservations, no fees. Equestrians can rent 10 sites (four sites have electric hookups) at the same rate as campground sites; no reservations are taken.

The park has a rustic dining lodge open daily from Memorial Day to Labor Day and weekends from April 1 to Memorial Day and Labor Day to October 31.

Nearby Attractions

Giant granite rocks a billion years old stand end to end like a train of circus elephants in the 129-acre **Elephant Rocks State Park** (tel. 314/697-5395) near Bellview. The swift waters of the Black River form another series of "shut-ins" in **Johnson's Shut-ins State Park** (tel. 314/546-2450) near Middlebrook. At the wilderness park of Johnson's, you'll find a major trail head for the 500-mile long Ozark Trail, which is under development. Missouri's highest point and highest waterfall are in **Taum Sauk Mountain State Park** (tel. 314/546-2450) near Ironton.

To the southeast lies **Lake Wappapello State Park** (tel. 314/297-3232) on an 8,600-acre lake on which you can boat, fish, and do other water sports. South of that is the town of **Poplar Bluff,** which features an art museum and a railroad museum.

Cape Girardeau, the region's largest city—and the nation's only inland cape—lies to the east on the Mississippi River. Outstanding views of the Mississippi are had from the cape, and a scenic train runs weekends during the summer.

Thousand Hills State Park

Restaurant　Cabins &　RV　Tent　Marina　Boating　Boat　Fishing
Cottages　Camping　Camping　Launch

Beach　Waterskiing　Picnic　Trails　Nature　Playground
Areas　Programs

Capsule Description: A large, wooded lakeside park with developed facilities.

Location: Northeast Missouri, about four miles west of Kirkville. From Kirkville, go west on Missouri Highway 6 about four miles to Highway 157, then south about 1¾ miles.

Address: Route 3, Kirkville, MO 63501 (tel. 816/665-6995 for the office, 816/665-7119 for the park concessionaire).

Area Contacts: Kirkville Chamber of Commerce, P.O. Box 251, Kirkville, MO 63501 (tel. 816/665-3766).

This park preserves more than 3,000 acres of an oak-hickory forest in rugged hills that are surrounded by rolling farmlands referred to as the "thousand hills." Running through this landscape is the Grand Divide. A divide, such as the Continental Divide, is an area where the surface water drainage is separated by higher ground. Here the divide roughly follows the north-south line of U.S. Highway 63, which is east of the park. Land west of the Grand Divide drains into the Missouri River while land on the east drains into the Mississippi River.

The park surrounds the 573-acre Forest Lake. This is a reservoir owned and administered by the city of Kirkville.

Activities

The lake is the center of activities here.

For boaters there's a marina that opens for the season the beginning of April. Many types of boats from ski boats and pontoon boats to paddleboats and canoes can be rented here, as well as boat slips. Since the city owns the lake, it charges for private-boat permits depending on the horsepower of the motor with fees going from $2 to $5 a day. There is a limit of 90 horsepower on motors and no jet skis are allowed on the lake.

Waterskiing, tubing, and windsurfing are all popular on the lake. Skis are available for rent at the marina.

For swimmers, the park beach operates from Memorial Day weekend through Labor Day weekend. There are lifeguards and a fee is charged. Some coves along the lake's 17 miles of shoreline are also designated for swimming.

The lake is stocked with catfish annually. Other catches include largemouth bass, bluegill, walleye, and crappie.

Walkers have three short trails available, moderate difficulty but only about a half mile each. For hikers there's one five-mile trail rated difficult. Most of the trails go through the forest where you're apt to see white-tailed deer and wild turkey, which are plentiful in the park, as well as beaver, raccoons, woodchucks, hawks, and eagles. A park naturalist is available year-round to conduct interpretive programs including a pontoon-boat tour of the lake.

An interesting place to visit is an area of Native American rock carvings that have been dated back as far as 400 A.D. These carvings include crosses, arrows, snakes, thunderbirds, and other animal representations, which are thought to be symbols that served as memory aids to help ancient tribes remember the order of ceremonial rituals. This petroglyph site is listed in the National Register of Historic Places.

Camping and Accommodations

The 14 housekeeping **cabins** are one- and two-bedroom with capacities of up to 8 people. All have air conditioning, heat, and color TVs. They are available March 1 through December 22. Rentals for two to four persons range from about $40 to $90 in off-season to about $43 to $100 during the May through September season. You can also get weekly rates at substantial savings during the off-season. Reservations are made through the park concessionaire.

All 72 **campsites** are on a first-come basis. Forty-five sites have electric hookups, the other 27 are basic sites with no hookups. Rates are $10 for electric sites and $6 for the basic ones.

The Dining Lodge, which serves both food and cocktails, is open from mid-February to December 22 and has seasonal hours. This lodge has a reputation as one of the best places to eat in the region and therefore is one of the busiest in the park system.

Nearby Attractions

The world's first school of osteopathic medicine, Kirkville College of Osteopathic Medicine, was founded in the nearby city of **Kirkville** in 1892 and is still graduating osteopaths. The school's museum (tel. 816/626-2121) tells the history of Dr. Andrew Taylor Still, the founder of this branch of medicine. The town is also the home of **Northeast Missouri State University** (tel. 816/785-4000), which offers campus tours.

Northwest of the park is **Novinger,** which features the **Coal Miners' Museum.**

Two towns to the southwest contain memories of two world-famous Missourians with vastly different careers. Walt Disney grew up in **Marceleine** and his elementary school—now bearing his name—displays his desk. A little farther west, in **Laclede,** is a state historic site containing the boyhood home (tel. 816/963-2525) of Gen. John J. Pershing, the World War I hero.

Montana

FLATHEAD LAKE
STATE PARK

Montana has 43 state parks.

Contacts

- Parks Division, Department of Fish, Wildlife & Parks, 1420 E. Sixth Ave., Helena, MT 59604 (tel. 406/444-2535).
- Montana Travel Promotion Division, Department of Commerce, 800 Conley Lake Rd., Deer Lodge, MT 59722 (tel. toll free 800/541-1447 outside Montana only or 406/444-2654).

General Information on Montana State Parks

The terrain of the Big Sky State varies from the horizon-to-horizon prairies of the Great Plains in the east to the rugged landscape of the Rocky Mountains in the west with mile-high valleys and peaks that are topped at a height of 12,799 feet at Granite Peak. The parks reflect this diversity. They also vary in size from one acre to almost 9,000 acres. About half the parks are open year-round; the rest are open seasonally, usually starting around May 1.

While fourth in area of the states, Montana has a population of only about 800,000—less than that of many major cities. And, even though it ranks up near the top of the list of agricultural states, there are vast areas of open country, a delight for those who relish the outdoors.

It also means wildlife is abundant. This includes the largest population of grizzly bears in the lower 48 states. More than 100 areas throughout the state are marked by a roadside sign showing a pair of binoculars, designating a Watchable Wildlife Area. If you see one, stop and look because this is an area where you have a good chance of doing what the sign claims—watching wildlife.

General Fees

An entrance fee of $3 per car is charged at 28 parks. A season pass costs $15. Entry by walking, bicycle, or motorcycle costs 50¢ per person.

Camping

Campsites are available at 22 parks. Some campgrounds are open all year, but fully operational only during the summer season. A summer-season reservation system was discontinued due to budget cuts. Now all campsites are on a first-come basis. (Perhaps the reservation system will be reinstated by the time you read this.) Camping fees run from $7 to $9 and include the park entrance fee. There are electric and water hookups at a limited number of sites. Electric costs $2 extra and water $1. Two camper units are allowed per site. A few primitive camper cabins are available in Lewis and Clark Caverns State Park.

Pets. Where pets are allowed, they must be attended and on a leash at all times. Sometimes these rules are relaxed in off-season. In most parks, pets are not permitted on trails, on swimming beaches, or in buildings.

Alcoholic beverages. Generally permitted in most parks. Some designated restricted areas, such as the caverns.

Discounts. Camping discounts are available for Montana residents who are 62 and older or disabled.

Flathead Lake State Park

RV Camping | Tent Camping | Marina | Boating | Boat Launch | Fishing | Beach | Waterskiing | Picnic Areas | Trails | Nature Programs | Bicycling

Capsule Description: Six small, developed park units on both shores of a major lake.

Location: Northwestern Montana, about 50 miles southwest of Glacier National Park. From Missoula, take U.S. Highway 93 north about 70 miles to Polson at the southern end of the lake. From there continue on U.S. 93 to the park units on the west shore or take Montana Highway 35 to the park units on the east shore.

Address: 490 N. Meridian Rd., Kalispell, MT 59901 (tel. 406/752-5501).

Area Contacts: The Flathead Convention and Vacation Association, 15 Depot Park, Kalispell, MT 59901 (tel. toll free 800/543-3105).

Glacier Country, Suite B, 945 4th Ave. East, Kalispell, MT 59901 (tel. toll free 800/338-5072 or 406/756-7128).

Glacier National Park, West Glacier, MT 59936 (tel. 406/888-5441).

Missoula Chamber of Commerce, P.O. Box 7577, Missoula, MT 59807 (tel. 406/543-6623).

About 12,000 years ago, receding glaciers dredged out a trough that today is the bottom of the largest natural freshwater lake west of the Mississippi River. Located at an elevation of 2,893 feet, the lake is 38 miles long, 8 to 15 miles wide, and has 185 miles of shoreline. Its deepest point is 339 feet. The lake is surrounded by forests with patches of cherry and apple orchards.

The state park consists of six small units, totaling 343 acres scattered along the shoreline, and Wild Horse Island, at more than 2,100 acres the largest island in the lake.

The park is open May 1 through September 30.

Activities

Some activities, like swimming, boating, and fishing, are common to all lakeshore units, while other activities can only be enjoyed at certain units. Following is a breakdown to help you pick the unit you want to visit.

EAST SHORE

Finley Point. Located in a secluded, mature conifer forest near the south end of the lake. Small marina and designated swimming area (no lifeguards).

Wayfarers. In a mature mixed conifer forest on northeast shore within walking distance of the resort town of Bigfork. Beach, walking trails.

Yellow Bay. Located in the middle of the east shore in an area of cherry orchards. Beach, interpretive trail.

WEST SHORE

Big Arm. This unit has the most facilities for visitors. Located on the lake's Big Arm Bay, it has a long pebble beach, interpretive trail and interpretive programs, and boat rentals. Flocks of Canada geese favor the Big Arm area for their summer stay. (The park's boat tours from the Big Arm to Wild Horse Island were also a victim of budget cuts. They may be back on by the time you read this, but, if not, commercial tours to the island can be taken from several towns around the lake.)

Elmo. This unit is in a relatively open area spotted with juniper trees. Long gravel beach and boat rentals.

West Shore. Located in a mature forest of fir, pine, and larch, this unit also has a number of glacially carved rock outcrops. Swimming, hiking.

WILD HORSE ISLAND

Access by boat is carefully regulated to protect the wildlife and the endangered plant species on the island. This wilderness island got its name because the Flathead Indians once used it to keep their ponies from being stolen by the Blackfeet tribe. Now it is home to some wild horse, which were imported to give meaning to the name, plus herds of Rocky Mountain bighorn sheep, mule and white-tailed deer, bald eagles, and huge flocks of geese and other waterfowl.

In addition to boating and swimming, there's an opportunity for just about every other water sport on the lake including waterskiing, jet skiing, and windsurfing. Anglers can expect a variety of catches including bull, lake, and cutthroat trout— a 42-pound lake trout caught here in 1979 still holds the Montana record—yellow perch, kokanee salmon, and Lake Superior whitefish. The southern half of lake is within the Flathead Indian Reservation. You'll have to get a tribal fishing license to fish these waters.

Camping

There are **campgrounds** in all six lakeside units with a total of more than 100 campsites. Most are multiuse sites, but there are a few for tents only. All are on a first-come basis. Camping fees are from $7 to $9. Electric and water hookups are available at Finley Point for $3 extra and the 15 campsites there include a boat slip.

Nearby Attractions

At the north end of the lake near the town of Bigfork, the Jewel Basin Hiking Area offers 38 miles of trails. A star summer attraction at the resort community of Bigfork is a summer musical repertory theater. On the west shore, near **Dayton,** is the state's only winery with a tasting room. On the south end of the lake, **Polson,** the county seat of Lake County, offers a couple of small museums, as well as tour boats on the lake and whitewater rafting trips on the Flathead National Wild and Scenic River.

South, near **Moiese,** is the **National Bison Range** (tel. 406/644-2211), where you can take a 19-mile self-guided auto tour to see the herd of 400 or so of these great shaggy animals, as well as deer, elk, bighorn sheep, and pronghorns.

Still farther south—best as an overnight trip— is **Missoula.** Attractions here include the campus of the University of Montana; the headquarters of the U.S. Forest Service smokejumpers, which can be toured during the summer; a rose garden; the center of the Rocky Mountain Elk Foundation; and several museums. In winter, you can ski 30 trails in the **Snowbowl Ski Area** (tel. 406/549-9777), and in summer ride the chair lift for a spectacular view.

Heading north, the town of **Whitefish** is the home of the **Big Mountain Ski Area** (tel. 406/862-2514), Montana's largest ski resort. In summer you can take a gondola ride to a mountaintop restaurant with a view of the main attraction in this area, the million-plus-acre **Glacier National Park** (tel. 406/888-5441). This park, about two hours' drive from Flathead Lake, reaches up to the Canadian border where it joins the Waterton Lakes National Park in Alberta, Canada, to create the Waterton-Glacier International Peace Park. Some of the more than 50 glaciers here are reasonably accessible. For a breathtaking view, drive the **Going-to-the-Sun Road.** Often rated as one of the most spectacular drives in America, the 55-mile scenic highway through Glacier crosses the Continental Divide.

Unfortunately, it's a fair-weather road only open during the summer. If you decide to overnight, accommodations are available in Glacier National Park during the summer and outside the park year round.

Nebraska

FORT ROBINSON
STATE PARK

EUGENE T. MAHONEY
STATE PARK

Nebraska has 87 state parks.

Contacts

- Division of State Parks, Nebraska Game and Parks Commission, P.O. Box 30370, Lincoln, NE 68503-0370 (tel. 402/471-0641).
- Travel and Tourism Division, Department of Economic Development, P.O. Box 94666, Lincoln, NE 68509-4666 (tel. toll free 800/228-4307).

General Information About Nebraska State Parks

As you go from east to west across the state, you move gently uphill from the productive agricultural plains, which gave Nebraska its nickname as the "Cornhusker State," to the rich grasslands of cattle and real cowboy country.

Along the way you may visit some of the state's thousands of miles of streams and more than 3,000 lakes. A number of state parks have been established specifically to turn these waters into recreational playgrounds.

The state straddles two time zones with approximately the eastern two-thirds in the central time zone and the western third, from just a little way west of the city of North Platte, in the mountain time zone.

General Fees

There is an entrance fee of $2.50 per vehicle. An annual entrance permit is available for $14.

Camping and Accommodations

Lodge rooms are available in two parks: Eugene T. Mahoney and Fort Robinson. Rooms go for from about $25 to about $65. Fort Robinson also has a variety of other lodgings (see listing below). Eight parks have housekeeping **cabins** that range from two to nine bedrooms and cost from about $35 to $170 per night. Lodging reservations are made directly to the parks and are accepted for two or more nights up to a year in advance.

More than two dozen parks have modern **campgrounds** with electric hookups. Most of these go for $4 to $6 plus $3 for the electricity. An exception is Eugene T. Mahoney State Park where RV campsites go for $13 including electric. This is the only park that accepts campsite reservations for a limited number of sites. There is a reservation fee of $3. All other campsites are on a first-come basis. A number of parks with minimum facilities have free campsites.

The lodging and camping season in most parks runs from early April until November; however, a few parks, like Eugene T. Mahoney and Platte River, are open year-round. Most primitive campsites are available year-round.

Pets. Where permitted, pets must be under control and on a leash. They are not permitted in lodge rooms, but may be allowed in some cabins.

Alcoholic beverages. In general, public consumption of alcoholic beverages is prohibited in all parks.

Fort Robinson State Park

Lodge/ Hotel Restaurant Cabins & Cottages RV Camping Tent Camping Primitive Camping Group Lodge Dormitories Non-Motorized Boating Only Fishing Swimming

Picnic Areas Trails Horse Trails Nature Programs Bicycling Tennis Playground X-Country Skiing Gift Shop

Capsule Description: A large, natural park with a historic section and many developed facilities.

Location: Northwestern corner of Nebraska. From Crawford, take U.S. Highway 20 west three miles. In mountain time zone.

Address: P.O. Box 392, Crawford, NE 69339 (tel. 308/665-2900).

Area Contacts: Chadron Chamber of Commerce, P.O. Box 646, Chadron, NE 69337 (tel. 308/432-4401).

Crawford Chamber of Commerce, P.O. Box 506, Crawford, NE 69339 (tel. 308/665-2604).

Crazy Horse, Walter Reed, Chief Red Cloud, Arthur MacArthur, and General Crook—these are but a few of the colorful men who played significant roles in carving Fort Robinson's place in western lore. An active army post from the Indian wars of the mid-1870s until after World War II, it became the nucleus of the present state park in 1955. The 1972 acquisition of more than 22,000 acres surrounding the historic post made it Nebraska's largest state park.

Activities

The list of things to do here goes on and on. Much of it is concentrated in the summer season and centered around or at least starts at the historic fort area.

For a fast orientation on the historic area, take the tour train that leaves on the hour from 10am to 4pm. For fun, there are also one- and two-hour Jeep trips, a stagecoach ride, short or long trail rides, and a hayrack ride. You can also sign up to combine those last two with a trail-ride breakfast or a hayrack breakfast.

If you prefer to do it on your own, you can rent a bike or hike. There are 15 miles of marked bike trails and a 12-mile hiking trail. If you don't want to hike the whole 12-mile trail, you can pick a segment and enter from any of four trailheads, each of which has a parking lot. You can also bring your own horse, rent a park stable stall, and ride the trails.

Also on your own you can tour the restored fort buildings. The fort takes up about 75 acres and is a

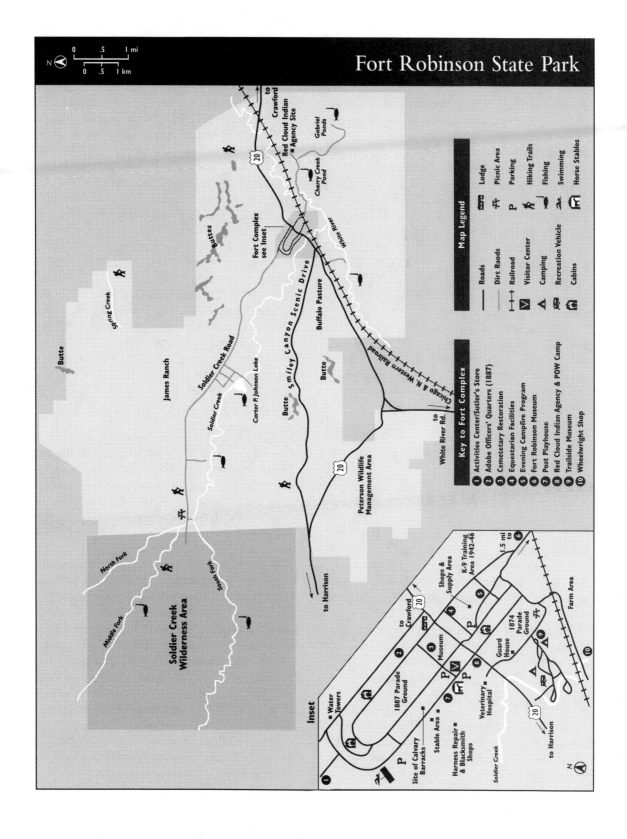

Fort Robinson State Park

Map Legend

- Roads
- Dirt Raods
- +++ Railroad
- Ⓥ Visitor Center
- ⚑ Camping
- ⚙ Recreation Vehicle
- ⌂ Cabins
- ⌂ Lodge
- ⚑ Picnic Area
- P Parking
- ⚑ Hiking Trails
- ⚑ Fishing
- ⚑ Swimming
- ⚐ Horse Stables

Key to Fort Complex

1. Activities Center/Sutler's Store
2. Adobe Officers' Quarters (1887)
3. Cemetetary Restoration
4. Equestarian Facilities
5. Evening Campfire Program
6. Fort Robinson Museum
7. Post Playhouse
8. Red Cloud Indian Agency & POW Camp
9. Trailside Museum
10. Wheelwright Shop

to Crawford

Red Cloud Indian Agency Site

Gabriel Ponds

Cherry Creek Pond

White River

20

Fort Complex see Inset

Smiley Canyon Scenic Drive

Buffalo Pasture

Chicago & N. Western Railroad

Spring Creek

Buttes

Butte

James Ranch

Soldier Creek Road

Soldier Creek

Carter P. Johnson Lake

Butte

Butte

Peterson Wildlife Management Area

20

to White River Rd.

to Harrison

North Fork

Middle Fork

South Fork

Soldier Creek Wilderness Area

Inset

Water Towers

1887 Parade Ground

Site of Calvalry Barracks

Stable Area

Harness Repair & Blacksmith Shops

Veterinary Hospital

Soldier Creek

to Harrison

to Crawford

20

Museum

Shops & Supply Area

K-9 Training Area 1942–46

1874 Parade Ground

Guard House

Farm Area

20

.5 mi to

2

3

7

4

5

8

9

10

6

N

National Historic Site. Here, in 1877, Crazy Horse was killed in an escape attempt; the army made its first attempt at becoming mechanized with a test (unsuccessful) of high-wheeled bicycles in 1897, the world's largest Remount Depot for army horses and mules was established after World War I, and the War Dog Reception and Training Center was established in World War II. There was also a German POW camp here during that war. Exhibit buildings include the officers' quarters, blacksmith shop, veterinary hospital, and the guardhouse. For a review of the fort's history, visit the Fort Robinson Museum. A second museum, the Trailside Museum, operated by the University of Nebraska State Museum, offers displays on area natural and geologic history.

Other summer activities include campfire slide and film programs, arts and crafts programs, a wildlife tour, historical tours, free rodeo events twice a week, plays put on by drama students from the nearby college at the Post Playhouse, and Chuckwagon Buffalo Stew Cookouts.

You can see the buffalo on the hoof plus elk and bighorn sheep in fenced pastures near the fort. On the trails you'll have a good chance of seeing deer, antelope, and wild turkey.

Fishing is good for bluegill, largemouth bass, and trout. In addition to the 68-acre Carter Johnson Lake, the park contains five miles of the White River, six miles of Soldier Creek, and several small fishing ponds. Rowboats can be rented at the lake.

There's no swimming in any of these waters, but there is an enclosed, heated pool with life-guards that's open during the summer. (Entrance fee.)

In the winter ice skating, cross-country skiing, and sledding are allowed, but you're on your own; no facilities are maintained for these sports.

Camping and Accommodations

The fort's former enlisted men's barracks is now the **Lodge.** Open from early April through late November, it has a restaurant, and 23 rooms that rent for $25 to $30.

There are 24 housekeeping **cabins** ranging from two to five bedrooms. These are in the officers' quarters built between 1874 and 1887 and rent for $50 to $80 per night. The newer (built in 1909) officers' quarters are seven brick houses that have from seven to nine bedrooms, and go from $120 to $145 per night. There are no TVs or phones in the cabins. Three miles west of the Lodge, in a wilderness area, the Peterson's Ranch House offers five bedrooms and the use of the barn and corral for $125.

The 1909 bachelor officers' quarters is now a group facility that will accommodate up to 60 people.

There are 150 **campsites** with electric hook-ups and another 100 without hookups. The electric sites go for $9 and the others for $6. All on a first-come basis; no reservations.

Backpack camping is permitted along the hiking trails and is free.

Nearby Attractions

A short drive to the east, just three miles east of **Chadron** on U.S. 20, is the **Museum of the Fur Trade** (tel. 308/432-3843). An 1841 fur trading post has been reconstructed on the museum grounds. Brochures on self-guided tours of Chadron and the surrounding Pine Ridge area are available from the Chadron Chamber of Commerce (tel. 308/432-4401).

To the southwest, a little farther afield, but still an easy daytrip from the park, is the **Agate Fossil Beds National Monument** (tel. 308/668-2211). It's located on Nebraska Highway 29 about 20 miles south of Harrison. The highlight here is the large number of exposed fossils, which you can see on a self-guided tour.

To the south on U.S. 385 about 2½ miles north of Alliance, is **Carhenge,** a whimsical re-creation of the world-renowned Stonehenge made with old cars.

For an all-day or overnight trip, South Dakota's **Black Hills** and **Mount Rushmore** are just about three hours' drive to the north.

Eugene T. Mahoney State Park

| Lodge/ Hotel | Restaurant | Cabins & Cottages | RV Camping | Tent Camping | Group Lodge Dormitories | Non-Motorized Boating Only | Fishing | Swimming |

| Picnic Areas | Trails | Horse Trails | Nature Programs | Bicycling | Tennis | Playground | X-Country Skiing | Gift Shop |

Capsule Description: A small, developed park between Nebraska's two largest cities.

Location: Eastern Nebraska on the Platte River. Take Exit 426 off I-80 and go west half a mile to park entrance. In central time zone.

Address: 28500 W. Park Hwy., Ashland, NE 68003 (tel. 402/944-2523).

Area Contacts: Dodge County Convention and Visitors Bureau, P.O. Box 182, Fremont, NE 68025 (tel. 402/721-2641).

Lincoln Convention and Visitors Bureau, P.O. Box 83737, Lincoln, NE 68501 (tel. toll free 800/423-8212 or 402/434-5335).

Omaha Convention and Visitors Bureau, 6800 Mercy Rd., Suite 202, Omaha, NE 68106-2627 (tel. toll free 800/332-1819 or 402/444-4660).

Listed as one of the twelve best parks in America by *Money Magazine,* Eugene T. Mahoney State Park is Nebraska's newest. Although most activities are concentrated in the summer season, this is the only state park where lodging, restaurant, and modern camping facilities are available year-round. The 720-acre park perches on wooded bluffs that overlook the confluence of the Platte River and Salt Creek. Its location between Nebraska's two largest cities and its proximity to I-80, which links the two, makes it readily accessible.

Activities

One of the places to visit here is the James Family Conservatory. A dual-purpose facility, part is devoted to displays of native Nebraska trees and shrubs, wildflowers and native grasses, aquatic resources and wildlife. It even has a small waterfall. The other part is a working greenhouse where plants are grown for parks and other Game and Parks Commission areas.

For a bird's-eye view of the park and the Platte River, climb the 70-foot tall observation tower in the north end near the group lodge. You can also get acquainted with the park at daily shows at the Administration Building Theater.

Parts of the seven miles of hiking trails are rated difficult because of fairly steep inclines. There are also five miles of equestrian trails and three miles of trails for mountain bikes. Wildlife often seen on the trails include deer and wild turkey.

There are two small lakes in the park. The 10-acre U.S. West Lake is open for fishing and has two fishing piers. Catches include bluegill, largemouth bass, trout, and channel catfish. However, since the initial stocking of the lake was only made in 1991, until the fish population matures and becomes well established, the rules are catch-and-release for all species except trout and channel catfish. Trout are stocked during fall and winter. No boating or swimming is allowed in the lake.

Fishing in the four-acre Owen Marina Lake is restricted to children under 16 years of age and handicapped adults. They can fish from the bank or the handicapped-accessible fishing bridge. The only boats allowed on this lake are paddleboats, which can be rented at the small marina. No fishing from these boats, and no swimming in the lake.

For swimmers, in season, there's an outdoor pool, with lifeguards, and a twisting water slide. (Entrance fee.)

Other things to do? How about taking a trail ride, playing a round on the 18-hole miniature golf course or driving a bucket of balls at the driving range, playing tennis or a variety of other sports, doing your thing at the Arts and Crafts Center, or enjoying a play in the park theater?

Come winter, as soon as the snow buildup is sufficient, about five miles of park trails are opened for cross-country skiing, plus you can ice-skate, ice-fish, go tobogganing or sledding, or take a horse-drawn sleigh ride through the woods.

Camping and Accommodations

There are 24 standard rooms in the **Lodge** that go for $55 per night and 16 loft rooms that cost $65. Four rooms are handicapped-equipped. The full-service restaurant is open every day.

The 41 housekeeping **cabins** all have air conditioning and heat, a deck, a fireplace, phone, and TV. Thirty-nine cabins are two-bedroom, the other two are four-bedroom. Standard cabins cost $80, deluxe cabins go for $90, and the four-bedroom cabins are $170 per night.

Reservations for the lodge and cabins may be made up to 12 months in advance for a two-night minimum and 14-day maximum stay.

Of the 149 **campsites** with electric hookups, 29 may be reserved up to a year in advance. The other 120, plus 20 primitive tent sites, are on a first-come basis. Sites with hookups go for $13. Tent sites are $5. The reservation fee is $3. Maximum reservation is 14 days.

A group lodge is available by reservation.

Nearby Attractions

Northeast, up Interstate 80 less than an hour away, is **Omaha,** Nebraska's largest city. Must-see and must-do attractions here include the **Henry Doorly Zoo** (tel. 308/733-8401) with an indoor rain forest, Thoroughbred and greyhound racing, professional sports, Boys Town, a wide variety of museums that cover everything from art to the history of the Strategic Air Command, and a planetarium at the Omaha branch of the University of Nebraska. Not to forget the **Omaha Livestock Market** and restaurants that specialize in Omaha steaks. You can take a cruise on the Missouri River or cross it and visit the neighboring city of Council Bluffs, Iowa.

In **Fremont,** to the northwest, you can take a 17- or 30-mile day-time ride on the **Fremont & Elkhorn Valley Railroad** (tel. 402/727-0615), or have dinner on the **Fremont Dinner Train** (tel. 402/727-0615).

To the southwest on Interstate 80 lies **Lincoln,** the capital of Nebraska. Sights here include the **State Capitol building** (tel. 402/471-2311), the **Governor's Mansion** (tel. 402/471-2244), the **Children's Zoo** (tel. 402/475-6742), and museums ranging from the **Museum of Nebraska History** (tel. 402/471-4754) to the **National Museum of Roller Skating** (tel. 402/483-7551).

Nevada

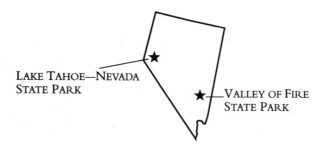

LAKE TAHOE—NEVADA
STATE PARK

VALLEY OF FIRE
STATE PARK

Nevada has 22 state parks.

Contacts

- Division of State Parks, Department of Conservation and Natural Resources, 123 W. Nye Lane, Carson City, NV 89710 (tel. 702/687-4370).
- Nevada Commission on Tourism, Capitol Complex, Carson City, NV 89710 (tel. toll free 800/638-2328 or 800/237-0774).

General Information on Nevada State Parks

Most of the world thinks of Nevada as a state made up of Las Vegas, Reno, and barren desert. On closer look, Nevada is a land of intriguing contrasts. Sure, there are those glittering, fast-paced cities and there are stretches of high desert, but for those who know it the desert can be a place of beauty and there are also mountain peaks that reach up to 13,000 feet sheltering cool alpine lakes.

Tourism is a major industry here, and the state parks are designed to offer both residents and visitors another view of the state.

GENERAL FEES
Not all parks have an entrance fee. Where there is one it is usually $3 to $4.

CAMPING
Although there are 16 parks with developed campgrounds, most have relatively few campsites, ranging in number from about 10 to 50. The sites are generally multiuse, cost about $8 per night, and are on a first-come basis—no reservations. In addition, most of these parks have some primitive sites that are available at a lower fee or, in some cases, no fee. Length of stay is limited to 14 days in any 30-day period.

Pets. Pets are allowed in most parks but must be kept on a leash not longer than six feet or under physical restraint at all times. In general, they are not allowed on beaches or in buildings.

Alcoholic beverages. Alcoholic beverages are permitted, but look for restrictions on types of containers, such as no glass on beaches.

Discounts. Nevada residents age 60 and older are entitled to a Senior Citizen's Permit which gives free entry to all parks.

Lake Tahoe–Nevada State Park

Primitive Camping | Boating | Boat Launch | Fishing | Beach | Waterskiing | Snorkeling & Diving | Picnic Areas | Trails | Horse Trails | Nature Programs | Bicycling | X-Country Skiing

Capsule Description: A largely wilderness park with some developed facilities on the lake.

Location: Western Nevada on the northeast shore of Lake Tahoe. From Carson City, take U.S. Highway 50 west to Nevada Highway 28 at the lake, then north to park headquarters at the Sand Harbor unit.

Address: P.O. Box 8867, Incline Village, NV 89452 (tel. 702/831-0494).

Area Contacts: Carson City Convention and Visitors Bureau, 1900 S. Carson St., Suite 200, Carson City, NV 89701 (tel. toll free 800/Nevada1 (800/638-2321) or 702/687-7410).

Incline Village/Crystal Bay Visitors and Convention Bureau, 969 Tahoe Blvd., Incline Village, NV 89451 (tel. 702/832-1606).

Lake Tahoe Visitors Authority, P.O. Box 272-127, Concord, CA 94527 (tel. toll free 800/AT-TAHOE (800/288-2463)).

Tahoe North Visitors and Convention Bureau, P.O. Box 5578, Tahoe City, CA 96145 (tel. toll free 800/TAHOE4U (800/824-6348) or 916/583-3494).

U.S.D.A. Forest Service, Lake Tahoe Basin Management Unit, 870 Emerald Bay Rd., Suite 1, South Lake Tahoe, CA 96150 (tel. 916/573-2600).

Insider Tips: The park has a music festival each weekend in July and a Shakespeare Festival in August nightly Tuesday to Sunday.

Lake Tahoe, the highest and largest alpine lake in North America—and possibly the best known—is 22 miles long, up to 12 miles wide, and has an average depth of close to 1,000 feet. Its name has been traced back to an Indian word meaning "Lake of the Sky." This fits since the lake is at an elevation of 6,226 feet, and the mountains sur-

rounding it go up another 4,000 feet. The eastern shore, amounting to about one-third of the shoreline, is in Nevada; the rest is in California. Both states have established parks both on their shorelines and in the lands back from the lake. Although it has been a resort lake for years, most of the resort development is concentrated at the north and south ends of the lake.

Lake Tahoe–Nevada State Park has a total of about 14,000 acres in five management areas. Three of these—Sand Harbor, Memorial Point/Hidden Beach, and Cave Rock—are actually on the lake. Spooner Lake and the Marlette/Hobart Backcountry are in the mountain wilderness.

Activities

The three-quarter-mile white sandy beach on the crystal-clear lake makes the lakeside Sand Harbor unit the most popular in the park. The entrance fee is $4 per vehicle. (No pets.) If you plan to visit this unit on a summer weekend, be warned: It is so popular that on summer weekends and holidays the vehicle gate is often closed by 11am because the parking lot is filled. Walk-ins are still allowed, but you may have a hard time finding a space where parking is permitted near the park.

Facilities in this unit include a half-mile self-guided nature trail and a natural amphitheater that is the site of the annual summer music and Shakespeare festivals.

You can swim (the top water gets up to about 68 degrees in summer), scuba-dive in Diver's Cove (below 12 feet the temperature drops rapidly), put your boat into the lake at the boat ramp (where the

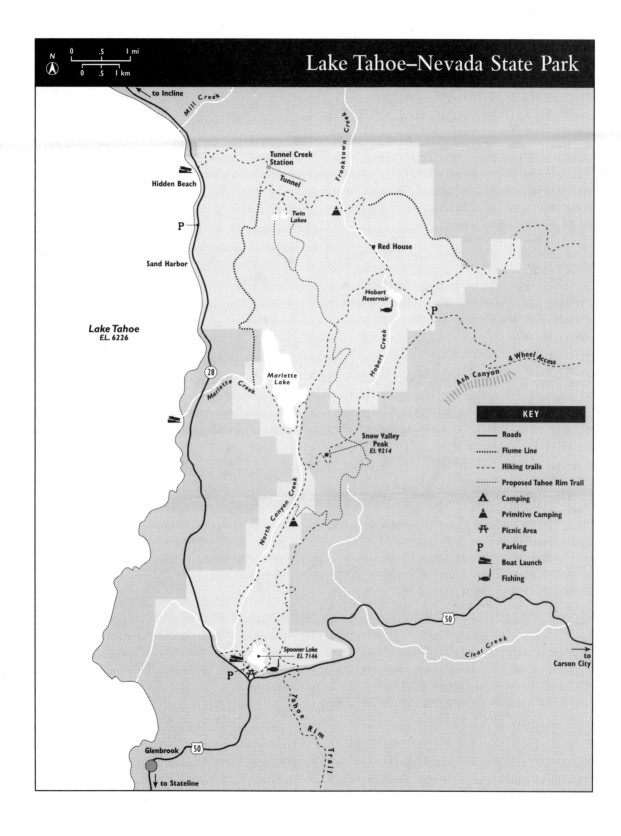

N

0   .5   1 mi
0   .5   1 km

to Incline

Mill Creek

Franktown Creek

Tunnel Creek
Station

Tunnel

Hidden Beach

P

Twin
Lakes

Red House

Sand Harbor

Hobart
Reservoir

Lake Tahoe
EL. 6226

P

Ash Canyon   4 Wheel Access

Marlette Creek

Marlette
Lake

Hobart Creek

28

Snow Valley
Peak
El. 9214

North Canyon Creek

KEY

Roads
Flume Line
Hiking trails
Proposed Tahoe Rim Trail
△ Camping
▲ Primitive Camping
⛱ Picnic Area
P Parking
🚤 Boat Launch
🎣 Fishing

50

Clear Creek

to
Carson City

Spooner Lake
EL. 7146

P

Tahoe Rim Trail

Glenbrook   50

to Stateline

parking lot is often filled shortly after the 8am gate-opening on summer weekends), or fish from a boat or the rocky shoreline. On the lake either a Nevada or California fishing license is OK.

Another park swimming and boating area is located at Hidden Beach, about two miles north of Sand Harbor. This is a small beach and no parking area. Between Sand Harbor and Hidden Beach, Memorial Point offers a scenic lookout and trails to the rocky shore.

Cave Rock, located on Highway 50 about three miles south of Glenbrook, has a boat ramp, a small beach, and a rocky shoreline that makes for good fishing because of the steep drop-off. Scuba diving is also permitted here. There is limited parking that quickly fills on summer weekends, and an entrance fee.

The Spooner Lake unit is located in a meadow in one of the summits of the Carson Range at the south end of the park, nine miles south of Sand Harbor near the junction of Highways 50 and 28. Sport fly-fishing for trout is the main attraction of the lake itself, but it's catch-and-release only. No motorized boats are allowed, but inflatables are. This unit is also a major trailhead for hikers, bikers, and equestrians who want to explore the back-country. These include a section of the Tahoe Rim Trail and the Flume Trail. Plans call for the Tahoe Rim Trail to eventually circle the entire lake and total about 150 miles. About 115 of those miles are maintained now. The section in the park runs north offering a number of choices that will take you to spectacular views of the lake as well as the backcountry Marlette Lake. The Flume Trail is a favorite with mountain bikers. It follows the route of a V-shaped flume used to carry water from Marlette Lake to Virginia City in the mid-1800s.

Many of the parks interpretive programs originate from Spooner because of its natural diversity and historical significance. Here is also the best place to view wildlife, especially deer. There's an entrance fee to this area.

In the winter, Spooner Lake becomes the center for 23 groomed, cross-country ski trails that add up to more than 60 miles. Operated by a

concessionaire; skis may be rented, lessons are available, and trail passes cost from $11 to $18 per day depending on a skier's age and whether it's a weekday or weekend.

In the backcountry area, Hobart reservoir is well known by fly-fishermen. Motorized vehicles are not allowed in this area.

Camping

The only camping in the park consists of three backpacking campgrounds in the Marlette/Hobart Backcountry area. These require a three- to six-mile hike in and consist of six tent sites at each.

Nearby Attractions

Since this is a day-use park, you will probably want to stay in one of the resort towns on the lake: **Stateline** or **Incline Village** in Nevada, or **South Lake Tahoe, Tahoe City,** or **Crystal Bay** in California. Among their other attractions, the Nevada cities offer gambling casinos with Las Vegas–style entertainment.

You may want to set aside a half day for a leisurely drive around Lake Tahoe. A narrated auto cassette tour is available for rent at the U.S. Forest Service's **Lake Tahoe Visitors Center** in South Lake Tahoe. This is just one of several cassette tours available; the center also offers free maps, brochures, and a variety of interpretive programs. The Forest Service operates several campgrounds around the lake.

If you want to take a sightseeing tour on the lake, two tour boats operate out of **Zephyr Cove** (tel. 702/588-4591) on Highway 50 north of Stateline.

In winter, the mountains north and west of the lake become ski country with almost two dozen resorts offering both downhill and cross-country skiing.

On the California side, two state parks are worth a visit: **D. L. Bliss** and **Emerald Bay** (tel. 916/525-7232). These two are connected and both have campgrounds, but they're open only in the summer. An attraction here is **Vikingsholm Castle,** a large home built of granite boulders and timbers to resemble a fortress like those used in ancient Scandinavia.

Both Carson City and Reno are easy daytrips away.

Carson City is the state capital and boasts a silver-domed Capitol Building. The **Nevada State Museum** (tel. 702/687-4811) is housed in the former U.S. Mint.

Reno is a little Las Vegas, with flashing neon, gambling, entertainment, and everything else you'd expect in a city that stays open and active 24 hours a day. Reno has several museums, including the **National Automobile Museum** (tel. 702/333-9300), a planetarium on the campus of the University of Nevada–Reno, and an arboretum.

Valley of Fire State Park

Visitor Center | RV Camping | Tent Camping | Primitive Camping | Picnic Areas | Trails | Horse Trails | Nature Programs | Bicycling

Capsule Description: A large desert park with a minimum of developed facilities.

Location: Southeastern Nevada, six miles northwest of Lake Mead and 55 miles northeast of Las Vegas. From Las Vegas, take I-15 north about 33 miles to Exit 75, then Nevada Highway 169 east 18 miles to park headquarters.

Address: P.O. Box 515, Overton, NV 89040 (tel. 702/397-2088).

Area Contacts: Boulder City Chamber of Commerce, 1497 Nevada Hwy., Boulder City, NV 89005 (tel. 702/293-2034).

Las Vegas Convention and Visitors Authority, 3150 Paradise Rd., Las Vegas, NV 89109-9096 (tel. 702/892-0711).

Insider Tip: Most mornings, you'll have a good chance of seeing wild burros near the east entrance.

The Valley of Fire derives its name from the fiery reflection of the sun off the eroded red sandstone formations that dominate the landscape. Nevada's oldest park, it spreads its 36,000 acres over the desert between I-15 and Lake Mead.

Erosion has created many diverse and fascinating formations, including Elephant Rock, the Beehives, and more than 400 arches.

Spring and fall are the preferred seasons for visiting here. Although winters are mild, temperatures can go down to freezing, and summer highs usually exceed 100 degrees. Springtime also sees the desert come alive with wildflowers.

Entrance to this park is free.

Activities

The more you know about the desert, the more you'll be able to see the beauty in it. A good place to start building your knowledge is watching the eight-minute film on the park at the Visitors Center before you start exploring. In addition to the film there are displays on desert life and, outside, a short self-guided nature trail, appropriately named the Cactus Trail.

There are only a few short designated trails in the park, leading to specific formations. One you can take from the Visitors Center is an easy half-mile round-trip walk to Mouse's Tank, a natural basin in the rock where rainwater collects. It is not named after the small rodent, but after an outlaw

Indian who hid out here in the 1890s. Near here are examples of prehistoric Indian rock writing.

There are no other trails designated strictly for hiking for the simple reason that the landscape is wide open and you can hike anywhere. The Visitors Center staff can suggest day hikes of varying length and terrain. Remembering, of course, that desert hiking requires understanding of a different set of rules than hiking in temperate areas. And backpackers who plan to stay overnight require approval from the park supervisor.

To preserve the fragile desert landscape, however, there are designated trails for equestrians and mountain bikers that hikers can also use. These are the seven-mile round-trip trail to the White Domes and the three-mile round-trip Fire Canyon/Silica dome trail.

Aside from the formations on these trails, most of the park's most distinctive formations can be seen from your car or with just a short walk from the main road. The Scenic Loop Road, for example, offers a two-mile trip around some of the valley's most interesting formations, such as Arch Rock and Piano Rock. And a short climb up some steps will take you to Atlatl Rock, the site of many Indian petroglyphs including a depiction of the *atlatl,* a notched stick used to add speed and distance to a thrown spear. The atlatl was a predecessor to the bow and arrow.

Shaded picnic areas, some with water, are located at several places along the main road.

Most desert animals are nocturnal, to avoid the heat of the desert day, so you probably won't see them. Park inhabitants include bighorn sheep, wild burros, and coyotes. Resident birds include ravens and the bird that made it as a famous cartoon character, the roadrunner.

Camping

Two campgrounds with 51 multiuse campsites are located near the west end of the park. No hookups. The 19 sites in Campground A have cold showers and regular restrooms. The rest, in Campground B, have water available and pit toilets. All have shaded picnic tables, but no other shade. No reservations.

Nearby Attractions

If the desert has dried you out and you're seeking water, head to the town of **Overton Beach** (tel. 702/735-1616) on Lake Mead, just 10 miles to the east. A number of small parks, part of the **Lake Mead National Recreation Area,** line the shores of the lake and offer swimming, fishing, and other water sports. With 600 miles of shoreline, Lake Mead is one of the largest man-made lakes in the western hemisphere. It was formed by **Hoover Dam** (tel. 702/293-8320) at Boulder City, about 70 miles south of the park. You can tour the dam every day but Christmas.

Then there's **Las Vegas.** About an hour's drive southwest on I-15, it offers all the gambling and entertainment you can take, plus sightseeing tours by bus, limo, helicopter, or plane, which will zoom you over the Grand Canyon. The city's museums range from the **Guinness World of Records Museum** (tel. 702/792-3766) to the **Liberace Museum** (tel. 702/798-5595) to the **Museum of Natural History** (tel. 702/384-3466) on the University of Nevada–Las Vegas campus. The **Lied Discovery Children's Museum** (tel. 702/382-5437) offers more than 100 hands-on exhibits for the kids.

New Hampshire

FRANCONIA NOTCH
STATE PARK

New Hampshire has 54 state parks.

Contacts

- Division of Parks and Recreation, New Hampshire Department of Resources and Economic Development, P.O. Box 1856, Concord, NH 03302-1856 (tel. 603/271-3255).
- Office of Travel and Tourism, New Hampshire Department of Resources and Economic Development, P.O. Box 1856, Concord, NH 03302-1856 (tel. 603/271-2666; toll free 800/386-4664 ext. 145 for free New Hampshire guidebook only, 800/258-3608 for recorded statewide events and ski conditions only, 800/262-6660 cross-country, 800/258-3608 alpine).

General Information on New Hampshire State Parks

Two of the many attractions of the Granite State are Mt. Washington, at 6,228 feet, the highest peak in the Northeast, and the granite profile of the Old Man of the Mountain at Franconia Notch. Both are in state parks.

New Hampshire has only 18 miles of shoreline on the Atlantic, but more than half that is public lands that includes a half-dozen beach parks. And since this is a state with rolling mountains, there are mountain parks, a number of which have popular ski areas. No matter where it is, each park seems to be designed to cover as many bases as possible. For example, the tiny Nansen Park has picnic sites, a boat launch for fishing the river, and a ski jump. Ski areas with chair lifts are set up to carry skiers up the slopes in winter and sightseers to bird's-eye viewpoints in the warmer months.

All parks are open year-round; however, some facilities only operate spring through fall.

GENERAL FEES

Many parks charge admission, but normally only during that park's high season. Discount coupon books are available.

CAMPING

There are about 1,500 developed campsites in about a dozen parks and another 100 primitive sites in four others. Most are for tent camping, but some will take RVs. Only a handful have hookups. Developed sites go for about $14 per night. Most sites are on a first-come basis, but a few RV sites may be reserved.

Pets. Pets are not permitted in some state parks. Where permitted, they must be on a leash and under control at all times.

Alcoholic beverages. Generally permitted. Rules vary from park to park depending on local laws. Statewide, liquor can only be purchased in state liquor stores.

Discounts. Special rates and other offerings are available to New Hampshire residents age 65 or older.

Franconia Notch State Park

Visitor Center | Restaurant | RV Camping | Tent Camping | Primitive Camping | Boat Launch | Non-Motorized Boating Only | Fishing | Beach

Snorkeling & Diving | Picnic Areas | Trails | Nature Programs | Bicycling | X-Country Skiing | Downhill Skiing | Snowmobiling | Gift Shop

Capsule Description: A large, developed park with a number of well-known tourist attractions, in the mountains surrounded by a national forest.

Location: North-central New Hampshire. I-93/U.S. Highway 3 (Franconia Notch Parkway) bisects the park. Exits 1, 2, and 3 all lead to various sections of the park.

Address: Franconia Notch State Park, Franconia, NH 03580 (tel. 603/823-5563 all year, 603/745-8391 for Flume Visitor Center mid-May through October only).

Area Contacts: Franconia/Easton/Sugar Hill Chamber of Commerce, P.O. Box 780, Franconia, NH 03580 (tel. toll free 800/237-9007 or 603/823-5661).

Lincoln/Woodstock Chamber of Commerce, P.O. Box 358, Lincoln, NH 03251 (tel. toll free 800/227-4191 or 603/745-6621).

White Mountains Attractions, P.O. Box 10, North Woodstock, NH 03262 (tel. toll free 800/346-3687 or 603/745-8720).

Insider Tip: This park was listed as one of the twelve best state parks in America by *Money* magazine.

Immortalized by Nathaniel Hawthorne, in his 1850 tale of "The Great Stone Face," the rock profile of the Old Man of the Mountain looks out over this 6,500-acre park set in the midst of an eight-mile-long, narrow, glacial valley with peaks reaching up to 5,000 feet on both sides. The park is surrounded by the 730,000-acre White Mountains National Forest.

The term "notch" is a local version of what would be called a mountain pass or gap in other areas. Since Franconia Notch is an important corridor between north and south, it was decided to include it in the Interstate highway system. This sparked two decades of controversy and, finally, compromise. To reduce the impact on the park and its natural beauty, the approximately eight-mile section of I-93 that goes through the park was built as a two-lane scenic parkway with a reduced speed limit. It is one of only two sections of the Interstate system in the country that is not up to that system's four-lane standard.

There is no admission to the park itself, so you can view the Old Man and a number of other natural features without paying for it; however, there are separate charges for the Flume, the Cannon Mountain Aerial Tramway, and the beach. If you plan to visit more than one of the admission areas in the park, ask about a combination ticket.

Activities

The Old Man is a rock profile made up of five ledges that measure 40 feet from chin to forehead and is 25 feet wide. It hovers majestically 1,200 feet over Profile Lake, a clear, 15-acre lake, sometimes called the Old Man's Mirror or the Old Man's Washbowl.

Another natural attraction here is the Flume, a gorge 12 to 20 feet wide with granite walls that rise to heights of 70 to 90 feet enclosing a swift flowing brook. A boardwalk goes through the gorge to the 45-foot Avalanche Falls.

The story of the Flume and other park attractions is told in exhibits at the Flume Visitor's Center. Here you can see a 15-minute film on the notch. Some of the park's interpretive programs are given here, in season. Open from mid-May through October, the center also has a cafeteria and gift shop. From here it's about three-quarters of a mile to the gorge. You can walk it or take a bus part of the way. The route takes you across one of the oldest covered bridges in the state.

Profile Lake is one of three glacial lakes in the park. It and Echo Lake are on the valley floor while Lonesome Lake is tucked into the mountains requiring a hike of about 45 minutes to reach it. Brook trout is the only species here with low-catch limits, so most fishing is catch-and-release. Fly-fishing only at Profile Lake and trolling motors only there to keep from disturbing the fly-fishermen. In the fall, you can watch brook trout use a fish ladder at Profile Lake as they head up the brook to the breeding pond to spawn.

Echo Lake has a swimming beach with lifeguards, and boat, canoe, paddleboat, and kayak rentals. Scuba diving and windsurfing are permitted in this lake, but no waterskiing. You can fish for the trout with regular gear here.

Access to hundreds of miles of hiking trails rated at all levels of difficulty begin in this park. Many of the trails stay within the park boundaries, including short, easy-to-walk nature trails as well as longer hiking trails. However, there are also connections to the many miles of trails in the surrounding national forest, and a section of the 2,034-mile Appalachian Trail—which runs from Springer Mountain, Georgia, to Mount Katahdin, Maine—goes through the notch. The Appalachian Mountain Club operates a mountain hut that'll accommodate 36 hikers near Lonesome Lake. (Reservations: tel. 603/466-2727.)

Bikers have a nine-mile paved trail that runs the length of the notch, and there are bikes for rent. The trail ties in with many miles of forestry roads for mountain bikers in the national forest.

Although you probably won't see them, normal residents of the park include black bears, deer, moose, porcupine, raccoons, bobcats, beavers, and even mink. Nearly 100 species of birds have been recorded in the park, including peregrine falcons that nest in Eagle Cliff, so called because eagles nested there until the late 1890s.

An 80-passenger aerial tram hoists you in a five-minute trip to the spectacular views of three states at the 4,180-foot summit of Cannon Mountain. If you want to see more, you can walk the 1,500-foot Rim Trail up there. This was the first passenger aerial tramway built in North America and had a great deal to do with building the skiing industry in the state.

In winter, the tram is one way to get up to the heights in the Cannon Mountain Ski Area. With an average snowfall of 156 inches a year and the highest vertical drop of any ski mountain in New Hampshire, this area offers 22 miles of downhill skiing on 35 trails, ranging from novice to expert. For families, the ski area has a nursery, child care, and ski-school programs for kids available during the season. Cross-country skiers have several miles of trails in the park and access to many more miles in the area. Snowboarding is also popular here. The New England Ski Museum is located at the foot of the tramway.

Camping

The 98 **campsites** in the Lafayette Campground are mostly for tents, but some will hold small RVs. However, there are no hookups and no reservations. Sites go for about $14 per night. There are seven RV sites with full hookups at Echo Lake. These cost about twice the fee at Lafayette and may be reserved by calling 603/823-5563. Campgrounds are open mid-May to mid-October. Free primitive camping is permitted November through April.

Nearby Attractions

To the south, in the towns of **Lincoln** and **North Woodstock,** you can see steam engines and trained bears at **Clark's Trading Post** (tel. 603/745-8913), tour the geological formations of **Lost River Gorge** (tel. 603/745-8031), or play in a water park, **Whale's Tale** (tel. 603/745-8810).

If you take the scenic Kancamagus Highway about an hour's drive to the east, you can visit **Mt. Washington,** at 6,288 feet, the highest peak in the Northeast. At the summit is the 52-acre **Mt. Washington State Park.** This mountain has earned the title of the "Home of the World's Worst Weather" by recording a world-record wind of 231 miles per hour and average temperature lows that would match temperatures in the Arctic. Days of clear visibility are rare on this mountain, but if you hit one you'll have a bird's-eye view from Canada to the Atlantic Ocean. A museum has exhibits that explain the mountain's harsh weather. The hale and hearty can hike or bike to the summit, or you can drive the auto toll road (tel. 603/466-3988), or ride the **cog railroad** (tel. toll free 800/922-8825 ext. 5) from the town of Bretton Woods.

In Franconia, north of Lincoln, is **Robert Frost Place** (tel. 603/823-5510), where the poet lived at one time; it's open Memorial Day to Labor Day.

New Jersey

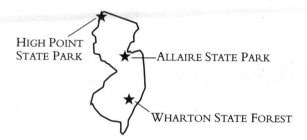

HIGH POINT STATE PARK

ALLAIRE STATE PARK

WHARTON STATE FOREST

New Jersey has 79 state parks.

Contacts

- Division of Parks and Forestry, Department of Environmental Protection and Energy, CN 404, 501 East State St., Trenton, NJ 08625-0404 (tel. 609/292-2797).
- Division of Travel and Tourism, Department of Commerce and Economic Development, CN 826, 20 West State St., Trenton, NJ 08625-0826 (tel. toll free 800/537-7397).

General Information on New Jersey State Parks

Too often, people think of New Jersey in terms of heavy industry and the densely populated towns across the river from New York City. But a short trip in almost any direction away from that area will quickly reveal that this state is much more than that. New Jersey has the third-largest park system in the country, managing a total of over 300,000 acres. Matching the state in diversity, the parks range from sandy beaches on the 127 miles of Atlantic shoreline to snow-covered mountains to pristine lakes to pine wilderness.

GENERAL FEES

There is an entrance fee to most parks during the summer season. This ranges from a $1 walk-in fee to about $3 up to about $8 per car depending on the day of the week and the popularity of the park. Some parks have a lower off-season entrance fee.

CAMPING AND ACCOMMODATIONS

There are campgrounds in 17 parks offering a total of close to 1,350 **campsites.** About 10 park campgrounds remain open all year; the rest are closed in the winter. Most sites are multiuse, but a few parks are tent only because the roads and sites cannot take large vehicles. No hookups. Campsites go for about $10 a night. A couple of parks also offer primitive/hike-in/boat-in sites at about $8 per night and three offer closed (four-sided) or open (three-sided) Adirondack-type lean-tos at $12 to $15.

Approximately one-third of the campsites in each campground can be reserved by calling the park direct. All others are on a first-come basis. Applications for reservations are accepted starting November 1. From June 15 through Labor Day, campsites must be reserved for exactly 7- or 14-night periods. The remainder of the year reservations are accepted from 2 to 14 nights. No phone reservations are accepted and there is a reservation fee of $7.

Six parks offer **cabins** that range in sleeping capacity from 4 to 12 persons. These may be reserved, with priority going to New Jersey residents. Since there are relatively few cabins, if demand dictates, and it often does in high season, a lottery is used to pick the winning reservations.

Reservation application must be submitted on a form available from the Parks and Forestry Division. Depending on location, size, and time of year, cabins rent from a low of about $30 up to $100 per night. Weekly rates are available.

Pets. In general, pets are permitted in day-use areas only. They are not allowed in campgrounds or swimming areas. Where permitted, they must be on a leash and under control at all times.

Alcoholic beverages. Alcoholic beverages are not permitted in state parks.

Discounts. New Jersey residents age 62 and older or totally disabled residents are eligible for a pass entitling them to free admission and free parking at all parks.

Allaire State Park

Visitor Center | RV Camping | Tent Camping | Non-Motorized Boating Only | Fishing

Picnic Areas | Trails | Horse Trails | Nature Programs | Bicycling | Golf | Playground | X-Country Skiing | Gift Shop

Capsule Description: A medium-sized park with a combination of preserved natural areas and developed facilities.

Location: Central New Jersey near the shore. From I-195, take Exit 31B and follow signs. From Garden State Parkway, take Exit 98. Follow Route 34 south to first traffic light. Turn right onto Allenwood Road. Proceed on Allenwood to Route 524 (Allaire Road). Turn right. Park entrance approximately one mile on the left.

Address: P.O. Box 220, Farmingdale, NJ 07727 (tel. 908/938-2371 or 908/938-2372).

Area Contacts: Greater Asbury Park Chamber of Commerce, P.O. Box 649, Asbury Park, NJ 07712 (tel. 908/775-7676).

Farmingdale Chamber of Commerce, P.O. Box 534, Farmingdale, NJ 07727 (tel. 908/294-4575).

Monmouth County Department of Promotion/Tourism, 25 E. Main St., Freehold, NJ 07728 (tel. toll free 800/523-2587).

Trenton Convention and Visitors Bureau, CN 206, Trenton, NJ 08625-0206 (tel. 609/777-1770).

Best known for its historic village, this 3,008-acre park also offers the opportunity for year-round recreational activities.

The village dates back to the early 1800s when it grew up around a pig-iron foundry that used the local bog-iron ore. During the 30 years that the village prospered, there were as many as 500 people living in the area. James P. Allaire, the owner, also had a foundry in New York City and it was there he personally cast the brass air chamber for Robert Fulton's famous *Clermont*.

The discovery of high grades of iron ore in Pennsylvania led to the decline of business and the furnace fires were extinguished in 1848. Over the next century the village earned the name the Deserted Village. It was donated to the state for a park in 1941, but there were no funds for restoration. Finally, in 1957, a nonprofit corporation started a continuing fund drive that got the restoration underway. It continues up to the present.

Activities

The village grounds are open all year, but during the summer, Allaire Village is a living museum. Most of the buildings are open and feature artifacts of the period of the village's heyday. Costumed interpreters demonstrate various 19th-century crafts. The Visitor Center and the Enameling Furnace Building feature rotating historical displays. Many historic events are re-created on weekends during the season.

The village opens weekends in May, then daily from Memorial Day to Labor Day, and weekends again well into October.

The Pine Creek Railroad, the only full-size, live-steam, narrow-gauge train in New Jersey, also operates in the park during the same months. Its less-than-a-mile route takes about 15 minutes to ride.

For golfers, there's an 18-hole course.

If you want to get back to nature, the park has 11 miles of marked trails including a self-guided nature trail. Some are designated for hikers only, but others are multiuse trails: hikers, horses, and mountain bikes. There are no stables in the park, but the horse trails begin and end near private stables. Hikers have a good chance of seeing white-tailed deer, raccoons, opossums, and other small animals.

During the winter, if there's enough snow—which doesn't happen every year—the trails are open for cross-country skiing.

More than 200 varieties of wildflowers have been cataloged in the park, and it is a good place for birding during the migrating seasons since it is a feeding and resting place for birds on the Atlantic Flyway. Observation blinds for birders and photographers are available in the park's wetlands.

Frequent trout stocking of the Manasquan River, which runs through the park, assures excellent fishing for anglers. Brook, brown, golden, and rainbow trout are all stocked. Other catches include largemouth bass, perch, and sunfish.

Children under 14 years of age may fish in the Village Mill Pond. Trout and various species of freshwater panfish are stocked here for them.

The river is also popular for canoeing. No rentals in the park, but there are some close by.

Camping

Fifty-five multiuse campsites are located in a wooded area about a mile from the village. No hookups. They are open all year and go for about $10. One-third of these sites may be reserved.

Nearby Attractions

There's no swimming in the park, but to the east, a half-dozen resort towns on the New Jersey shore are just a short drive away. Probably the best known of these is **Asbury Park.** In addition to the town's famed boardwalk and beach, it claims to be the birthplace of saltwater taffy.

To the northeast, near the junction of U.S. 9 and New Jersey Route 33, is **Monmouth Battlefield State Park** (tel. 908/462-9616). Here, on June 28, 1778, after the bitter winter at Valley Forge, Washington led his army to victory against the British.

If you have kids, take I-195 west to Exit 16, then south a mile to **Six Flags Great Adventure** (tel. 908/928-2000), the state's largest theme park. Continue west on I-195 and you'll soon be in **Trenton,** the state capital. Sights worth a visit here include the second-oldest **capitol building** (tel. 609/292-2121) in the U.S. and the **New Jersey State Museum** (tel. 609/292-6300).

High Point State Park

Visitor Center

Cabins & Cottages

RV Camping

Tent Camping

Primitive Camping

Group Camping

Group Lodge Dormitories

Non-Motorized Boating Only

Fishing

Beach

Picnic Areas

Trails

Horse Trails

Nature Programs

Bicycling

Playground

X-Country Skiing

Snowmobiling

Capsule Description: A large, natural park with developed facilities.

Location: The extreme northwest corner of the state, at the New York and Pennsylvania borders. From Sussex, take New Jersey Route 23 eight miles northwest to the park entrance.

Address: 1480 State Rte. 23, Sussex, NJ 07461 (tel. 201/875-4800).

Area Contacts: Skylands Region Tourism Council, 3117 Rte. 10 East, Denville, NJ 07834 (tel. 201/366-6889).

Insider Tip: You can avoid the admission charge, which is collected from Memorial Day to Labor Day, by visiting on any Tuesday, a free day.

Forming the northwestern border of the state is the Kittatinny ridge, 36 miles long, narrow, and relatively flat with an average height of 1,600 feet. The appropriately named High Point State Park caps the summit of this ridge at 1,803 feet.

High Point was dedicated as New Jersey's first state park in 1923. In the late 1920s, a 220-foot obelisk was built on the highest point. Dedicated to New Jersey's war heroes, it has 200 steps inside that go to the top where a small window offers hearty climbers a panoramic view. Unfortunately, the windows do not open and it's a difficult task to get to them for cleaning, so the view is rarely worth the effort. On the other hand, the view from the base of the monument is almost as spectacular. You can see a large section of northern New Jersey's farms and woodlands to the east and south, and, on a clear day, Pennsylvania's Pocono Mountains on the west, and New York's Catskill Mountains on the north.

One sight that pops up from a variety of viewpoints in the park is the hulk of the old High Point Inn. Founded in the late 1880s, it went through various restorations, including being turned into the summer mansion of the Kusers, who donated the land for the park to the state, winding up as the park office. Unfortunately, it was closed because of excessive maintenance costs and now sits as a reminder of a bygone era.

In the 1930s, the depression-era Civilian Conservation Corp (CCC) built much of the 14,000-acre park's basics, including the dams that formed two of the park's three lakes—the other is a glacial lake.

In addition to being the state's first state park, it is also the site of the state's first natural area. The 850-acre Dryden Kuser Natural Area, located in the north end of the park, starts at the New York State border and extends south about a mile. It features a distinctive bog, locally called the Cedar Swamp. The self-guided Cedar Swamp Trail makes a mile and a half loop around the bog.

Activities

For hikers, there are 10 color-marked trails in the park plus a stretch of the Appalachian Trail. In distance they vary from less than a half mile to over four miles and range from easy walking to difficult rocky terrain that will offer a challenge to those who want it. In addition, there is a 1½-mile self-guided loop nature trail around the bog in the natural area, and the section of the 2,100-mile Maine-to-Georgia Appalachian Trail corridor runs north and south on the east side of the park.

All but two of the trails are also open for equestrians and mountain bikers.

In winter, provided the snow is deep enough, several of the trails are open for cross-country skiing. There are also snowmobile trails that extend into the adjoining state forest, and dog sledding is becoming a popular winter activity.

There are observation platforms for birders and nature photographers. Birders have spotted close to 90 species including more than a half-dozen varieties of hawks. Among the animals you might see in the park are white-tailed deer, black bears, river otters, weasels, mink, raccoons, skunks, and porcupines.

There is a swimming beach on Lake Marcia, the 20-acre natural lake. Lifeguards are on duty during the summer and swimming is permitted only when they are on duty. You can fish this lake, too, but only from the shore; no boats. Rowboats with electric trolling motors are permitted on the other two lakes—Steenykill and Sawmill. Catches include largemouth bass, catfish, perch, and, in Sawmill only, trout. You can also canoe on these two, although most canoeists prefer the Delaware River, which is about four miles from the park.

Camping and Accommodations

There are two six-bunk rustic **cabins** with fireplaces on Lake Steenykill available from mid-May through mid-October. They go for about $42 a night but are rented by a reservation lottery. For groups, there's one cabin accommodating up to 32 people.

Some of the 50 **campsites** are on one of the lakes. Although the sites can be used for both tent and RV camping, there are no hookups and most sites are in areas that do not have maneuver room for a large RV. The campground is open from April through October and sites cost $10 per night. Primitive camping is permitted in sites along the Appalachian Trail.

Nearby Attractions

Adjacent to the park on the west and south are the **Delaware Water Gap National Recreation Area** (tel. 717/588-2451) and the **Stokes State Forest** (tel. 201/948-3820).

Going east and south, on easy daytrips, you can visit **Action Park** (tel. 201/827-2000) in Vernon, a theme park with a wave pool and other rides; **Fairy Tale Forest** (tel. 201/697-5656) in Newfoundland, and the **Space Farm Zoo and Museum** (tel. 201/875-5800) in Beamerville. In winter, both **Vernon Valley** (tel. 201/827-2000) and **Craigmeur** (tel. 201/697-4500) in Newfoundland offer downhill skiing.

Interested in a calm or white-water trip on the Delaware? Head for the **Port Jervis**, New York, area, just a few miles north of the park. **White-Water Willies** (tel. toll free 800/233-7238) and **Silver Canoe Rentals** (tel. toll free 800/724-8342) offer canoe, kayak, and raft trips.

Wharton State Forest

Visitor
Center

Cabins &
Cottages

RV
Camping

Tent
Camping

Primitive
Camping

Group
Camping

Boat
Launch

Non-
Motorized
Boating
Only

Fishing

Beach

Picnic
Areas

Trails

Horse
Trails

Nature
Programs

Bicycling

Playground

Gift Shop

Capsule Description: A huge wilderness park with some developed facilities.

Location: South-central New Jersey. From U.S. Highway 30, take New Jersey Route 542 at Hammonton about eight miles northeast to Visitors Center at Batsto.

Address: RD no. 9 Batsto, Hammonton, NJ 08037 (tel. 609/561-0024 for the office, 609/561-3262 for the Visitors Center).

Area Contacts: Atlantic City Convention and Visitors Bureau, 2314 Pacific Ave., Atlantic City, NJ 08401 (tel. 609/348-7100).

Greater Atlantic City Region Tourism Council, P.O. Box 7457, Atlantic City, NJ 08404 (tel. 609/345-1722).

Greater Hammonton Chamber of Commerce, P.O. Box 554, Hammonton, NJ 08037 (tel. 609/561-9080).

With about 109,000 acres spread across three counties in the state's Pine Barrens region, this is the largest park in the state system.

From its beginnings in about 1766, through the Revolutionary War and well past the War of 1812, the bog-iron industry flourished in the Batsto area, producing all sorts of iron products from pipes to firebacks to cannonballs. But by the mid-1800s this industry had died and the village of Batsto died with it. Today, Batsto has been restored as a historic site where you can catch a glimpse into the life of this early iron-making settlement.

In 1876, John Wharton moved here and started buying up land. It was his intention to dam several of the streams that feed the four rivers that run through the forest, create reservoirs, and pipe and sell the water to Philadelphia, 40 miles away. But the New Jersey Legislature, aware of the value of its water resources, refused to allow it to be exported. So, Wharton gave up his grandiose scheme and went into timber and agriculture. The state acquired the land from the Wharton estate in the 1950s.

Recreational areas have been developed at Atsion, Batsto, and Crowley Landing, but the majority of the park remains undeveloped in order to preserve the natural habitat. There are three designated natural areas in the forest.

Activities

The Batsto Historic Site consists of some 39 restored buildings including a general store, blacksmith shop, sawmill, gristmill, mansion, and worker's cottages. The oldest operating post office in the state is in the restored village post office. There's a park entrance fee from Memorial Day to Labor Day, but once inside the park you can poke around the historic site for free, except for a fee for tours of the 36-room Batsto Mansion.

Nearly 200 miles of sand roads in the park are open year-round for hiking, horseback riding, and mountain biking. The 50-mile-long Batona Trail

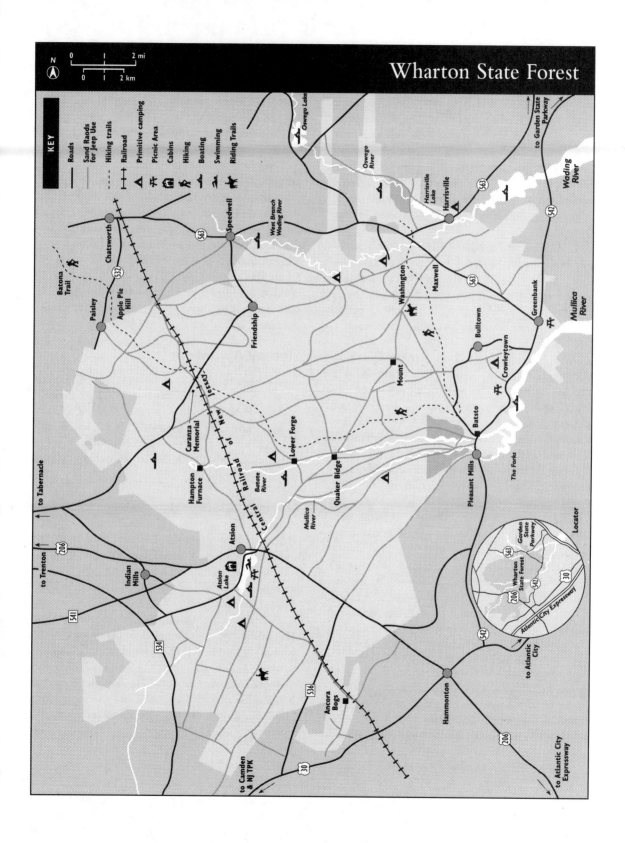

Wharton State Forest

KEY

——	Roads
——	Sand Roads for Jeep Use
----	Hiking trails
‡‡‡	Railroad
▲	Primitive camping
⌂	Picnic Area
🏠	Cabins
🚶	Hiking
🚣	Boating
🏊	Swimming
🏇	Riding Trails

0 — 1 — 2 mi
0 — 1 — 2 km

N

Locator

Batona Trail

Paisley

Chatsworth

Apple Pie Hill

Speedwell

West Branch Wading River

Oswego Lake

Oswego River

Harrisville Lake

Harrisville

563

542

to Garden State Parkway

Wading River

Mullica River

Greenbank

Washington

Maxwell

563

Bulltown

Crowleytown

Batsto

Friendship

Mount

Lower Forge

Quaker Bridge

Hampton Furnace

Caranza Memorial

Batsto River

Mullica River

Pleasant Mills

The Forks

Atsion

Atsion Lake

Indian Mills

541

534

206

to Trenton

to Tabernacle

Railroad of New Jersey

Central

536

30

Ancora Bogs

Hammonton

206

to Atlantic City Expressway

to Camden & NJ TPK

537

to Atlantic City

542

563

206

542

30

Garden State Parkway

Wharton State Forest

Atlantic City Expressway

goes through the park near Batsto on its way across the Pine Barrens wilderness from Lebanon State Forest to Bass River State Forest. The trail crosses a number of roads, so, if you just want to hike a piece of it, you can probably reach a good starting point by car. Horses and mountain bikes are not permitted on this trail. There is also a mile-long self-guided nature trail in the Batsto Natural Area. A brochure for this is available at the Batsto Nature Center.

If you're a hearty hiker with a yen for a bird's-eye view, the Batona Trail will take you to an 85-foot fire tower at Apple Pie Hill in the northern section of the park. On the way you'll pass close by a unique memorial to a Mexican pilot, Emilio Caranza—considered the Lindbergh of Mexico—who crashed here.

The Mullica, one of four rivers that flow through the park, is classified as a National Wild and Scenic River. This a favorite park for canoeing. Conveniently located entry and exit points on the rivers make it easy to have trips of varying length. Only electric trolling motors are permitted in the park. There is one public ramp, at Crowley Landing on the Mullica River, but powerboats can only use it to go down river, not up into the park. Canoes, small boat, and paddleboat rentals are available from **Adams Canoe Rental** (tel. 609/268-0189) in the Atsion area. The lake there is also popular for windsurfing.

You can fish anywhere in the park where it's not specifically prohibited by signs. Catches include bass, pickerel, catfish, perch, and sunfish.

You can swim at Atsion Lake. From Memorial Day to Labor Day, lifeguards are on duty and an entrance fee is charged ($5 per car weekdays; $7 per car on weekends and holidays).

Camping and Accommodations

Nine **cabins,** located on the shore of Atsion Lake, are available from April 1 through October 31.

Seven can accommodate four persons and the other two eight persons. The smaller cabins rent for $28 per night, the larger for $56. Weekly rates are available. Reservations must be submitted on the Parks and Forestry form.

There are nine camping areas, but all but two are for groups. The two family camping areas are: 50 **campsites** at the Atsion Lake Recreation Area and 49 sites at Godfrey Bridge. Campgrounds are open all year and one-third of the sites may be reserved. Multiuse, but no hookups. Depending on location and facilities, sites go for $8 to $10.

Two primitive camping areas, with about 50 sites each, can be reached by canoe or backpacking.

Nearby Attractions

From the park, the Jersey Shore is about 20 miles away (30 minutes by car), and you can easily make a daytrip to some of the resort towns such as **Margate City** or **Ocean City** for some saltwater swimming. At the southern end of Ocean City, **Corson's Inlet State Park** has a free beach; you can also buy a daily beach tag in Ocean City for $3.

A major lure is the glitter and entertainment of **Atlantic City,** at the southeastern end of U.S. 30. Revitalized by gambling, Atlantic City has five miles of beaches, a world-renowned boardwalk (dating from 1870), and resort hotels and casinos, such as **Caesar's** (tel 609/348-4411) and the **Taj Mahal** (tel. 609/449-1000).

Northwest of Atlantic City on U.S. 30 in **Egg Harbor City,** the **Renault Winery** (tel. 609/965-2111) has a champagne and wine glass museum.

North of Absecon on U.S. 9 is the town of **Smithville,** with an **antique center** (tel. 609/652-4044), restaurants, and amusement rides.

New Mexico

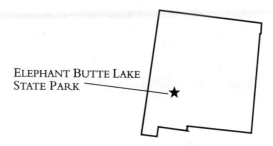

Elephant Butte Lake State Park

New Mexico has 37 state parks.

Contacts

- New Mexico State Parks and Recreation Division, P.O. Box 1147, Santa Fe, NM 87504 (tel. 505/827-7465; toll free 800/451-2541 in New Mexico only).
- New Mexico Department of Tourism, 491 Old Sante Fe Trail, Lamy Building, Santa Fe, NM 87503 (tel. toll free 800/545-2040).

General Information on New Mexico State Parks

Called "The Land of Enchantment," New Mexico is also a land of contrasts that range from the Chihuahuan Desert in the south to the vast eastern plains to the high mountains of the north. The parks are scattered throughout the state to provide an opportunity to enjoy this wide variety of terrain and environments. They offer the chance for outdoor activities that include desert hikes and rock-hounding, all sorts of water sports in the 15 lake parks, and skiing in the mountains.

Most parks are open all year.

Three groups of Native Americans call this state home: Pueblo, Apache, and Navajo. However, each is a nation itself. They live within the state under their own sovereign rule on lands that belong to them. A number of their villages are within an easy drive of state parks and visitors are welcome.

General Fees

Most parks have an entrance or day-use fee of about $3 per vehicle. Annual passes are available. Walk-ins are free.

Camping

Four parks have **cabins** available through concessionaires. They may be reserved and go for about $60 to $80 a night.

There are **campgrounds** in all the parks except two day-use-only parks and two nature center parks. Some sites have hookups. Campsites range from $6 to $13 depending on facilities. Reservations are accepted only at Elephant Butte Lake State Park and then only on a small number of sites. There is a reservation fee of $7. All others are on a first-come basis. Annual camping permits are also available. Camping is limited to 14 days in any 20-day period.

Pets. Where pets are permitted, they must be on a leash no more than 10 feet long and under control at all times. Pets are not allowed in the two nature center parks or Smoky Bear Historical State Parks.

Alcoholic beverages. Although alcoholic beverages are permitted in most parks, there are exceptions where consumption may be prohibited.

Discounts. Annual entrance and camping permits are available at a discount to senior citizens, age 62 and older, and handicapped/disabled persons.

Elephant Butte Lake State Park

Visitor Center   Restaurant   Cabins & Cottages   RV Camping   Tent Camping   Primitive Camping   Marina   Boating

Boat Launch   Fishing   Swimming   Waterskiing   Snorkeling & Diving   Picnic Areas   Trails   Nature Programs   Bicycling   Playground

Capsule Description: A large, lake park with developed facilities.

Location: Southwest New Mexico. Take Exit 76 off I-25. Follow signs through the city of Truth or Consequences about five miles to the park entrance.

Address: P.O. Box 13, Elephant Butte, NM 87935 (tel. 505/744-5421).

Area Contacts: Truth or Consequences/Sierra County Chamber of Commerce, P.O. Box 31, Truth or Consequences, NM 87901 (tel. 505/894-3536).

Insider Tip: In the off-season, campers can get seven days for the price of five.

The park covers the shoreline of the largest body of water in the state, a reservoir impoundment of the Rio Grande covering 35,000 surface acres. With that as a desert draw, it's no wonder that this park has the highest number of visitors of any New Mexico state park. Over holiday weekends, like Memorial Day weekend, it has enough visitors to rank as the second-largest populated area in the state.

Fortunately, the 24,500-acres of parkland stretches out along the 40-mile long man-made lake with 200 miles of shoreline, so even on the major holidays, if you want peace and quiet, you can find it.

Although fossils of the stegomastodon, the primitive relative of today's elephant, have been found here, the lake is not named after them. Instead it refers to the eroded core of an ancient volcano from when this was a land of fire millions of years ago. Now an island in the lake, it resembles the shape of an elephant's head. (Fossils of the Tyrannosaurus rex dinosaur have also been discovered in area rock formations.)

Activities

Swimming, boating, waterskiing, fishing—if it's a water sport, you can find somewhere to do it here. Most of the facilities are around the Visitor Center and the dam area at the south end of the lake, but the lake is open just about anywhere you want to go. For example, there's no designated swimming area, you just go in anyplace the water looks inviting. Some of the beach areas can all but disappear, however, when the lake is high. The lake is three miles across at its widest point.

For boaters there are three full-service marinas—the one near the dam includes a restaurant—and three boat-launching ramps, one with 10 lanes. All types of water-sports equipment can be rented at the marinas from jet skis to paddle bikes to windsurfing gear. Classes on how to use them are offered. During the year there are a number of races and competitions for just about every type of boat and water vehicle.

Fishing is good in the lake for black, white, and striped bass; crappie; catfish; and walleyed pike. A state-record striped bass weighing in at 54 pounds 4 ounces was taken here. You can also try for trout in the river and scuba diving for game fish is allowed.

For your time on land, you can hike or bike the shoreline and there's a marked nature trail, a little over half a mile long, near the Visitor Center. A free guide to the trail is available. A designated birdwatching area is found on an overlook near the dam. More than 100 species of birds have been seen in the area ranging from the bald eagle to a variety of hummingbirds. Away from the congested area, you have a good chance of spotting mule deer and wild turkey. West of the restaurant is a walk shaded by grape vines that drape over a natural stone-columned arbor.

During high season the staff conducts interpretive and nature programs.

Camping and Accommodations

A concessionaire rents 19 **cabins** with kitchenettes near the dam. They cost $60 to $80 per night. For information and reservations call 505/894-2073.

There are 106 multiuse **campsites** with electric and water hookups. Twenty of these can be reserved between February 15 and September 30. Most sites are close together and there is virtually no shade, but the site picnic tables are covered. Developed campsites go for about $11.

Nearby Attractions

The nearby town with the unique moniker was originally called Hot Springs—many resorts here still offer mineral baths—but then in 1950, Ralph Edwards, producer of the most popular radio game show of the time, asked the town to change its name to that of the show, "Truth or Consequences." The townspeople cast their votes, and the yeas had it. Each May since then, Ralph Edwards comes to visit the town of **Truth or Consequences** and a festival is held. The **Geronimo Museum** (tel. 505/894-6600) on Main Street has exhibits on Native American history, a Spanish Heritage Room, and a Ralph Edwards Room.

Northwest of Truth or Consequences are two "ghost towns"—**Winston** (38 miles) and **Chloride** (42 miles). Both are reached by car via I-25 and New Mexico Highway 52. In these old cowboy towns, you'll see abandoned buildings and the pit of an old silver mine in Chloride.

The historic gold-, silver-, and copper-mining towns of **Hillsboro** and **Kingston** lie southwest of Truth or Consequences. Take I-25 and New Mexico 152 to get to them; Hillsboro is 32 miles away; Kingston, 41 miles. An inactive gold mine sits outside of the one-street town of Hillsboro, which offers an art gallery, museum, café, and motel. The surrounding country has cattle ranches.

New York

NIAGARA RESERVATION
STATE PARK

SARATOGA SPA STATE PARK

WATKINS GLEN STATE PARK

LETCHWORTH STATE PARK

JONES BEACH STATE PARK

New York has 200 state parks.

Contacts

- Office of Parks, Recreation, and Historic Preservation, Empire State Plaza, Albany, NY 12238
  (tel. 518/474-0456).
- Department of Environmental Conservation, 50
  Wolf Rd., Albany, NY 12233 (tel. 518/457-
  2500, for Adirondack Park camping information).
- Division of Tourism, Department of Economic
  Development, One Commerce Plaza, Albany
  12245 (tel. toll free 800/CALL-NYS [800/225-
  5697] or 518/474-4116).

General Information on New York State Parks

The Empire State offers an empire of state parks
encompassing over 260,000 acres and a variety
that's hard to beat. Among its many claims to fame,
the state park system contains the nation's oldest
state park, Niagara Reservation; the largest
bathing facility complex in the world at Jones
Beach State Park; the largest publicly operated golf
facility in the country at Bethpage State Park; and
Artpark, the only state park in the nation dedicated entirely to the visual and performing arts.
Among its other firsts are the first state historic site
in America at Washington's Headquarters in

Newburgh, and the first state nature center in the
Trailside Museum at Bear Mountain.

And all this does not include the area loosely
known as Adirondack State Park, which comes
under the jurisdiction of the Department of
Environmental Conservation. Adirondack Park
covers six million acres—about the size of
Connecticut—the largest wilderness area east of
the Mississippi. This park is not one of the *100
Best-Loved,* however, only because it is not feasible
to cover in terms of this book. Larger in size than
all but two national parks (both in Alaska), it has
more than 100 towns and villages with hundreds
more private than public recreational facilities
within its boundaries, all of which puts it outside
our scope.

GENERAL FEES

There is a day-use/admission fee of about $4 a car
for the beach parks and $3 for nonbeach parks. In
most parks it's only collected during the summer
season, Memorial Day weekend to Labor Day.
There's a small additional fee for the use of park
pools.

CAMPING AND ACCOMMODATIONS

Three parks have a **hotel/inn.** The ones at Bear
Mountain and Saratoga Spa are open all year. The
inn at Letchworth is only open from April until
early November.

There is a total of 765 **cabins** in about two

dozen of the parks. Most are rustic cabins with minimum facilities. Some are winterized, but the majority are only for summer rental. Reservations from early June through Labor Day may be made for one or two full weeks only. Most cabins have a capacity of four persons; however, a number will hold six and eight. Fees range from about $30 to $70 per night with weekly rates about four times the daily rate.

More than 8,300 **campsites** are available in the parks. Most sites are multiuse. The basic fee runs from $9 to $15 with additional charges for hookups, when available.

Reservations for cabins and campsites may be made up to 90 days in advance by calling toll free 800/456-CAMP (800/456-2267). There is a reservation fee.

Pets. Restrictions on pets vary widely. Check with the park before you visit. Where they're permitted, you must have current proof of rabies inoculation, and they must be on a leash and under control at all times.

Alcoholic beverages. Alcohol is generally allowed except in bathing facilities, public buildings, or in parking lots. However, here too restrictions vary. For example, alcoholic beverages are not permitted in any state park in the New York City region and there are periods when alcoholic beverages are not allowed in certain areas of parks in other regions.

Discounts. The Golden Park Program provides New York State residents age 62 or older free entry to state parks and recreation areas any weekday, excluding holidays, as well as reduced fees for some activities. The Access Pass provides New York State residents who have certain permanent disabilities free entry to state parks and recreation areas and free use of many of their facilities.

Jones Beach State Park

Restaurant Marina Boating Fishing Swimming Beach Picnic Areas Nature Programs Golf Tennis Playground Gift Shop

Capsule Description: An Atlantic Ocean beach park with bathhouses, which include showers and toilet facilities; a restaurant; snack bars; two Olympic size swimming pools; an outdoor theater for concerts; an 18-hole pitch-putt golf course; an 18-hole miniature golf course; lighted tennis courts.

Location: South shore of Long Island, approximately 33 miles east of New York City. From New York City, take the Long Island Expressway to Northern State Parkway east, then to Meadowbrook Parkway south to the park entrance.

Address: P.O. Box 1000, Wantagh, NY 11793 (tel. 516/785-1600).

Area Contacts: Long Island Convention and Visitors Bureau, Eisenhower Park, 1899 Hempstead Tpk., Suite 500, East Meadow, NY 11554-1042 (tel. toll free 800/441-4601 or 516/794-4222).

New York Convention and Visitors Bureau, 2 Columbus Circle, New York, NY 10019 (tel. 212/397-8222).

Insider Tips: User surveys have consistently confirmed that this is the cleanest and safest bathing beach anywhere in the New York Metropolitan area. For peace and quiet, seek out the designated radio-free beaches at fields 1, 2, or 6. Each fall, the park features a chrysanthemum display along the field 4 beach walkway from Labor Day to Columbus Day.

Located on a barrier reef, five miles from the Long Island mainland, this 2,400-acre park has six miles of natural white sand beaches with facilities that include eight ocean-surf bathing areas, a calm-water bay bathing area, two Olympic-size swimming pools, and an outdoor theater seating 11,000 for summer concerts.

Robert Moses, called the "master builder" of the state parks and parkways, designed this park to give visitors the feel of being on a cruise ship. The 1½-mile boardwalk resembles a ship's promenade, dotted with masts and shuffleboard decks. The garbage receptacles even look like ship funnels.

The park opened in 1929 and several buildings are in the art deco style popular at that time. Its distinctive West Bathhouse, which surrounds one of the Olympic-size pools, and the 231-foot-high water tower, a park landmark modeled after the St. Mark's Bell Tower in Venice, are both in the National Register of Historic Places.

Although the park hosts up to 200,000 visitors on a busy summer weekend day, it's large enough to comfortably accommodate this crowd.

The park is open every day in the year, but the entrance fee, $4 per car, is only collected from Memorial Day weekend through Labor Day. No pets or alcoholic beverages are allowed.

Activities

This is a beach park that could be a model for beach parks.

For one thing, all the swimming areas and the pools have lifeguards on duty during the season from Memorial Day weekend through the weekend after Labor Day. You have a choice of surf swimming, bay swimming in Zach's Bay on the back side of the island, or paying the small extra fee to use one of the two pools.

Want a break from swimming? There's a one-mile physical fitness course by the boardwalk, an 18-hole pitch-putt golf course, and 18-hole lighted miniature golf course, lighted tennis courts, other sports courts and fields. Five evenings a week you can dance at the park bandshell.

There are no specific hiking trails, but you can walk the boardwalk or the beach. Beach walks are especially popular during the off-season. There's a bike trail on the bay side of the park. The West End Environmental Interpretive Center offers free nature programs in the spring. For birders, there are birdwatching areas and a bird checklist. Jones Beach includes habitats for a number of shorebirds and waterfowl including terns, gulls, egrets, herons, ducks, geese, the snowy owl, and the endangered piping plover, which usually nests on the beach from April through August.

For fishermen, there are four large fishing piers or you can try your luck from shore or boat. No license is required for saltwater fishing. Catches usually include striped bass, bluefish, flounder, and fluke. The park has no boat launch, but there is a 76-slip marina.

In addition to snack bars in each beach area, there's a full-service restaurant and cocktail lounge at the mall by the water tower, and an ice-cream parlor upstairs at the West Bathhouse.

Each summer, about 50 concerts, many by top entertainers from country to rock, are held at the Jones Beach Theater, which overlooks Zach's Bay. For schedules and ticket information call 516/221-1000.

Even on busy summer days, you'll probably find a secluded spot to relax between the guarded beaches here.

Camping and Accommodations

This is a day-use only park. There are no overnight accommodations.

Nearby Attractions

On a barrier island to the east of Jones Beach, **Fire Island** is known for its beaches, bars, and discos.

To get there from Jones Beach, you drive east on Ocean Parkway to the Robert Moses Causeway. At **Robert Moses State Park** (tel. 516/669-0449), you'll have to park your car at field 5, and then walk east down the dirt road to the town of **Kismet.** The historic **Fire Island Light House** (tel. 516/321-7028) will guide your way to Kismet. Other Fire Island towns are **Ocean Beach, Saltaire,** and **Sailor's Haven. Cherry Grove** is popular with gays.

The **Hamptons** are where the "beautiful people" of Manhattan summer, and here you'll find beaches, dining, and shopping. Southhampton's **Parrish Art Museum** (516/283-2118) displays changing exhibits of 19th- and 20th-century American Art. The **Southhampton Historical Museum** (tel. 516/283-2494), on Meeting House Lane, is in a former sea captain's house. East Hampton is often dubbed "America's Most Beautiful Village." The **Pantigo Windmill** (tel. 516/324-0713) and the **Hook Windmill** are two of East Hampton's 19th-century windmills. To get to the Hamptons from Jones Beach, take the Meadowbrook Parkway to the Long Island Expressway to Exit 70; it's about an hour's drive.

At the tip of Long Island is **Montauk,** with beaches, restaurants, and accommodations from deluxe resorts to cheap motels. You can climb **Montauk Lighthouse** (1796) to look out on the waters of the Atlantic. From the center of the Hamptons to Montauk, it's about an hour's drive on Montauk Highway (Route 27A).

Letchworth State Park

| Visitor Center | Lodge/ Hotel | Restaurant | Cabins & Cottages | RV Camping | Tent Camping | Group Camping | Fishing | Swimming |

| Picnic Areas | Trails | Horse Trails | Nature Programs | Playground | X-Country Skiing | Snow-mobiling | Gift Shop |

Capsule Description: A large, scenic river park with well-developed facilities.

Location: Western New York, about 35 miles south of Rochester. The park may be entered all year from the towns of Mount Morris and Castile, and during the summer, also from Perry and Portageville.

Address: Castile, NY 14427 (tel. 716/493-3600).

Area Contacts: Greater Rochester Visitors Association, 126 Andrews St., Rochester, NY 14604-1102 (tel. 716/546-3070).

Livingston County Chamber of Commerce, 53 Main St., Mount Morris, NY 14510 (tel. 716/658-2520).

Wyoming County Tourist Promotion Agency, 30 North Main St., P.O. Box 502, Castile, NY 14427-0502 (tel. 716/493-3190).

Insider Tip: The Inn offers take-out picnic lunches.

Racing through the heart of this 14,350-acre park is the Genesee River. Hemmed into a 17-mile canyon, between gorge walls that tower up to 600 feet, it roars over three major waterfalls, one of them 107 feet high.

Although facilities are scattered all up and down the river, the main area of the park is at the south end. Here is a museum, a restored Seneca Council House, with displays that document the rich heri-

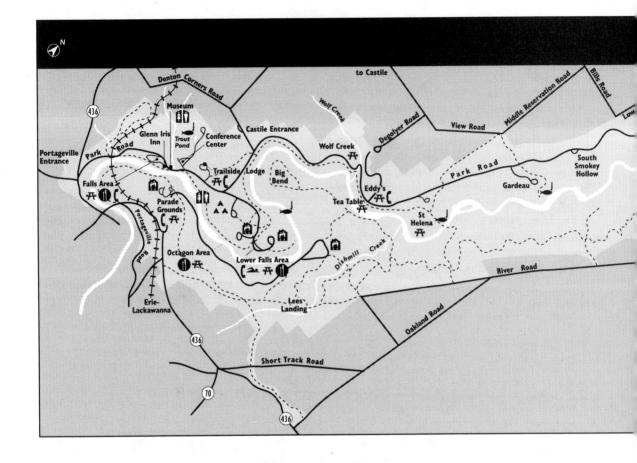

tage of those Native Americans in this area; and the restored Glen Iris Inn, which was the center of area activities in the 1860s when it was the home of William Pryor Letchworth.

Activities

A favorite activity here is taking in the scenic beauty of the river, and a favorite spot to do this is at the Middle Falls—the highest of the three major falls—especially when they are illuminated at night.

Hikers have more than 20 marked trails to choose from, ranging from several half-mile trails to the seven-mile Gorge Trail. About half are rated easy and the rest moderate. Some trails are open for horseback riding. In addition, a section

of the Finger Lakes Trail, a wilderness trail that goes from the Catskills to the Allegheny Mountains, crosses the park. In winter, some of the trails are open for cross-country skiing and snowmobiling.

Deer and wild turkeys are frequently seen in the park and birders have recorded more than 200 species here, including an occasional bald eagle. Over 140 of them are nesting species.

The river is off-limits for swimming—in fact, entering the river within the park is prohibited—but the swimming pool is open and lifeguards are on duty from the end of June through Labor Day weekend.

There's no boat fishing either, but bank fishing is permitted at designated access points, and, in spring, the Trout Pond is open. Want to feel the

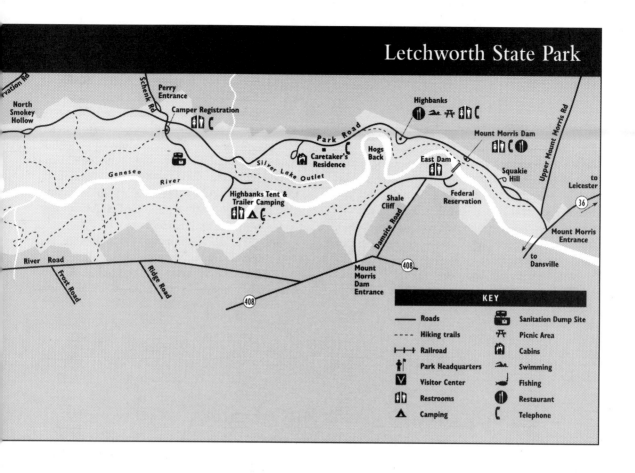

power of the roaring river? During high season, a concessionaire offers a raft trip on a 5½-mile Class II section at the south end of the park.

Also during the summer there are interpretive programs and campfire programs. In July and August, there's usually a concert or entertainment of some kind on Wednesday evenings.

Camping and Accommodations

The historic **Glen Iris Inn** has 14 rooms and suites in the main building, some furnished with antiques. Seven additional kitchenette rooms are located in the adjoining motel. The inn is open April through October. A double costs about $65, suites about $125. The highly rated restaurant serves a continental menu. The inn is located at the Middle Falls, and some rooms offer great views of the river.

Of the 82 **cabins,** about half are one- or three-room kitchenettes—rustic, with no inside water. These sleep from four to six people and rent for $18 to $46 per night. Some have wood-burning stoves. The other half are three-room cabins, with kitchenettes and flush toilets, fireplaces, and screened porches for about $65 per night. Some of these also have electric heat. During high season, most cabins must be rented for a minimum of one week with a limit of two weeks. Most cabins are available from late April until mid-October. Fifteen cabins remain available during the winter.

There are 270 multiuse **campsites** with electric hookups. Most sites are in the woods and well separated for privacy. Pets are permitted in two of the eight campground loops. Campsites cost about $15 per night.

Nearby Attractions

Just to the south of the park are the locks of the historic **Genesee Valley Canal,** which connected the Erie Canal with the Allegheny River. At the north end of the park, you can see the **Mount Morris Dam,** and then go into the village of Mount Morris to visit the **1838 mansion** (tel. 716/658-3548) of Gen. William Augustus Mills, the town father.

Easy daytrips can be made to nearby towns of **Wyoming,** which has more than 70 buildings in the National Register; **Arcade,** where you can take a 90-minute excursion on the steam passenger train of the **Arcade & Attica Railroad** (tel. toll free 800/841-2418); or **Geneseo** to visit the **National Warplane Museum** (tel. 716/243-0690) or stroll through that city's historic district.

A little farther north is a reconstructed 19th-century recreated village in the **Genesee Country Museum** (tel. 716/538-6822) at **Mumford.** Also at the museum is the **Gallery of Sporting Art,** a collection of paintings and sculptures that have hunting and fishing themes.

Only 35 miles to the north is **Rochester,** the third-largest city in the state. Sometimes called "The Picture City," since it is the home of Eastman Kodak, it offers museums, performing arts, and professional sports.

Niagara Reservation State Park

Visitor Center   Picnic Areas   Nature Programs   Gift Shop

Capsule Description: A small, visitor-oriented park that encompasses the American section of Niagara Falls.

Location: Western New York, at the city of Niagara Falls. Take U.S. Highway 190 north from Buffalo to the city of Niagara Falls, then the Robert Moses State Parkway west into the park.

Address: P.O. Box 1132, Niagara Falls, NY 14303-0132 (tel. 716/278-1770).

Area Contacts: Niagara Falls Convention and Visitors Bureau, 310 4th St., Niagara Falls, NY 14303 (tel. toll free 800/421-5223 or 716/285-2400).

Niagara Frontier State Park and Recreation Region, Prospect Park, P.O. Box 1132, Niagara Falls, NY 14303-0132 (tel. 716/278-1770).

Niagara Falls Canada Visitors and Convention Bureau, 5433 Victoria Ave., Niagara Falls, ON, Canada L2G 3L1 (tel. toll free 800/56-FALLS or 905/356-6061).

Insider Tips: Paying the car parking fee here entitles you to park free that same day at the other parks in the area, like Fort Niagara. The best way to enjoy the special effects in the film at the Festival Theatre is to look straight ahead and let your peripheral vision work its wonders.

You might say this is where the U.S. state park systems began. There had been city parks and even county parks before it, but when it was officially dedicated on July 15, 1885, Niagara Reservation became the first state park in the country.

As you watch the hundreds of thousands of

gallons of water that race furiously over the falls each second, what you are witnessing is the mingling of waters from the four upper lakes surging through the narrow gap of the Niagara River on a journey to Lake Ontario, the St. Lawrence River, and the Atlantic.

Geologists estimate that this all started when the glaciers retreated about 12,000 years ago. The Great Lakes watershed looked for an outlet to the sea and the Niagara River was born. At that time the falls were about seven miles closer to Lake Ontario, near the town of Lewiston. Because the soft shale underneath the hard caprock of the falls is slowly eroding away by the force of the water, the edge of the falls is constantly undermined and periodically breaks off. Each year the falls retreat another one to four feet toward Lake Erie.

Niagara Reservation State Park consists of about 435 acres, of which about 300 acres are under water.

Activities

The ideal way to visit this park would be to start at the Festival Theatre in the Schoellkopf Geological Museum and be wowed by the 20-minute film *Niagara Wonders*. Then, when you've recovered from the film's special effects, take the time to look at the museum displays, which correct a few of the filmmaker's exaggerations. One thing you'll find out is that less than 10% of the water actually flows over the American falls. The river splits around Goat Island, and the border with Canada is just on the other side of that island, so the other 90% flows over the Canadian Horseshoe Falls. Next, go to the Great Lakes Garden outside the Visitor Center. It takes a little imagination, but here you can walk through a living map of grass and flowers representing the Great Lakes, and see where Niagara's water comes from and where it goes. Now that you have the background to understand them, walk down to the falls.

That's the ideal way, but it's doubtful you'll be able to resist the temptation to head for the roar and the rising mist and walk down to stand at the edge of the falls first. After all, it's what you've come to see, and at Prospect Point, where the rushing water is just a step away from you, you'll truly experience being at the falls.

There are other views, of course.

For the big picture, go to the Observation Tower at Prospect Point. It rises 100 feet over the cliff and gives a bird's-eye view of the American and Canadian falls as well as the river. The tower elevator then goes down to the base of the American falls for a close-up view.

A more dramatic and closer view is offered on the half-hour cruise of the *Maid of the Mist,* which lives up to its name by taking you past the American falls and into the mist and thundering waters at the base of the Canadian Horseshoe Falls.

For an even closer view, walk over to Goat Island and take the Cave of the Winds Tour. Or, if you prefer, take the Viewmobile over. This little open-air train makes a 45-minute narrated circuit of the park, and your ticket lets you get off and on at any stop. While on Goat Island, go to Terrapin Point where you can have a just-a-step-away experience of the Horseshoe Falls. North of the Horseshoe Falls are the tiny Three Sisters Islands, which are connected by small bridges. When crossing the first bridge to them, look for a flock of ducks that usually nests here, adapting to their environment by paddling against the rushing waters to hold their position.

For the Cave of the Winds Tour, you'll be dressed from head to toe in heavy-weather gear, ride an elevator down into the gorge, walk on wet platforms to a point as close as you can safely get to rocks at the base of the Bridal Falls, and crane your neck back as you look up through the spray at the tons of water thundering down at you from 180 feet above. In winter, when it's too hazardous to walk the platforms, you can still take the elevator down for a view from the gorge.

Viewing the falls and wandering the park grounds is free, but everything else requires you to buy a ticket. You can save a few dollars by buying a Master Pass that gets you into all the attractions.

Camping

Niagara Reservation has no campsites. Two regional state parks with multiuse campsites are **Four Mile Creek** (tel. 716/745-3802) in Youngstown, 12 miles north of Niagara Reservation; and **Evangola** (tel. 716/549-2316), in Angola, 50 miles south.

Nearby Attractions

The park is in downtown **Niagara Falls, New York,** and just across the bridge from **Niagara Falls, Ontario.** Both these cities have a wide variety of accommodations, restaurants, and attractions—from tacky to tasteful. Among the better places on the American side are the **Aquarium** (tel. 716/285-3575), which is just an overpass away from the park museum; the **Native American Center for the Living Arts** (tel. 716/284-2427); the **Wintergarden** (tel. 716/286-4943), a seven-story indoor tropical park; the

art museum on the campus of Niagara University (tel. 716/286-8200); the **Niagara Power Project** (tel. 716/285-3211), across the road from that university; and historic **Fort Niagara State Park** (tel. 716/745-7611), which dates back to before the Revolutionary War. You can also take a boat ride on the Erie Barge Canal or the Upper Niagara River from nearby towns of **Lockport** and **North Tonawanda.** The **New York State Artpark** (tel. 716/754-4375) is at the village of **Lewiston,** about a 10-minute drive from Niagara Falls; it's dedicated to presenting the finest in performing and visual arts programs. While Artpark operates year-round, its primary season is during June, July, and August.

From the Canadian side, you'll get a spectacular view of the falls from several towers. Here, too, are a number of tourist-type museums, an IMAX theater, a **cable car** (tel. 905/356-2241) that goes over the river's whirlpool and rapids, and a **Marineland theme park** (tel. 905/356-8250).

Saratoga Spa State Park

Visitor Center | Lodge/ Hotel | Restaurant | Swimming | Picnic Areas | Trails | Nature Programs | Bicycling

Golf | Tennis | Playground | X-Country Skiing | Gift Shop

Capsule Description: A National Historic Landmark park with outstanding facilities.

Location: Northeast New York, one mile south of downtown Saratoga Springs. Take Exit 13N off I-87 and go north three miles to the park.

Address: P.O. Box W, Saratoga Springs, NY 12866 (tel. 518/584-2535).

Area Contacts: Adirondack Regional Chambers of

Commerce, 136 Warren St., Glens Falls, NY 12801 (tel. 518/798-1761).

Albany County Convention and Visitors Bureau, 52 S. Pearl St., Albany, NY 12207 (tel. toll free 800/258-3582 or 518/434-1217).

Saratoga County Promotion Agency, 494 Broadway, Suite 212, Saratoga Springs, NY 12866 (tel. toll free 800/526-8970 or 518/584-3255).

For centuries people have been drawn to the carbonated mineral waters found here and nowhere else east of the Rockies. Recognizing this, in 1803, Gideon Putnam built a hotel for spa visitors. By the mid-19th century, "taking the waters" at Saratoga was *the* thing to do in high society. The flood of wealthy visitors made business so good that by the early 1900s overpumping was threatening the springs. To preserve this natural resource, the State Reservation was formed in 1909 to acquire the land and protect the springs. But it wasn't until 1962 that this area actually was designated as a state park.

You can still take a mineral bath here, but this 2,033-acre park is now also known for its diverse cultural, aesthetic, and recreational resources. It's also famed for its classical architecture of an earlier era that has earned it a listing as a National Historic Landmark.

Activities

The two Roosevelt Mineral Bath Houses, named after Franklin D. Roosevelt who was governor when they were started, are open all year. The older Lincoln Bathhouse is only open during July and August. Both bathhouses, with their graceful columns and landscaped grounds and walkways, have been restored to their original splendor. In the Roosevelt, the baths are given in private rooms; in the Lincoln, in semiprivate. Depending on the season and the day of the week, a bath alone costs from about $10 to $15, a bath and massage from $30 to $40.

If you prefer to be in cool water, there are two swimming pools: the Olympic-size Peerless Pool with a separate diving and wading pool; and the smaller Victoria Pool, which also has a separate diving pool. These are open from the third Saturday in June to Labor Day, with lifeguards always on duty.

And rounding out the facilities that come in pairs, there are also two golf courses: a championship 18-hole course and an executive 9-hole par-29 course.

Other exercise-type facilities include an easy walking trail of less than two miles and a bike trail of about the same length, with bikes for rent at the hotel; certified 5- and 10-kilometer running courses; and four hard-top and four clay tennis courts. In the winter there are about six miles of groomed trails for cross-country skiing and some downhill ski and sledding areas. You can ice-skate at Victoria Mall near the pool complex. A complete ski shop provides ski and skate rentals as well as individual and group instruction.

Although you probably won't see much of them, park residents include white-tailed deer, beaver, and red fox. What you have a better chance of seeing, in season, is the Karner Blue butterfly. A 200-acre management area is set aside in the park for this endangered species. In season, the park staff will provide tours. An interpretive nature walk on a three-quarter-mile trail is also offered along with other walking tours, including ones explaining both the history of the spa and the springs.

Among the park highlights in the summer are the activities at the **Saratoga Performing Arts Center** (tel. 518/587-3330). This is the summer home of the New York City Ballet, the New York City Opera, and the Philadelphia Orchestra. These, plus guest concert artists, classical to popular, put on a series of performances that start on weekends in early June, accelerate to almost daily programs in July and August, then taper off again to end in early September.

Adding to the cultural galaxy are performances and exhibits at the **National Museum of Dance.** This is the only museum in the country devoted exclusively to professional American dance—from ballet to Broadway, modern to jazz, ethnic to tap. The permanent collection honors dancers ranging from Bill "Bojangles" Robinson and Fred Astaire to George Balanchine and Isadora Duncan.

And to round it all out, the Home Made Theater, a local theater group, usually puts on three productions a year in the Spa Little Theater.

Accommodations

The Georgian-style **Gideon Putnam Hotel** has more than 100 units that range from standard rooms to large parlor suites. Rates are seasonal, with the highest from late July through August, during the performing arts center and Saratoga racing seasons. For those five or so weeks, a double costs up to $250 per night and a large suite over $400. The rest of the year the rates drop by more than half, winding up at a low of about $100 for a double and $150 for a large suite on a weekend between November 1 and April 30. (Call toll free 800/732-1560.) The hotel restaurant has a good reputation.

Nearby Attractions

Founded in 1863, the **Saratoga Racecourse,** also called the New York Racing Association (tel. 518/584-2600), is the oldest racecourse in America. From late July through August, you can see Thoroughbreds blaze to a photo finish in the oldest continous meet in the country. In August, world-class polo matches and the Saratoga Cutting Horse Spectacular are also held here. Near the racecourse is the **National Museum of Racing and Hall of Fame** (tel. 518/584-0400), which has hands-on exhibits on the "sport of kings."

Across the road from the racecourse is the **Saratoga Raceway** (tel. 518/584-2110), with harness racing from March through November, and a **Harness Hall of Fame** (tel. 518/587-4210).

The city of **Saratoga Springs** also offers a **children's museum** (tel. 518/584-5540) and a **city historical museum** (tel. 518/584-6920),

which is in an old casino building. The fossils of prehistoric plants at the **Petrified Sea Gardens** (tel. 518/584-7102) are a national registered landmark, on Route 29, about three miles southwest of the city. In the town of Ballston Spa, a few miles south, is the **National Bottle Museum** (tel. 518/885-7589).

In Glens Falls—an easy daytrip to the north— is the well-known **Hyde Collection of Art** (tel. 518/792-1761) ensconced in a 1912 villa; Rembrandt, Rubens, and Picasso are represented. Just a little northwest of Glens Falls is the resort of **Lake George Village.** The **Lake George Steamboat Co.** (tel. 518/668-5777) offers one-to-four-hour cruises of the 32-mile-long lake from May to October. Kids may want to visit several fun parks or a water park here.

To the west of Saratoga, on Route 32, are the battlefields of the **Saratoga National Historical Park** (tel. 518/664-9821). Here, in two engagements in the fall of 1777, the American forces led by Gen. Horatio Gates defeated the British under Gen. John Burgoyne. These victories are considered the turning point of the Revolution since they persuaded France to join the side of the hardpressed colonists.

South of Saratoga is Albany, the state capital. Places to visit include the 1898 French Renaissance-style **capitol building** (tel. 518/474-2418), the **Institute of History and Art** (tel. 518/463-4478), the **Observation Deck** on the 42nd floor of the Corning Tower Building in Empire Center (tel. 518/474-2418), the **New York State Museum** (tel. 518/474-5877), and the 1761 **Schuyler Mansion** (tel. 518/434-0834), and the 1798 **Ten Broeck Mansion** (tel. 518/436-9826).

Watkins Glen State Park

Visitor Center RV Camping Tent Camping Group Lodge Dormitories Non-Motorized Boating Only Fishing Swimming Picnic Areas Trails Nature Programs Playground

Capsule Description: A natural gorge park with developed facilities.

Location: Finger Lakes region of western New York. On New York Highway 14 at the Village of Watkins Glen at the south end of Seneca Lake.

Address: P.O. Box 304, Watkins Glen, NY 14891 (tel. 607/535-4511).

Area Contacts: Schuyler County Chamber of Commerce, 1000 N. Franklin St., Watkins Glen, NY 14891 (tel. 607/535-4300).

Corning Chamber of Commerce, 42 E. Market St., Corning, NY 14830 (tel. 607/936-4686).

Finger Lakes Association, 309 Lake St., Penn Yan, NY 14527-1831 (tel. toll free 800/548-4386).

Ithaca/Tompkins County Convention and Visitors Bureau, 904 E. Shore Dr., Ithaca, NY 14850 (tel. toll free 800/284-8422).

Watkins Glen began to form about 12,000 years ago. By the end of the Ice Age, glaciers had excavated an immense trough in an ancient river valley, leaving behind the 35-mile-long Seneca Lake, the deepest of the Finger Lakes. Glen Creek flows into the lake. On the way it descends 400 feet within a two-mile run, rushing over 19 waterfalls between 300-foot cliffs. Over the years the creek has slowly eroded the gorge that is the centerpiece of this park, a process that continues today.

Activities

The main activity in this 1,000-acre park is walking the scenic Gorge Trail, which is open from mid-May until mid-November. There are three entrances to the trail: Main, South, and Upper.

Most visitors walk uphill from the main entrance and return. However, you can take a shuttle bus to the Upper Entrance and walk the 1½ miles back downhill to the Main or take a shorter walk from the South entrance back to the Main. The shuttle-bus system is advised if you are not in good physical condition since the Gorge Trail is steep in places and there are more than 800 stone steps along it.

In high season, guided walks are led by park staff twice a day. If you want to do it on your own, a free brochure will guide you to the main points. A path follows the gorge, going over and under waterfalls including the Central Cascade, the highest waterfall in the gorge, which plunges more than 60 feet.

From mid-May through mid-October, there is a high-tech sound and light show called TIMESPELL presented in the gorge. It tells the story of the billions of years of the earth's history that led to the creation of this natural wonder. Admission is charged.

The two other trails in the park are open all year. North of the gorge is the Indian Trail. The South Rim Trail is also part of the Finger Lakes Trail, which, in turn, is a section of the Appalachian Trail.

Also during the summer there is an active recreation program with guest naturalists, arts and crafts, cultural programs, and campfire programs. The park's Olympic-size swimming pool is open from mid-June to Labor Day with lifeguards on duty.

There's no swimming in the two small lakes in

the gorge, but they can be fished. Catches include pickerel, largemouth bass, perch, panfish, and in the spring, rainbow trout. Each lake is about five acres. Canoes are permitted, but you have to portage them in.

The park has a Carry-In-Carry Out program for trash. You're issued a refuge bag at the ticket booth and asked to put all your picnic or other trash in it and take it out of the park with you. There are no trash cans.

Camping

The 302 multiuse **campsites** do not have hookups. Located in a wooded section of the park, sites are generally well separated and spacious. The campgrounds are open from mid-May to Columbus Day. Sites may be reserved through the central reservation system and cost about $10 per night. Sites not reserved are available on a first-come basis.

Nearby Attractions

The village of **Watkins Glen** is known worldwide for the international sports car races that are held there every summer. You can also fish or enjoy other water sports on Seneca Lake as well as take cruises on it. Several wineries offering tours are located in the area.

A short daytrip to the east is the city of **Ithaca,** located on the southern end of Cayuga Lake, another of the slender Finger Lakes. This is the home of **Cornell University** (tel. 607/254-INFO), which offers a number of museums, galleries, and other places worth a visit including the Laboratory of Ornithology and a botanical garden.

To the south, another short daytrip is **Corning** where the main attraction is the **Corning Glass Center complex** (tel. 607/974-8271). One ticket gets you in to see the Corning Museum of Glass, the Hall of Science and Industry, and the Steuben Glass Factory.

North Carolina

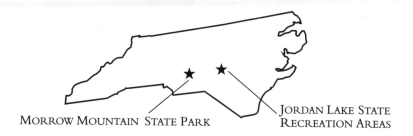

MORROW MOUNTAIN STATE PARK

JORDAN LAKE STATE
RECREATION AREAS

North Carolina has 34 state parks.

Contacts

• Division of Parks and Recreation, North Carolina Department of Environment, Health, and Natural Resources, P.O. Box 27687, Raleigh, NC 27611-7687 (tel. 919/733-PARK [919/733-7275]).
• Travel and Tourism Division, 430 N. Salisbury St., Raleigh, NC 27611 (tel. toll free 800/VISIT-NC [800/847-4862]).

General Information on North Carolina State Parks

Encapsulating the variety of the state, the terrain of North Carolina's state parks include Mount Mitchell, at 6,684 feet, the highest peak in the eastern United States, and Carolina Beach on the 300 miles of Atlantic shoreline. Between these extremes of elevation, as the land changes from the western mountains to rolling hills and plains as it slopes to the sea, there are parks that take advantage of all the varied landscape offers.

All North Carolina parks are designated wildlife preserves, which means no hunting or trapping.

GENERAL FEES

There is a $3 entrance fee to the three recreation areas located on reservoirs: Falls Lake, Jordan Lake, and Kerr Lake. Entrance to all the other parks is free.

CAMPING AND ACCOMMODATIONS

Only two parks, Hanging Rock and Morrow Mountain, have modest cabins with kitchen facilities for rent, available by reservation only. In high season, from June through Labor Day, they rent by the week only for about $270. April through May and September through October they are available at a day rate of $55.

Fourteen parks have developed campgrounds. Most campsites are multiuse but only the campsites at the three recreation areas on the reservoirs have electric and water hookups and accept reservations for a stay of seven days or longer. Without hookups the sites go for $9; with, for $14. Six of the parks with developed campgrounds and eight others also have primitive campsites that go for $5. All of the primitive campsites and selected developed campsites at Jordan Lake and Kerr Lake are open all year. All other campgrounds are only open from March 15 through November 30.

Pets. Pets must be under control and on a leash no longer than six feet. They are not allowed in cabin, bathhouse, or swimming areas.

Alcoholic beverages. The public use or display of alcoholic beverages is prohibited in all parks. In some parks the restriction goes further in that the possession or consumption is prohibited.

Jordan Lake State Recreation Areas

 RV Camping
 Tent Camping
 Primitive Camping
 Group Camping
 Marina
 Boating
 Boat Launch
 Fishing

 Beach
 Waterskiing
 Picnic Areas
 Trails
 Nature Programs
 Playground

Capsule Description: A large park with several units on a large reservoir.

Location: Central North Carolina. From Raleigh, take U.S. Highway 64 west about 20 miles. This highway bisects the lake.

Address: 280 State Park Road, Apex, NC 27502 (tel. 919/362-0586).

Area Contacts: Asheboro Chamber of Commerce, P.O. Box 2007, Asheboro, NC 27204 (tel. 910/626-2626 or tel. toll free 800/626-2672).

Chapel Hill–Carrboro Chamber of Commerce, P.O. Box 2897, Chapel Hill, NC 27515 (tel. 919/967-7075).

Durham Convention and Visitors Bureau, 101 E. Morgan St., Durham, NC 27701 (tel. toll free 800/446-8604 or 919/687-0288).

Raleigh Convention and Visitors Bureau, P.O. Box 1879, Raleigh, NC 27602 (tel. 919/834-5900 or toll free 800/849-8499).

The park's title refers to "recreation areas" in the plural because there are six units, adding up to about 4,000 acres, along the shoreline of this 14,000-acre federal reservoir.

This park is the largest summertime home of the bald eagle in the eastern United States. The number of eagles has increased dramatically since the reservoir was opened in 1983 because it offers vast undisturbed areas that provide the migrating eagles with a mature forest for roosting and an abundant supply of fish.

Activities

Although summer is the best time to see the eagles, some are there all year and interpretive programs on the bald eagle are given throughout the year. You can join one of the programs or do your eagle-watching on your own. The eagles congregate at the north end of the lake. Your best chance of seeing them is in the early morning or early evening. The best spots for seeing them are: the bridge crossing Northeast Creek on Hwy. 751, or the North Carolina Wildlife Resources observation deck located on Hwy. 751, five miles south of I-40.

The eagles aren't the only ones the lake offers an abundant supply of fish. Throw a line in the water and you have a good chance of catching largemouth bass, crappie, catfish, and other panfish, all of which are plentiful. The best fishing is in March through June and in the fall of the year.

All types of boating, from power to sail, are popular on the lake, as are waterskiing, windsurfing, and tubing. All the units have boat-launch sites and a concessionaire operates a marina at the Crosswinds unit that offers boat launching, slips and mooring, fishing and pontoon boat rentals, services and supplies.

There are swimming beaches in all the units, but no lifeguards. And for hikers, there are trails in most of the units.

Camping

About half of the 1,050 **campsites** have electric and water hookups. Most sites are located along the shoreline and all campgrounds have a swimming area. Reservations are accepted for a stay of seven days or longer. Shorter stays are on a first-come basis. The maximum stay in one campsite is two weeks. Sites cost $9 to $14 depending on facilities.

There are 24 primitive sites that require a hike from the nearest parking space of from a half mile to a mile, also 11 group camping areas, each of which can accommodate up to 30 persons.

Nearby Attractions

The more than a thousand campsites in the park and four interesting cities within an hour's drive make this an ideal base for daytrips.

About 45 minutes' drive to the west is **Asheboro.** Just south of that town on North Carolina Highway 159, is the **North Carolina Zoological Park** (tel. 910/879-7000). Considered the world's largest natural habitat zoo, it's designed to re-create the natural environments of the major continents complete with native plants.

A little more than a half hour's drive to the north or east gives you a choice of going to Chapel Hill, Durham, or Raleigh.

The heart of **Chapel Hill** is the campus of the University of North Carolina (tel. 919/962-2211), the oldest state university in the country. Places to visit on the 720-acre campus include Old East, the oldest state university building in the country, dating from 1793; the five-acre arboretum; and the planetarium. **The North Carolina Botanical Garden** (tel. 919/962-0522) is also in this city.

A star attraction in **Durham** is **Duke University** (tel. 919/684-8111), spread over two campuses that total 8,000 acres. Its chapel, memorial gardens, and art museum are worth a campus visit. Off campus, the ancestral home of the Duke family, who made their fortune in tobacco, is preserved as the **Duke Homestead State Historic Site** (tel. 919/477-5498), which includes a tobacco museum, farm buildings, and historical exhibits. Also in Durham is the **North Carolina Museum of Life and Science** (tel. 919/220-5429), which features a number of hands-on exhibits and a train ride the kids will enjoy.

You can visit the Executive Mansion, the State Capitol and the State Legislative Building in **Raleigh,** the capital of North Carolina. Among the museums here are the state museums of history, natural sciences, and art.

Morrow Mountain State Park

| Cabins & Cottages | RV Camping | Tent Camping | Primitive Camping | Boating | Boat Launch | Fishing | Swimming | Picnic Areas | Trails | Horse Trails | Nature Programs |

Capsule Description: A large, hilly, river/lakeside park with some developed facilities.
Location: Central North Carolina, about six miles east of Albemarle. From Albemarle, take either North

Carolina Highway 24/27 east and Valley Drive or Highway 740 north and Morrow Mountain Road.
Address: 49104 Morrow Mountain Rd., Albemarle, NC 28001 (tel. 704/982-4402).
Area Contacts: Albemarle Chamber of Commerce,

P.O. Box 909, Albemarle, NC 28002 (tel. 704/982-8116).

Charlotte Convention and Visitors Bureau, 122 E. Stonewall St., Charlotte, NC 28202 (tel. toll free 800/231-4636 or 704/331-2700).

Concord Chamber of Commerce, P.O. Box 1029, Concord, NC 28026 (tel. 704/782-4111).

Insider Tip: Parking can be a problem at the top of Morrow Mountain on summer weekends and holidays. If the parking lot is full, you'll have to descend the mountain missing the view from the overlook.

The 4,693-acre park is located in one of the oldest mountain ranges in the eastern United States. The hills form a stark contrast to the rolling countryside of this section of North Carolina. Not that these are like the high mountains farther west. The hills are now worn down to rounded ridges, with the highest elevation of the four major peaks in the park at 936 feet, but still steep and rugged in places.

On the east side, the park borders the junction of three rivers and the north end of the 5,000-acre Lake Tilley, a power company reservoir.

Established in 1935, many of the facilities were constructed by the Civilian Conservation Corps (CCC) and the Works Project Administration (WPA) during the last days of the Depression.

Activities

Hikers have a choice of nine trails adding up to a total of 15 miles and ranging from easy to moderate to strenuous. The easy trails include the Laurel Trail, a self-guided nature trail on which many of the trees of the upland hardwood forest are identified. On the other end, the Sugarloaf Mountain Trail, although less than three miles long, climbs the slopes of the second-highest mountain in the park and includes a number of steep sections.

For equestrians, there are 16 miles of bridle trails available for day use only—no overnight horse camping. All bridle trails may also be used by hikers.

Much of the park has been left as a natural area

so the diversity of the park's wildlife is best observed on the trails where you may see white-tailed deer, raccoons, and a variety of other smaller animals. Park inhabitants also include the great blue heron and many songbirds, with occasional sightings of ospreys and bald eagles. If you're interested in wildlife observation or photography, ask the rangers about using the observation blind on the easy-to-walk Three Rivers Trail. Good bird's-eye views of the area can be had from the scenic overlooks at the top of Morrow Mountain and on the Rocks Trail.

The nature museum, near the park office, is open daily during the summer and weekends the rest of the year, offering regularly scheduled interpretive programs.

History buffs may enjoy a visit to the homesite of Dr. Francis Kron, located at the foot of Fall Mountain. Dr. Kron emigrated from Prussia to America in 1823 and was the first medical doctor to settle and practice medicine in this area. His home, office, infirmary, and greenhouse are restored to appear as they did in the 1870s.

Rowboats and canoes can be rented at the park boathouse during the summer. There's also a boat ramp if you bring your own. Fishing is good in all the local waters with catches of bluegill, perch, catfish, crappie, and largemouth, striped, and white bass.

From the park, there aren't any swimming access areas on the rivers or lake, but there is a swimming pool open from June through Labor Day.

Camping and Accommodations

Six rustic wooden cabins are located in a wooded section of the park. Each cabin has two bedrooms, bathroom, living room with fireplace, and kitchen. They are for family use only and will accommodate up to six persons. Available from March through November, reservations are accepted by the week only from early June through Labor Day. The rest of the year they may be rented by the night with a two-night minimum. Weekly rates are $250, nightly $55.

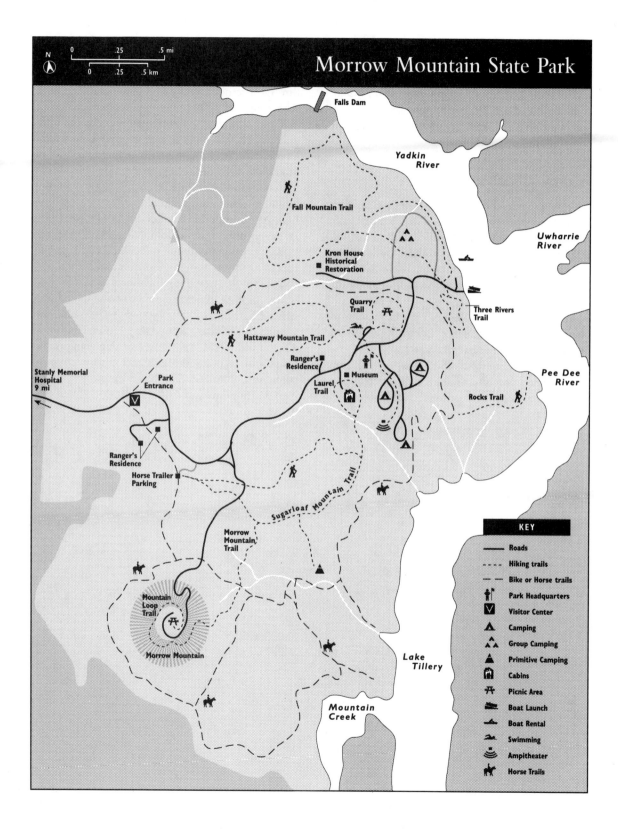

Morrow Mountain State Park

Falls Dam

Yadkin River

Uwharrie River

Fall Mountain Trail

Kron House Historical Restoration

Quarry Trail

Three Rivers Trail

Hattaway Mountain Trail

Pee Dee River

Ranger's Residence

Museum

Laurel Trail

Rocks Trail

Stanly Memorial Hospital 9 mi

Park Entrance

Ranger's Residence

Horse Trailer Parking

Sugarloaf Mountain Trail

Morrow Mountain Trail

Mountain Loop Trail

Morrow Mountain

Lake Tillery

Mountain Creek

KEY

——	Roads
----	Hiking trails
– –	Bike or Horse trails
⚲	Park Headquarters
Ⓥ	Visitor Center
⛰	Camping
⛰⛰	Group Camping
▲	Primitive Camping
⌂	Cabins
⛩	Picnic Area
⛴	Boat Launch
⛵	Boat Rental
🏊	Swimming
🔊	Ampitheater
🐎	Horse Trails

0 .25 .5 mi
0 .25 .5 km

N

There are no hookups at the multiuse campsites in the three campground loops. Sites are on a first-come basis and cost $9. For backpackers, there are four hike-in sites, and there's also a small tent camping site for youth groups.

Nearby Attractions

An easy drive to the east is the **North Carolina Zoo** (see "Nearby Attractions" in Jordan Lake section, above), south of Asheboro. Closer in, off Highway 731 just past Mount Gilead, is the **Town Creek Indian Mound State Historic Site** (tel. 910/439-6802), a reconstructed 16th-century Indian ceremonial center.

You may possibly strike gold if you go west to Georgeville, just outside of Locust. The **Reed Gold Mine State Historic Site** (tel. 704/786-8337) is a short detour off Highway 24/27 on your way to Charlotte. Gold was discovered here in 1799 resulting in the nation's first gold mine.

Year round you can tour the mine; and from April through October, you can pan for gold and keep what you find.

Continuing west, **Charlotte** is the state's largest city. Places worth a visit include **Discovery Place** (tel. 704/372-6261), the largest museum of science and technology in the state; **the Mint Museum of Art** (tel. 704/337-2000), in the building that was originally a branch of the U.S. Mint built to handle the gold discovered at the nearby Reed Gold Mine; and, for the kids, **Carowinds** (tel. 704/588-2600), a theme park.

Just to the north of Charlotte is **Concord,** where, despite its name, you'll find the **Charlotte Motor Speedway** (tel. 704/455-3200) and the **Concord Motor Speedway** (tel. 704/782-4221), both NASCAR tracks. If you like industrial tours, you can go through the **Philip Morris plant** (tel. 704/788-5000) and the nearby **Cannon Mills plant** (tel. 704/939-2000).

North Dakota

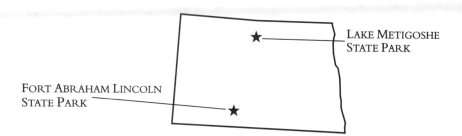

FORT ABRAHAM LINCOLN
STATE PARK

LAKE METIGOSHE
STATE PARK

North Dakota has 18 state parks.

Contacts

- North Dakota Parks and Tourism Department, 1835 Bismarck Expwy., Bismarck, ND 58504 (tel. toll free 800/807-4723 for camping reservations only).
- North Dakota Tourism Promotion, Liberty Memorial Building, 2nd floor, 604 E. Blvd., Bismarck, ND 58505 (tel. toll free 800/HELLO-ND [800/435-5663]). *Note:* If you can't get the parks information you want here, they can transfer the call to the parks headquarters or a state park.

General Information on North Dakota State Parks

Sometimes, when looking at this state's far-north location on the border with Canada, it's a little hard to recall that it became part of the United States as one of the territories in the Louisiana Purchase in 1803. And, as a result, it was one of the early stopovers for Lewis and Clark, who wintered here the following year.

North Dakota is truly in the heart of North America; the geographical center of this continent is located near the city of Rugby close to the Canadian border. The state also is divided by two time zones, with the east and northwest in the

central time zone and the southwest following mountain time.

Its state parks, although small in number, are scattered geographically to provide recreational opportunities for all sections of the state. The parks are open all year and in the winter they are connected to more than 250 miles of cross-country skiing and snowmobile trails.

GENERAL FEES

Depending on the level of services provided at each park, there is a vehicle entrance fee of $2 or $3 during the summer season, and $1 to $3 in the off-season.

CAMPING

There are more than 1,100 campsites available. Some 200 of these may be reserved during the period from Memorial Day through Labor Day by calling the 800 number. All other campsites are on a first-come basis. Some of the parks have modern campsites with hookups. Most parks also have primitive camping. Campsite fees range from $8 to $12 depending on hookups. This includes the park entrance fee. The reservation fee is $5.

Rent-A-Camp sites, providing all you need for basic camping except blankets, are available at most major parks. The cost is from $18 to $23, depending on extras you want to rent.

Pets. Pets are permitted just about everywhere but in swimming area, but they must be on a leash not over six feet in length and under control at all times.

Alcoholic beverages. Generally permitted except inside park buildings.

Discounts. North Dakota residents age 60 and older are eligible to purchase a Senior Citizen Passport which provides free admission to any North Dakota state park.

Fort Abraham Lincoln State Park

 Visitor Center
 RV Camping
 Tent Camping
 Boating
 Fishing
 Waterskiing
 Picnic Areas
 Trails
 Nature Programs
 X-Country Skiing
 Snow-mobiling
 Gift Shop

Capsule Description: A historic park with developed facilities.
Location: South-central North Dakota. From Bismarck, take I-94 west to Exit 155 at Mandan, then south four miles on North Dakota Highway 1806.
Address: Route 2, Box 139, Mandan, ND 58554 (tel. 701/663-9571).
Area Contacts: Bismarck-Mandan Convention and Visitors Bureau, P.O. Box 2274, Bismarck, ND 58502 (tel. toll free 800/767-3555 or 701/222-4308).

In the early 1870s, as the Northern Pacific Railroad pushed west through the Dakota Territory, an infantry post was established here to protect the frontier settlements and the railroad work parties. It was soon recognized that infantry was no match for the swift-moving Sioux horsemen, so a cavalry post was authorized in 1873. The infantry and cavalry posts together were called Fort Lincoln and Lt. Col. George Armstrong Custer was sent to command this post and several others in the Middle District of the Department of Dakota. His troops were the 7th Cavalry. Three years later, as part of a 1,000-man army lead by Gen. Alfred Terry, Custer led his ill-fated 7th Cavalry from here on an Indian campaign that ended when he

and 265 of his men died at the Battle of Little Bighorn.

As the frontier moved west, the fort declined in importance and was abandoned in 1891. In 1907, Theodore Roosevelt was the prime mover in turning the land over to the North Dakota Historical Society. In the 1930s the Civilian Conservation Corps (CCC) helped develop the park, and when the Department of Parks and Recreation was created in 1965, Fort Lincoln became a state park.

In addition to the fort, the ruins of On-A-Slant Indian Village, occupied by the Mandan Indians from approximately 1650 to 1764, lie within the park boundaries.

Activities

The Visitor Center/Museum in this 1,000-acre park features exhibits and audiovisual programs that tell the story of this area from the Mandan Indians, through the visit of the Lewis and Clark Expedition, the fur trade, railroad and homesteading eras, to the birth and death of the military post. Interpretive programs are given every weekend during the summer and tours are given by guides in period costumes. After dark on summer weekends, films on natural and cultural history are shown in the amphitheater by the campgrounds.

In its heyday, the fort had 78 buildings. All were destroyed by the turn of the century; however, parts of the fort have been reconstructed and are open to visitors. These include the Victorian-style home of George and Libby Custer, the commissary storehouse, and the central barracks on Cavalry Square; and three infantry blockhouses perched on the bluffs overlooking the Missouri River. Guided tours are given of the Custer home and you can follow a self-guided interpretive trail around the rest of the fort.

Between the cavalry and infantry posts are several reconstructed earth lodges on the ruins of the On-A-Slant Indian Village, which got its name because it sloped toward the river. The Mandans were a peaceful, sedentary agricultural tribe. Smallpox epidemics in 1781 and again in 1837 almost wiped out the tribe. Today, the remaining descendants live with two other tribes in the Fort Berhold Reservation northwest of here.

Also between the two posts is the Ridgeline Nature Trail. This is a self-guided trail of about three-quarters of a mile. The scenic overlook at the north entrance to the park gives an excellent view of the Missouri River. This is also a wildlife viewing area where, especially in fall, you may see white-tailed deer, fox, hawks, and geese. For serious hikers, the Lewis and Clark National Historic Trail passes by the park.

In the winter there is a 1½-mile, groomed cross-country ski trail and sledding hills in the park and a 22-mile snowmobile trail begins in the park and goes south to Fort Rice.

The Heart and the Missouri rivers come together here and boating, waterskiing, and fishing are popular. Walleye and pike are common catches on both rivers in summer. In winter, you can ice fish on the Heart River. A paddlewheel riverboat from the port of Bismarck docks at the state park daily and offers river excursions. A trolley will take you on a nine-mile scenic tour of both the Heart and Missouri rivers on a round-trip from the park to Mandan.

Camping

Nestled in the trees along the banks of the rivers, 56 of the 95 **campsites** have electric hookups. Fees are $12 with hookup, $9 without. Some sites may be reserved during the summer season.

Nearby Attractions

A bridge over the Missouri River joins the sister cities of Bismarck and Mandan. The capital of **Bismarck** is home of one of the tallest state capitol buildings in the country. At 19 stories, it's known as the **"Skyscraper of the Prairies"** (tel. 701/328-2000). For a good view of those prairies, try the observation tower on top. Other places worth visiting here are the **Former Governor's Mansion State Historic Site** (tel. 701/328-3567), the **North Dakota Heritage Center** (tel. 701/328-2666), and the zoo (tel. 701/223-7543).

North of Mandan about 30 miles is **Cross Ranch State Park** (tel. 701/794-3731). This small, mostly natural, state park gives access to a 5,000-acre nature preserve that's home to the Centennial Buffalo Herd.

Lake Metigoshe State Park

 Cabins & Cottages
 RV Camping
 Tent Camping
 Primitive Camping
 Group Lodge Dormitories
 Boating
 Boat Launch
 Fishing
 Beach

 Waterskiing
 Snorkeling & Diving
 Picnic Areas
 Trails
 Nature Programs
 Bicycling
 Playground
 X-Country Skiing
 Snow-mobiling

Capsule Description: A lakeside park with developed facilities.

Location: North-central North Dakota on the Canadian border. From Dunseith, take U.S. Highway 291/North Dakota Highway 3 north to Highway 43, then west to the park. From Bottineau, go east on North Dakota Highway 5 about two miles to the Lake Road, then north about 12 miles to the park.

Address: Route 1, Box 359, Bottineau, ND 58318 (tel. 701/263-4651).

Area Contacts: Bottineau Chamber of Commerce, 103 East 11th St., Bottineau, ND 58318 (tel. 701/228-3849).

Greater Rugby Area Chamber of Commerce, P.O. Box 288, Rugby, ND 58368 (tel. 701/776-5846).

Insider Tip: In winter, a warming hut is open by the sledding hill.

Nestled in the scenic Turtle Mountains on the North Dakota/Manitoba border, this is one of the most popular year-round vacation spots in the state. The 1,141-acre park offers a variety of terrain ranging from sandy beaches and marshlands to heavily wooded hills rising high above Lake Metigoshe and three smaller lakes.

Activities

In the summer, water sports are king here. The park has two miles of shoreline on the 1,619-acre Lake Metigoshe offering swimming (a beach, but no lifeguards), boating, jet and waterskiing, snor-

keling, windsurfing, and fishing. In addition to a boat launch, there's a courtesy dock with eight slips on a first-come basis.

You can rent a canoe in the park, and canoeing is popular on the three smaller lakes, including Eromosh, a 350-acre lake that's cut through the middle by the U.S./Canada border. The most northern reaches of Lake Metigoshe also cross the border, so if you want to fish the Canadian sections of either of these lakes, you'll need a Manitoba fishing license in addition to a North Dakota license. Catches include pike, walleye, muskie, and perch, with the pike and walleye stocked periodically by the North Dakota Game and Fish Department. Come winter, ice fishing is popular.

The Old Oak Trail, a self-guided nature trail about three miles long, was the first trail in the state to be designated as a National Recreation Trail. It's rated moderate in difficulty. Like all North Dakota parks, this is a wildlife sanctuary making it a good place to spot white-tailed deer, beaver, muskrat, mink, and other small animals, and possibly even a moose. There's also an observation tower on School Section Lake where you can bird-watch. More than 100 species are known to nest in the park area and during the migratory seasons many waterfowl stop over on this 115-acre lake where motorized boats are not allowed.

There are about 12 miles of other hiking trails here, with about half that distance open for bikes. Come the snow and these trails become part of four groomed cross-country ski trails. (Skis can be rented in the park.) They are also part of the state's snowmobile trail system. Only about five miles of snowmobile trails are in the park itself, but they connect with many miles of groomed trails in the area.

During the summer there are campfire and other nature programs on the weekends.

The park is also the home of the Turtle Mountain Environmental Learning Center, which offers programs from April through December. Aimed at increasing the awareness, understanding, and appreciation of students for the environment, its hands-on programs are also open to adult groups.

Camping

Out of 142 multiuse **campsites,** 90 have electric and water hookups, of which 42 may be reserved. Sites with hookups are available from about mid-May through September and cost $12 per night. The other 52 sites have no hookups and go for $9. Eighteen of these may be reserved. Sites without hookups are available year-round. This park has the Rent-A-Camp program.

The group camp includes dorms and a kitchen/dining hall. There are also three primitive camping areas that can be reached by vehicles.

The recent purchase of an additional 300 acres between the park and the Canadian border has added cabins, a dining hall, and hike-in campsites to the park. These are in the process of being incorporated into the park facilities and may be available by the time you read this.

Nearby Attractions

Commemorating the centuries of peace along the world's longest undefended international boundary, the **International Peace Garden** (tel. 701/263-4390) sits half in the States and half in Canada. It's about 20 miles east of Lake Metigoshe State Park on U.S. 281/North Dakota 3, just north of Dunseith. On the landscaped grounds (2,300 acres) are a floral clock, a peace tower, an arboretum, formal gardens, and hiking trails. During the summer, the **International Music Camp** (tel. 701/263-4211 or 701/838-8472) holds concerts, plays, and dance productions here in the gardens.

To the south of the park, the city of **Rugby** is the geographical center of North America. The **Geographical Center Museum** (tel. 701/776-6414) is open from May through October. The **Victorian Dress Museum** (tel. 701/776-2189) displays period costumes. The **county courthouse** is listed in the National Register of Historic Sites.

Ohio

MAUMEE BAY STATE PARK

MOHICAN STATE PARK

SHAWNEE STATE PARK

Ohio has 72 state parks.

Contacts

- Division of Parks and Recreation, Ohio Department of Natural Resources, 1952 Belcher Dr., Bldg. C-3, Columbus, OH 43224-1386 (tel. 614/265-7000).
- Division of Travel and Tourism, Ohio Department of Development, P.O. Box 1001, Columbus OH 43266-0001 (tel. toll free 800/BUCKEYE [800/282-5393]).

General Information on Ohio State Parks

Although Ohio ranks 35th in size of the states, its state park system ranks in the top five in number of parks and, spread over 207,000 acres, the top 10 in park acreage. Many of its parks are connected to water: the old canals, rivers, inland lakes, and seven parks alone along the state's 230 miles of shoreline on Lake Erie.

For serious hikers, the Buckeye Trail touches a number of parks. This 1,200-mile trail loops through all four corners of the state, going through 40 of Ohio's 88 counties.

The Ohio State Fair, held annually in Columbus, is the largest state fair in the United States.

GENERAL FEES

There is no charge for entrance to any of the Ohio State parks.

CAMPING AND ACCOMMODATIONS

Eight parks have resort **lodges:** Burr Oak, Deer Creek, Hueston Woods, Maumee Bay, Mohican, Punderson, Salt Fork, and Shawnee. They offer a total of about 700 rooms. Rates vary from park to park, season to season, and weekday to weekend, but the maximum allowable charge for a double in high season goes from about $75 to $106. Off-season rates are lower. For reservations call toll free 800/AT-A-PARK (800/282-7275).

There are also **cabins** for rent at those eight parks. Reservations for cabins in all of these parks except Mohican (see Mohican listing, below) may be made up to a year in advance by calling toll free 800/AT-A-PARK. In addition, cabins are available at Buck Creek, Cowan Lake, Dillon, Geneva, Hocking Hills, Lake Hope, Pike Lake, and Pymatuning. Reservations for these are made directly though the individual park.

A cabin is a cabin is a cabin is not quite correct in this case. The 535 "cabins" range from the town-house design with gas-burning fireplaces at Maumee Bay to rustic sleeping cabins and "cabents," hexagonal wood structures with fabric roofs. Sizes run from one- to four-bedroom, but most are two-bedroom. A half-dozen parks only open the cabins seasonally; the others are open all year. During June, July, and August cabins are available on a weekly basis only. For a two-bedroom family housekeeping cabin that sleeps six and is available all year, the rental rate runs from about $65 to $100 a day or $335 to $500 a week.

The more than 9,000 family **campsites** located in 55 parks are designed to appeal to a wide variety of camping tastes. While some pads accommodate motor homes up to 35 feet long, others are secluded and ideal for a tent. Most campsites are on a first-come basis; however, some parks accept reservations. Depending on park facilities and hookups, campsites go for $7 to $15 per night. Camping is limited to no more than 14 days in any 30-day period.

For $11 to $22 a night you can Rent-A-Camp, which provides a large tent that sleeps four adults and other essential equipment. Rent-A-Camp sites are available in 23 parks from May through September. Reservations are accepted after March 1, by mail only.

Only four parks have primitive camping. It's on a first-come basis and free of charge.

Almost 400 miles of bridle trails weave through state parklands. Seven parks offer equestrian camping facilities and bridle trails. Another nine parks have bridle trails available for day use.

Group camps are available in more than 30 parks with capacities ranging from a low of 40 to a high of 700. These are reserved directly through the individual park.

Pets. Where permitted, pets must be on a leash not longer than six feet and under control at all times. Pets are not allowed in lodges, cabins, on beaches or any swimming area, in wildlife-display areas, and in some campgrounds. However, for $1 per night, pet camping is available in designated areas of all state park campgrounds and in most horsemen's camps.

Alcoholic beverages. Public display or consumption of alcoholic beverages is prohibited except in the lounges/bars of the resort lodges.

Discounts. Ohioans 60 years of age or older and Ohioans 18 years or older who are totally and permanently disabled are eligible for the Golden Buckeye card. Cardholders are given a 50% discount on camping Sunday through Thursday, a 10% discount on camping Friday and Saturday, and a 10% discount on all cabins and lodge reservations. Ohio veterans with a total and permanent VA disability and Ohio residents who are former prisoners of war are exempt from camping fees.

Maumee Bay State Park

Lodge/Hotel · Restaurant · Cabins & Cottages · RV Camping · Tent Camping · Marina · Boating · Fishing · Swimming · Beach · Waterskiing · Snorkeling & Diving · Picnic Areas

Trails · Horse Trails · Nature Programs · Bicycling · Golf · Tennis · Fitness Center · Playground · X-Country Skiing · Gift Shop

Capsule Description: A resort park on Lake Erie.

Location: Northwestern Ohio, just east of Toledo. From Toledo, take Ohio Route 2 east to North Curtice Road, then north three miles to the park.

Address: 1400 Park Rd. no. 1, Oregon, OH 43618 (tel. 419/836-7758; toll free 800/AT-A-PARK (800/282-7275) for lodge and cabin reservations only).

Area Contacts: Greater Toledo Convention and Visitors Bureau, 401 Jefferson Ave., Toledo, OH 43604 (tel. toll free 800/243-4667).

Ottawa County Visitors Bureau, 109 Madison, Suite E, Port Clinton, OH 43452 (tel. toll free 800/441-1271).

An older park, it now boasts the newest of Ohio's eight resort lodges. On its 1,450 acres you'll find a little bit of everything for visitors: boating, golf, swimming, fishing, hiking, nature programs, and winter sports. In addition to the man-made recreational facilities, the park encompasses a wetlands area, a habitat that contains more species of wildlife than any other habitat type.

Activities

This is a resort park in every sense of the word. For starters, there's an 18-hole "Scottish Links"–style golf course; tennis courts; indoor and outdoor pools; a fitness center with racquetball courts; sauna; whirlpool; sports courts; and two sand beaches, one on Lake Erie and the other on the park's 57-acre inland lake. Other amenities include

an amphitheater that seats 3,000 for a variety of entertainment programs, a boardwalk and observation blind for nature-viewing of the wetlands, and a state-of-the-art nature center. The nature center features hands-on displays, viewing windows, a theater for nature programs, and a remote-video monitoring system that transmits activities from the wetlands back to the center so those who cannot physically make the trip there can experience wetland life.

For those who want to see more of the natural side of the park, besides the two-mile boardwalk trail, there are three other land-based trails. All are rated easy and vary in length from about three to seven miles. The seven-mile trail is hard-surfaced and can be used for biking. Bikes for rent include tandems. For equestrians there's a two-mile bridle trail.

In winter, the park is open for cross-country skiing, with skis for rent at the lodge. And the area known as Big Hill lives up to its name for sledding.

Deer, fox, muskrat, raccoon, groundhog, and a myriad of wetlands frogs, turtles, and snakes are all residents. More than 300 species of birds have been recorded, including a variety of shorebirds, waterfowl, and songbirds. Ring-necked pheasants densely populate the meadows area of the park.

Lake Erie offers unlimited opportunities for boaters. There is a marina in the park with 32 slips. The inland lake is suitable for sailing, canoeing, and other nonmotorized boat use. Canoes, paddle-boats, rowboats, and sailboats are available for rent.

Lake Erie is known as "the walleye capital of the world." But that's not all you can catch. Channel catfish, drum, smallmouth bass, and yellow perch are plentiful. Bluegill and bass are among the fish taken from the inland lake, along with catfish and crappie, which are stocked periodically.

Camping and Accommodations

A two-story, native-stone fireplace welcomes guests to the massive beam and glass lobby of the **lodge** that overlooks Lake Erie. The 120 guest rooms all have balconies. A double rents for about $106 in high season. Children 18 and younger stay free when staying in the same room as their parents. The lodge has a full-service restaurant.

Sixteen of the **cabins** are two-bedroom, four are four-bedroom. These are classified as "resort cottages," the highest category, and come with a gas fireplace, central heat and air, TV, and phone. The high-season cost is $115 a day or $525 a week for the two-bedroom, and $150 a day and $600 a week for the four-bedroom.

Reservations for the lodge and cabins are made through toll free 800/AT-A-PARK (800/282-7275).

The 256 **campsites,** all with electric hookups, cost $12 per night. There are also Rent-A-Tent sites for a $22 fee. In the winter, 76 campsites remain open with reduced facilities available.

Nearby Attractions

Three national wildlife refuges exist in Ohio and they are all within a short distance of this park. Information on **Cedar Point, West Sister,** and **Ottawa National Wildlife Refuges** may be obtained by calling 419/898-0014.

To the east, less than an hour's drive away, there are places worth a visit in the **Port Clinton** area. For the kids, or the kid in you, there's the **African Safari Wildlife Park** (tel. 419/732-3606), near Port Clinton, and the **Cedar Point Amusement Park** (tel. 419/627-2350), with ten roller coasters.

In the town of Sandusky, boat trips are given by **Newman Boat Line** (tel. toll free 800/876-1907) to **Kelleys Island,** one of the largest of the 20 islands in Lake Erie, and across the lake to **Leamington, Ontario.**

It only takes a few minutes to drive west from the park to **Toledo.** Sights here include the **Toledo Art Museum** (tel. 419/255-8000), the **botanical gardens** (tel. 419/536-8365), and the **zoo** (tel. 419/385-5721). Walks can be taken in the downtown riverfront area and past the Victorian homes in the historic **Old West End neighborhood.** Sometimes getting around is half the fun; Toledo offers horse-drawn carriage rides in the downtown area, a 1930-era excursion train, a canal boat, an 1880s trolleycar replica, and a stern-wheeler excursion boat.

Mohican State Park

Lodge/ Hotel   Restaurant   Cabins & Cottages   RV Camping   Tent Camping   Primitive Camping   Group Camping   Non-Motorized Boating Only   Fishing   Swimming

Picnic Areas   Trails   Nature Programs   Tennis   Playground   X-Country Skiing   Gift Shop

Capsule Description: A park with a lodge and other developed facilities on a river and small lake.

Location: Northeast Ohio. Take Exit 165 off I-71 to Ohio 97. Go east about 20 miles to Ohio 3, then north about a quarter mile to the park entrance. Or, from Loudonville take Ohio 3 southwest to the park entrance.

Address: 3116 State Rte. 3, Loudonville, OH 44842 (tel. 419/994-5125; 419/994-4290 for cabin and campsite reservations only).

Area Contacts: Coshocton County Convention and Visitors Bureau, P.O. Box 905, Coshocton, OH 43812 (tel. toll free 800/338-4724 or 614/622-9315).

Greater Cleveland Convention and Visitors Bureau, 50 Public Square, Suite 3100, Cleveland, OH 44113 (tel. toll free 800/321-1001 or 216/621-4110).

Greater Columbus Convention and Visitors Bureau, 10 W. Broad St., Suite 1300, Columbus, OH 43215 (tel. 614/221-6623 or toll free 800/354-2657).

Wayne County Convention and Visitors Bureau, 377 West Liberty St., Wooster, OH 44691 (tel. 216/264-1800).

Insider Tip: You'll have a good chance of observing a variety of wildlife at the feeding station along the self-guided nature trail.

The 1,294-acre park was cut out of the Mohican State Memorial Forest that still surrounds it, providing a 5,400-acre natural wilderness buffer against the cultivated world outside with impres-

sive stands of oaks, maples, and a dozen other varieties of trees.

One of the highlights here is the narrow gorge of the Clearfork on the Mohican River, which runs through the park. Clearfork Gorge, more than a thousand feet wide at the top with steep cliff walls over 300 feet tall, is a Registered National Natural Landmark.

Activities

The Mohican is considered one of the finest canoeing rivers in the state. Canoes and kayaks are for rent at the park's canoe livery, which is open daily May through September and weekends in April and October. Rental includes radio-dispatched transportation for pickup. The five miles of the river in the park are popular for tubing, too. Reservations are required on off-season weekends and strongly suggested during June though August, the prime river season. Call toll free 800/HI-CANOE (800/442-2663).

The river is also noted for smallmouth bass fishing and an annual trout derby—trout is stocked twice a year. Largemouth bass, carp, crappie, catfish, perch, and bluegill are abundant in the river and in Pleasant Hill Lake, which is above the dam, near the lodge.

For swimmers, there's an Olympic-size pool located in the campgrounds for cabin and camping guests, and both indoor and outdoor pools for lodge guests.

The only markings of the border between the park and the forest lands is red paint on trees, so the designated trails often lead from one to the other. The Lyons Falls Trail, for example, which was once a stagecoach trail, starts in the park and goes to two falls in the forest. There are over 12 miles of hiking trails within the park, most rated moderate in difficulty, and another 30 miles in the forest. In addition to the falls, there are trails leading to such attractions as Clearfork Gorge and the lake dam. About 10 miles of the trails are open for cross-country skiing in winter. There is also a two-mile self-guided nature trail in the park. According to local history, John Chapman, immortalized as Johnny Appleseed, tended apple orchards and planted trees here in the 1800s. But much more of the tree planting was done by the Civilian Conservation Corps (CCC) in the 1930s. Although there are no bridle trails or snowmobile trails within the park boundaries, you can enjoy both sports in the forest. The park has no designated bike trails, but bikes can be ridden on the paved roads. The lodge rents bikes.

The park/forest area is the home of a number of white-tailed deer, raccoons, opossum, skunks, and red fox. In the not too distant past, wild turkey had almost disappeared from this area, but now it can be seen in significant numbers. Of particular interest to birders is the abundance of nesting warblers in the Clearfork Gorge. More than 15 species nest here in spring and summer.

Camping and Accommodations

All 96 **lodge** rooms have private balconies and TV. Children under age 10 stay free in their parents' rooms. Amenities include a dining room that has a lake view, lounge and bar, sauna, gift shop, two tennis courts, and the two pools. A double costs $85 in high season. For reservations call 800/AT-A-PARK.

The 25 family **cabins,** located in a wooded area along the river, are all two-bedroom that sleep six. Heated, they are available year-round. Reservations for these cabins must be made directly

through the park by calling 419/994-4290. This is also the number to call for those of the **campsites** that may be reserved. One hundred fifty-three of the 177 sites have electric hookups. These go for $15 per night, nonelectric for $7. There are 24 sites in a primitive camp, which go for $10 during peak season, $7 during low season. No reservations.

Nearby Attractions

An easy daytrip to the northwest in Lucas—12 miles—is **Malabar Farm State Park** (tel. 419/892-2784). Here you'll find the largest working farm in a state park. You can take a guided tour of the **32-room mansion** of Pulitzer Prize–winning author Louis Bromfield, where Humphrey Bogart and Lauren Bacall were married in 1945. The **Malabar Inn,** a restaurant in an 1820 stagecoach inn, is on the park grounds.

A little farther northwest in **Mansfield,** you can visit the **Living Bible Museum** (tel. 419/524-0139); the 47 acres of the **Kingwood Center and Gardens** (tel. 419/522-0211); the **Oak Kill Cottage** (tel. 419/525-1878), considered one of the most perfect examples of Gothic houses in the nation; or take a carousel ride in **Richland Carousel Park** (tel. 419/522-4223), then tour the nearby Carousel Works where wooden carousels are produced.

To the east in **Holmes County,** near the town of Berlin, you can visit an example of an **Amish farm and home.** Amish communities are scattered throughout the area and north toward **Wooster.** At the **Ohio Agricultural Research and Development Center** (tel. 216/263-3779) in Wooster, you can amble in the arboretum and rhododendron and rose gardens daily during daylight hours.

At **Coshocton**—to the southeast, also an easy daytrip—is the living museum of the **Roscoe Village** (tel. 614/622-9310), where you can take a **horse-drawn canal-boat ride** around this restored 1830s Ohio–Erie Canal town.

And if you want all the sights and activities of a major city, you have choices. Go northeast about 1½ hours on I-71 to **Cleveland,** or about the same distance to the southeast on I-71 to state capital at **Columbus.** You can make a daytrip of these cities, but a stay overnight would probably be better.

Shawnee State Park

Lodge/ Hotel   Restaurant   Cabins & Cottages   RV Camping   Tent Camping   Primitive Camping   Marina   Boating   Fishing   Beach   Snorkeling & Diving   Picnic Areas

Trails   Horse Trails   Nature Programs   Golf   Tennis   Fitness Center   Playground   Gift Shop

Capsule Description: A resort park surrounded by a large forest.

Location: South-central Ohio, near the Kentucky border. From Plymouth, take U.S. Highway 52 west to Ohio Route 125 to the park.

Address: 4404 State Rte. 125, Portsmouth, OH 45663-9003 (tel. 614/858-6652).

Area Contacts: Portsmouth Convention and Visitors Bureau, P.O. Box 509, Portsmouth, OH 45662 (tel. 614/353-1116).

Insider Tip: The terminus of the Ohio Historic Canoe route is in the park.

This is another park that owes much of its attractiveness to being surrounded by a state forest. The park itself is just 1,165 acres, but it knifes into the heart of the 60,000-acre Shawnee State Forest, the largest of Ohio's 20 state forests. This area was once the hunting grounds of the Shawnee Indians. Historians note that the word Shawnee means "those who have silver" and this tribe conducted considerable trade in that precious metal.

One small section of the park is detached from the main section and the forest. It sits on U.S. 52 on the Ohio River, about five miles from the main park, and features a marina and a golf course.

Activities

There are two small lakes in the park. The 48-acre Turkey Creek Lake has a swimming beach (no lifeguards) and boat livery where you can rent canoes, paddleboats, and electric boat motors. This lake is a favorite with area scuba divers. There's another swimming beach (no lifeguards) on the 20-acre Roosevelt Lake. Only electric motors are allowed on boats on both lakes. The lakes are stocked regularly so anglers can expect good catches of largemouth bass, catfish, bluegill, crappie, and trout. A trout derby is held annually. In the winter the lakes are popular for ice skating and ice fishing.

The marina offers access to the Ohio River where there are no boating restrictions. This is a full-service marina with more than 100 docks for boats up to 60 feet long. The river is popular for boating, waterskiing, and fishing.

The golf course, adjoining the marina is an 18-hole, par-72 championship course.

When thinking of hiking, the park and the forest should be considered as one, since there are no barriers between them. Within the park itself there are only three small trails. Two of these are one-mile loop nature trails rated easy to moderate in difficulty. The other, the Lookout Trail, a mile round-trip rated moderate to difficult, goes to higher ground for a bird's-eye view. For serious hikers, there are trails all over the state forest, including the 42-mile Backpack Trail that makes a wide loop through the forest with the park at its center. Much of the trail is over rugged terrain and rated moderate to difficult. There are primitive campsites along this trail.

The forest also has more than 70 miles of bridle trails and a horsemen's camp with 58 campsites that are on a first-come basis.

If you like to drive narrow, gravel forest roads—especially if you have a four-wheel-drive vehicle—you might want to try the Panoram Scenic Drive that winds through the park and the surrounding forest. This road is most popular during the spring blossom and fall colors seasons.

Camping and Accommodations

The **lodge** has 50 guest rooms, with furnishings crafted by local artisans. It has a full-service dining room, fitness center, indoor pool, whirlpool, sauna, and two tennis courts. The high-season rate on a double is $78.

The 25 family housekeeping **cabins** here are all two-bedrooms that sleep six. They go for $89 per night. Lodge facilities are available to cabin guests. Reservations for the lodge and cabins are made through 800/AT-A-PARK.

All but three of the 107 **campsites** are multiuse with electric hookups. Those three are for tents only. Electric sites go for $11, the nonelectric for $7. For reservations call 614/858-4561 during the high season and 614/858-6652 in the off-season. Pet camping is available for a limited number of sites.

Nearby Attractions

The nearby city of **Portsmouth** sits at the confluence of the Scioto and Ohio rivers. Here you can see several houses dating to the early 1800s, a historic district, and the **Southern Ohio Museum and Cultural Center** (tel. 614/354-5629).

Oklahoma

QUARTZ MOUNTAIN
RESORT AND STATE PARK

LAKE MURRAY
RESORT AND STATE PARK

BEAVERS BEND AND
HOCHATOWN STATE PARKS

Oklahoma has 55 state parks.

Contacts

· Division of State Parks, Oklahoma Tourism and Recreation Department, Box 60789, Oklahoma City, OK 73146-0789 (tel. toll free 800/652-6552, 800/654-8240 for resort and cabin reservations only).

General Information on Oklahoma State Parks

The name of the state comes from two Choctaw Indian words meaning "Red People." This is appropriate since Oklahoma has one of the largest Native American populations in the country with 36 tribal headquarters and representatives from 67 tribes residing in the state. Counties, towns, and streets throughout the state are named for Indian leaders and tribes. This is carried on in the parks with names like Arrowhead, Cherokee, and Roman Nose.

The history of the state can also be traced through its state parks, from the ancient markings on the Heaverner Runestone to the dinosaur remains at Black Mesa. Closer to our time, you can experience Robbers Cave, hideout to many outlaws, or Red Rock Canyon, winter camp for both Indians and settlers.

Many of the parks are located on lakes. Oklahoma boasts that it has more man-made lakes than any other state and 2,000 more miles of shoreline than the Atlantic and Gulf coasts combined.

GENERAL FEES
Admission to the parks is free.

CAMPING AND ACCOMMODATIONS
Five parks are designated as resort parks with a **lodge** or inn: Lake Murray, Lake Texoma, Quartz Mountain, Roman Nose, and Sequoyah. Together they offer close to 350 rooms and suites. Rates are seasonal, from a low in the winter from December through February, to a high in the summer from May 15 through September 15. Rates also vary with location within the resort, such as lakeside or poolside, making high-season rates for a double range from about $58 to $75. In the winter season, the same room goes for about $40. Children, 18 and under, are free when they stay with parents in the same room.

The five resort parks also have 235 **cabins** for rent, and nine other parks add another 180 cabins. Cabin size and facilities vary widely but most are one- or two-bedroom. A one-bedroom sleeps four and a two-bedroom sleeps six. There are a few larger cabins in the system that sleep more. Some have kitchens and some have fireplaces. Most cabins have seasonal rates. In summer the rental range on a simple one-bedroom in the resort parks goes from about $63 to $68. Rates are generally lower in the nonresort parks.

For resort and cabin information and reservations call toll free 800/654-8240.

All but nine smaller parks have campgrounds, the other 46 offering a total of close to 6,600 campsites. The majority of the sites are multiuse and designated as "modern" when they have three-way hookups, "semimodern" with electric and water hookups only, and "primitive/unimproved" when there are no hookups. About 40 of the parks have either modern or semimodern sites, some with a combination of both. Modern cost $13 per night, semimodern $10, and unimproved $6. Most parks accept reservations, which are made directly to the park and may be made up to a year in advance. At Roman Nose State Park you can rent a teepee, with electric and water, that sleeps four for $15.

Group camps, most with dormitory buildings, are available in more than a dozen parks.

Pets. Pets must be on a leash not longer than 10 feet and under control at all times. They are not permitted in the lodges or other public buildings, but are allowed in some cabins. Free kennels are available in some of the resort parks.

Alcoholic beverages. No alcoholic beverage stronger than 3.2% alcohol is permitted.

Discounts. The base rate on campsites is discounted 50% for all Oklahoma residents age 62 and older and for out-of-state visitors age 62 and older if their resident state reciprocates the same discounts to Oklahoma senior citizens. The base rate for campsites is also discounted 50% for persons 100% disabled. Members of the National Camping and Hiking Association and Good Sam Clubs should inquire about camping discounts. These are reviewed annually and may or may not be in effect.

Beavers Bend and Hochatown State Parks

Restaurant | Cabins & Cottages | RV Camping | Tent Camping | Primitive Camping | Group Lodge Dormitories | Marina | Boating | Boat Launch | Fishing

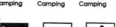

Beach | Waterskiing | Snorkeling & Diving | Picnic Areas | Trails | Nature Programs | Golf | Tennis | Playground | Gift Shop

Capsule Description: Adjoining parks with developed facilities on a river and a lake.

Location: Southeastern corner of Oklahoma near the Arkansas and Texas borders. From Broken Bow, take U.S. Highway 259 north seven miles to Oklahoma Highway 259A, then east three miles.

Address: Beavers Bend State Park, P.O. Box 10, Broken Bow, OK 74728 (tel. 405/494-6300 or 405/494-6538 for reservations).

Area Contacts: Broken Bow Chamber of Commerce, 214 Martin Luther King, Broken Bow, OK 74728 (tel. 405/584-3393).

Hugo Chamber of Commerce, 200 S. Broadway, Hugo, OK 74743 (tel. 405/326-7511).

Kiamichi Country, P.O. Box 638, Wilburton, OK 74578 (tel. toll free 800/722-8180 or 405/326-5598).

Insider Tip: The river below the powerhouse is off-limits to any water use, even wading.

Mountains, forests, 300-foot high cliffs, and a trout-fishing river—this is Oklahoma?

Yes, it is. Beaver Bend State Park encompasses part of the Mountain Fork River that runs through pine and hardwood forests in the Kiamichi Mountains. Adjoining it is Hochatown State Park on the 14,200-acre Broken Bow Lake, an Army Corps of Engineers lake. Together the two parks total more than 5,200 acres. Although these parks are separated administratively, they are usually considered as one by visitors, and by this book.

Activities

In season, the cool waters of the river are stocked with rainbow trout every two weeks. Bass and crappie are also among the regular catches here. The 22-mile-long lake with 180 miles of shoreline offers a wider selection of species of bass and crappie plus channel and flathead catfish and a variety of sunfish.

At a marina on the lake, in season, concessionaires rent all types of water craft including small fishing boats, bass boats, party barges, ski boats, canoes, kayaks, and even paddleboats, bumper boats, and tubes. They also offer whitewater canoe trips that go out of the park, and war canoe tours. There are also overnight boat slips for rent.

For swimmers, there are beaches on both the river and the lake (no lifeguards). The lake is also popular with scuba divers.

On land, guided trail rides and hayrides are available. There's both a regulation 18-hole golf course and a miniature course, plus tennis courts. This is also the home of the Forest Heritage Center Museum, which is designed to show man's continuing relationship with the forest. Diorama exhibits here take you on a journey from the prehistoric forests of the Mesozoic era through projections of 21st-century forestry. The park also has a separate nature center with year-round campfire and other programs by a naturalist.

The two short nature trails—three-fourths of a mile and one mile—are both rated easy to moderate for walkers. For hikers the 26-mile David Boren trail can be taken in shorter bits and pieces. Sections of this trail are rated from easy to difficult. Hikers have a good chance of seeing white-tailed deer, beaver, mink, and raccoon. Birders can expect to see quail, dove, and a variety of other birds including waterfowl during migrating season and bald eagles that winter here from November through mid-March.

Construction of a bike trail is in the works; meanwhile, bikes can be rented at the Forest Heritage Center and ridden on paved roads.

You can enjoy a view of the river from the deck of the full-service restaurant in Beavers Bend.

Camping and Accommodations

There are plans to build a new 40-room lodge on the lake in the near future. Perhaps it will be completed by the time you read this. Meanwhile, Beavers Bend has 47 rental **cabins** either in wooded groves or overlooking the river. There are 11 one-bedroom cabins that sleep two, 22 cabins able to sleep four, and 14 cabins able to sleep six. All are housekeeping cabins with kitchens, heat and air-conditioning, some with fireplaces; no phones or TV. A one-bedroom cabin with a river view, the most expensive, goes for about $58 in high season and every weekend and $48 on weekdays in December through February. Park-view cabins are cheaper. For reservations call toll free 800/654-8240 or directly to the park at 405/494-6538.

Beavers Bend has 110 semimodern multiuse **campsites** with electricity and water and 68 unimproved sites. Hochatown has 21 modern sites with three-way hookups, 28 semimodern with electricity and water, and 165 unimproved sites. Modern cost $13, semimodern $10, and unimproved $6. Call 405/494-6300 for reservations.

Nearby Attractions

Native American artifacts are at the heart of two places to visit in **Broken Bow. The Memorial Indian Museum** (tel. 405/584-6531) has an outstanding collection of Caddo Indian pottery, and the **Gardner Mansion** (tel. 405/584-6588) was the home of a Choctaw Chief. A little further south, in **Idabel,** is the **Museum of the Red River** (tel. 405/286-3616) with exhibits dedicated to Native Americans.

Another daytrip to the east is **Hugo** where you can take the longest scenic passenger ride in Oklahoma at the **Hugo Heritage Railroad and Frisco Museum** (tel. 405/326-6630).

Lake Murray Resort and State Park

Lodge/Hotel | Restaurant | Cabins & Cottages | RV Camping | Tent Camping | Primitive Camping | Group Lodge Dormitories | Marina | Boating | Boat Launch | Fishing | Swimming | Beach

Waterskiing | Snorkeling & Diving | Picnic Areas | Trails | Horse Trails | Nature Programs | Bicycling | Golf | Tennis | Playground | Gift Shop

Capsule Description: A resort park on a lake.

Location: South-central Oklahoma, six miles south of Ardmore near the border with Texas. Take Exit 29 off I-35, go east on U.S. Highway 70, to Scenic Route 77, then south to the park. (Scenic 77 circles the park.)

Address: 3310 S. Lake Murray Dr., no. 1, Ardmore, OK 73401 (tel. 405/223-4044 for the office and camping reservations; toll free 800/654-8240 or 405/223-6600 for lodge and cabin reservations).

Area Contacts: Ardmore Chamber of Commerce, P.O. Box 1585, Ardmore, OK 73402 (tel. 405/223-7765).

Lake Country, P.O. Box 456, Davis, OK 73030 (tel. 405/369-3392).

Tishomingo Chamber of Commerce, 101 S. Capitol, Tishomingo, OK 73460 (tel. 405/371-2175).

Insider Tip: *Condé Nast Traveler* has named Lake Murray one of the top 100 swimming holes in the nation.

In the early 1930s, in the depths of the depression, William H. "Alfalfa Bill" Murray, one of Oklahoma's most colorful governors, decided to take advantage of Franklin D. Roosevelt's New Deal to help the people of his state. He arranged for the state to buy the land and got the federal government to provide thousands of Works Progress Administration (WPA) and Civilian Conservation Corps (CCC) workers to transform a forest into a man-made recreation lake. The result was the 6,500-acre lake and the 12,496-acre state park, both named after him, which combined to make the first, and largest, state park in Oklahoma. To round it out, long after Governor Murray's time, the first lodge in the state park system was constructed here in 1957.

Lake Murray is strictly a state recreational lake—no power or flood control involved and no private homes or development, so much of the 115 miles of shoreline has a wilderness appearance. Fed by natural springs and local creeks, against a sandstone bottom, the water generally stays clear and remarkably blue.

"Alfalfa Bill's" plans for the park were not a total success. He started construction of a rock tower modeled on the tower of a castle on the Rhine River. This was to be a summer home for the governor in those pre–air conditioning times. But, the federal government thought it too expensive and stopped the funding before it could be completed. It was finally completed in the 1950s, and today, known as Tucker Tower, is a museum.

Activities

While the workmen were building the lake, they discovered a large meteorite that is among the exhibits of Oklahoma geology and wildlife you can now see in this museum. The top of the tower is the best place to get a bird's-eye view of the lake. The tower is also the park's nature center with a full-time naturalist who conducts programs and guided walks throughout the year.

Water sports are a large part of the activities here. There are boat launches all around the lake and at the marina you can rent fishing boats with motors and pontoon boats. Nearby, at the Water Sports Center, you can rent all sorts of water toys: paddleboats, canoes, sailboats, Windsurfers, water skis, yak boards, and water bikes. You can also take an hour tour of the lake on a pontoon boat or, if you have a group of 25 or more, on a houseboat.

You can boat fish or throw in a line off the fishing piers located at most of the campgrounds, including one pier that's handicapped-accessible. Or, if the weather's not the best, you can fish in a heated indoor marina. Florida, largemouth, and smallmouth bass and channel catfish are all stocked. These, plus crappie, are the main catches.

There are three swimming areas on the lake (no lifeguards) and a pool near the lodge (with lifeguards in season). The pool is free to lodge and cabin guests, but there's a fee for everyone else.

On land, your options are equally diverse. There's an 18-hole regulation golf course, a minia-ture golf course, and a Frisbee golf course, tennis courts, and bike rentals.

The park riding stables offers trail rides and hayrides. The stables are only for rental horses, but there are times when you can bring your own horse. This is when the area set aside for bird-dog field trials is not in use. Then the 32 miles of field-trial trails and the field-trial barn stalls are available. But call first.

There are also 26 miles of motorcycle trails.

Three short trails in the park are for walkers: the two-mile self-guided Buckhorn Interpretive Trail, the 1½-mile Anadarche Nature Trail, and an unnamed ¾-mile trail near one of the campgrounds. All are rated easy.

Animal residents of the park include whitetailed deer, turkeys, raccoons, armadillos, beavers, and other small animals. Among the many species birders should be able to spot are a variety of herons, cranes, ducks, geese, roadrunners, and an occasional bald eagle.

The park is also the home of the Heritage Arts and Crafts workshops where you can take classes in folk arts ranging from quiltmaking to storytelling.

To round out the facilities, there is a chapel open 24 hours for meditation, a remote-control aircraft flying area, and a 2,500-foot airstrip for real planes.

Camping and Accommodations

The 54 guest rooms in the **Country Inn** go for $58 to $75 in high season. A suite costs $150 all year. The inn has a restaurant and a lounge/bar.

The 88 **cabins** come in a wide variety of styles, furnishings, sleeping capacity—from 2 to 14—and prices. In high season, a Country Cottage that sleeps four goes for $68, a Villa that sleeps four is $78, and the same on the lakefront is $98. A family cabin that sleeps 14 costs $225 per night in high season and $125 in the winter season.

Reservations for the inn and cabins may be made through the 800 number or the park reservation number.

The eight **campgrounds** scattered around the

lake offer a total of 268 improved sites. The breakdown is: 35 semimodern sites with two way hookups that may be reserved, 182 semimodern, and 51 modern with three-way hookups that are on a first-come basis. Unimproved/primitive camping is unlimited with some sites that may be reached by car or boat. Modern sites are $13, semimodern $10, and unimproved $6. There's an extra charge of $1 for reservations, which may be made by calling the park at 405/223-4044. Three of the eight campgrounds remain open in the winter.

Three group camps with cabins are available. Each will accommodate 160 to 190 people.

Nearby Attractions

Ardmore, just up the road to the north, has a **doll museum** (tel. 405/223-8290) at the Ardmore Public Library; some of the dolls date back to the early 1700s. A center for the visual and performing arts is also found in Ardmore.

In **Marietta,** about nine miles south of the park, you'll find the first courthouse built in Oklahoma after statehood, a pioneer museum, and the **Marietta Bakery** (tel. 405/276-3312), a cookie factory.

Two small cities to the east worth a daytrip visit are Durant and Tishomingo. Attractions in **Durant** include the **Fort Washita Historic Site** (tel. 405/924-6502) on the shore of Lake Texoma. **Tishomingo** is the capital of the Chickasaw Nation and features several museums including the **Chickasaw Council House Museum** (tel. 405/371-3351).

It takes about two hours to drive I-35 north to **Oklahoma City** and about the same time south to the **Dallas/Fort Worth Metroplex.**

Quartz Mountain Resort and State Park

 Lodge/Hotel
 Restaurant
 Cabins & Cottages
 RV Camping
 Tent Camping
 Primitive Camping
 Group Lodge Dormitories
 Marina
 Boating
 Boat Launch
 Fishing
 Swimming

 Boat Launch
 Fishing
 Swimming
 Beach
 Waterskiing
 Picnic Areas
 Trails
 Nature Programs
 Golf Tennis Playground Gift Shop

Capsule Description: A resort park on a mountain lake.

Location: Southwestern Oklahoma, 17 miles north of Altus. From Altus, take U.S. Highway 283/Oklahoma Highway 6 north to Oklahoma 44 then one mile to 44A to the park.

Address: Route 1, Box 40, Lone Wolf, OK 73655 (tel. 405/563-2238 for the office; toll free 800/654-8240 or 405/563-2424 for lodge/cabin reservations).

Area Contacts: Altus Chamber of Commerce, P.O. Box 518, Altus, OK 73522 (tel. 405/482-0210).

Anadarko Chamber of Commerce, P.O. Box 366, Anadarko, OK 73005 (tel. 405/247-6651).

Great Plains Country, P.O. Box 249, Burns Flat, OK 73624 (tel. toll free 800/627-4882.

Lawton Chamber of Commerce, P.O. Box 1376, Lawton, OK 73502 (tel. 405/355-3541).

Insider Tip: The Lodge offers Eagle Watch programs in January and February.

They are not high, but the rugged, granite formation of the Quartz Mountains take on a look of majesty as they rise in the midst of the high, dry plains of southwestern Oklahoma. The 4,540-acre park sits on the shore of the 6,770-acre Altus-Lugert Lake amid the pinkish-red granite hills and woodlands.

Quartz Mountain State Park is in a region that has the unusual distinction—at least for Oklahoma—of having been under five flags. First it was Spanish, then French, included in the Louisiana Province, which was sold to the United States but claimed successively by Mexico and the Republic of Texas. It became part of the U.S. again when Texas entered the Union, but as a Texas county. It wasn't until 1896 that the Supreme Court ruled that this area belonged to the U.S. not the old Republic of Texas, and the land was assigned to the Oklahoma Territory.

For two weeks every summer, the park is home to the Oklahoma Summer Arts Institute. Two-hundred students, who have passed rigorous auditions, receive intensive training from masters in dance, acting, music, photography, and creative writing. Faculty demonstrations and student performances in the evenings are open to the public.

Activities

The lake offers the opportunity for a wide variety of water sports including boating, waterskiing, jet skiing, and tubing. There's a full-service marina on the lake. Fishing boats, ski boats, and jet skis can be rented. Fishing is good for striper, bass, and crappie. Canoe and paddleboat rentals are on the three-quarters of a mile of river that runs through the park. Campers and day-use visitors can swim at two beach areas (no lifeguards). Lodge guests have use of both an outdoor and an indoor pool.

You can find plenty of places to hike in the park, but there's only one designated trail. It goes about a mile up a mountain and is rated moderate to difficult.

Wildlife in the park includes white-tailed deer, raccoons, and other small animals. Among the birds seen here are osprey, vultures, migrating waterfowl, and, in winter, bald eagles.

Other land-based facilities include an 18-hole golf course, a miniature golf course, and tennis courts. On the north shore there is an Off-road Vehicle Area, including sand dunes, open in the summer to motorcycles, ATVs, and other off-roaders. An ORV Area permit costs $4 a day.

Camping and Accommodations

The **lodge** has 45 rooms and suites. Rooms rent for $58 in summer and the suites cost $125 in the same high season. There are also six one-bedroom **cabins** that sleep four, and eight two-bedroom units that sleep six. All have TVs, but since this is the mountains and reception is poor, they are for VCR use only. No phones. A one-bedroom costs $68 in high season, a two-bedroom $88. The lodge has a full-service restaurant.

Of the 114 multiuse **campsites,** 20 are modern sites with three-way hookups and the rest are semimodern with electric and water hookups. In addition, there are almost unlimited sites to put up tents. Modern sites cost $13, semimodern $10, unimproved tent sites $6. All are on a first-come basis; no reservations.

A 10-cabin group camp can sleep up to 125. Contact the park office for reservations.

Nearby Attractions

For the kids, a water slide and go-kart track are located just outside the park.

You can learn about the under-five-flags history of this area of Oklahoma at the **Museum of the Western Prairie** (tel. 405/482-1044) in nearby **Altus.**

About 30 miles southeast is the **Wichita Mountains Wildlife Refuge** (tel. 405/429-3222) where you can see herds of buffalo and longhorn cattle. The **home of Quanah Parker** (tel. 405/429-3420), the last major chief of the Comanches to surrender, is in **Cache,** near the refuge.

Just past this wildlife refuge is **Fort Sill** (tel. 405/442-8111), the U.S. Army's Field Artillery

School. The Old Post here has 43 buildings that date back to the 1870s and are now a National Historic Landmark. Geronimo, the famed Apache leader, is buried here. A few miles south of the fort is the city of **Lawton,** which features several museums including the **Museum of the Great Plains** (tel. 405/581-3460).

If you want to know more about the Native Americans who live here, the place to go is **Anadarko.** It's about 60 miles northeast of the park, a long daytrip but worth it. Here, in **Indian City USA** (tel. 405/247-5661), are authentic reconstructions of the villages of seven tribes that lived on the plains.

Oregon

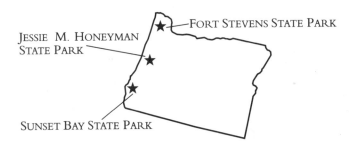

JESSIE M. HONEYMAN STATE PARK

FORT STEVENS STATE PARK

SUNSET BAY STATE PARK

Oregon has 200 state parks.

Contacts

- State Parks and Recreation Department, 1115 Commercial St. NE, Salem, OR 97310-1001 (tel. 503/378-8605).
- Oregon Tourism Division, Economic Development Department, 775 Summer St. NE, Salem, OR 97310 (tel. toll free 800/547-7842).

General Information About Oregon State Parks

Variety is definitely the way of life in Oregon, starting with the scenery. From the hundreds of miles of beaches along the Pacific to the mountain ski resorts to the semiarid high desert in the east, the state offers a bountiful supply of changing and contrasting landscapes. The state parks, which consistently rate among the top 10 in the nation for annual attendance, are designed to offer prime examples of each variety for your enjoyment.

In addition to the parks, the parks system maintains the Oregon Coast Trail, a hiking trail that extends the length of the state between the Oregon-California border and the Columbia River. Paralleling this, generally following U.S. Highway 101, is the Oregon Coast Bike Route maintained by the Department of Transportation.

GENERAL FEES

Entrance fees are collected at about three dozen of the more popular parks during the high season from May 1 through September 30. Most fees are $3 per vehicle. Annual permits are available for $20.

CAMPING

Fifty parks have campgrounds. Reservations are accepted for the 3,700 campsites in 13 of these parks from Memorial Day weekend through Labor Day weekend. The rest of the year they are on a first-come basis. An additional 2,600 campsites in the other 37 parks are on a first-come basis all year.

Up-to-the minute information on campsite availability at all state parks may be obtained from the Oregon State Park Campsite Information Center. Inside Oregon, except in the Portland area, call toll free 800/452-5687. Out-of-state and in the Portland area, call 503/238-7488. The center operates from the first Monday in March through Labor Day weekend from 8am to 4:30pm weekdays. This is for information only; no reservations.

Reservations must be made directly to the 13 reservation parks on a standard application form available from the parks, state police, and many chamber of commerce visitor information centers. They are accepted from the second Monday in January until Labor Day. Fees run about $14 for tent sites and $16 for sites with hookups. Reduced rates are available off-season.

Special campsites designed for hikers and bicyclists are available in 20 parks, most along the coast where they connect with the coast hiking and biking trails. There are also group camps in 14 parks and horse camps in four parks.

Pets. Pets are welcome in most parks as long as they are under control and kept on a leash not more than six feet long. Generally, they are not permitted in buildings.

Alcoholic beverages. Alcoholic beverages are allowed.

Fort Stevens State Park

RV Camping · Tent Camping · Group Camping · Boating · Fishing · Swimming · Beach · Trails · Nature Programs · Bicycling · Playground

Capsule Description: A historic park with developed facilities.
Location: Northernmost point on the Oregon coast at the mouth of the Columbia River about 10 miles west of Astoria. From Seaside, take U.S. Highway 101 north and follow signs to the park.
Address: Hammond, OR 97121 (tel. 503/861-3170).
Area Contacts: Greater Astoria Area Chamber of Commerce, P.O. Box 176, Astoria, OR 97103 (tel. 503/325-6311).

Portland/Oregon Visitors Association, 26 SW Salmon, Portland, OR 97204 (tel. 503/222-2223 or toll free 800/962-3700).

Seaside Chamber of Commerce, P.O. Box 7, Seaside, OR 97138 (tel. toll free 800/444-6740).
Insider Tip: A Civil War reenactment takes place over the Labor Day weekend—a major event.

In 1863, in response to the presence of British and Confederate sea raiders in the area, President Lincoln ordered the construction of fortifications at the mouth of the Columbia River. The fort served to protect the area from the Civil War until 1947. Near the end of its career, in World War II, it earned the unique distinction of being the only military installation in the continental United States to be fired on since the War of 1812. On the night of June 21, 1942, less than seven months after Pearl Harbor, a Japanese submarine fired 17 shells in the vicinity of the fort. The shelling caused no damage, and since the sub was out of range, the fort did not return fire.

Now the historic fort is the centerpiece of this 3,800-acre park.

Activities

From May through September, the fort becomes a living history museum with costumed personnel acting the part of residents during the fort's Civil War years. During the summer there are tours, some conducted on army trucks, and programs, or you can take a self-guided walking tour all year. The fort museum contains maps and displays as well as artifacts from archeological digs. A good view of the Columbia River can be seen from the commander's station and several other locations in the park.

Aside from exploring the historic section, the park offers a number of other things to do.

For hikers there are five miles of trails in the park or you can take your first steps down the hundreds of miles of the Oregon Coast Trail from its origin point here. There are also eight miles of paved bike trails and the Coast Bike Route is nearby. In summer, the park naturalist conducts a variety of nature programs including bike nature tours.

A walk along the beach will lead you to the wreck of the *Peter Iredale,* an iron, four-masted, English bark that ran aground during a storm in 1906.

The three small lakes in the park add up to about 56 acres. Swimming is allowed at the two beaches on Coffenbury Lake, the largest of the three. Powerboats are permitted on this lake but speeds are limited to 10 miles per hour. The lakes are stocked with trout and anglers can also expect to catch large and smallmouth bass, bluegill, and crappie. Or you can go saltwater fishing from the jetty and try for salmon, sturgeon, ling cod, sea perch, and a variety of others.

This is also a birders' paradise since more than 300 species of migrating and resident birds have been recorded here. For an especially good view of the many seabirds, try the observation platform at the South Jetty. A wildlife observation platform is found near Swash Lake. On land, Roosevelt Elk and black-tailed deer are occasionally seen in the woods.

And, of course, a most popular activity in spring and winter is watching the migrating whales.

Camping

Of the 604 campsites: 213 have three-way hookups, 130 have electric and water, and 261 are tent sites with water available. Most sites are in the woods with little separation between them. All can be reserved during the high season and reservations are strongly recommended on summer weekends, holidays, and during the entire month of August. Fees range from $14 to $16.

There are seven group camps each holding a maximum of 25 people. These are tent only.

Nearby Attractions

Astoria, to the east, was the first permanent U.S. settlement west of the Rocky Mountains. Ornate Victorian architecture abounds in this scenic port town with some of the houses now serving as bed-and-breakfast inns. Among the several museums here, the **Columbia River Maritime Museum** (tel. 503/325-2323) has displays covering more than 200 years of maritime history. The last U.S. Coast Guard lightship on the Pacific coast is also moored at the museum dock. If you feel energetic, you can climb the 166 steps to the top of the Astoria Column for a bird's-eye view of the river and across into Washington. The 4.1-mile Astoria Bridge over the Columbia is the longest continuous truss span bridge in the world.

The **Jewell Meadow Wildlife Refuge** (tel. 503/755-2264) is 22 miles southeast of Astoria on Highway 202. On the scenic drive through this refuge you'll see hundreds of Roosevelt elk that live here.

Another easy daytrip is to take Highway 101 south along the coast to the resort town of **Seaside,** which is famed for its Prom, a mile-and-a-half street for strolling paralleling the beach. This town marks the westernmost end of Lewis and Clark's 2,000-mile journey from St. Louis, Missouri, to the sea in 1804–06.

For an overnight, head for **Portland,** often rated as one of America's most livable cities. Among the many things to see and experience here are the **Oregon Museum of Science and Industry** (tel. 503/797-4000); the **World Forestry Center** (tel. 503/228-1367); the **American Advertising Museum,** the first museum in the United States devoted to advertising, the weather machines in **Pioneer Courthouse Square** (tel. 503/223-1613); the **Japanese Gardens** (tel. 503/223-1321); **Metro Washington Park Zoo** (tel. 503/226-1561); and a sprinkling of **microbreweries,** each offering its own distinctive brews. The City of Roses also lays claim to **Mill Ends Park,** the world's smallest dedicated park at just 24 inches, and the only extinct volcano within a continental U.S. city.

Jessie M. Honeyman State Park

RV Camping Tent Camping Group Camping Boating Fishing Swimming Beach Waterskiing

Snorkeling & Diving Picnic Areas Trails Nature Programs Bicycling Playground

Capsule Description: A small natural park with developed facilities.

Location: Western Oregon, on the coast. From Florence, take U.S. Highway 101 south about three miles to the park.

Address: 84505 Hwy. 101, Florence, Oregon 97439 (tel. 503/997-3641 or 503/997-3851).

Area Contacts: Florence Area Chamber of Commerce, P.O. Box 26000, Florence, OR 97439 (tel. 503/997-3128).

Lower Umpqua Chamber of Commerce, P.O. Box 11, Reedsport, OR 97467 (tel. 503/271-3495).

It's fitting that this park is named as a memorial to Jessie M. Honeyman. The founder of the Oregon Roadside Council in 1932, she was a tireless worker, right up until her death at the age of 96, to preserve and display Oregon's scenic beauty. And this park is a beautiful gem.

The 522-acre park contains three sparkling freshwater lakes, towering sand dunes—it's the northern gateway to the Oregon Dunes National Recreation Area—and a forest that bursts into color with a profusion of rhododendrons in spring and early summer.

Activities

Although the ocean is just about two miles away—you can see it from the top of the dunes—the two larger lakes in this park are a major draw for visitors.

For swimmers there are three small beaches (no lifeguards), and the clear waters are popular with both snorkelers and skin divers. There are three boat ramps and waterskiing is permitted on Woahink Lake, the larger of the three. Canoes and paddleboats can be rented.

Fishing is good from both bank and boat for trout, perch, and bass.

The one marked trail in the park is dual use for both hikers and bikers. It is an easy trail going between the campgrounds and the two larger lakes. Although not a trail, a favorite for hikers is climbing the dunes, some of which have piled up several hundred feet high. And, of course, a seasonal delight is the blossoming of rhododendrons in the forest. May is normally the best month for viewing the profusion of these flowers.

In the summer season, there are a number of interpretive, nature, and campfire programs.

Camping

The 381 **campsites** are almost all in the woods, close together, but most are separated by abundant vegetation. The sites are all multiuse, with 67 having three-way hookups and 75 with electric and water hookups. The other 239 have no hookups. Reservations may be made for the period Memorial Day to Labor Day only. They are accepted starting the second Monday in January but must be on the standard reservation form. The rest of the year, sites are on a first-come basis. Sites cost $12 to $16 per night depending on facilities.

Primitive camping is available in a hike/bike camp that holds about 30, and there are six tent camps for groups that hold about the same number.

Nearby Attractions

The park is set in the midst of myriad forests, lakes, rivers, dunes, and near the ocean, so there's plenty of nature for roaming in the immediate vicinity of the park.

Close by, to the north on Highway 101 is **Florence.** Here you'll find a doll museum featuring several thousand rare and unusual dolls and a pioneer museum. You could rent and drive a dune-buggy, or you can rent a horse to ride the dunes the old way. The Old Town, by the harbor, is a restored area with shops.

Five miles north of Florence is the **Darlingtonia Botanical Wayside,** Oregon's only rare plant sanctuary. An 18-acre park in a bog, it's named for its resident insect-eating cobra lily (*Darlingtoniona californica*).

Just a few miles further north from the habitat

of those carnivorous plants are two other sights worth a visit. **Sea Lion Caves** (tel. 503/547-3111) is a commercial attraction that lets you go down into a huge cave that's the year-round home of hundreds of barking and bawling Steller sea lions. In spring and summer, the sea lions usually sun on the rocky ledges outside the cave, but the rest of the year, the cave is close to standing room only.

From the cave you can see the other local attraction, Oregon's most photographed lighthouse, the **Heceta Head Lighthouse.** Standing on this headland for more than 90 years, it's earned a listing in the National Register of Historic Places. It's said that the caretaker's cottage is haunted.

Bordering Honeyman to the west and sweeping south for more than 40 miles is the **Oregon Sand Dunes Recreation Area** (tel. toll free 800/283-CAMP). The Dunes offer hiking, dune-buggy riding, fishing, boating, and birding—more than 240 species have been sighted here. Just about everything you'll need to do these things can be obtained in the nearby towns like **Reedsport.** Also near Reedsport you can visit the **Dean Creek Elk Viewing Area.**

Sunset Bay State Park

| Visitor Center | RV Camping | Tent Camping | Group Camping | Boat Launch | Fishing | Swimming | Beach | Snorkeling & Diving | Picnic Areas | Trails | Playground |

Capsule Description: A trio of small, contiguous, scenic coastal parks with a variety of developed facilities.

Location: The southern coast of Oregon, starting about 12 miles southwest of the towns of Coos Bay/North Bend. From Coos Bay follow signs to Charleston and Sunset Bay State Park. Sunset Bay, Shore Acres, and Cape Arago State Parks are all on the Cape Arago Highway along the coast.

Address: Sunset Bay State Park, 10965 Cape Arago Hwy., Coos Bay, OR 97420 (tel. 503/888-4902).

Area Contacts: Bandon Chamber of Commerce, P.O. Box 1515, Bandon, OR 97411 (tel. 503/347-9616).

Bay Area Chamber of Commerce, P.O. Box 210, Coos Bay, OR 97420 (tel. toll free 800/824-8486).

Insider Tip: Plans to illuminate the gardens at Shore Acres for occasional night openings are in the works—it's worth inquiring about at the time of your visit.

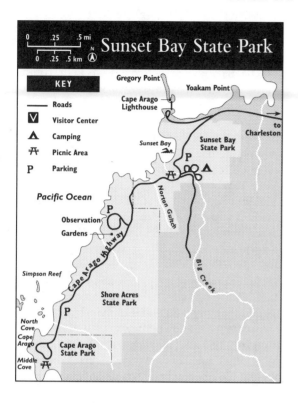

This is the least populated stretch of the Oregon coastline, where the sand dunes that dominated much of the coast to the north stop and some of the state's most ruggedly beautiful seascapes begin. The sandstone cliffs enclosing Sunset Bay make it one of the safest swimming areas on that coast. Shore Acres offers both historic formal gardens and a glass-enclosed observation area for watching the wild waves and whales. And Cape Arago is the site of a lighthouse and a popular viewpoint for spotting seals and sea lions as well as migrating whales.

Activities

A major part of the 395-acre Sunset Bay State Park is given over to the campgrounds, so it has become the center for activities in the three parks. Because of its protected cove it offers an ideal place for swimming on a coast where most beaches have warning signs about dangerous currents and un-

dertows. The beach has a gradual slope and the shallow, wind-protected nature of the bay allows the water to stay warmer than at other more exposed beaches. Skin diving is popular here. There are restrooms, but no showers at the beach, and no lifeguards. There is a boat-launching area at the north end of the beach. Fishermen find the main catches are rockfish and perch. This is a favorite spot for shell-hunters, too, as fossil shells can usually be found at low tide at the bottom of the steep sandstone cliffs along the north and south walls.

A branch of the Oregon Coast Trail takes hikers off the main route to connect these three parks, and the Coast Bike Route diverts from U.S. Highway 101 north of Coos Bay for a more scenic route that goes through the nearby town of Charleston, within five miles of the parks.

Shore Acres, the next park south, is the largest of the three with 736 acres. Its historic gardens, started as part of the summer home of the Louis J. Simpson family in the early 1900s, are filled with exotic plants brought in from around the world. The gardens include a Japanese garden, a 100-foot lily pond, and other formal gardens that showcase a variety of plants including roses, with several new varieties developed here, rhododendrons, azaleas, and climbing wisteria. The Simpson mansion is gone, but its cliff-top site is now occupied by a glass-enclosed observation shelter with a spectacular view of the rugged coastline. Offering good viewing at any season, it's an ideal place to watch the dramatic action as high waves crash on the rocks during winter storm season. There is an information center/gift shop at this park; however, it's volunteer-staffed and open only when volunteers are available. (Pets are not permitted at Shore Acres.)

The final part of the park trio, bordering south of Shore Acres, is the rugged headland of the 134-acre Cape Arago State Park. The original lighthouse here was constructed in 1866; however, wave erosion led to its abandonment and the present lighthouse was built in 1934. Steep trails lead down to the south, middle, and north coves. All three park have excellent observation areas for whale-watching—gray whales in spring and winter and killer whales in early summer—but the viewpoint in this park is especially good for observing sea lions, harbor seals, and elephant seals on the offshore rocks. You can also see cormorants and oyster-catchers on those rocks, plus there are frequent sightings throughout the parks of peregrine falcons, bald eagles, brown pelicans, and a variety of shorebirds.

Camping

The 137 campsites at Sunset Bay are broken down to 29 with three-way hookups, 34 with electric and water, and 74 tent sites with water available. Fees range from $14 to $16 and all sites may be reserved from Memorial Day through Labor Day. Reservation forms for this period are accepted starting the second Monday in January. The rest of the year all sites are on a first-come basis.

There's a small hiker/biker camp near the main campground at Sunset Bay, and a group camping area at both Sunset Bay and Cape Arago.

Nearby Attractions

The coastal dunes end north of Coos Bay, but it's an easy daytrip up U.S. Highway 101 to visit them at the **Oregon Dunes National Recreation Area** (tel. 503/997-3641). This recreation area stretches north for more than 40 miles, encompassing 14,000 acres of dunes, some 500 feet high.

More than half this area is open to ATVs—you can bring your own, rent one, or arrange a dune-buggy tour with a commercial operator.

The nearby joined towns of **North Bend/Coos Bay** are small in size, but offer restaurants, accommodations, and shopping; a couple of small museums; and a Coast Guard cutter and a Myrtlewood factory you can tour—Myrtlewood is a product unique to the South Coast. Major wood products are shipped through the bustling port of Coos Bay.

Between Coos Bay and the parks is the small town of **Charleston** where you can charter boats at the marina for fishing and tours. Nearby is the **South Slough National Estuarine Reserve** (tel. 503/888-5558). With freshwater streams, saltwater marshes, a forested island, and hiking trails, this 4,400-acre reserve has quite a different terrain than the sand dunes to the north.

To the south, down Highway 101, the town of **Bandon** proudly proclaims itself the "Storm-Watching Capital of the World." During the storm season, January to April, lectures and programs on weather phenomena are given. Bandon is Oregon's cranberry capital, too. Several viewpoints along Bandon's coast are outstanding for whale, seal, and bird watching. South of the town is the **West Coast Game Safari Park.** Populated by 450 animals representing 75 species, it lays claim to being America's largest wild animal petting park.

Pennsylvania

RICKETTS GLEN
STATE PARK

PYMATUNING
STATE PARK

OHIOPYLE STATE PARK

Pennsylvania has 114 state parks.

Contacts

• Bureau of State Parks, Department of Environmental Resources, P.O. Box 8551, Harrisburg, PA 17105-8551 (tel. toll free 800/63-PARKS [800/637-2757]).
• Bureau of Travel Marketing, Department of Commerce, Room 453 Forum Building, Harrisburg, PA 17120 (tel. toll free 800/VISIT-PA [800/847-4872]).

General Information on Pennsylvania State Parks

As the birthplace of the Declaration of Independence and the Constitution, site of Lincoln's Gettysburg Address, and home of the Liberty Bell, it's evident that Pennsylvania has played a dynamic role in forging our nation. It was also a transition state in the eastern part of the country in its early years since its southern border is the Mason–Dixon Line, which originally separated the North and South, and the Allegheny Mountains, which run diagonally from the southwest to the northeast, were the barrier that separated the East from the Midwest.

Pennsylvania's state park system had its start in 1893 when the first park was established at Valley Forge. Today the system encompasses more than 277,000 acres of property and has reached the enviable goal of locating a state park within 25 miles of every citizen of the state.

GENERAL FEES
There are no entrance fees to the state parks.

CAMPING AND ACCOMMODATIONS
There are 276 **cabins** located in 26 parks. These are of three types: modern, rustic, and special. The 126 modern cabins were built in recent years by the Pennsylvania Conservation Corps. They are two-bedroom sleeping six and three-bedroom sleeping eight, of log construction, furnished and carpeted, with heat. These rent by the week only for between $270 to $320 for nonresidents in summer. During the other three seasons of the year, half-week rentals are available for some cabins at about half the rent. The modern cabins are open all year.

The rustic cabins were built of log, stone, and wood by the Civilian Conservation Corps (CCC) in the 1930s. They vary in size, sleep two to eight, have sparse furnishings, wood stoves for heat, and no indoor bathroom. They rent for between $85 and $180 a week for nonresidents in summer. Half-week rentals are available the rest of the year, but some rustic cabins are closed from mid-December through mid-April.

The special units are six former large residences in five parks that have been converted to cabins.

These sleep eight to twelve, are open all year, and rent for about $250 a week in season for non-residents.

Contact the Bureau of State Parks or the individual parks for detailed cabin information and reservation forms.

Fifty-seven parks offer more than 7,000 **campsites.** Seventeen parks accept reservations for the period Memorial Day to Labor Day, another 14 accept them only for holiday weekends, and the remainder are on a first-come basis. Campsites with modern sanitary facilities available cost $9 per night for residents, $11 for nonresidents; those with primitive sanitary facilities

go for $7 and $9. There's a $2 additional charge for an electric hookup, when available, and $3 reservation fee. Maximum stay is 14 consecutive nights.

Pets. Pets are permitted if on a leash no more than six feet in length and under control at all times. They are not permitted in swimming or camping or cabin areas.

Alcoholic beverages. Alcoholic beverages are prohibited.

Discounts. Camping discounts are available for both resident and nonresident senior citizens and the physically challenged.

Ohiopyle State Park

RV Camping | Tent Camping | Non-Motorized Boating Only | Fishing | Swimming | Picnic Areas | Trails | Nature Programs | Bicycling | Playground | X-Country Skiing | Snow-mobiling | Gift Shop

Capsule Description: A large, natural park containing a white-water river and developed facilities.
Location: Southwestern Pennsylvania near the Maryland and West Virginia borders. From Uniontown, take U.S. Highway 40 southeast to Farmington, then Pennsylvania 381 four miles north to the park.
Address: Box 105, Ohiopyle, PA 15470 (tel. 412/329-8591).
Area Contacts: Laurel Highlands, Inc., Town Hall, 120 E. Main, Ligonier, PA 15658 (tel. toll free 800/925-7669).

Greater Pittsburgh Convention and Visitors Bureau, 4 Gateway Center, Suite 514, Pittsburgh, PA 15222 (tel. toll free 800/366-0093).
Insider Tip: Most of the scenic overlooks at Ohiopyle can be reached by car.

Old records indicate the name Ohiopyle was derived from an Indian word meaning "white frothy waters," a reference to the falls on the

Youghiogheny River. In 1754, it was these falls that forced George Washington, then fighting for the British, to abandon his search down the river for a water supply route he could use to help him capture Fort Duquesne, now Pittsburgh, from the French.

The focal point of this 19,000-acre park is the 14 miles of the Youghiogheny River Gorge that passes through its heart. The "Yough" is considered among the best white-water boating rivers in the east, and its narrow, heavily-forested, 1,700-feet deep gorge provides spectacular views. The small village of Ohiopyle is located in the middle of the park. Here you'll find a general store that serves hot meals and a gas station.

Activities

The river is divided into two segments by the falls. The "Middle Yough," upstream of the falls, is a nine-mile stretch that includes Class I and II rapids, excellent for canoeing for skilled canoeists. The "Lower Yough," about 7½ miles below the falls, is white water with numerous Class III and IV rapids that are run with sturdily constructed rubber rafts, closed-deck canoes, and kayaks. Four authorized concessionaires provide guided tours on the lower segment. Experienced paddlers can also rent rafts, but if you plan to rent you'll need to reserve a launch permit (fee) from the park office. These are used to control the number of boaters on the river at any one time. Permits are sometimes booked solid on weekends so try to reserve your put-in time early. Canoe rentals are available for use on the Middle Yough.

The more than a dozen designated hiking trails in the park add up to 41 miles. The longest is 17 miles and the shortest just half a mile long. The 3½-mile Beech Trail is a self-guided nature trail. These trails take you to various scenic overlooks with panoramic views, and, in season, to areas blanketed with wildflowers, mountain laurel, and blooming rhododendron. Four of the shorter trails are in the Ferncliff Natural Area, a 100-acre peninsula formed by a loop in the river. The peninsula, a National Natural Landmark, is famed for both the variety of plants and the number of rare plants. Foreshadowing reality, an 1875 map of the Ohiopyle region shows the peninsula as a "future park."

The park is also the southern terminus of the 70-mile Laurel Highlands Hiking Trail and a way point on the Yough River Trail, a hike and bike trail that is still being developed. Eventually this trail will connect Pittsburgh with Washington, D.C.

Nine miles of an abandoned railroad right-of-way that parallels the river has been converted to a hard-surfaced bike and hike trail. Rental bikes are available.

You can't swim the river, at least not intentionally, but there are a scattering of swimming holes in the park, including one with a natural rock slide. (No lifeguards.)

The Yough is a good bass river, plus it's stocked to provide good wilderness trout fishing. You can also fish for trout in some smaller streams if you don't want to try the foamy waters of the river.

In spring, summer, and fall you can attend a variety of park programs on subjects ranging from area history to nature topics to white-water boating.

In winter, 30 miles of trails are open for cross-country skiing and there are areas for snowmobiling, tobogganing, and sledding. More than 18,000 acres are open for training dogs from Labor Day through late May.

Camping

The 225 **campsites** are available all year. There are no hookups, but, with the exception of 27 walk-in sites, most are multiuse. All are reservable with reservations accepted anytime during the year. These cost $9 for residents, $11 for nonresidents.

The Ohiopyle Youth Hostel is also here.

Nearby Attractions

Frank Lloyd Wright's **Fallingwater** (tel. 412-329-8501), one of the most famous houses in the world, is located just north of the park on Highway 381. Its name comes from its location over a waterfall. Tours are given daily April through mid-November, and most holidays and weekends the rest of the year.

To the southwest are Fort Necessity, Laurel Caverns, and the Touchstone Center for Crafts. On July 3, 1754, the opening battle of the war between England and France for control of the North American continent was fought at **Fort Necessity** (tel. 412/329-5512). Located 11 miles east of Uniontown on U.S. 40, the restored fort is now a National Battlefield. **Laurel Caverns** (tel. 412/438-3003), in the same area, is the largest cave in Pennsylvania. It's a maze cave with 2.3 miles of passages. You can take a guided tour or explore it on your own (after signing a release). Although **Touchstone** (tel. 412/329-1370), a 63-acre mountain retreat, is primarily a center for instruction by renowned artists and craftspeople; year-round activities are open to visitors.

A little farther afield, but still an easy daytrip from the park, is **Pittsburgh.** Once infamous for its industrial pollution, in recent years Pittsburgh has been cleaned up and reborn and is now a city worth visiting. The opening of the **Andy Warhol Museum** (tel. 412/237-8300) has attracted the attention of the art world, as well as visitors from around the world. Other sights to see are the zoo, the aviary, the Biblical Botanical Gardens, a variety of museums, the Carnegie Science Center, and professional sports.

Pymatuning State Park

Restaurant   Cabins & Cottages   RV Camping   Tent Camping   Group Camping   Boat Launch   Non-Motorized Boating Only   Fishing   Beach

Snorkeling & Diving   Picnic Areas   Trails   Nature Programs   Bicycling   Playground   X-Country Skiing   Snow-mobiling

Capsule Description: A large lakeside park with developed facilities.

Location: Northwest Pennsylvania on the border with Ohio. Take the Meadville exit from I-79. Go west on U.S. Highway 6/322 through Jamestown to the park office near the dam at the south end of the lake.

Address: Box 425, Jamestown, PA 16134 (tel. 412/932-3141).

Area Contacts: Crawford County Tourist Association, 969 Park Avenue, Meadville, PA 16335 (tel. 814/333-1258).

Erie Area Chamber of Commerce, 1006 State St., Erie, PA 16501 (tel. 814/454-7191).

Mercer County Tourist Promotion Agency, 1 W. State St., Sharon, PA 16146 (tel. toll free 800/637-2370).

Pymatuning State Park, Box 1000, Andover, OH 44003 (tel. 216/293-6329).

Youngstown/Mahoning County Convention and Visitors Bureau, 101 City Centre One, Youngstown, OH 44503-1810 (tel. toll free 800/447-8201 or 216/747-8200).

Insider Tip: The park restaurant, which was destroyed by fire, is being rebuilt and may be open by the time you read this.

The name "Pymatuning" has been traced back to the Iroquois Indians. Loosely translated it means "The Crooked-Mouth Man's Dwelling Place." According to authorities, "crooked-mouth" refers to a deceitful person rather than a facial disfigurement. Specifically, it's believed the name refers not to a man but to a woman. The Erie Indians lived here before the Iroquois and their queen had a reputation for crooked dealings.

But everything is aboveboard in this park now. The 17,000-acre, 16-mile long Pymatuning Lake lies on the state lines of Pennsylvania and Ohio with three-quarters of the shoreline (north, east, and south) occupied by Pennsylvania's Pymatuning State Park, and the other quarter of the shoreline (west) in the Ohio state park of the same name.

Activities

One of the most popular activities at this park is fish-watching. This occurs at several points along the Linesville Causeway, which crosses the northeastern finger of the lake. At the north end of the causeway you can watch the fish through portholes in the Visitors Center at the Fish Hatchery.

The hatchery is one of the largest in the country, so all the species propagated in the state can be seen here. As an example of its size, it produces an average of 100 million walleye fry each spring for distribution to lakes throughout the state. Even more popular is fish-watching at the feeding station at the spillway near the southern end of the causeway. Here the feeding frenzy packs the fish in so tightly that the ducks in the area—at least those not smart enough to get out of the way—actually walk on the fishes' backs.

Between these two locations, on an island midway across the Linesville Causeway, is the Waterfowl Museum. In season, American bald eagles nest near the museum.

Since the lake is stocked from the hatchery, the catches are usually good for walleye, carp, crappie, muskie, and largemouth and smallmouth bass, among others. Fishing licenses issued by either Pennsylvania or Ohio are honored anywhere on the water, but if you fish from the shore you'll need the license from the state you're standing in.

Boating is just as good, especially sailing and windsurfing, however only nonpowered boats and boats with no more than 10 horsepower motors are permitted. There are three marinas where you can rent pontoon boats, fishing boats, canoes, and paddleboats.

The five guarded beaches are open from Memorial Day through Labor Day. Scuba diving is permitted, but you need a park permit.

Although the park property covers all of the shoreline, it never goes very deep inland and in places, barely clears the waterline. As a result, designated hiking trails are limited to just about three miles. The same is true for bike trails. There are no designated equestrian trails, but horseback riding is permitted on park roads.

There is a wildlife observation blind on the hiking trail where you may see deer, wild turkeys, and small game. But you don't have to go far to see waterfowl. Several thousand make the park their year-round home and as many as 20,000 Canada geese and ducks stop here during migration.

On weekends in summer there are a number of interpretive and campfire programs. The amphitheater at the Jamestown Campgrounds is also used for nature programs, nature films, and entertainment.

In winter the park offers ice skating, ice fishing, ice boating, sledding, and snowmobiling. There's also a 4.7-mile cross-country ski trail. Ice skates, cross-country equipment, and snowmobiles can be rented.

Camping and Accommodations

The 19 modern **cabins** are open all year. Sixteen are two-bedroom sleeping up to six and three are three-bedroom sleeping up to eight. The cabins are all lakeside and each has its own dock. No TV or phones. In summer they may be reserved for a minimum of a week, and that's also the maximum stay. In the off-season they may be rented for from one night up to two weeks. Rents range from $270 to $320 a week for nonresidents in high season.

With 657 **campsites** in three campgrounds, this is one of the largest camping areas in the state. Most sites are multiuse and about 200 have electric hookups. Sites can be reserved only during the three major holiday weekends. Sites go for $9 to $11 plus $2 for the electric hookup. For groups, there's a tent camping area with a capacity of 400.

Nearby Attractions

If you want to play in a larger lake, head north. Less than an hour away is the city of **Erie, Lake Erie,** and **Presque Isle State Park** (tel. 814/871-4251), a day-use park with beaches on a sandy peninsula jutting seven miles into the lake. The city offers several museums, a planetarium, a zoo, and a water park.

South, less than an hour away, is **Youngstown, Ohio.** Sights to see here include the Ford Nature Education Center, the riverside gardens, a restored gristmill, and several museums.

Ricketts Glen State Park

 Visitor Center
 Cabins & Cottages
 RV Camping
 Tent Camping
 Group Camping
 Boat Launch
 Non-Motorized Boating Only
 Fishing
 Beach

 Snorkeling & Diving
 Picnic Areas
 Trails
 Horse Trails
 Nature Programs
 X-Country Skiing
Snow-mobiling

Capsule Description: A large natural park with developed facilities.

Location: Northeastern Pennsylvania. From I-80, take Exit 35 (east of Bloomsburg) to Pennsylvania 487, then go 30 miles north to the park.

Address: RD 2, Box 130, Benton, PA 17814-8900 (tel. 717/477-5675).

Area Contacts: Columbia-Montour Tourist Promotion Agency, Inc., 121 Paper Mill Rd., Bloomsburg, PA 17815 (tel. toll free 800/847-4810 or tel. 717/784-8279).

Endless Mountain Visitors Bureau, RR 6, Box 132A, Tunkhannock, PA 18657-9232 (tel. toll free 800/769-8999 or tel. 717/836-5431).

Lycoming County Tourist Promotion Agency, 454 Pine Street, Williamsport, PA 17701 (tel. toll free 800/358-9900).

Scranton/Lackawanna County Visitors and Convention Bureau, P.O. Box 431, Scranton, PA 18501 (tel. 717/342-7711).

There are at least 25 distinct waterfalls in this 13,050-acre park, 22 of them named. These falls range in size from low single cascades, such as Oneida Falls, which only falls 13 feet, to the many-tiered Ganoga Falls, the highest in the park, dropping a total of 94 feet. Adams Falls, often classed as the most beautiful falls in the park, plunges over three picturesque cascades of 18, 25, and 10 feet high.

Most of the falls are on two branches of Kitchen Creek that cut through the deep gorges of Ganoga Glen and Glen Leigh to unite at "Waters Meet" and then flow through Ricketts Glen. These all require that you hike in to see them. Adams Falls, on the other hand, is the only falls you can reach from the road. It's about 100 yards south of the parking area on Pennsylvania 487, about a mile east of the Red Rock intersection.

Activities

The falls are a major attraction even though you have to hike in to see them. The 20 miles of trails vary in difficulty from fairly level to steep hills. A series of trails, covering a total of seven miles, parallel the streams as they course their way down to the Glens. There's also a half-mile self-guided nature trail. In addition to the dramatic scenery, on these trails you have a good chance of seeing deer. Occasionally you might also spot a black bear. The trails will take you by trees over 500 years old—ring counts on fallen trees revealed ages as old as 900 years—many over 100 feet in height. The area represents the meeting ground of the southern and northern hardwoods, so the variety of trees is extensive. For a bird's-eye view, head for Red Rock Mountain. The scenic overlook there, appropriately called Grand View, is located at 2,449 feet, the highest point on the mountain.

Horse owners have a network of five miles of bridle trails; however, there are no overnight facilities for horses.

In summer, the interpretive programs frequently include guided walks as well as campfire programs.

The 245-acre Lake Jean is in the northern section of the park. A small, guarded beach there is open for swimmers from Memorial Day weekend to Labor Day. Scuba diving is permitted. Only nonpowered or electric powerboats can be used on the lake, and sailing and windsurfing are popular here. During the summer, you can rent canoes, paddleboats, and rowboats. Fishing is good in the lake for warm-water game fish and panfish. There are several creeks in the park where trout may be caught, and Mountain Springs Lake, a 40-acre lake owned by the state fish commission, which adjoins the eastern end of the park, offers an additional opportunity for catching trout and panfish.

Come winter, snowmobiles can zoom along a 21-mile trail, plus there's ice fishing on Lake Jean and sledding in several areas of the park. The snowmobile and hiking trails may also be used for cross-country skiing.

Camping and Accommodations

Seven of the 10 modern **cabins** sleep six while the other three sleep eight. They are fully equipped for year-round use, but do not have TV or phones. They may be reserved and rent for $270 to $320 a week for nonresidents in high season.

The 120 **campsites** are all multiuse, but without hookups. Located in the woods, there is good separation between sites. All sites may be reserved. From mid-April to mid-October, they go for $9 to $11. The rest of the year the bathhouse and other facilities close down and the sites rent as primitive for $7 to $9.

Nearby Attractions

Do you fancy a romantic drive through covered bridges? To the west of the park in nearby **Sullivan County,** several are easy daytrips. To the south, on Pennsylvania 487, about 10 miles north of Bloomsburg, you can check out what are believed to be the only twin covered bridges in the country. Still farther south, the **Bloomsburg Historic District** has more than 600 structures in the center of town.

If you have any Little Leaguers in the family, a trip west to **Williamsport** should be on your agenda. This is the home of the **Little League Baseball International Headquarters** (tel. 717/326-1921) and its museum. The kids, and grown-ups, should also enjoy the toy train collection at the **Lycoming County Historical Museum** (tel. 717/326-3326).

To the east is **Scranton.** Things to do in this major city include taking a steam-train ride at the **Steamtown National Historic Site** (tel. 717/961-2033) and going 300 feet below ground to tour the **Lackawanna Coal Mine** (tel. toll free 800/238-7245).

Rhode Island

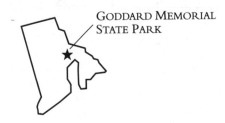

GODDARD MEMORIAL
STATE PARK

Rhode Island has 24 state parks.

Contacts

- Division of Parks and Recreation, Department of Environmental Management, 2321 Hartford Ave., Johnston, RI 02919-1713 (tel. 401/277-2632).
- Rhode Island Tourism Division, 7 Jackson Walkway, Providence, RI 02903 (tel. toll free 800/556-2484).

General Information on Rhode Island State Parks

The smallest state in the nation, just 48 miles long and 37 miles wide, the Ocean State still offers 400 miles of coastline and thousands of acres of beautiful parks, a number of them on the state's six major islands.

In general the parks are small, too—the largest only about 2,000 acres—and most are for day use only. Perhaps this is because in this compact state, everything is in easy reach, including overnight accommodations.

GENERAL FEES

There is an entrance/parking fee to the state parks of $2 per car for residents and $4 per car for nonresidents. If there's a senior in the car (65 and older) it's half price. The fee at state beaches is usually higher and varies for weekday, weekend, and holidays. Normally, this fee is only collected from May 1 through September 30.

CAMPING

There are campsites in five parks: Burlingame (755), Charlestown (75), Fishermen's Memorial (182), George Washington Camping Area (72), and Ningret Conservation Area (30). Fees range from $8 to $12 per night; with various hookups they cost from $10 to $16. Sites may be reserved.

Pets. Some parks permit pets, but they are not allowed on any beaches. Where allowed they must be under control at all times and on a leash not longer than six feet.

Alcoholic beverages. No alcoholic beverages are allowed.

Discounts: Resident and nonresident senior citizens, age 65 and older, are eligible for discounts on entrance and other fees, including golf.

Goddard Memorial State Park

Boating Boat Launch Fishing Beach Picnic Areas Trails Horse Trails Nature Programs X-Country Skiing

Capsule Description: A small wooded park with developed facilities on a saltwater bay.

Location: In East Greenwich, south of Providence on Narragansett Bay. From Route 1, take Route 1A to Ives Road in East Greenwich and follow signs east to the main entrance.

Address: Ives Road, Warwick, RI 02818 (tel. 401/884-2010).

Area Contacts: Greater Providence Convention and Visitors Bureau, 30 Exchange Terrace, Providence, RI 02903 (tel. toll free 800/233-1636).

Warwick Department of Economic and Community Development, City Hall, 3275 Post Rd., Warwick, RI 02886 (tel. 401/738-2000).

Insider Tip: As this is the only state park in Rhode Island that offers such a diversity of facilities and activities in a single park, it's extremely popular. Expect traffic jams on summer weekends and holidays; to avoid them, arrive early.

The seeds for this park were literally planted more than 120 years ago. In the 1870s, Henry Russell, the owner of the land, started a project to turn the barren sand dunes into a shady woodland. He began by planting acorns. He'd fill his pockets with acorns and on his walks stop frequently to punch three holes in the ground placing an acorn in each; one for the squirrels, one for the worms, and one for a tree. Later he raised a large variety of seedling trees to transplant into the dry sandy ground. Russell continued this for 30 years, and, after his death, Robert Goddard, who inherited the property, continued tree planting for another 20 years.

In 1927, the land was given to the state for a park. As a result, today you can picnic, ride horses, hike, or just stroll this seaside park in the shade of huge, old trees.

Activities

Most visitors come to this 472-acre day-use park to picnic and swim.

Picnicking is so popular here that, from March 15 on, the more than 350 picnic tables—155 with fireplaces and the rest with portable stove sites—can be reserved up to 60 days in advance for a fee of $2 per table.

Swimming is from the beach on the saltwater Greenwich Bay. Lifeguards are on duty from 10am to 6pm during the summer season.

At the beach, there's also a nature display including a terrarium and salt- and freshwater aquariums. During the summer, a park naturalist conducts a variety of programs and nature walks. The renovated Carousel building here is used as a performing arts center.

For boaters and fishermen, there's a boat launch for shallow-draft boats into the bay. Catches include bluefish, striped bass, and blackfish.

Land-bound activities include golf on a nine-hole course, horseback riding on 18 miles of trails (bring your own horse) through the woods of oaks, maples, walnut, pine, and a variety of other trees. You can walk or hike the same trails, all fairly level, as long as you understand that horses have the right of way.

In winter, the park is open for cross-country skiing (no groomed trails), ice skating, and sledding.

Nearby Attractions

Everything is nearby. You can go in any direction and find some place of interest worth a visit.

The capital city of **Providence,** for example, is just minutes to the north. One way to see that city is on a self-guided walking tour with tapes and tour booklets provided by the **Providence Preservation Society** (tel. 401/831-7440). Places to visit include Benefit Street's **"Mile of History,"** an impressive concentration of original colonial homes; the art center and other buildings at **Brown University** (tel. 401/863-1000), the seventh-oldest college in the nation; the **Rhode Island School of Design** (tel. 401/454-6100); the zoo; museums; and the **State Capitol building** (tel. 401/277-2357).

In the opposite direction, the historic, palatial mansions of **Newport,** the "Yachting Capital of the World," are just a half hour or so away. Other sights to see here are as diverse as can be and include the **International Tennis Hall of Fame** (tel. 401/849-3990); **Green Animals Topiary Garden** (tel. 401/847-1000); the **Naval War College Museum** (tel. 401/848-8306); **Touro Synagogue** (tel. 410/847-4794), the oldest synagogue in the U.S.; and the **White Horse Tavern** (tel. 401/849-3600), the oldest operating tavern in the U.S.

South Carolina

SANTEE STATE PARK

HUNTING ISLAND STATE PARK

South Carolina has 47 state parks.

Contacts

- South Carolina Division of State Parks, Department of Parks, Recreation & Tourism, 1205 Pendelton St., Columbia, SC 29201 (tel. 803/734-0156).
- South Carolina Division of Tourism, Department of Parks, Recreation & Tourism, P.O. Box 71, Columbia, SC 29202 (tel. toll free 800/451-8188 or 800/346-3634).

General Information on South Carolina State Parks

From the fury of cascades that fall several hundred feet as the rivers plunge down from the Blue Ridge escarpment in the west through the evergreen countryside of the Midlands to the miles of beaches and resort islands on the Atlantic coast, South Carolina offers a diversity of terrain and recreational opportunities that's reflected in its state parks.

South Carolinians took an active part in the Revolutionary War with 137 battles and skirmishes fought here, more than in any other state. On December 20, 1860, in Charleston, the Ordinance of Secession was passed, making South Carolina the first state to secede from the Union, and the first shots of the Civil War were fired on Fort

Sumter in Charleston Harbor. Much of this history is also preserved in the state parks and historic sites.

GENERAL FEES

Most of the year, admission/parking is free at all state parks except Charles Towne Landing and Old Santee Canal. However, during the peak summer season, an admission/parking fee of $2 or $3 is charged at a dozen or so of the busier parks.

CAMPING AND ACCOMMODATIONS

There's an 80-room resort **lodge** at Hickory Knob, 150 **cabins** available at 13 parks, and close to 2,900 **campsites** in 33 parks.

Cabins may be reserved for the current year at any time by contacting the park of your choice. Reservations for the following year are initially accepted by mail requests only during the period from October 20 through the first Monday in November. (Requests postmarked before October 20 will be returned without action.) After the first Monday in November, in-person reservations will have first priority, phone reservations second priority, and mail requests third. Cabins are one-, two-, and three-bedroom. Rates depend on a number of factors including: size, facilities, season, weekday or weekend, area, and location within the park. For example, a two-bedroom goes from less than $40 per night at Poinsett State Park in the Midlands to around $80 on the ocean at Hunting

Island to about $90 at Devil's Fork in the mountains. Weekly rates usually result in a savings of at least one night's rent.

With the exception of a limited number of reservable campsites at Edisto Beach State Park and two handicapped sites at all the other parks, campsites are on a first-come basis, no reservations. Sites have water and electric hookups and cost $9 to $15 per night. A few parks have tent sites available without hookups for a lower rate.

Pets. Where allowed, pets must be on a leash no longer than six feet or otherwise restrained and under control at all times. Pets are not permitted in cabins or cabin areas.

Alcoholic beverages. Public display or consumption of any beverage of alcoholic content, including beer and wine, is prohibited unless specifically authorized by the parks division.

Discounts. South Carolina residents who are age 65 or older, legally blind, or totally disabled may use certain state park facilities without charge. Some discounts are available for non-residents age 65 or older.

Hunting Island State Park

Visitor Center · Cabins & Cottages · RV Camping · Tent Camping · Group Camping · Boating · Boat Launch · Fishing · Beach · Picnic Areas · Trails · Nature Programs · Playground

Capsule Description: A large oceanside park with developed facilities on a secluded barrier island.

Location: On the Atlantic Ocean near the southeast corner of the state, about midway between Charleston and Savannah, Georgia. From I-95 take U.S. Highway 21 exit east to Beaufort, then continue about 16 miles southeast to the park. U.S. 21 ends in the park.

Address: 1775 Sea Island Pkwy., Hunting Island, SC 29920 (tel. 803/838-2011).

Area Contacts: Charleston Trident Convention and Visitors Bureau, P.O. Box 975, Charleston, SC 29402 (tel. toll free 800/868-8118 or tel. 803/853-8000).

Greater Beaufort Chamber of Commerce, P.O. Box 910, Beaufort, SC 29901 (tel. 803/524-3163).

Lowcountry and Resort Islands Tourism Commission, P.O. Box 366, Hampton, SC 29924 (tel. 803/943-9180).

Insider Tips: On hot muggy days, the mosquitoes swarm about you, so pack some repellent. From April through October, loggerhead turtles are spotted on the beach at night. Once each June, the park's naturalist offers a guided all-night beach walk—for those age 17 and older—to look for nesting turtles; reservations are required.

The island got its name from the time it was used for hunting deer, small game, and waterfowl. Today there's no hunting, so this barrier island, approximately three miles long and one mile wide, offers refuge to those creatures. The semitropical park encompasses 5,000 acres of sandy beach, maritime forest, and saltwater marsh. It possesses the best-developed slash pine–palmetto forest in the state and is a good place to see the state tree, the palmetto palm.

One of the few remaining lighthouses on the south Atlantic coast is on the island. Built in 1875, it was active until 1933.

Activities

There's close to four miles of beaches with life-guards on duty in two swimming areas from Memorial Day through Labor Day.

Fisherman can put a line in the ocean or in the lagoon on the back side of the island. Surf fishing is popular and an 1,120-foot-long fishing pier on the southern tip of the island lays claim to being the longest freestanding pier on the East Coast. There's a charge to fish off the pier from March through November. Catches include sea trout, flounder, drum, and bass. A popular crabbing spot is the end of the boardwalk over the marsh. The quarter-mile boardwalk is also a good place to see marsh wildlife including alligators, sea otters, and sea turtles.

White-tailed deer and raccoons are abundant and frequently seen by park visitors, especially on the four miles of hiking trails and the two nature trails in the forest. You can also bike these trails. More than 125 species of birds have been sighted here including significant numbers of herons, terns, pelicans, and egrets.

The park naturalist conducts beach walks, nature hikes, and other programs throughout the year. There are also recreational programs daily during the summer. On lighthouse tours, the hearty can climb the 181 stairsteps to the top for a bird's-eye view of the area. You can see displays on the cultural and natural history of the area at the park visitor's center.

Camping and Accommodations

The five two-bedroom **cabins** sleep six and the 10 three-bedroom sleep 10. All are just off the beach and have screened porches, air-conditioning and heat, but no TV or phones. Two two-bedroom and two three-bedroom have fireplaces. Daily rentals run from about $65 to $80, weekends from about $180 to $225, and a full week from $360 to $450.

The 200 multiuse **campsites** all have water and electric hookups. They are on a first-come basis, but there are plans to put in a reservation system, so check it out before you go. Summer rates are $15.

Primitive camping is available for organized groups.

Nearby Attractions

The area around the nearby town of **Beaufort** was discovered by Spanish explorers 100 years before the Pilgrims landed at Plymouth Rock. A number of informative and offbeat tours of old homes and museums in this historic town are offered; arrangements can be made through the Greater Beaufort Chamber of Commerce (tel. 803/524-3163). The Spirit of Old Beaufort conducts walking tours, the Point will escort you around by van, and Black Stones Barge Tours will take you by water. Carriage Tours of Beaufort will draw you by horse and carriage. Gullah Geechie n Mahn is an African American heritage tour. A military museum worth a visit is the **Parris Island Museum** (tel. 803/525-2951) at the nearby Marine Corps Recruit Depot (tel. 803/524-5881). Exhibits here tell the history of the Marine Corps from World War I to Desert Storm.

South of the park is **Hilton Head,** one of the best-known resort areas on the East Coast—but you have to make a big U-shaped loop around Port Royal Sound to get there. There are more than 20 championship golf courses among the recreational facilities in the Hilton Head area.

A little farther south, but still an easy daytrip from the park, is **Savannah,** often rated as one of the most beautiful antebellum cities in the South. The historic riverfront district is well worth a walking tour.

A longer daytrip—or an overnighter—to the north will take you to charming **Charleston,** a city that rivals Savannah in both history and beauty. Standing here are more than 70 pre–Revolutionary War buildings—plus more than 100 from the late 1700s, and 600 others built before the mid-1800s. In addition to the chance to step back into our architectural past, Charleston offers several museums; Fort Sumter (tel. 803/883-3123); the Citadel (tel. 803/953-5000), one of the last three military state colleges in the nation; and so many churches that the city is often nicknamed "The Holy City."

Santee State Park

 Visitor Center
 Restaurant
 Cabins & Cottages
 RV Camping
 Tent Camping
 Group Camping
 Boating

 Boat Launch
 Fishing
 Beach
 Picnic Areas
 Trails
 Nature Programs
 Bicycling
 Tennis
 Playground

Capsule Description: A natural park with developed facilities on the largest lake in South Carolina.

Location: Midway between Charleston and Columbia on Lake Marion, approximately three miles northwest of Santee. Take Exit 98 off I-95 onto South Carolina Highway 6. Go west to Route 105, then northwest to Route 82, which goes to the park.

Address: Route 1, Box 79, Santee, SC 29142 (tel. 803/854-2408).

Area Contacts: Charleston Trident Convention and Visitors Bureau, P.O. Box 975, Charleston, SC 29402 (tel. 803/853-8000).

Santee Cooper Counties Promotion Commission, P.O. Drawer 40, Santee, SC 29142 (tel. toll free 800/227-8510 outside South Carolina or 803/854-2131).

Greater Columbia Convention and Visitors Bureau, P.O. Box 15, Columbia, SC 29202 (tel. toll free 800/264-4884).

Insider Tip: Golfers will be pleased to know that—though there is no golfing in Santee—four courses open to the public are within five miles of the park.

Santee was the local Indian word for "Great River." The Santee was great, but also dangerous, periodically flooding and destroying crops and property. In 1938 work was started to control the river and provide electricity to this depression-ravaged rural area by building two lakes, Marion and Moultrie, now known jointly as the Santee Cooper Lakes after the two rivers that were dammed. At the time, it was the largest earth-moving project in history. Marion, the largest lake in the state, is 43 miles long and covers more than 110,000 acres. It's connected to the 12½-mile-long, 60,000-acre Lake Moultrie by a 6½-mile-long canal, a link in the waterway chain that permits small boats to go from here to Charleston and the sea.

Together, the lakes have 450 miles of shoreline. Since this is a magnet for commercial development, a policy has been set to preserve at least 70% of the area surrounding the lakes in a natural state. Part of that 70% is this 2,500-acre park on the southern shore of Lake Marion.

Activities

Boating and fishing are the main attractions. The lakes are open to all size and type boats. Fishing boats are available for rent year-round, but gas motors are required and are not available for rent. If you don't want to boat, you can fish from the park pier.

Fishermen flock to these lakes lured by a number of record catches including world records for an Arkansas blue catfish weighing 109.4 pounds and a channel catfish weighing 58 pounds. Several state record fish have also been landed here.

Catches include bream, crappie, catfish, and a variety of bass including striped bass, normally a saltwater fish. The striped bass story goes back to when the dams across the Santee and Cooper rivers were completed in 1941. Then it was discovered that stripers that had come up the rivers from the ocean to spawn had been trapped and could not return to the sea. Turned out that the fish quickly adapted to the freshwater lakes and since then stripers have been spawning and living here year-round.

For land activities, there are three tennis courts (two lighted), a guarded beach on a small swimming lake, where you can also rent paddleboats in season; about four miles of hiking trails and a one-way, 3.8-mile mountain bike and hiking trail. The park nature center, which is open year-round, features a 250-gallon aquarium housing fish native to the lakes. The park naturalist conducts a number of programs and walks all year. One of these, on weekends in the fall, is a tour of the limestone caverns in a remote area of the park. There are also recreational programs during the summer.

A section of the park is designated as a management area for an endangered bird, the red cockaded woodpecker. In this area the nesting trees are marked so you have a good chance of spotting this rare bird. Other birds and animals you'll probably see include wild turkey, white-tailed deer, egrets, and many, many waterfowl that fly over from the national wildlife refuge across the lake.

Camping and Accommodations

Of the 30 **cabins** for rent, 10 are located on piers extending into the waters of Lake Marion, while the remaining 20 are located in a moss-draped wooded area along the lakeshore. These two-bedroom cabins can accommodate up to six persons, have heat and air-conditioning, and are fully furnished including cable TV. Each pier-based cabin has boat-docking facilities while each land-based has a deck.

Cabins may be reserved for a period of one week (Monday to Monday) during June, July, and August. They can be rented for less than a week the rest of the year. Rents run about $55 per night or $330 a week.

Two **camping** areas with a total of 150 multi-use sites are located near the lakeshore. All have water and electrical hookups. Rents are about $12 per night. All on a first-come basis; no reservations.

Also on the lakeshore is a full-service restaurant, which is open year-round.

Nearby Attractions

To see more wildlife or fish up close: the **Santee National Wildlife Refuge** (tel. 803/478-2217) is just across the lake; the **Dennis Wildlife Center** (tel. 803/825-3387) on the east shore of Lake Moultrie is a center for the state's striped bass program and for deer research; and the **Orangeburg National Fish Hatchery** has aquariums. Flower lovers will want to visit the **Edisto Memorial Gardens** (tel. 803/534-6821) in Orangeburg and see the black swans and six million irises in the **Swan Lake Iris Gardens** (tel. 803/778-7720) at Sumter. Those interested in Revolutionary War history have the small, but interesting **Fort Watson** (tel. 803/478-2217), three miles north of Santee; and the tomb of "The Swamp Fox," Gen. Francis Marion, north of the diversion canal near Eadytown.

Farther afield, but still a fast hour or so trip away on the nearby I-26 are both Columbia to the northwest and Charleston to the southeast. Among the sights to see in Columbia, the capital city, are the **Governor's Mansion** (tel. 803/737-1710), the **State House** (tel. 803/734-2430), the fifteen antebellum buildings that make up the **Lexington County Museum Complex** (tel. 803/359-8369), the **South Carolina State Museum** (tel. 803/737-4595), the **University of South Carolina** (tel. 803/777-0169), and the **Riverbanks Zoo** (tel. 803/779-8717), which has been ranked among the top zoos in the country. The principal sights of historic Charleston are covered in the listing for Hunting Island State Park, above.

South Dakota

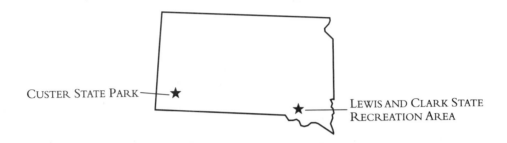

CUSTER STATE PARK

LEWIS AND CLARK STATE
RECREATION AREA

South Dakota has 41 state parks.

Contacts

- Division of Parks and Recreation, Department of Game, Fish and Parks, 523 E. Capitol Ave., Pierre, SD 57501-3182 (tel. 605/773-3391).
- South Dakota Department of Tourism, 711 E. Wells Ave., Pierre, SD 57501-3369 (tel. toll free 800/732-5682 [800/SDAKOTA], 800/952-2217 in South Dakota).

General Information on South Dakota State Parks

The Dakotas are the land of the famous Sioux or Dacotah Indians and the state is named for that tribe.

Going from east to west, across the seemingly endless amber waves of grain, South Dakota builds in elevation from the low plains in the east to the rolling plains of mid-state to the famed Black Hills in the west where there are 18 peaks rising above 7,000 feet. The state parks are scattered across the state to take full advantage of its varied terrain, geological wonders, and celebrated legends. The parks are open all year.

South Dakota is divided into two time zones, central and mountain, roughly along the north-south line of the Missouri River.

Every state has its state tree, state song, and other official symbols. South Dakota may be the only state with an official state jewelry. Called Black Hills Gold, it is manufactured exclusively in that section of the state.

GENERAL FEES

There is a $2 daily entrance fee for all parks except Custer. At Custer, a temporary permit good for up to five days costs $3 per person or $8 per vehicle from May through October and $2 per person or $5 per vehicle the rest of the year. An annual permit is available for $15.

CAMPING AND ACCOMMODATIONS

Lodges, motel rooms, and a variety of housekeeping and sleeping cabins, mostly concessionaire-operated, are available in Custer State Park and Lewis and Clark State Park. Rates on these vary widely with facilities and season from a high-season rate of about $50 a weekday night for a motel room at Lewis and Clark to $75 to $200 a day for a double room at the State Game Lodge at Custer State Park. In high season cabin rates run from about $60 to $300 a day, once again depending on size and facilities. In addition, five parks have basic camping cabins: Lewis and Clark, Newton Hills, Snake Creek, West Whitlock, and Oakwood Lakes. These all have electricity and go for about $22 a night. Reservations are made through the individual park.

There are more than 2,300 campsites available in 37 parks. In addition, more than half the parks have a Rent-A-Tent program. Fees run from $5 for a basic campsite to $10 for a modern campsite with electric hookup at Custer. Thirty parks accept reservations. They may be made by phone, mail, or in person to the individual park for a one-time reservation fee of $6. Some parks have a minimum stay on weekends and over holidays.

Pets. All pets must be under immediate control and on a leash not longer than 10 feet. Pets are prohibited from posted areas at beaches.

Alcoholic beverages. Alcoholic beverages are permitted as long as their use does not violate any state law.

Custer State Park

Visitor Center   Lodge/ Hotel   Restaurant   Cabins & Cottages   RV Camping   Tent Camping   Group Camping   Boating   Boat Launch   Fishing

Beach   Waterskiing   Picnic Areas   Trails   Horse Trails   Nature Programs   Bicycling   Playground   X-Country Skiing   Snow-mobiling   Gift Shop

Capsule Description: One of the largest state parks in the 48 contiguous states with vast natural areas and developed facilities.

Location: Southwestern corner of the state, in the Black Hills. From Rapid City, take U.S. Highway 16 south to 16A to the park. From the city of Custer, take 16A east to the park.

Address: HC83, Box 70, Custer, SD 57730-9705 (tel. 605/255-4515 for information, (tel. toll free 800/710-CAMP) (800/710-2267) for camping reservations, or toll free 800/658-3530 for resort reservations).

Area Contacts: Black Hills, Badlands & Lakes Association, 900 Jackson Blvd., Rapid City, SD 57702 (tel. 605/341-1462).

   Custer County Chamber of Commerce, 447 Crook St., Custer, SD 57730 (tel. 605/673-2244 or tel. toll free 800/992-9818).

   Rapid City Convention and Visitors Bureau, P.O. Box 747, Rapid City, SD 57709 (tel. toll free 800/487-3223).

Insider Tips: In July, the bison breeding season begins, and the adult bulls battle for breeding rights. This continues until late August or early September. You

may become a spectator at some of these fights, but do it from the safety of your car.

   You can get one of the best panoramic views of the Black Hills from the observation deck atop the 6,023-foot peak of Mount Coolridge. From this lookout you can see Mount Rushmore, the Crazy Horse Memorial, Harney Peak, and the Needles. To get there you have to drive a fairly steep, 1.2 mile gravel road with switchbacks—it's worth the drive in a car, but don't try it if you have a large RV.

In 1874, Lt. Col. George Armstrong Custer led an army expedition of 1,200 men on a reconnaissance into Sioux territory in the Black Hills. Among the things the troops discovered was gold. The area was off-limits to settlers, but the discovery set off an illegal, but condoned, gold rush into Indian country.

The city, county, and this state park are named after this flamboyant cavalry officer, Civil War hero, and frontier legend, who led his troops against the Sioux at the Little Bighorn two years later.

In recent years, Custer State Park has become almost as legendary as the man it's named after because of another symbol of the frontier. On its 73,000 acres of rolling grassland and pine-covered mountains roams one of the largest public herds of buffalo. About 1,500 of these great, shaggy animals range freely in a large section of the park. There would be more of them, and there has been in the past, but it was found that this is close to the ideal herd size for the available range. Any more and the grasses are soon overgrazed. So early each October there's a Buffalo Round-up and the herd is thinned and culled for an auction on the hoof in November.

Activities

Although you may see buffalo in many areas of the park, the best chance is on the Wildlife Loop Road, an 18-mile circle through open grasslands and rolling hills. Buffalo are the prime attraction, but you'll probably also see deer, elk, antelope, mountain goats, bighorn sheep, and wild burros that may come up to your car to beg for edible handouts; plus some of the 186 species of birds that have been spotted here including eagles, hawks, and wild turkey. The best time to make this swing is early morning or evening when the animals are most active. A caution: Buffalo may look docile, but they are wild and a mature bull can weigh a ton, turn on a dime, and easily outrun you to your car. So keep your distance, preferably inside your car. You can also leave the driving to someone else and, for a fee, take a Buffalo Safari Jeep Ride that goes out into the wildlife grazing areas.

Two other scenic drives in the park are well worth the slow ride on roads with hairpin curves, over pigtail bridges, and through narrow tunnels. The Needles Highway lives up to its name by threading 14 miles of a needle-eye road through a forest of towering, jagged granite spires. These pinnacles attract rock climbers who scale them like kids shimmying up flagpoles. If you're interested in doing this, there's a climbing school in the park that offers both instructions and guided climbs.

Along here you can get a good view of Harney Peak, at 7,242 feet the highest peak between the Rockies to the west and the European Alps far, far to the east. Iron Mountain Road is a 17-mile route that begins in the park and goes to Mount Rushmore. Along the way there are a number of scenic overlooks offering panoramic views of the Black Hills and granite tunnels that frame the mammoth sculpted faces of Washington, Jefferson, Roosevelt, and Lincoln.

If you prefer to explore the park on foot, there are miles and miles of trails. Among these are three trails leading to the summit of Harney Peak and 22 miles of the 111-mile South Dakota Centennial Trail pass through the park. Most of these trails are also open for mountain bikes, which can be rented in the park, and there are four marked horse trails plus you can ride the park segment of the Centennial Trail. There's a 30-site horse camp at French Creek Nature Area. In addition, a concessionaire offers trail rides and overnight pack trips on stable horses.

Four lakes and three major streams are all stocked with brown, rainbow, and brook trout and Stockade Lake also has perch, bass, and bullhead. There are fishing docks and rowboats for rent. For straight fun, you can also rent a paddleboat. Three of the lakes have sandy swimming beaches and waterskiing is popular on the fourth. There's even some rafting on the streams in high-water years.

The two visitors centers are open during peak season (May through September or October). Both have a variety of historic and wildlife displays. Park naturalists lead nature walks and gold-panning excursions, there are hayrides, chuckwagon cookouts, barn dances, movies, and other entertainment, including live theater at the Black Hills Playhouse during the summer.

Among the historic sights in the park are the Gordon Stockade, a replica of an 1874 log stockade where costumed interpreters demonstrate life in that era; and the cabin of Charles Badger Clark, South Dakota's first poet laureate and author of "A Cowboy's Prayer."

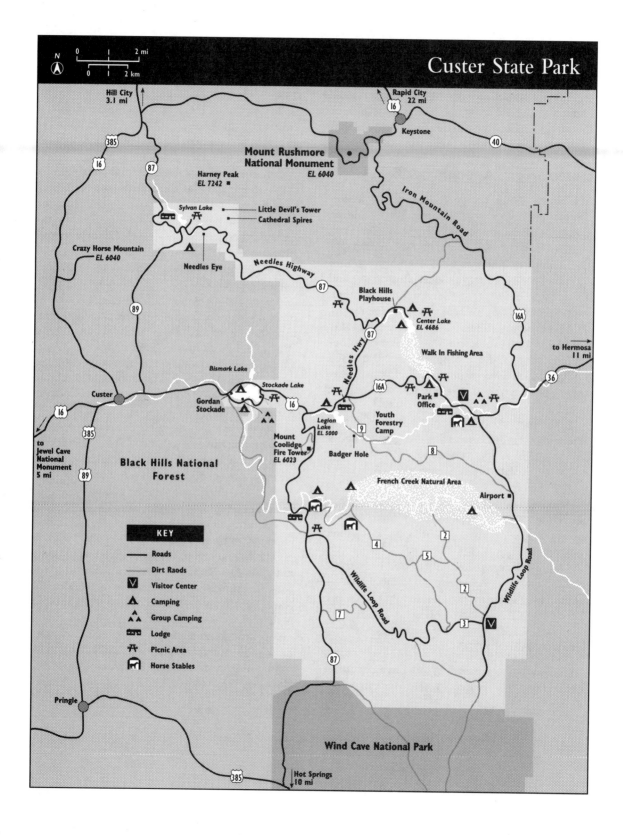

Custer State Park

N

0   1   2 mi

0   1   2 km

Hill City
3.1 mi

Rapid City
22 mi

16

Keystone

385

40

16

87

Mount Rushmore National Monument
EL 6040

Harney Peak
EL 7242

Iron Mountain Road

Sylvan Lake

Little Devil's Tower
Cathedral Spires

Crazy Horse Mountain
EL 6040

Needles Eye

Needles Highway

89

87

Black Hills Playhouse

16A

Center Lake
EL 4686

Walk In Fishing Area

to Hermosa
11 mi

Bismark Lake

Needles Hwy

16A

36

Stockade Lake

Park Office

Custer

Gordan Stockade

16

Legion Lake
EL 5000

9

Youth Forestry Camp

16

385

Mount Coolidge Fire Tower
EL 6023

Badger Hole

8

to Jewel Cave National Monument
5 mi

89

Black Hills National Forest

French Creek Natural Area

Airport

4

2

5

KEY

—— Roads

—— Dirt Raods

V Visitor Center

▲ Camping

▲▲ Group Camping

Lodge

Picnic Area

Horse Stables

Wildlife Loop Road

2

7

3

V

Pringle

87

Wildlife Loop Road

Wind Cave National Park

385

Hot Springs
10 mi

Weather closes down much of the park in winter, but you can still ice-fish the lakes and do cross-country skiing and snowmobiling in some areas of the park, including the Needles Highway, which is closed to vehicle traffic.

Camping and Accommodations

The **State Game Lodge & Resort** is listed on the National Register of Historic Places since it was once the Summer White House for Pres. Calvin Coolidge and was visited by Pres. Dwight D. Eisenhower. The resort has seven hotel rooms, 40 motel rooms, eight housekeeping cabins, and 13 sleeping cabins. The **Sylvan Lake Resort,** overlooking that alpine lake, has 35 lodge rooms, 19 housekeeping cabins, and 12 sleeping cabins. **Legion Lake Resort,** also lakeside, has 12 housekeeping cabins and 13 sleeping cabins. **Blue Bell Lodge,** which is a mini dude ranch, has 13 housekeeping cabins and 16 sleeping cabins. There's a restaurant at each resort.

Rates match facilities and cover the gamut from a sleeping cabin at Legion Lake that goes for about $60 per night in high season to a four-bedroom cabin at the State Game Resort that costs about $300 per night.

Almost all the resorts open in late April or May and close down in September or October, but usually a few cabins are kept open for winter sportsmen.

Of the 330 **campsites,** all but 40 are multiuse. No hookups. Fees range from $8 to $10. Reservations may be made for the calendar year by calling 605/255-4000 after January 1.

Nearby Attractions

To the south of the park is **Wind Cave National Park** (tel. 605/745-4600) where you can take a variety of guided tours of the cave, which has 66 miles of known underground passages. A little farther south, in **Hot Springs,** you'll be able to swim in a large natural warm-water indoor pool or go watch a dig where they've unearthed bones of 20,000-year-old mammoths.

Among the places featured in **Custer City,** to the west, are the **National Museum of Woodcarving** (tel. 605/673-4404) and a **Flintstone's amusement park** (tel. 605/673-4079) for the kids. Farther west is the **Jewel Cave National Monument** (tel. 605/673-2288). More than 85 miles of passages in this cave rank it as the second-longest cave in the U.S.

About six miles north of Custer City is the ongoing project of cutting out the colossal mountain carving of the Sioux Chief Crazy Horse. When, and if, it's finished, this will be the largest sculpture in the world—563 feet high, 641 feet long—much larger than the heads on Mount Rushmore. The **Indian Museum of North America** is close by.

Directly north of the park are the presidents on **Mount Rushmore** (tel. 605/574-2523). What may be the best-known mountain in America draws more than 2½ million visitors a year. Among the things you can do in **Keystone,** the nearest city to Rushmore, is take a helicopter ride to see the mountain. Or you can dig for gold there in an authentic gold mine.

The largest city in the area, and second largest in the state, is **Rapid City** to the northeast of the park. Tourism is big business here and among the places to visit are a wooden church that's an exact replica of an 800-year-old church in Norway; a drive-through wildlife park with bears, mountain lions, and other animals; and an air and space museum at the entrance to **Ellsworth Air Force Base** (tel. 605/385-7631).

Lewis and Clark State Recreation Area

 Lodge/ Hotel Restaurant Cabins & Cottages RV Camping Tent Camping Group Camping Marina Boating Boat Launch Fishing

 Beach Waterskiing Picnic Areas Trails Horse Trails Nature Programs Bicycling Playground X-Country Skiing Snow-mobiling

Capsule Description: A lakeside resort park with well-developed facilities.

Location: Southeast corner of the state. From U.S. Highway 81 at Yankton, take South Dakota Highway 52 four miles west to the park.

Address: RR 1, Box 240, Yankton, SD 57078-9207 (tel. 605/668-2985 or tel. toll free 800/700-2261 for reservations only). Only accept reservations 90 days in advance.

Area Contacts: Dakota Heritage and Lakes Association, 818 East 41st Street, Sioux Falls, SD 57105 (tel. 605/336-2602).

Sioux Falls Convention and Visitors Bureau, P.O. Box 1425, Sioux Falls, SD 57101-1425 (tel. 605/336-1620 or tel. toll free 800/330-2072).

Sioux City Convention and Tourism Bureau, P.O. Box 3183, Sioux City, Iowa 51102 (tel. 712/279-4800 or tel. toll free 800/593-2228).

Yankton Area Chamber of Commerce, P.O. Box 588, Yankton, SD 57078 (tel. toll free 800/888-1460).

Insider Tips: The park is divided into three units: The first two are the Yankton and Midway units, which are next to each other, and the third is the Gavin's Point unit, a short distance away. Ask about the resort's off-season package plans that include accommodations and a fishing-boat rental.

This is the state's most popular recreation area and it's not hard to understand why. With six miles of shoreline on a 33,000-acre lake that stretches more than 20 miles up the Missouri River, the 864-acre park offers a modern motel, cabins, campgrounds, trails, swimming beaches, a marina, and a variety of lake and shore activities. Lewis and Clark probably would have loved to have this here when they came through on their famous expedition in 1804. It would have been, and is, a great stopover on any journey.

Activities

Naturally, boating is close to the top of the list here, especially since there's a 373-slip marina that can accommodate boats up to 50 feet long, and there are 14 lanes for boat launching. You can rent canoes, fishing boats, pontoon and sailboats, plus water skis, jet skis, and other water recreation equipment. The marina also offers lake excursions and has a restaurant overlooking the lake.

The freshwater reservoir is fished primarily for walleye, bass, and crappie.

In addition to about a half mile of guarded sandy beaches, there's a swimming pool for resort guests.

There's a lot of space to roam around on foot or bike, but only a mile or so of marked hiking trails. Bike rentals are available. For horsemen and women, there are seven miles of equestrian trails.

During the summer, daily organized programs include nature hikes, campfire programs, educational talks, and movies.

In winter, the park is open for ice fishing, cross-country skiing, and snowmobiling.

Camping and Accommodations

The 24 **motel** units have TV, microwaves, and refrigerators. A double rents for $48 per weekday night in season (late May to early September) and $70 per night on weekends. There's a two-night minimum during high season. The rest of the year a double costs $35 anytime. Children under 12 stay free in parents' room.

There are 10 two-bedroom and three-bedroom modern **cabins** with kitchen and TV. The two-bedroom sleep eight and go for from $95 to $110, depending on length of stay, and $125 on holiday weekends. The three-bedrooms sleep 10 and go for $100 to $120 and $135 on holiday weekends. Off-season the two-bedrooms are $80 per night and the three-bedroom $90.

Several rustic, sparsely furnished camping cabins are available in the summer for $22 per night.

Most of the 292 **campsites** have electrical hookups. They are $10 per night with electric, $7 without, and may be reserved.

Nearby Attractions

Close by, you can tour the **Gavens Point Dam** (tel. 402/667-7875), which backs up the lake, as well as the **national fish hatchery and aquarium** near the dam.

The **Dakota Territorial Museum** (tel. 605/665-3898), in nearby **Yankton,** is an exact replica of several of the buildings that made up the old Dakota Territorial Capitol. In summer, you can take a cruise on the Missouri aboard a paddlewheeler berthed in this town.

Sioux City, Iowa, is about an hour's drive from the park to the southeast. This city, of about 80,000, has an art center, theaters, museums, a symphony orchestra, and both greyhound and Thoroughbred racing.

Sioux Falls is South Dakota's largest city—it's just under two hours' drive from Lewis and Clark park to the northeast. Here you'll find the falls that give the city its name, the **Great Plains Zoo** (tel. 605/339-7059), about a dozen museums, and a fine arts center.

Tennessee

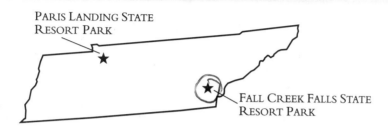

PARIS LANDING STATE RESORT PARK

FALL CREEK FALLS STATE RESORT PARK

Tennessee has 50 state parks.

Contacts

- State Parks Division, Tennessee Department of Conservation, 401 Church St., LC Tower 7th Floor, Nashville, TN 37243 (tel. toll free 800/421-6683).
- Tennessee Department of Tourist Development, P.O. Box 23170, Nashville, TN 37202 (tel. toll free 800/836-6200 or 615/741-2158).

General Information on Tennessee State Parks

Today, Tennessee is probably best known throughout the world either for Nashville, the capital of country music, or Memphis, the home of the legendary Elvis Presley.

But in the past it was best known for its marksmen. Following the lead of adoptive native son, Andrew Jackson, so many long rifle marksmen from Tennessee volunteered for the War of 1812 that Tennessee earned the title "the Volunteer State." This tradition was carried by men like Davy Crockett who was among the Tennessee volunteers who went to help fight for the Texans in their war for independence from Mexico. In the Civil War, Tennessee joined the Confederacy and their marksmanship won the respect of Union troops. However, a number of Tennesseans stayed with the Union, including Andrew Johnson who became president when Lincoln was assassinated. In World War I, the tradition continued with Sgt. Alvin York, the backwoods marksman who became one of the most decorated soldiers of that war. Much of the history of these marksmen is preserved in both national and state parks.

A state of rugged, natural beauty, it offers a great diversity of terrain from the Smoky Mountains in the east to the Mississippi Delta in the west. The state parks reflect this diversity. And no matter where you are in Tennessee, you're no more than an hour's drive from a state park.

The state is divided into two time zones, eastern and central, with the zone line cutting the state just west of Chattanooga.

GENERAL FEES
There are no entrance or parking fees.

CAMPING AND ACCOMMODATIONS
Seven parks have an inn: Fall Creek Falls, Henry Horton, Montgomery Bell, Natchez Trace, Paris Landing, Pickwick Landing, and Reelfoot Lake. The number of rooms range from 20 at Natchez Trace to 100 at Paris Landing. These offer full resort amenities including a restaurant, swimming in a lake or pool, and, in four parks, a golf course. A double room costs about $65 per night in high season (March through November) and about $50 the rest of the year.

Rustic and modern cabins are available in 16 parks. Rates vary, according to the type and size cabin, from about $40 to $95 per night. Weekly rates are cheaper, and during the period Memorial Day to Labor Day, priority is given to weekly reservations.

Inn and cabin reservations are made directly to the individual park.

There are 2,600 campsites available in 40 parks. Most of these are multiuse with water and electric hookups. Depending on facilities and season, fees range from about $6 to $12 per night. Most sites are on a first-come basis; however, reservations are accepted in a dozen parks and may be made up to a year in advance. There is a $5 reservation fee.

Pets. Pets must be under physical control and on a leash at all times. They are not allowed in inns or cabins.

Alcoholic beverages. The public display or consumption of alcoholic beverages is prohibited.

Discounts. Tennessee senior citizens are entitled to a discount on campsites in some parks, provided the vehicle is registered to the senior. Senior discounts are also available to non-residents who possess the Federal Golden Age Passport and those from states that have a reciprocal senior discount agreement with Tennessee.

Fall Creek Falls State Resort Park

Lodge/Hotel · Restaurant · Cabins & Cottages · RV Camping · Tent Camping · Group Lodge Dormitories

Non-Motorized Boating Only · Fishing · Swimming · Trails · Horse Trails · Nature Programs · Bicycling · Golf · Tennis · Fitness Center · Playground · Gift Shop

Capsule Description: A large, natural lakeside park with resort facilities.

Location: Eastern Tennessee, about 50 miles north of Chattanooga and 18 miles west of Pikeville. From Pikeville take Tennessee Highway 30 west to the park.

Address: Route 3, Pikeville, TN 37367 (tel. 615/881-3297 for the park office, 615/881-3241 for the inn).

Area Contacts: Chattanooga Area Convention and Visitors Bureau, 1001 Market St., Chattanooga, TN 37402 (tel. toll free 800/322-3344).

Pikeville-Bledsoe County Chamber of Commerce, P.O. Box 205, Pikeville, TN 37367 (tel. 615/447-2791).

McMinnville-Warren County Chamber of Commerce, P.O. Box 574, McMinnville, TN 37110 (tel. 615/473-6611).

Insider Tip: The resort has earned a listing in *Better Homes and Gardens* magazine as one of America's 30 Favorite Family Vacation Resorts. In summer, guided tours conducted by the park's naturalist fill up fast. Sign up at the nature center early, even a day in advance.

Fall Creek Falls is only one of five falls in this 16,800-acre park. However, its plunge of 256 feet, into a shaded pool at the base of its gorge, makes it the highest waterfall east of the Rocky

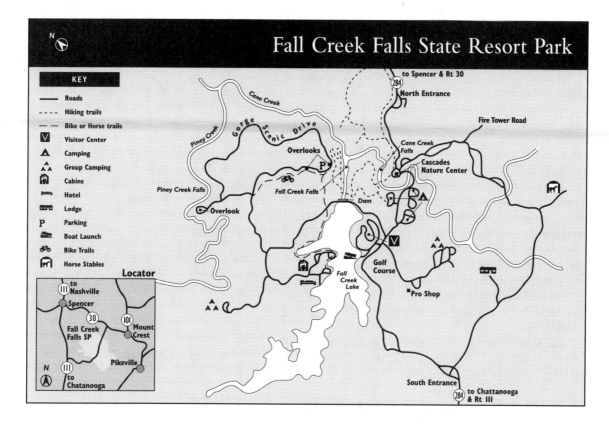

KEY

— Roads
- - - - Hiking trails
— — Bike or Horse trails
V Visitor Center
▲ Camping
▲▲ Group Camping
Cabins
Hotel
Lodge
P Parking
Boat Launch
Bike Trails
Horse Stables

Locator

Mountains. The other, smaller, falls are just as impressive.

Much of the park is covered by an oak and hickory forest that gives way to tulip poplar and hemlock forests in the gorges. All this scenic splendor serves as a memorable backdrop for the resort activities at the state's second-largest park.

Activities

More than 9,000 acres of the park are a designated state natural area. If you want to explore this fine example of nature's lovely handiwork, a good place to start is at the nature center near Cane Creek Falls. A short audiovisual show here will give you the broad picture of the park. A full-time ranger-naturalist can fill in the details, answer questions, and arrange special tours. You can reinforce this with a walk on the self-guided nature trail near the center. There's also a self-guided nature trail along the park's lengthy scenic loop

you can take in your car. On this drive you can stop at several scenic overlooks. During the summer, nature and recreation programs are presented daily.

Hikers will find miles and miles of trails that wind through the woods, fields, gorges, and along the lakeshore. There are seven day-use trails ranging in length from ¼ mile to about 4½ miles. You can combine these to suit your hiking desires. One trail takes you to the overlook at Fall Creek Falls. From here, another trail—a bit more strenuous, but rewarding—takes you to the pool at the base of these falls. For the more adventuresome, there are two longer trails of about a dozen miles each with campsites. If you plan to overnight on these, you'll need a permit.

A three-mile-long paved bicycle trail leads from the inn to the falls. Rental bikes are available. There are two designated equestrian trails, but they are only for the use of horses rented from the park stable.

Once you get in the woods away from the resort area, you'll have a good chance of seeing deer, raccoons, and other small animals.

The park surrounds a 365-acre lake that's open for boating and fishing, but not swimming. For that there's an Olympic-size public swimming pool ($2) open Memorial Day to Labor Day.

Canoes, paddleboats, and small fishing boats with electric trolling motors can be rented at the lake. No privately owned boats are permitted, but you can bring your own electric trolling motor. Bank and pier fishing are also popular. In addition to the state fishing license, lake fishing permits ($1.50) are required of all fishermen except registered inn and cabin guests. The lake has yielded two state-record fish: the largest bluegill and the largest channel catfish. Largemouth bass are also plentiful here.

On land, there are lighted tennis courts, ball fields, a recreation center, crafts center, and other recreation facilities in the Village Green Complex around the park headquarters.

The 18-hole, par-72 golf course has been named one of the top 25 public courses in America by *Golf Digest* magazine.

Camping and Accommodations

The 70 rooms in the three-story **inn** all have a lake view, a private balcony or patio, a phone and a color TV. Amenities include a recreation room and an exercise/fitness room. A double rents for about $65 per night in high season and about $50 in off-season. There is a full-service restaurant in the inn.

There are 10 lakeside **cabins,** where you can fish from the porch, and 10 other cabins on a hill close to the lake. All are two-bedroom that sleep eight, have central heat and air, color TV, phones, and fireplaces. In season these are available only on a weekly rental of $475. Off-season you rent them

by the day for about $70 on weekdays to about $95 on weekends.

Inn and cabin guests have their own pool.

The 227 **campsites** are in three campgrounds. All have water and electric hookups and rent for $12 per night. They are on a first-come basis; no reservations. The stay limit is two weeks.

The park also has two group lodges, open year-round, and two group camps with 21 rustic cabins open March through October.

Nearby Attractions

In nearby **Pikeville,** a number of historic and stately homes have earned a listing in the National Register of Historic Places. The town also lays claim to being the "Pumpkin Capital of the World."

To the west, near McMinnville, are **Cumberland Caverns Park** (tel. 615/668-4396); you can tour these impressive caverns and enter the "Hall of the Mountain King."

South at **Dunlop,** you can arrange a llama pack trip, take hang gliding instruction, visit a display of hundreds of model trains and a museum that features more than 200 beehive coke ovens at an early coal mine site.

Farther south—possibly too far for a daytrip, but an easy overnighter—is **Chattanooga.** Lots to see and do here. For example, you can see an electronic re-creation of the Battle of Chickamauga; visit a number of Civil War battlesites here and in northern Georgia; take what claims to be the world's steepest passenger railway to the top of Lookout Mountain; visit the **Tennessee Aquarium** (tel. 615/265-0695) and the **National Knife Museum** (tel. 615/892-5007); take a cruise on the Tennessee River; ride a historic railway; take a half-mile, personally controlled sled ride down a mountain; or take a simulated hang-gliding flight.

Paris Landing State Resort Park

Lodge/ Restaurant RV Tent Primitive Boating Boat Fishing Swimming Beach
Hotel Camping Camping Camping Launch

Waterskiing Snorkeling Picnic Trails Nature Golf Tennis Playground Gift Shop
& Diving Areas Programs

Capsule Description: A lakeside resort park.

Location: Northwestern Tennessee on the border with Kentucky. From Paris, take U.S. Highway 79 northeast 16 miles to the park.

Address: Route 1, Box 77 Buchanan, TN 38222 (tel. 901/644-7358 for the park office, fax 901/642-4140, 901/642-4311 for the inn).

Area Contacts: Land Between the Lakes, 100 Van Morgan Dr., Golden Pond, KY 42211-9001 (tel. 502/924-5602).

Paris/Henry County Chamber of Commerce, P.O. Box 8, Paris, TN 38242-0008 (tel. toll free 800/345-1103 or tel. 901/642-3431).

Insider Tip: Golf packages are available through the inn.

This 841-acre park is on the western shore of the 200,000-acre Kentucky Lake, one of the largest man-made lakes in the world. It's named for a steamboat and freight landing on the Tennessee River dating back to the mid-1800s.

Activities

Kentucky Lake is big enough to handle yachts, sailboats, cruisers, runabouts, and just about any other type of pleasure craft you can put in the water. The park's full-service marina can handle them all and also rents fishing boats and motors, pontoon boats, ski boats, Scat Cats, and Waverunners. Naturally, the lake is also popular for other water sports from windsurfing to snorkeling and skin diving.

Fishing is good for largemouth, smallmouth, and spotted bass; bream, catfish, and crappie. If you don't want to boat, there's a fishing pier.

Swimmers have a choice of a lake beach, without lifeguards, or a guarded public Olympic-size swimming pool (fee) open from early summer through Labor Day.

The 18-hole, par-72 golf course has been carved out of 300 acres of woods, hills, and hollows adjacent to the lake. Special golf packages are available over the winter season.

Other resort facilities include a 14-station archery range, two lighted tennis courts, and a variety of recreational courts. During the summer recreation directors run a number of programs and activities including outdoor entertainment on Saturday nights.

This is not a hiker's park, with only about 1½ miles of trails; however, the park has an agreement to use the trails and the interpretive facilities at the nearby Tennessee Valley Authority's (TVA) 170,000-acre Land Between the Lakes, a national recreation area.

Camping and Accommodations

The **inn** has 100 rooms, most providing a commanding view of the lake. During high season, from April through November, a double costs about $65 on weekends, a little lower on weekdays. It has a restaurant and a private pool for guests.

At the time of this writing, a number of **cabins** were under construction at the park. Call for details.

The 46 **campsites,** all in the woods, have water and electric hookups and rent for $12 per night. They are on a first-come basis; no reservations. There are also some primitive sites that rent for about half the developed-site fee. Group camping is allowed in the primitive area.

Nearby Attractions

You won't see much wildlife in this resort park, but you don't have to go far to satisfy that interest. To the south is the **Tennessee National Wildlife Refuge** (tel. toll free 800/372-3928). White-tailed deer, opossums, raccoons, and skunks are commonly sighted here, and, though seldom seen, muskrats, beavers, and minks are present in significant numbers. Each fall and winter, migrations bring more than 150,000 ducks and 75,000 Canada geese. Bald eagles nest in the reservation, and the tree-nesting wood duck is making a population comeback here.

Want more? Head north to the **Land Between the Lakes.** Nestled between Kentucky and Barkley lakes, this 270-square-mile recreation area has a population of deer, wild turkey, otter, beaver, even a 200-acre Buffalo Range. Other sights on this peninsula worth a visit are the **Homeplace,** a living history farm that depicts life in the 1850s, and **Empire Farm,** a demonstration farm.

Northwest of the park, in **Murray, Kentucky,** is the **National Museum of the Boy Scouts of America** (tel. 502/762-3383), on the grounds of Murray State University.

To the southwest, in nearby **Paris,** you can take a walking tour of the historic downtown, centered around the oldest courthouse still in use in the state. For something completely different, visit the 65-foot scale **model of the Eiffel Tower** in the town park.

To the east, in **Dover,** is **Fort Donelson National Battlefield** (tel. 615/232-5706), the site of Ulysses S. Grant's first major Union victory in the Civil War. You can also take a riverboat cruise here.

Texas

PALO DURO CANYON STATE PARK

DAVIS MOUNTAINS STATE PARK

BRAZOS BEND STATE PARK

Texas has 136 state parks.

Contacts

- Texas Parks and Wildlife Department, 4200 Smith School Rd., Austin, TX 78744-3291 (tel. toll free 800/792-1112 for information or 512/389-8900 for reservations).
- Division of Travel and Information, Texas Department of Transportation, P.O. Box 5064, Austin, TX 78763-5064 (tel. toll free 800/ 452-9292 for information).
- Texas Department of Commerce travel kit (tel. toll free 800/888-8TEX [800/888-8839]).

General Information About Texas State Parks

One Texas writer claims that Texans don't brag. "It just sounds that way when we tell the truth about our state."

He may be right. Texas is the largest state in the nation not covered by snow and ice most of the year. It measures around 800 miles in both length and breadth—as big as all New England with New York, Pennsylvania, Ohio, and Illinois thrown in— and has more than 600 miles of coastline that includes some of the best-rated beaches in the world. Its wide diversity of environments makes it the home of more than 5,000 species of wildflowers, and 550 species of birds have been sighted here, three-fourths of all the American species. Although

it contains three of the most populous cities in the nation—Dallas, Houston, and San Antonio—it also has a deer population that exceeds 2.5 million and more than 200,000 alligators.

Historically, Texans claim the first Thanksgiving in the New World was in the El Paso area in 1598, years before the Pilgrims got around to it. And they won their independence from Mexico in what may be the shortest decisive battle in history—the Battle of San Jacinto, on April 21, 1836, which lasted 18 minutes.

The Republic of Texas lasted from 1836 to 1845 when Texas was annexed into the Union. The sheer size of Texas was recognized by the annexation treaty, which gave the new state the right to divide into four more states. Texans have never exercised that right, although there are some Texans who bring it up when they get annoyed by the state government. Geographically, the state is like four states. In the east are the vast pine forests, in the west the desert and mountains—Texas has 91 mountains more than a mile high with the highest soaring to 8,749 feet—in the north are the wide open plains of the Panhandle, and in the south the Gulf Coast and the lush semitropics of the Rio Grande Valley.

The state parks are as varied as Texas itself. There are beach parks, mountain parks, desert parks, the Texas State Railroad State Historical Park (tel. 903/683-2561), much of which is not much wider than the track of this railroad that runs 25-miles-long; and the battleship *Texas*. In size, they range from the .006-acre burial site of Davy Crockett's wife to the 268,000-acre Big Bend Ranch.

GENERAL FEES

Entrance fees per vehicle are based on park classification as a high-use park ($6), medium use ($4 to $5), or low use ($2 to $3). If you go in individually by foot, horse, bike, boat, or bus, the fee is $1 to $3 for an adult and 50¢ to $1 for 12 or under.

The Texas Conservation Passport, which costs $25, not only gives you free admission to the recreational parks, but also waives the tour fee at historical parks and offers several other extra benefits.

CAMPING AND ACCOMMODATIONS

Inn and **motel** accommodations are available at Indian Lodge at Davis Mountains State Park, San Salomon Springs Courts at Balmorhea State Park, and the Landmark Inn in Castroville. A double runs from $40 to $55.

Six parks have **cabins**: Bastrop, Caddo Lake, Daingerfield, Garner, Lake Brownwood, and Possum Kingdom. These range in capacity from two to six persons. Some are air-conditioned, some have fireplaces. Depending on park and facilities, they rent from $35 to $80 per night. Bastrop, Daingerfield, and Lake Brownwood also have rus-

tic lodges for small groups of eight to about 25. Some parks also have screened shelters that can be rented for overnight lodging for about $15 to $25.

There are **campgrounds** in 75 parks. Most campsites are multiuse with a variety of hookups ranging from water only to three-way. Fees are based on both the park's use category and the hookups provided, ranging from $6 to $12 for a water-only site to $10 to $16 for a three-way. Ten parks also offer equestrian campsites.

Reservations for campsites and all accommodations except Indian Lodge (see below) may be booked through the Central Reservation System (tel. 512/389-8900).

Pets. Pets must be on a maximum six-foot leash and attended at all times. They are not permitted in cabins or any other buildings or in swimming areas.

Alcoholic beverages. Public consumption or display of an open container of alcoholic beverages is prohibited.

Discounts. The State Parklands Passport, which exempts the holder from entrance fees, is available to anyone 65 or older and veterans with 60% or greater VA disability.

Davis Mountains State Park

| Lodge/
Hotel | Restaurant | RV
Camping | Tent
Camping | Primitive
Camping | Swimming | Picnic
Areas | Trails | Nature
Programs | Playground | Gift Shop |

Capsule Description: A mountain park with an inn and other facilities.

Location: West Texas in the Davis Mountains, four miles northwest of Fort Davis. Going east on I-10 from El Paso, take Exit 176 to Texas Highway 118 to the park. Going west on I-10 from Fort Stockton, take Exit 209

to Texas Highway 17, then south to Fort Davis to Texas 118, then northwest four miles to the park.

Address: P.O. Box 1458, Fort Davis, TX 79734 (tel. 915/426-3337). Indian Lodge (tel. 915/426-3254).

Area Contacts: Alpine Chamber of Commerce, 106 N. Third Street, Alpine, TX 79831 (tel. 915/837-2326). Fort Davis Chamber of Commerce, P.O. Box

378, Fort Davis, TX 79734 (tel. toll free 800/524-3015 or tel. 915/426-3015).

Insider Tips: If you attend a Star Party at the McDonald Observatory, dress warmly—the mountain air can get quite cool after the sun goes down. The Lodge and restaurant are normally closed the middle two weeks in January for maintenance.

The 2,677-acre park is located in the rolling foothills of the Davis Mountains, the most extensive mountain range in Texas. Between the desert plains grasslands of lower elevations and the woodlands of the intermediate elevation, it has the flora and fauna of both represented. However, the park ecosystem is predominantly grassland with few flowering plants, except during wet years when wildflowers bloom in abundance. Much of the park was built by the Civilian Conservation Corps (CCC) in the 1930s.

The mountains, the county, the town, and the nearby fort were all named after Jefferson Davis when he was U.S. Secretary of War. Nestling comfortably at 5,000 feet, Fort Davis has the distinction of being the highest town in the state.

Activities

The most popular place in the park is Skyline Drive, a scenic road that winds its way up to overlooks at 6,000 feet on the park's highest peaks. You can drive up or hike it. From here you can see Mount Livermore, at 8,382 feet the second-highest peak in the state, and the famous McDonald Observatory on the top of Mount Locke. At night, for a small fee, you can do your own stargazing on Skyline Drive.

A hilly, 4½-mile hiking trail connects the park with Fort Davis National Historic Site. There is also an eight-mile trail north of Highway 118 that is open only to holders of a Texas Conservation Passport. The passport is also your passport to watch bird-banding operation in spring and fall.

Next to the park's small Interpretive Center is an observation point by a wildlife watering station. Here you should see mostly small animals and a variety of birds, like white-wing doves, curved-bill thrashers, and the Montezuma quail, once abundant, but now rare in Texas. Larger animals you might see in the park include the mule deer and javelina.

During the summer, campfire programs are presented on weekends on topics ranging from natural history to Indian lore.

Camping and Accommodations

Indian Lodge was originally constructed by the CCC in 1933 in Southwestern pueblo style from adobe, Texas cedar, native plants, and river cane. The 39 rooms are a blend of CCC craftsmanship and more modern renovations. Many of the older rooms have walls 18 inches thick and some have adobe fireplaces (now only decorative). All rooms have color TV with cable, heat, and air conditioning, and there's a heated pool for guests.

Reservations are made directly to the lodge (tel. 915/426-3254). They are accepted up to one calendar year in advance and many weekends are booked solid that far ahead. A standard double costs $55 per night. There are seven suites of various type that rent for $70 to $85 for two persons and $10 extra for each additional adult. The inn restaurant is full service and open to guests and visitors.

There are 37 pull-through RV campsites with three-way hookups, 20 multiuse with water and electric, and 41 with water only. About 70% of the sites have good shade. Sites cost $6 to $14 per night. They may be reserved through the central reservation number.

Nearby Attractions

Although seemingly away from everything, the park is actually an excellent jumping-off place for a number of easy daytrips.

The town of **Fort Davis** offers a couple of small but interesting museums and a national historic site that features the restored 1854 fort (tel. 915/426-3224). More than two dozen original fort buildings have been restored in the 460-acre site. During the summer, park rangers and volunteers dress up in military and civilian costumes.

Approximately three miles south of the town of Fort Davis on Highway 118 is the **Chihuahuan Desert Research Institute** (tel. 915/837-8370) with an arboretum and a desert garden containing more than 500 species of plants from the region.

If you go north 13 miles on Highway 118, you'll reach the **McDonald Observatory** (tel. 915/426-3263). Atop 6,791-foot Mount Locke, this is one of the world's great observatories. Guided tours are given twice a day in summer and once a day in winter, or you can take a self-guided tour. Star parties, using small telescopes, are given each Tuesday, Friday, and Saturday starting at sunset. A public-viewing night is held monthly—on the Wednesday when the moon is at its fullest—using the observatories 107-inch telescope, the largest telescope in the world available to the public. Reservations for this monthly event are required and should be made six months in advance.

To the south, **Alpine** offers the **Museum of the Big Bend** and a rock-hunting ranch where you can pick up gemstones from amethysts to opals for about 50¢ a pound. Also to the south, you can see and try to come up with an explanation for the mysterious Marfa Ghost Lights.

Brazos Bend State Park

Visitor Center | RV Camping | Tent Camping | Primitive Camping | Picnic Areas | Trails | Nature Programs | Bicycling | Playground | Gift Shop

Capsule Description: A large natural park with some developed facilities.

Location: Southeast Texas, approximately 50 miles southeast of Houston. From Houston, take Texas Highway 288 south to Rosharon, then west on Farm Road (FM) 1462 to the park. Or, from U.S. Highway 90 at Richmond, take Farm Road (FM) 762 approximately 20 miles southeast to the park.

Address: 21901 FM 762, Needville, TX 77461 (tel. 409/553-5101).

Area Contacts: Greater Houston Convention and Visitors Bureau, 801 Congress, Houston, TX 77002 (tel. toll free 800/231-7799).

Rosenberg-Richmond Chamber of Commerce, 4120 Ave. H, Rosenberg, TX 77471 (tel. 713/342-5464).

West Columbia Chamber of Commerce, P.O. Box 837, West Columbia, TX 77486 (tel. 409/345-3921).

Insider Tips: Spring is the best time for alligator-viewing. This is when alligators come out to bask in the sun.

There are not many state parks where they hand you a listing of "Alligator Etiquette" when you come through the gate. That's necessary because Brazos State Park is one of the best places in Texas to see alligators in their natural setting. The 4,897-acre park is not a zoo and the 200 to 300 alligators that make this their home are not tame or under any type restraint, so knowing how to alligator-watch safely is important.

Alligators may be the best known, but they aren't the only residents. The park is also home to 20 other species of reptiles and amphibians, 23 species of mammals including white-tailed deer, bobcats, raccoons, gray foxes, and feral hogs; and more than 270 species of birds have been sighted here.

In other words, this is a park to see wildlife up close. The reason for this abundant and diverse wildlife population is the diversity of the land that has forests, which include huge moss-draped live oaks; six lakes totaling about 800 acres, about three miles of the Bravos River, and freshwater marshes.

From the swamps to the stars—the park is also home to the George Observatory of the Houston Museum of Natural History, where you can take part in regular public stargazing programs.

In the early 1800s, the parkland was part of Stephen F. Austin's first colonial land grant from Mexico. The grant that started it all.

Activities

Wildlife-watching is high on the list of things to do here. Not just the alligators, but the herds of deer and the dozens of other animals, plus the ducks, herons, egrets, cranes, and other birds that either live here or migrate through and often number in the thousands. To help you get up close, there are about 20 miles of hiking trails, a one-mile self-guided nature trail, and 11 miles of hike and bike trails (mountain bikes only). To give you a better view, these trails lead to a three-story observation tower, a 60-foot boardwalk extending into a pond, and seven platforms that are for both wildlife observation and fishing.

Guided nature walks and other nature programs are given on weekends year-round. There is also an Interpretive Center with exhibits that will tell you all you need to know about alligators.

The most important thing you need to know right away is you don't feed or annoy alligators. People who feed them "train" them to associate humans with food—and the humans could become the food. Do not assume they are slow-moving or sluggish. They can run up to 23 miles per hour—faster than you can—so it's wise to stay at least 30 feet from an alligator. Also, if you love your pet, keep it on a leash and don't let it in the water. No human deaths from alligators have been reported in Texas, at least not up to the time this book went to press, but a few pets who decided to go up and smell out a seemingly quiet alligator or swim in their waters are now merely statistics.

Scary? If you obey those rules, it shouldn't be. And you'll have a good chance of being rewarded with a close-up view of a creature in the wild that has ancestors going back 65 million years.

Of course, unlike most water-blessed parks, swimming and boating are prohibited here. You can fish, though, as long as it's from the banks, two T-shaped lighted fishing piers, or the fishing platforms. Catches include perch, bass, crappie. One lake is stocked with rainbow trout in winter.

Want to turn your eyes to the heavens? On Saturday nights, weather permitting, volunteer astronomers hold stargazing programs at the George Observatory using the 36-inch telescope—so powerful it can only focus on one section of the Andromeda galaxy at a time—and several smaller telescopes. Passes for stargazing through the 36-incher are usually distributed about 5pm for viewing after sunset. The smaller telescopes, which are often trained at planets, don't require viewing passes. The observatory is open late in the day on Saturday if you want to visit the exhibit hall.

Camping and Accommodations

There are 14 screened **shelters** that may be used overnight. These consist of a slab, picnic table, fire ring, grill, and are provided with electricity. You have to bring cots and everything else. They cost $18 to $20 per night.

The 42 multiuse **campsites** have electric and water hookups. There are also 35 sites with water primarily for tent campers. Sites go for $7 to $15. Campsites and shelters can be reserved through the central reservation number.

Nearby Attractions

Among the points of interest in **Rosenberg-Richmond,** to the north, is the **Fort Bend County Museum Complex** (tel. 713/342-1256), which includes several buildings from the 1800s and the county museum.

About 25 miles south is **West Columbia.** Founded in 1826, it served briefly as the capital of the Texas Republic in 1836. A reconstruction of the few pioneer buildings that made up this capital are located in the center of town. It is also the site of the **Varner-Hogg State Historical Park** (tel. 409/345-4656), a plantation park featuring a mansion built in the early 1800s.

To the northeast, less than an hour away, is **Houston,** the largest city in the state, offering entertainment, cultural attractions, sports, and shopping.

Palo Duro Canyon State Park

Visitor Center   RV Camping   Tent Camping   Picnic Areas   Trails   Horse Trails   Nature Programs

Capsule Description: A large natural canyonlands park with some developed facilities.

Location: Northwestern Texas, in the Panhandle. From Canyon, take Texas 217 east 12 miles to the park. From Amarillo, take I-25 south to Exit 106, then Texas Highway 217 east to the park.

Address: Route 2, Box 285, Canyon, TX 79015 (tel. 806/488-2227).

Area Contacts: Amarillo Convention and Visitors Bureau, P.O. Box 9480, Amarillo, TX 79105 (tel. 806/373-7800; toll free 800/692-1338 in Texas only).

Canyon Chamber of Commerce, P.O. Box 8, Canyon, TX 79015 (tel. toll free 800/999-9481 or tel. 806/655-1183).

Insider Tip: When you descend to the bottom of the Palo Duro Canyon, you'll see layers of earth that are 90 million years old.

The most dramatic scenery on the relatively flat High Plains of Texas are the inverted mountains—the dozen or so canyon gorges cut through the Panhandle by the Red River and its tributaries. The Prairie Dog Town Fork of the Red River, a seemingly insignificant stream, over a few million years of time, has carved out the rugged, scenic Palo Duro Canyon, 120 miles long, plunging to a depth of almost 800 feet. The largest and best known of the canyons, it's often cited as Texas's

scaled-down version of the Grand Canyon. What some consider the most spectacular portion of that canyon lies within the 16,402-acre Palo Duro Canyon State Park.

Historians are pretty much in agreement that Spanish explorer Francisco Vásquez de Coronado and his men, on their fruitless search for the fabled Seven Cities of Cibola, were the first white men to see the canyon. Coronado is credited with naming one of the canyon's landmarks *El Faro,* "The Lighthouse." It is not known if he also gave the canyon its name, but *palo duro,* is Spanish for "hard wood," referring to the cedar growing here, which the Indians used to make bows and arrows.

In 1874, this was the site of the last major battle with the Indians in Texas. U.S. troops attacked a large encampment of Comanches, Cheyennes, Kiowas, and Arapahos. The battle itself was inconclusive in terms of casualties, but the troops captured and destroyed more than a thousand Indian horses and mules, putting the most fierce horsemen of the Plains afoot. Dispirited, the Indians eventually returned to their reservations in Oklahoma.

Activities

One of the joys in this park is watching the colors of the multihued clays and rocks of the canyon

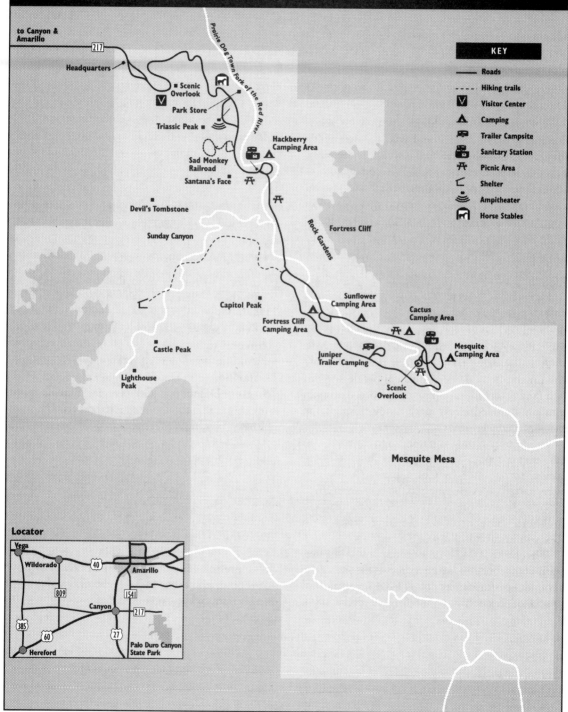

Palo Duro Canyon State Park

N

| 0 | .25 | .5 mi |
| 0 | .25 | .5 km |

KEY

— Roads
- - - - Hiking trails
V Visitor Center
▲ Camping
Trailer Campsite
Sanitary Station
Picnic Area
Shelter
Ampitheater
Horse Stables

to Canyon & Amarillo

217

Headquarters

Prairie Dog Town Fork of the Red River

Scenic Overlook

Park Store

Triassic Peak

Hackberry Camping Area

Sad Monkey Railroad

Santana's Face

Devil's Tombstone

Sunday Canyon

Rock Gardens

Fortress Cliff

Capitol Peak

Fortress Cliff Camping Area

Sunflower Camping Area

Cactus Camping Area

Mesquite Camping Area

Castle Peak

Juniper Trailer Camping

Scenic Overlook

Lighthouse Peak

Mesquite Mesa

Locator

Vega

Wildorado

40

Amarillo

809

1541

Canyon

217

385

60

27

Hereford

Palo Duro Canyon State Park

walls change with changes in the angle of the sun. There are a number of named formations that are particularly interesting to watch, such as the Spanish Skirts, so named because the colors in the clay layers resemble the folds and ruffles in a Spanish dancer's flared skirt. Early morning and just before sunset are the best times to watch these visual pyrotechnics.

At the interpretive center you can learn about the area geology, history, and wildlife. Park wildlife includes mule deer and aoudad sheep. The aoudads are mountain sheep that trace their ancestry back to the rugged mountains of North Africa. Part of the state's longhorn herd is also located in this park. For birders, more than 200 species of birds have been sighted here.

There are miles of both hiking and equestrian trails, many to scenic overlooks offering panoramic vistas. One, for example, is a 4.6-mile (round-trip) trail for both hikers and riders to the Lighthouse scenic overlook. There are no stables for visitors, but you can bring in your own horse for a day-trip or rent one from the park stables.

A scenic drive takes you down to and along the canyon floor. Here you can also ride the Sad Monkey Railroad, a miniature railroad that takes you on a guided two-mile journey through the canyon.

In addition to the natural sights in the park, you can visit a replica of a primitive dugout home similar to one used by Col. Charles Goodnight, who started his cattle ranch in the canyon in 1876. Goodnight was one of the men who first ran longhorn cattle herds on the long drives from Texas to markets in Kansas.

The park's 1,742-seat outdoor amphitheater, with a 600-foot cliff as a backdrop, is the site of the summer performances of *TEXAS,* a musical drama of Texas history. Performed every night except Sunday from early June through mid-August, this show has been running since the mid-1960s and played to more than 2½ million visitors. Reservations are recommended (tel. 806/655-2181), with tickets going for $6 to $14. Admission to the park is free to theater patrons after 5:30pm. For an additional charge you can have a barbecue dinner before the performance.

Camping

The six **campgrounds** offer 53 multiuse campsites and 20 trailer sites with water and electric hookups, and 43 tent sites with water available. Sites go for $7 to $15 and may be reserved through the central reservation number.

Nearby Attractions

Canyon, a short drive to the west, features the **Panhandle-Plains Museum** (tel. 806/656-2244). You can also take a guided tour of the museums and other buildings at **West Texas State University.**

Among the points of interest worth a visit in **Amarillo,** to the northwest, are the **Don Harrington Discovery Center** and **Planetarium** (tel. 806/355-9547); the **American Quarter Horse Heritage Center** and **Museum** (tel. 806/383-4712); and for the kids, Storyland Zoo and Wonderland Park (tel. 806/383-4712). If you're in Amarillo on a Tuesday, visit the livestock auction, one of the world's largest. From Amarillo you can also arrange to take a trip back to Palo Duro as part of **Cowboy Morning** or **Cowboy Evening.** These two popular ranch events include a huge cowboy breakfast or dinner prepared on a campfire and demonstrations by working cowboys of roping, branding, and other cowboy skills. All on the rim of the canyon.

Utah

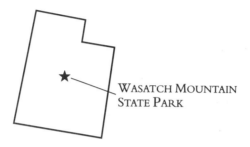

WASATCH MOUNTAIN
STATE PARK

Utah has 50 state parks.

Contacts

- Division of Parks and Recreation, Department of Natural Resources, 1636 W. North Temple, Salt Lake City, UT 84116 (tel. 801/538-7221; toll free 800/322-3770 for reservations only).
- Utah Travel Council, Council Hall, Capitol Hill, Salt Lake City, UT 84114-1102 (tel. toll free 800/200-1160).

General Information on Utah State Parks

One of Utah's advertising slogans is "Discover the diversity." That hits the mark. Utah definitely offers a diversity, starting with the terrain. Most of the state lies on a plateau above 4,000 feet in elevation. Its many mountain ranges top out around 13,000 feet and are crowned by King's Peak at 13,528 feet. Over 500 inches of snow fall on Utah's mountain ski resorts each year. It also has forests, the Great Salt Lake and thousands of other not salty lakes, and deserts.

Nearly 80% of Utah's land is administered by government agencies for public use. In addition to its state parks, Utah contains five national parks, seven national forests, six national monuments, two national recreation areas, one national historic site, millions of acres of U.S. Bureau of Land Management lands, and 3.3 million acres of Indian reservations.

The diversity in the state parks carry over to sports that include all the normal seasonal choices plus the not-so-normal river running and sand-dune sliding.

GENERAL FEES

The entrance fee to most parks is $3 per vehicle.

CAMPING

There are about 1,200 campsites ranging from modern with three-way hookups to primitive. Reservations may be made three to 120 days in advance by calling toll free 800/322-3770 during the normal business week. Sites cost $7 to $15 per night depending on facilities.

Pets. Pets are allowed in most state parks provided they are confined or on a leash no longer than six feet in length. They are not permitted on developed beaches, golf courses, or in park buildings or lakes and streams.

Alcoholic beverages. Alcoholic beverages are permitted is most parks; however, no containers over one gallon are allowed and no keg beer.

Wasatch Mountain State Park

| RV Camping | Tent Camping | Primitive Camping | Group Camping | Trails | Horse Trails | Nature Programs | Bicycling | Golf | X-Country Skiing | Snow-mobiling |

Capsule Description: A large, mountain wilderness park with developed facilities.

Location: North central Utah, about 50 miles east of Salt Lake City. From Salt Lake City, take I-80 east to the U.S. Highway 40/Heber exit. Go south on U.S. 40 to Heber City, approximately 17 miles; then take Utah Highway 113 west to Midway, and follow signs to the park. (Approximately seven miles from Heber to the park.)

Address: PO Box 10, Midway, UT 84049 (tel. 801/654-1791).

Area Contacts: Heber Valley Chamber of Commerce, 475 N. Main, Heber, UT 84032 (tel. 801/654-3666).

Mountainland, 2545 N. Canyon Rd., Provo, UT 84604 (tel. 801/377-2262).

Salt Lake City Convention and Visitors Bureau, 180 S. West Temple, Salt Lake City, UT 84101-1493 (tel. 801/521-2822).

Insider Tips: Advance reservations for the park's 27-hole golf course are made by calling 801/654-0532 or 266-0268. Tee times for Saturday through Monday must be arranged by the preceding Monday; play Tuesday through Friday must be reserved the preceding Saturday. At the campground amphitheater, free programs are offered June through August on Friday and Saturday evenings.

This 22,000-acre park is poised on the east slope of the Wasatch Mountains at an elevation of 6,000 feet. The largest park in the state, it is open year-round.

Activities

Although there are endless trails in the park and nearby national forests, not many are signed hiking trails. The one self-guided nature trail, 1.2 miles in length, requires a moderate climb from 6,100 feet to 6,320 feet elevation. Several of the roads in the park are open to bikes, motorcycles, and horseback riders. Since much of the park is wilderness, hikers have a good chance of seeing mule deer, elk, moose, and small animals such as raccoons and porcupines. Larger birds include eagles and red-tailed hawks.

The Utah section of the Great Western Trail is adjacent to the park. While still under development, much of the Utah section is open. This trail will eventually stretch from Mexico to Canada, with separate trails for hikers, horses, and mountain bikes.

One of the park's summer claims to fame is its USGA-sanctioned, 27-hole golf course. The par-72 course has 10 lakes located throughout tree-lined fairways.

There's a fishing pond, but it's only for kids under 12 who can try their skill or luck for rainbow trout. For adult fishing and other water sports, Deer Creek State Park is just a short drive south. This park, on the Deer Creek Reservoir, offers fishing for perch, bass, and stocked rainbow trout, sailing, swimming, boating, and water-skiing.

It's a different story in winter when Wasatch Mountain Park turns into Utah's finest and most complete snowmobiling facility. The park, in cooperation with the U.S. Forest Service and the Utah Department of Transportation, offers miles of groomed snowmobile trails that connect with other area trails to add up to a total of close to 90 miles. Trail facilities include parking, restrooms, warming stations, and designated play areas. The

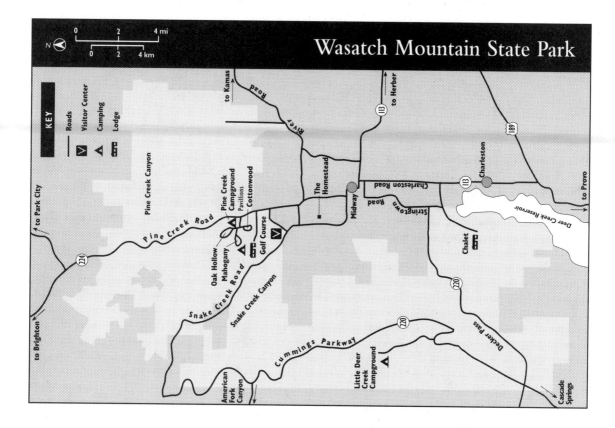

park also has a seven-mile groomed Nordic ski track with diagonal stride and skating lanes. Nordic ski equipment and snowmobiles can be rented and guided snowmobile tours can be arranged.

Camping

The **campgrounds** are open from May through October. Of the 122 campsites, 40 are designated tent sites and the rest are multiuse with three-way hookups on 66 sites and water and electric hookups on the rest. Sites may be reserved through the central reservation system and cost $11 to $15 per night.

Seventeen primitive sites, in a mountain campgrounds reached over about 10 miles of unimproved road, are $8 per night.

The group camp has both RV and tent-camping space and a dining building with a capacity of 100 in summer and 50 in winter.

Nearby Attractions

In nearby Midway, you can visit the **state fish hatchery** (tel. 801/654-0282). At **Heber City,** you can take a steam-train excursion on the **Heber Valley Historic Railroad** (tel. 801/ 654-5601) through the Heber Valley and Provo Canyon.

To the southwest is **Provo,** an easy daytrip from the park. Three places worth a visit on the way are Sundance, Bridal Veil Falls, and the Timpanogas Cave National Monument. **Sundance** (tel. 801/-225-4107) is a ski resort area where Robert Redford has his film institute, which holds a world-renowned film festival each January. At **Bridal Veil Falls** you can ride a tramway up 1,700 feet from the canyon floor for a bird's-eye view of double falls. The **Timpanogos caves** (tel. 801/756-5239), open from mid-May to mid-October, are three large, colorful limestone caverns connected by man-made tunnels. In spite of a vigorous hike of about 1½ miles required to reach the cave, it's still a popular attraction.

The must-see place in Provo is **Brigham Young University** (tel. 801/378-4636). One of the largest church-affiliated (Mormon) universities in the world, with about 27,000 students, it has a number of museums and other buildings worth a visit. Also in Provo is the **McCurdy Historical Doll Museum** (tel. 801/377-9935), which exhibits more than 3,000 dolls.

Park City, to the north of Wasatch Mountain Park, has long been a popular ski resort area.

To the northwest is **Salt Lake City,** the state capital. Among the things to do here are: take a tour of **Temple Square** (tel. 801/240-2534) and visit some of the impressive buildings belonging to the Mormon Church that are open to non-Mormons (and perhaps hear the famed Mormon Tabernacle Choir), tour the **capitol building** (tel. 801/538-3000) and the **Governor's Mansion** (tel. 801/538-1000), and take a self-guided tour of the **State Arboretum** (tel. 801/581-5322) on the campus of the **University of Utah** (tel. 801/581-7200).

Vermont

GROTON STATE
FOREST PARKS

Vermont has 50 state parks.

Contacts

- Department of Forests, Parks and Recreation, 103 S. Main, 10 South, Waterbury, VT 05671 (tel. 802/241-3655).
- Department of Travel and Tourism, 134 State St., Montpelier, VT 05602 (tel. toll free 800/837-6668).
- Vermont Chamber of Commerce, P.O. Box 37, Montpelier, VT 05601 (tel. 802/223-3443).

General Information on Vermont State Parks

The French explorer Samuel de Champlain described this area as *les verts monts* (the green mountains), and the compacted version of his words became the state name.

A quiet, almost pastoral state now—except during ski season—it had a boisterous beginning when Ethan Allen and his Green Mountain Boys organized to protect their colonial lands from a takeover by the New York Colony. This spilled over into a fight against the British and they joined with a force lead by Benedict Arnold to capture Fort Ticonderoga from the British in 1775, giving the colonists one of their first victories in the Revolutionary War.

After that war, because of the land dispute with

New York, Vermont decide not to join the other states in the new nation. For 14 years, until 1791, it was an independent republic. Its constitution was ahead of its time, outlawing slavery and granting the right to vote to all men without regard to wealth or property.

Still small in population today—a little over 500,000—the state has made a strong and successful effort to provide a park system that locates parks within easy reach of all its people. But a small population means small budgets, so most parks are normally only open from about mid-May to mid-October. In winter, many park lands are open for ski touring and snowmobiling, but there are few groomed trails and campgrounds and other facilities are closed.

GENERAL FEES

Most parks have an entrance fee of $1.50 per person for those 14 years and older, $1 from 4 through 13 years of age.

CAMPING AND ACCOMMODATIONS

There is one ranch house that operates as a guesthouse in Groton State Forest. (See listing below.)

Thirty-five parks have **campgrounds** with a total of 2,200 campsites. There are no hookups. Most campgrounds open officially the Friday preceding Memorial Day and close the Tuesday following Labor Day. If weather permits, some open earlier and close later. Sites may be reserved directly through the individual park. Preseason reservations of six or more nights will be accepted beginning January 2 at department headquarters or one of the four regional offices. After May 15, three or more nights' reservations are accepted directly by the parks. Maximum stay is normally 21 days. Sites cost $10 to $12. A number of parks also have lean-tos available that rent for $14 to $16 per night. There is a $3 reservation fee. Group camping areas are available for organized groups in eight parks. These are open year-round, except during the November deer hunting season. Primitive camping is permitted in many remote areas.

Pets. Pets are allowed only at designated campsites. All domestic animals must be restrained on a leash at all times. Proof of current rabies vaccination is required. Animals are not allowed in day-use areas, parking lots, or parked cars.

Alcoholic beverages. Alcoholic beverages are permitted. Kegs can only be brought in by a licensed caterer.

Discounts. Vermont residents age 62 and older may obtain the Green Mountain Passport that entitles them to free admission to any state day-use area.

Groton State Forest Parks

 Lodge/ Hotel
 RV Camping
 Tent Camping
 Primitive Camping
 Boating
 Boat Launch
 Fishing
 Beach

 Picnic Areas
 Trails
 Nature Programs
 Playground
 X-Country Skiing
 Snow-mobiling

Capsule Description: A large forest with a number of smaller state park units within its borders.

Location: Northeastern Vermont. From I-91, take U.S. Highway 302 west one mile past Groton to Vermont Highway 232, then north four miles to the park.

Address: RD, Groton, VT 05046 (tel. 802/584-3820). (January to April: Region IV, 324 N. Main, Barre, VT 05641; tel. 802/479-4280).

Area Contacts: Central Vermont Chamber of Commerce, P.O. Box 336, Barre, VT 05641 (tel. 802/229-4619).

St. Johnsbury Chamber of Commerce, 30 Western Ave., St. Johnsbury, VT 05819 (tel. 802/748-3678 or toll free 800/639-6379).

Insider Tip: Several mountain tops are accessible by trails. Owl's Head, elevation 1956 feet, is best known for its panoramic views of the area. The road that goes almost to the summit of Owl's Head is open to cars in summer.

At 28,000 acres, Groton is only second largest in size, but the largest recreational facility operated by the parks service. A scenic and rugged place, its bedrock is granite similar to that of the White Mountains of New Hampshire. It contains 2,000 acres of lakes, brooks, streams, and ponds, including the three-mile-long Lake Groton.

The Civilian Conservation Corps (CCC) laid much of the groundwork for the park during the 1930s: developing campgrounds and other facilities and building forest roads, including the one that's now Vermont 232 and one to the scenic overlook at the summit of Owls Head Mountain.

There are 10 separate facilities set in a mix of hard- and softwood forest.

Activities

About 35 miles of trails, of varied degrees of difficulty, invite hikers to explore the forest. The trail system connects most major points of interest and is well marked with blue paint for hikers and snowshoers, and orange reflectorized diamonds for cross-country skiing and snowmobiling in winter. There are no designated mountain bike or horseback trails, but they may use the old railroad bed and logging roads.

Before exploring, you might want to visit the Nature Center where displays give you information on the park's history, geology, and its bird and animal inhabitants, which include moose and white-tailed deer as well as a variety of songbirds. A self-guided half-mile nature trail starts at the center and loops back to it. In the summer, a park naturalist gives nature programs and conducts nature and canoe hikes.

The lakes, ponds, brooks, and streams offer opportunities for swimming, boating, and fishing. There are several places to swim—no lifeguards—but only Boulder Beach has a bathhouse and concession stand. Boat launches vary from car-top to trailer launches. Just about any type watercraft are allowed except personal watercraft like jet skis. Rowboats, canoes, and paddleboats can be rented at several locations.

Brook trout, rainbow trout, and smallmouth bass are the main catches. At the Seyon Ranch unit, only fly fishing is allowed. In winter, you can try ice fishing.

Camping and Accommodations

Private and semiprivate sleeping quarters (from two to four people in a room) can be rented at the rustic **Seyon Ranch House,** with up to three meals a day. The ranch accommodates up to 15 overnight guests and up to 30 diners. Lodging is about $15 per person and meals run from about $6 for breakfast to $15 for dinner. From May to October, reservation requests should be directed to the park (tel. 802/584-3829); the rest of the year to the region office (tel. 802/479-3241). This is mainly a small group facility—sometimes known as Vermont's Camp David since it's used by the governor and cabinet—but individual reservations are accepted on a space-available basis up to two weeks in advance.

There are 169 multiuse **campsites** and 54 lean-tos at various campgrounds in the park. No hookups. They rent for $10 to $16 and can be reserved through the Northeast Region office (324 N. Main, Barre, VT 05641; tel. 802/479-4280) in the off-season or directly to the park after May 15.

Nearby Attractions

The sights to see in the area go from cream and sugar to granite.

Cabot, to the northwest, is where you can tour the **Cabot Creamery** (tel. 802/563-2231) and a maple sugarhouse. At **Barre,** to the west, you can watch derricks capable of lifting 100-ton granite blocks out of the 27-acre hole called the **Rock of Ages Quarry** (tel. 802/476-3121), and watch craftsmen cut and polish these rough stones into things of beauty.

As evidence that high tech grows here as well as maple syrup, **St. Johnsbury,** to the north, has been known for its precision-weighing devices since the platform scale was invented here in the 1830s. You can't see that part of this town's industry, but you can visit the **Maple Museum** (tel. 802/748-5141) and the **Fairbanks Museum and Planetarium** (tel. 802/748-2372).

Montpelier, to the west, is the state capital. Sights here include the **State House** (tel. 802/828-1110), where you can visit the legislative chambers, and the **Vermont Historical Society Museum** (tel. 802/828-2291).

Virginia

DOUTHAT STATE PARK

SEASHORE STATE PARK AND NATURAL AREA

Virginia has 36 state parks.

Contacts

- Division of State Parks, Department of Conservation and Recreation, 203 Governor St., Suite 302, Richmond, VA 23219 (tel. 804/786-1712 or tel. toll free 800/933-7275 in state—outside of Richmond).
- Virginia Tourism Development Group, 910 E. Byrd St., Richmond, VA 23219 (tel. toll free 800/847-4882 or tel. 804-786-4484).

General Information on Virginia State Parks

Since Sir Walter Raleigh named this area after Elizabeth, the Virgin Queen, Virginia has played a major role in the history of our nation, especially in the early years. The first permanent English settlement in America was at Jamestown. Virginia was among the first colonies to rebel against England, and the Revolutionary War ended here with the British surrender at Yorktown in 1781. The state has produced eight presidents, starting with George Washington.

During the Civil War, Richmond became the capital of the Confederacy and the state's location on the Union border and its proximity to Lincoln's capital in Washington, D.C., made it the major battleground of that war.

Going west from Virginia's 112 mile Atlantic shoreline, the landscape gradually rises across rolling hills to the Blue Ridge and Allegheny mountains. Parklands represent the many landscapes from seashore to mountains. The foundation for the current park system was laid by the Civilian Conservation Corps in the 1930s. Carefully preserved buildings made of hand-hewn logs, roads, and other facilities are still in use today, tributes to the skilled handiwork of the men of the CCC.

Parks are open year-round, but most campgrounds/cabins and some other facilities are not available in the winter.

GENERAL FEES

Day-use parking fees range from $1 to $2.50 depending on the park and the day of the week. Fees are collected on weekends from about the end of March to Memorial Day, then daily through Labor Day weekend, and weekends again through the end of October. With the exception of a few parks, like Seashore, there's no parking charge the rest of the year.

CAMPING AND ACCOMMODATIONS

Seven parks offer a total of 140 rustic housekeeping **cabins:** Claytor Lake, Douthat, Fairy Stone, Hungry Mother, Seashore, Staunton River, and Westmoreland. These are available in the following sizes: one-room, one- and two-bedroom, and overnight. The overnight cabins, which are only at Westmoreland State Park, do not have kitchens or bathrooms; all the others do. They may be reserved for a minimum rental period of one week and a maximum of two consecutive weeks at one park. Any cabins not reserved are available on a first-come basis for a minimum of two nights. Weekly rates start at about $195 for a one-room, up to $250 for a one-bedroom, and from about $320 to $420 for a two-bedroom. The overnight cabins are about $25 per night.

There is one lodge with a capacity of 15 at Douthat State Park. It rents for about $550 per week.

Nineteen Virginia state parks have a total of more than 1,500 **campsites** ranging from primitive to those with electric and water hookups. Developed sites go for about $9 to $20 depending on the park and facilities. Primitive sites are $6. The maximum camping period is 14 days in any 30-day period. Most campgrounds are closed in the winter.

All cabins and campsites may be reserved in person at the individual park or at the division headquarters in Richmond. There is a $6 reservation fee. Telephone and mail reservations may only be made through the Ticketmaster Reservation Center: phone 804/490-3939 or write for an application form from Ticketmaster Reservation Center (State Parks), P.O. Box 62346, Virginia Beach, VA 23466. There is an $8 reservation fee for Ticketmaster phone or mail reservations.

Pets. Pets are allowed almost everywhere, including in cabins and campgrounds. Outside they must be on a leash no longer than six feet. At night they must be kept in cabins, tents, or vehicles. A $3 per night pet fee is charged for each pet in a cabin or campsite.

Alcoholic beverages. The display or consumption of alcoholic beverages is prohibited.

Douthat State Park

Visitor Center   Restaurant   Cabins & Cottages   RV Camping   Tent Camping   Group Camping   Group Lodge Dormitories   Boat Launch   Non-Motorized Boating Only

Fishing   Beach   Picnic Areas   Trails   Nature Programs   Bicycling   X-Country Skiing   Gift Shop

Capsule Description: A natural park in the mountains with some developed facilities.

Location: Western Virginia, four miles north of Clifton Forge. Take Exit 27 off I-64 to Virginia 629, then go four miles north to the park.

Address: Route 1, Box 212, Millboro, VA 24460 (tel. 703/862-7200).

Area Contacts: Allegheny Highlands Chamber of Commerce, 241 W. Main St., Covington, VA 24426 (tel. 703/962-2178).

Bath County Chamber of Commerce, P.O. Box 718, Hot Springs, VA 24445 (tel. toll free 800/628-8092 or tel. 703/839-5409).

Lexington Visitors Bureau, 106 E. Washington, Lexington, VA 24450 (tel. 703/463-3777).

The 4,493-acre park is nestled in the Allegheny Mountains near the border with West Virginia.

Douthat was one of the original six Virginia state parks to be opened in 1936. Much of the park was built by the men of the Civilian Conservation Corps (CCC) and many of the structures built by the CCC are still in use. You'll find striking examples of their craftsmanship in such things as hand-carved wooden doorknobs and hinges as well as hand-wrought iron T-hinges, light fixtures, and door and shutter latches.

In 1986, on the 50th anniversary of the park, it was designated a National Registered Historic Landmark.

Activities

There are 40 miles of hiking trails in the park, most are short, many less than a mile in length, including a self-guided nature trail that's about half a mile long, but they interconnect so you can pick your own distance. In addition several connect to even longer hiking trails in the George Washington National Forest, which surrounds the park. A number of the trails offer panoramic views from scenic overlooks.

Besides the small animals common to the area, the park is the home of a number of white-tailed deer, and an occasional black bear may be spotted.

Mountain bikes can be used on most of the hiking trails.

In winter, the trails are open for cross-country skiing, but they are not groomed.

If you want to know more about the park and its CCC builders, go to the visitors center. Originally constructed by the CCC, the center is open daily from Memorial Day weekend through Labor Day and features exhibits on the work of the CCC plus the park's plant and animal life.

During the summer season, for a small fee you can swim at the guarded beach on the 50-acre Douthat Lake. The lake is also open for boating and fishing. The only power permitted on the boats, however, is electric motors. Paddleboats and 14-foot johnboats can be rented on the lake.

Fishing is especially good for brook, brown, and rainbow trout, which are restocked about twice a week in both the lake and the adjoining creek in the summer. Other catches include smallmouth and largemouth bass, catfish, crappie, and sunfish.

Summer also offers a number of interpretive programs including nature hikes, paddleboat tours of the lake, and, occasionally, mountain storytellers and musicians.

The park restaurant, one of the original CCC facilities, overlooks the lake and is open for lunch and dinner daily during the high season, and weekends in April, May, and September.

Camping and Accommodations

Of the 30 rustic **cabins,** 25 are CCC-built log cabins and the other five are cinderblock. All have rustic furniture and fireplaces. No heat/air conditioning, TV, or phones. All the one-room and one-bedroom cabins are log. They rent for from about $195 to about $220 per week. The two-bedrooms are both log and block and rent for around $320 per week.

There is also the CCC-built log **lodge** with six bedrooms that sleeps up to 15 persons. It rents as a unit for about $550 per week.

There are no hookups on the 116 multiuse **campsites** located in three campgrounds. The fee on these is $8.50 per night.

All cabins, campsites, and the lodge may be reserved in person at the park or the parks division office in Richmond, or by phone or mail through Ticketmaster (see phone number and address on page 267).

Nearby Attractions

There's a lot to see in the park, and a lot more to see close by.

A short drive to the north, in **Hot Springs,** is **The Homestead** (tel. 703/839-1766), one of the most famous resorts in the East. The warm springs baths here, and some other facilities, are open to nonguests for a fee. In winter, this is also a place for downhill skiing and other winter sports. There are more public baths in **Warm Springs,** just a little farther north.

Just outside the park, to the south, in **Clifton Forge,** you can visit the **Allegheny Highlands Arts and Crafts Center** (tel. 703/862-4447) and the **Chesapeake and Ohio Railroad Historical Society Archives** (tel. 703/863-1415).

To the southwest, in **Covington,** is the **Humpback Bridge,** built in 1835 and now the nation's only surviving curved-span covered bridge. Here, too, is a reconstruction of **Fort Young,** which was designed by George Washington.

A little farther to the west, just across the West Virginia border, is another famous resort, **The Greenbrier** (tel. 304/536-1110) in **White Sul-**

phur Springs, which is worth a visit just to walk the grounds or eat in its restaurant.

An easy daytrip to the east is **Lexington,** the home of Robert E. Lee and one of his most celebrated generals, "Stonewall" Jackson. Both are buried here: Jackson in a cemetery named after him, and Lee in the Chapel of Washington and Lee University, where he served as president from 1865 to his death in 1870.

Another famous general, George C. Marshall, is honored here in a museum dedicated to him at the **Virginia Military Institute** (tel. 703/464-7000), the oldest state-supported military college in the nation.

For the equestrian-minded, Lexington is the home of the **Virginia Horse Center** (tel. 703/463-4300).

Seashore State Park and Natural Area

Visitor Center · Cabins & Cottages · RV Camping · Tent Camping · Boating · Boat Launch · Fishing · Beach · Picnic Areas · Trails · Nature Programs · Bicycling

Capsule Description: A beach park on Chesapeake Bay with developed facilities.

Location: On Chesapeake Bay east of Norfolk. From I-64, take Exit 227 to U.S. Highway 13, go north to U.S. Highway 60, then east to the park.

Address: 2500 Shore Dr., Virginia Beach, VA 23451 (tel. 804/481-2131).

Area Contacts: Colonial Williamsburg Foundation, P.O. Box 1776, Williamsburg, VA 23187 (tel. toll free 800/447-8679 (800/HISTORY)).

Norfolk Convention and Visitors Bureau, 236 E. Plune Street, Norfolk, VA 23510 (tel. toll free 800/368-3097).

Virginia Beach Department of Convention and Visitor Development, 2101 Parks Ave., Suite 500,

Virginia Beach, VA 24351 (tel. toll free 800/822-3224 (800/VA-BEACH)).

Insider Tips: Parking is limited, and lots are usually filled early on weekends and holidays from mid-April to Memorial Day. Your walk on the Bald Cypress Nature Trail is enhanced by reading the trail booklet on sale at the Visitor Center for 50¢.

Another of Virginia's six original parks built by the Civilian Conservation Corps (CCC) and opened in 1936, the 2,890-acre Seashore State Park is now the most visited park in the system. In 1965 the park's natural area was included in the National Register of Natural Landmarks because it is the northernmost location on the East Coast where subtropical and temperate plants grow and thrive together.

Activities

Among the 19 miles of hiking trails here, the Bald Cypress Nature Trail is not only the most popular in the park, it's the most-hiked trail in the state. Although rarely crowded, it is hiked by an estimated 300,000 visitors a year.

What's the attraction? Mainly that it offers an easy 1½-mile walk through majestic and relaxing bald cypress swamps and various pine and hardwood forests that have little changed since the first English settlers saw the area in the 17th century. Among the intriguing sights on this trail is the natural engineering of the bald cypress trees growing in the swamp water, particularly their wide base that helps support the trees in the unstable bottom, and the Spanish moss draped over the trees. Seashore State Park is the northern limit of the Spanish-moss growth range.

Among the other trails, the longest is the Long Creek Trail, which crosses through some salt marshes and is five miles one-way. The shortest is the quarter-mile High Dune Trail, which takes you up and over a dune ridge.

The Cape Henry Trail is the only one open to bicyclists. Packed and easily ridden, with only some moderate hills, it is about six miles in length one-way. You can rent a bike in the park.

A wide range of birds can be seen on these trails, including osprey, great blue heron, green heron, great egret, pileated woodpecker, and a variety of songbirds. In migrating season, these are joined by large numbers of other waterfowl. Swamp creatures you might see include the chicken turtle, which gets its name from its long neck, and a number of species of frogs.

The park Visitors Center is normally open from April through November. Exhibits explain the habitats of the park wildlife. Interpreters conduct guided nature hikes, beach walks, and campfire programs in season.

A pristine beach stretches about 1¼ miles on the bay side of the park. There are no lifeguards and swimming is restricted to registered guests in the campgrounds and cabins from April through October.

Fishing and crabbing are both popular here, with the fishing options ranging from surf to bay to the ocean. Surf-fishing gear can be rented. Catches run the gamut of saltwater fish. For boaters, there's a four-lane back-in boat ramp.

Camping and Accommodations

The park has 20 two-bedroom **cabins** available for rent, each with a fireplace, but no TV or phone. Only one cabin has heat and air conditioning. It rents for about $420 a week while the others rent for about $380 per week.

Of the 235 **campsites,** 90 can accommodate trailers and RVs. The rest are for tents only. No hookups.

Cabins and campsites may be reserved in person at the park or the parks division office in Richmond, or by phone or mail through Ticketmaster (see phone number and address on page 267).

Nearby Attractions

Virginia Beach is known as a vacation playland. Among its many offerings you can sample are oceanfront cruises, a lighthouse built in 1791 and several homes dating from 1680 to the mid-1700s, a zoo, the waterpark Ocean Breeze (tel. 804/422-4444), several museums, and the international headquarters for the work of psychic Edgar Cayce.

Norfolk is the home of the largest naval base in the world. You can tour designated ships on weekends. There's also a botanical garden (tel. 804/640-6879) and a number of museums. Here, too, you can take a cruise on a three-masted tall ship or a harbor cruise that includes a water view of the naval base.

A longer excursion, but still within the daytrip range, will take you north on I-64 through the Hampton Roads Bridge-Tunnel to **Busch Gardens** and **Colonial Williamsburg.**

Washington

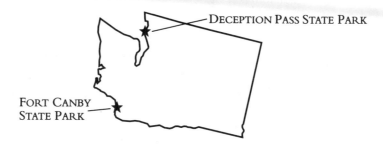

DECEPTION PASS STATE PARK

FORT CANBY
STATE PARK

Washington has 141 state parks.

Contacts

- Washington State Parks and Recreation Commission, Public Affairs Office, 7150 Cleanwater Lane, Tumwater, WA 98504 (tel. 206/902-8563).
- Tourism Development Division, Department of Trade and Economic Development, 101 General Administration Bldg., Olympia, WA 98504 (tel. 206/586-2102; toll free 800/544-1800 for travel packet only).

General Information on Washington State Parks

Volcanoes and a rain forest; a tropical country? No, just a little of the varied geography of Washington, the state that makes up the northwest corner of our nation.

Punctuating the Cascades and the Olympics, the two major mountain ranges in the state, are five snowcapped volcanic cones including Mount Rainier, at 14,411 feet, the highest peak in the state, and Mount St. Helens, which literally blew more than 1,000 feet of its top off in 1980. The temperate rain forest is on the Olympic Peninsula, bathed in more than 100 inches of rain a year.

Washington also has 10,000 miles of saltwater shoreline, making ferryboat commuting a way of life in some sections of the state, while inland there are wheat fields on rolling plains and orchards that make it the largest producer of apples in the country.

The park system encompasses more than 233,000 acres touching all these areas. Most parks are open year-round, although some close for the winter from October through March. Parks remaining open often have limited facilities.

As in many states, the park system got its start from the work of the men of the depression-era Civilian Conservation Corps (CCC), a foundation Washington acknowledges at the CCC Interpretive Center at Deception Pass State Park (see below).

GENERAL FEES
Most parks have an entrance fee of about $3.

CAMPING AND ACCOMMODATIONS
There are 24 two-story, turn-of-the-century **homes** associated with the conference facilities at Fort Worden State Park, and concessionaire-operated cabins at Sun Lakes State Park. For information on these, contact the parks commission headquarters in Olympia. Fort Worden, Fort Columbia, and Fort Flagler state parks all have dorm-style youth **hostels.** For information contact the American Youth Hostel, Inc. (tel. 206/281-7306).

Eighty parks have **campgrounds.** About 75%

of the campsites are classed as "standard" sites. Primarily designed for tents, these will accommodate trailers or RVs within certain size limitations. Sites classed as "utility" have an assortment of hookups, which may include a combination of water, electricity, and/or sewer. Standard sites are $10 per night and utility $14.

Campsites in 68 parks are on a first-come basis; however, reservations may be made for sites in the other 12 parks for the period from the Friday before Memorial Day through Labor Day. For information on the specific parks and the reservation system, contact the parks commission headquarters in Olympia.

More than half the parks with campgrounds have group camping areas available.

Pets. Pets must be on a leash not longer than eight feet and under control at all times. They are not permitted on designated swimming beaches or in most buildings.

Alcoholic beverages. Alcoholic beverages are permitted only in designated campgrounds and picnic areas or where concessionaires are licensed to sell such beverages.

Discounts. Resident senior citizens may purchase a pass ($30) that allows 30 nights of camping in the off-season, from Labor Day to May 1. Disabled persons and limited-income senior citizens may obtain a pass that gives a 50% discount on year-round camping fees. Disabled veterans are offered a pass for free, year-round camping.

Deception Pass State Park

| RV Camping | Tent Camping | Primitive Camping | Boating | Boat Launch | Fishing | Beach | Picnic Areas | Trails | Nature Programs |

Capsule Description: A natural park with some developed facilities, near the San Juan Islands.

Location: Northwest Washington, about 60 miles north of Seattle, and 18 miles west of Burlington, on opposing ends of two islands. From Seattle, take I-5 north to the Burlington exit, then Washington Highway 20 west to the park. (*Note:* Stay on Highway 20; do not take Spur 20.)

Address: 5175 N. State Hwy. 20, Oak Harbor, WA 98277 (tel. 206/675-2417).

Area Contacts: Anacortes Chamber of Commerce, 819 Commercial Ave., Anacortes, WA 98221 (tel. 206/293-3832).

Northwest Washington Tourism Association, c/o Mount Vernon Chamber of Commerce, P.O. Box 1007 or 220 E. College Way, Suite 174 Mount Vernon, WA 98273 (tel. 206/428-8547).

Oak Harbor Chamber of Commerce, P.O. Box 883, Oak Harbor, WA 98277 (tel. 206/675-3535).

Seattle/King County Convention and Visitors Bureau, 800 Convention Place, Seattle, WA 98101 (tel. 206/461-5840).

Tourism Victoria, 812 Wharf St., Victoria, BC, Canada V8W 1T3 (tel. toll free 800/663-3883 or 604/382-2127).

Insider Tip: One of the lesser known overlooks is the Marshlands Environmental Overlook by Cranberry Lake—no spectacular vistas, but an interesting view of a marsh environment. You can reach it from the Sand Dune Trail.

Capt. George Vancouver first named this area Port Gardner in 1792. However, shortly after he discovered he'd been deceived. What he thought was

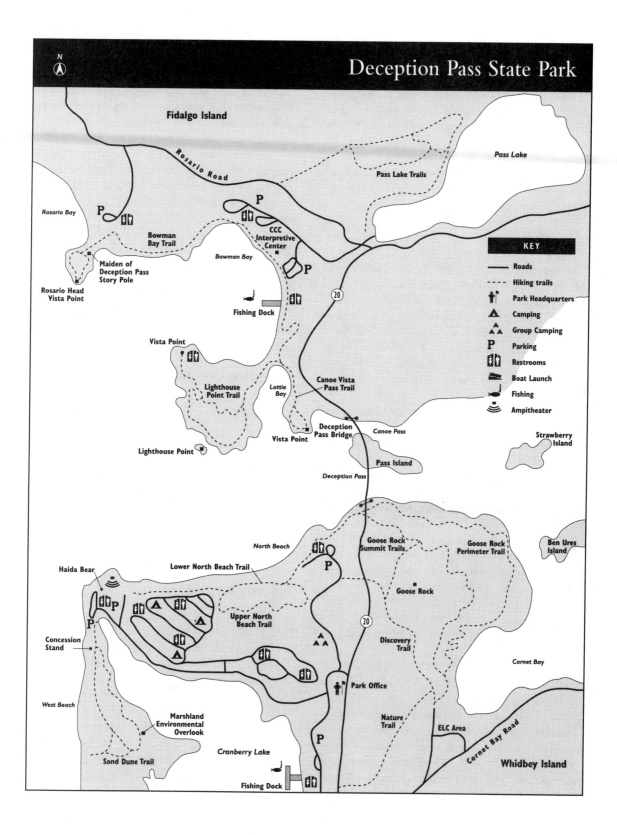

Deception Pass State Park

N

Fidalgo Island

Rosario Road

Pass Lake

Pass Lake Trails

Rosario Bay

P

Bowman
Bay Trail

P

CCC
Interpretive
Center

Maiden of
Deception Pass
Story Pole

Bowman Bay

P

Rosario Head
Vista Point

(20)

Fishing Dock

Vista Point

Lighthouse
Point Trail

Lottie
Bay

Canoe Vista
Pass Trail

KEY

— Roads
- - - Hiking trails
Park Headquarters
Camping
Group Camping
P Parking
Restrooms
Boat Launch
Fishing
Ampitheater

Lighthouse Point

Vista Point

Deception
Pass Bridge

Canoe Pass

Strawberry
Island

Pass Island

Deception Pass

Ben Ures
Island

North Beach

Goose Rock
Summit Trails

Goose Rock
Perimeter Trail

Haida Bear

Lower North Beach Trail

P

P

P

Upper North
Beach Trail

Goose Rock

Concession
Stand

P

West Beach

Marshland
Environmental
Overlook

Discovery
Trail

Cornet Bay

Park Office

Nature
Trail

ELC Area

Cornet Bay Road

Sand Dune Trail

Cranberry Lake

P

Whidbey Island

Fishing Dock

an inlet was actually a narrow passage between two islands, so he renamed the waterway Deception Pass. The island to the south of the pass is called Whidbey in honor of one of Vancouver's officers, and the island to the north is named after the Spanish explorer Salvador Fidalgo. The 4,000-acre park sits on the southern end of Fidalgo Island and the northern end of Whidbey Island with the two parts connected by a bridge.

Activities

The Deception Pass Bridge, a National Historic Monument, is actually two spans anchored on Pass Island, in between the two larger islands. Like much of the park, it was built by the Civilian Conservation Corps (CCC) in 1935. The view from the bridge is a favorite for photographers. You can't park on the bridge itself, but there's a parking area on the south end and you can walk back onto it.

The 11 trails in the park offer a total of 16 miles for hiking through Douglas fir and cedar forests and along the fjordlike shoreline. Five of the trails are on Fidalgo Island, the other six on Whidbey. In addition, there's a guided nature trail, about half a mile long, just south of the park office. The trails vary in difficulty from easy to strenuous. The numerous scenic overlooks, offer the opportunity for excellent views of the San Juan Islands, and, on the trails, there are two tributes to the Native Americans who used to live here: the Haida Bear Totem and the Maiden of Deception Pass story pole.

Park wildlife you're likely to see include black-tailed deer, raccoons, sea otters, bald eagles, osprey, a variety of waterfowl and migratory birds, including loons, in season.

Fishing is permitted on all three park lakes. Pass Lake—restricted to fly fishing for trout 18 inches or larger—and Cranberry Lake are open year-round. Heart Lake is only open in the spring for the trout season. Both brown and rainbow are in the lakes. There are no restrictions on boat motors on Heart Lake; however, no motors are permitted on Pass Lake and electric motors only on Cran-

berry Lake. There are three freshwater and two saltwater boat-launching sites and a fishing pier on Cranberry Lake and a saltwater pier at Bowman Bay. Saltwater catches include salmon and ling cod.

For swimming, there's a guarded saltwater beach. Scuba divers can explore the underwater marine park in Bowman and Rosario bays.

The park's and the state's debt to the CCC is explained in the CCC Interpretive Center, which is open during the summer. Exhibits here tell about the men who built the park and how they did it.

For groups, the Cornet Bay Environmental Learning Center is nestled in a forested area on Whidbey Island. Cabins and other facilities here permit groups to stay and study the park's ecosystem.

Camping and Accommodations

There are 16 sleeping cabins at the Environmental Learning Center; however, these are for groups only.

The 246 multiuse and five primitive **campsites** are all in forested areas. There are no hookups and all are on a first-come basis; no reservations. The standard campsites go for $10 per night, primitive for much less. The campgrounds are extremely popular in the summer and fill up quickly, so early arrival is suggested, and it might be a good idea to call ahead to see if there are any vacancies.

Nearby Attractions

The natural beauty of this whole area makes it a remarkable place for daytrip explorations.

You can start right on the southern island that hosts the park. To the south, on **Whidbey Island,** are a number of interesting small towns and small state parks. Near the middle of the island is **Ebey's Landing National Historical Reserve** (tel. 360/678-6084), a 22-square-mile area of historic sites including 91 nationally registered historical structures. A little farther south is **Rhododendron State Park,** a 200-acre wild rhododendron forest. A ferry at **Clinton,** at the southern end of the island, makes a 20-minute crossing to **Mukilteo,** which puts you within a half-hour drive of **Seattle.** A daytrip to Seattle is possible but wouldn't be leisurely; so if you really want to see Seattle, make it an overnight trip.

A major business in the **Sagit Valley,** on the mainland to the east, is the growing of tulips. In spring, the fields are abloom with that flower.

Going north, on Fidalgo Island, you can visit **Anacortes,** a quaint town with a historic area to

wander. A county ferry at the north end of the island will quickly take you to the next island, **Guemes,** where you can catch a state ferry to several of the San Juan Islands and to the port of **Sidney,** on Vancouver Island, British Columbia. From Sidney, it's a short drive south on to **Victoria,** a city famed for being more British than Britain. The San Juan Islands could be done as a daytrip from the park, but Victoria is definitely an overnighter.

Fort Canby State Park

Visitor Center · RV Camping · Tent Camping · Primitive Camping · Group Lodge Dormitories · Boating · Boat Launch · Fishing · Picnic Areas · Trails · Nature Programs

Capsule Description: A natural park with developed facilities.

Location: Southwestern tip of Washington at the mouth of the Columbia River. From Longview, take Washington Highway 4 west to U.S. Highway 101, then south to Loop 100 at Ilwaco and follow signs three miles to the park. From Astoria, Oregon, take U.S. 101 north to Ilwaco, then Loop 100 to the park.

Address: P.O. Box 488, Ilwaco, WA 98624 (tel. 206/642-3078).

Area Contacts: Long Beach Peninsula Visitors Bureau, P.O. Box 562, Long Beach, WA 98631 (tel. toll free 800/451-2542).

Astoria Warrenton Area Chamber of Commerce, P.O. Box 176, Astoria, OR 97103 (tel. toll free 800/535-3637or tel. 503/325-6311).

Southwest Washington Tourism, P.O. Box 876, Longview, WA 98632 (tel. 206/425-1211).

Insider Tips: The Visitor Center at nearby Fort Columbia State Park is in the former commanding officer's residence. Its display of antique furnishing represents a typical upper-middle class residence

at the turn of the century. Note the contrast between these quarters and the nearby enlisted men's barracks.

During the 1800s, the high waves and a treacherous river bar at the mouth of the Columbia River led to the loss of so many ships and lives this area became known among seaman as the "Graveyard of the Pacific." As early as 1788, an English explorer who failed to cross the bar named the nearby headlands Cape Disappointment.

To secure America's claim to the area and find overland routes to the Pacific, the Lewis and Clark Expedition followed the Columbia to its mouth and the cape in 1805. To cut down on shipwrecks, the Cape Disappointment Lighthouse began operating in 1856, and in 1862 a fort, later named Fort Canby, was built on the cape to protect the entrance to the Columbia.

Dredging and other engineering work has made the bar less dangerous today. The fort was deactivated following World War II, after close to 90 years of service, but the Cape Disappointment Lighthouse is still in operation—making it the oldest lighthouse still in use on the West Coast. At this writing, there are plans to deactivate the lighthouse and turn it over to the state, where, like the cape itself, now a National Historic District, it will be part of the 1,881-acre Fort Canby State Park.

Fort Canby is the administrative headquarters for a number of satellite parks on the Long Beach Peninsula and in other areas in the vicinity. These smaller parks offer additional facilities available for visitors to Fort Canby.

Activities

One of the main features of the park is the Lewis and Clark Interpretive Center. Located high on Cape Disappointment, the center overlooks the mouth of the mighty Columbia River and the Pacific Ocean. You can take in this view through the center's large picture windows. In winter in the comfort of the center, you can whale-watch and witness the fury of the winter waves as they crash against the rocks.

The center's walk-through design lets you follow the route and adventures of Lewis and Clark, see examples of their gear, and relate the help the historic expedition received from Indian tribes along the way. In addition to the exhibits, multimedia presentations highlight various aspects of the 8,000-mile, 2½-year journey.

The center is open daily in summer and at least on weekends the rest of the year. There are plans to keep it open daily all year. As a bonus, the U.S. Coast Guard station on the cape is occasionally open for visitors.

The best way to see this southwestern tip of the state, still much the way Lewis and Clark saw it, is on the number of trails of varying length that explore the forests of spruce and pine, and the headlands. There is also about two miles of ocean beach inside the park for walking. But no swimming. The waters are too dangerous here. The trails give you the best chance of seeing black-tailed deer, beaver, an occasional black bear, and during migratory season, trumpeter swans that winter here, and a variety of other birds.

In season, there are campfire and nature programs on most weekends.

Ocean fishing from the beach, jetty, or a boat can yield salmon, ling cod, rock bass, and sea perch. Two small freshwater lakes in the park are good fishing holes for largemouth bass and perch. The park boat launch is on the relatively quiet Baker Bay off the river. Fishing tackle and some gear may be rented.

Camping

Of the 250 multiuse **campsites,** 60 have three-way hookups and the rest have no hookups. Fees are $14 with hookups, $10 per night without. There are also a few primitive hike and bike sites available. This is one of the 12 state parks that accept reservations. Reservations are accepted after January 1 for the period April through September only. For information on reservation procedures, contact the park.

Nearby Attractions

The vacation area of **Long Beach Peninsula,** to the north, is a 26-mile stretch of beach with several towns and some small state parks with beach access.

Among the attractions in the nearby town of **Ilwaco** is the **World Kite Museum** (tel. 206/642-4020), which displays more than 600 kites from around the world, including what is reported as the largest collection of Japanese kites outside of Japan. Kite flying is popular along the open beaches.

Continuing north, the town of Long Beach features a boardwalk close to half a mile long with observation platforms. **Oysterville,** a national historic district, dates back to the 1850s when it supplied shiploads of oysters to San Franciscans. **Willapa Bay** is still a major producer of oysters and **South Bend,** on the mainland, across the bay, calls itself "The Oyster Capital of the World."

Other sights on the peninsula include cranberry bogs, a large rhododendron nursery, a state fisheries laboratory, and a national wildlife refuge.

To the southeast, on U.S. 101, is **Fort Columbia State Park** (tel. 206/642-3078), which has an interpretive center that tells the story of the Columbia River, early exploration, the military in the area, and the local Chinook Indians.

The nearest large town is **Astoria, Oregon,** across the Columbia River. (See Fort Stevens State Park, Oregon.)

West Virginia

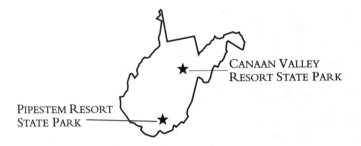

CANAAN VALLEY
RESORT STATE PARK

PIPESTEM RESORT
STATE PARK

West Virginia has 46 state parks.

Contacts

· West Virginia Division of Tourism and Parks, State Capitol Complex, Bldg. 6 Rm. B564 Charleston, WV 25305 (tel. toll free 800/ 225-5982 [800/CALL-WVA]).

General Information on West Virginia State Parks

If the name West Virginia brings to mind hillbillies and feuds in backwater hollers, you are way behind the times. The days of mountain isolation are long gone and now the hollers are luring visitors to the rugged beauty of the Mountain State.

In the early 1800s this was a neglected part of Virginia where the citizens were always talking of splitting off and going their own way. Virginia's secession from the Union provided the catalyst to turn disgruntled feelings into action. In 1861, the western counties not only declared Virginia's secession from the Union void, they seceded from Virginia. When Confederate forces were driven out in 1863, West Virginia became the 35th state in the Union.

In general, the terrain ranges from hilly to mountainous. Not mountainous like the Rockies—Spruce Knob, the highest point in the state, is only 4,861 feet high—but rather rugged

folds of ridges, hills, and valleys that make for intriguing and virtually unspoiled scenery. This topography also makes the state a magnet for white-water enthusiasts with seven rivers rated high for rafting.

In order to provide low-cost vacation possibilities for its citizens, as well as lure out-of-state tourists, in addition to campgrounds, West Virginia has built resorts with lodges and cabins, golf courses, and other resort-type facilities in a number of its parks. One of its parks is also among the state's most popular downhill ski resorts.

GENERAL FEES
There is no entrance or parking fee at the state parks.

CAMPING AND ACCOMMODATIONS
Eight parks have **lodges:** Blackwater Falls, Cacapon, Canaan Valley, Hawks Nest, North Bend, Pipestem, Twin Falls, and Tygart Lake. These range in size from 20 rooms at Tygart Lake to 250 rooms at Canaan Valley. Depending on the park, a double room goes from an off-season low of about $35 to an in-season high of about $75.

With the exception of Hawks Nest, all these parks also have cabins, plus there are cabins in eight other parks and forests. **Cabins** fall into four classifications: modern, standard, economy, and rustic, with the majority falling in the first two categories. At certain parks, modern cabins are open year-round; however, most are open only from the end of March until mid-December. Most standard and economy cabins are available from mid-April until the end of October. Rustic cabins have a wide variety of seasons. Cabin capacities go from two to eight or even ten. From the beginning of June through Labor Day, cabins may be reserved only on a weekly basis. For two persons the prices go from about $300 to $400. For larger families or groups, the largest are the four-bedroom cabins at Canaan Valley and Pipestem and the two-story cabins at Cass Scenic Railroad. These rent from about $500 to $650 a week. There is a $15 reservation fee.

More than two dozen parks have **campgrounds.** Some sites have hookups, but most do not. Sites go for $6 to $14 depending on the park and facilities. About a dozen parks accept camping

reservations; the rest are on a first-come basis. There's a $5 reservation fee.

For information on reservations at lodges, cabins, or campgrounds—or any other information you want to know about the parks or other recreation facilities in the state—call toll free 800/CALL-WVA. One number does it all, including connecting you with the park of your choice.

Pets. Pets must be on a leash and under control at all times. They are not permitted in lodges, cabins, or most other buildings and not in swimming or ski areas.

Alcoholic beverages. Rules vary from park to park. In most parks alcoholic beverages are permitted; in others there's no public display except in licensed areas like lodge lounges or dining rooms.

Canaan Valley Resort State Park

| Visitor Center | Lodge/ Hotel | Restaurant | Cabins & Cottages | RV Camping | Tent Camping | Fishing | Swimming | Picnic Areas | Trails |

| Nature Programs | Bicycling | Golf | Tennis | Fitness Center | Playground | X-Country Skiing | Downhill Skiing | Gift Shop |

Capsule Description: A large resort park with all the amenities.

Location: Northeast West Virginia. On West Virginia Highway 32 south of Davis.

Address: Route HC70, Box 330, Davis, WV 26260 (tel. 304/866-4121; toll free 800/622-4121 or 800/CALL-WVA for reservations).

Area Contacts: Potomac Highlands Convention and Visitors Bureau, P.O. Box 1459, Elkins, WV 26241 (tel. 304/636-8400).

Tucker County Convention and Visitors Bureau, P.O. Box 565, Davis WV 26260 (tel. toll free 800/782-2775).

Insider Tip: The resort offers a number of package plans that amount to good bargains. These range from golf packages to mid-week family getaways during the ski season.

This 6,000-acre park, located in the scenic Allegheny Mountains valley it is named after, has something to offer year-round, from hiking to swimming and golf to downhill skiing, all in a resort setting.

Activities

There are 18 miles of hiking trails in the park. Most are relatively short—from half a mile up to 2½ miles—and range from easy to difficult hiking through forests of hardwoods. The 2½-mile Bald Knob Trail is the only one rated as most difficult, but it also leads to a spectacular view of Canaan Valley from the top of the knob. There are also scenic overlooks on several of the other trails, perhaps not quite as spectacular, but still offering a dramatic panoramic view of the mountains. If you want more challenging trails, you can take the eight-mile (one-way) trail north through the national forest across Canaan Mountain to Blackwater Falls State Park, or one of the park trails that connects with the Allegheny Trail, which snakes its way along highland crests for close to 200 miles.

Although white-tailed deer are common sights in the park, you'll have the best chance of seeing them and other animals, like wild turkey, black bear, and beaver, on the trails. In spring and fall, the park is also a stopover for migrating Canada geese and other waterfowl, which spill over from the nearby Dolly Sod Wilderness Area, the second-largest inland wetland in the country.

For the nature lover, there is a nature center and the park staff conducts frequent nature programs and guided walks. But nature programs are only part of the array of activities that include everything from symphony concerts to square dancing and tours to areas outside the park.

Fishing is not a major attraction here, but the river and streams in the park do offer trout and other native fish.

The center of the resort facilities, at least until the snow falls, is the 18-hole, par-72 championship golf course. It's especially popular in the summer when the cool mountain air averages a high of only 75 degrees. Other facilities include six lighted tennis courts, an outdoor Olympic-size pool, an indoor heated lap pool, 19-hole miniature golf course, and a fitness center with sauna and hot tub.

In warm weather, at least one of the four ski center chair lifts is open for scenic rides. Come winter, from about November to March, all four get a workout carrying skiers to the top of the runs. There are 21 slopes and trails here, for skiers from beginner to expert, with the longest run 1¼ miles and a vertical drop of 850 feet. Some areas are lighted for night skiing. Ski instruction and ski rentals are available on the mountain. In addition to downhill skiing, the resort offers 18 miles of cross-country trails ranging from a beginner's loop to advanced terrain, ice skating, and snowboarding. Equipment rentals are available for all these sports. Since this is a popular family resort, there are ski programs for children and a nursery available during the day.

Camping and Accommodations

The 250 units in the **lodge** include six suites. All have TV and phones and all the amenities of a good hotel room. The lodge has a restaurant and lounge. (There are also restaurants at the golf course and the ski area, in season.) Depending on the season, a double costs from about $50 to $75. There are also 15 modern cabins: 8 two-bedroom, 3 three-bedroom, and 4 four bedroom. A two-bedroom rents year-round for around $500 a week. Reservations may be made by calling the park or toll free 800/CALL-WVA.

The 34 multiuse **campsites** all have three-way hookups. Sites cost $14 per night.

Nearby Attractions

One place close by, just a few minutes north up Highway 32, is **Blackwater Falls State Park** (tel. 304/259-5216), which offers several activities not available at Canaan Valley Resort, specifically lake swimming, boating, and fishing; rental riding horses; and carriage rides on weekends in season. (This park also has a 55-room lodge, 25 additional cabins, and 65 campsites that are open from April through October.)

Interested in white-water rafting? Outfitters in **Davis** and other towns can set you up for that experience. And if you want to try your hand at rock climbing, head southeast for **Seneca Rocks.** The climbing school (tel. 304/567-2600) here gives both lessons and guided tours.

To the southwest, in **Elkins,** you can attend concerts and dances put on at **Elkins College** (tel. 304/636-1900) by the Augusta Heritage Arts Workshops, or even take short courses they give in Appalachian arts, crafts, and music.

More directly south, but still within an easy daytrip, are the **National Radio Astronomy Observatory** (tel. 304/456-2011) in **Green Bank** and the **Cass Scenic Railroad State Park** (tel. 304/456-4300). Free guided tours are given at the observatory daily during the summer and weekends in early fall. The whole turn-of-the-century company logging town of Cass, which is listed in the National Register of Historic Places, is in the state park. You can stay in the restored historical homes and ride the steam trains on a 1½-hour trip to nearby **Whittaker Station** or a 4½-hour trip to **Bald Knob,** the second-highest point in the state. For reservations for the train and accommodations, call toll free 800/CALL-WVA.

Pipestem Resort State Park

| Visitor Center | Lodge/ Hotel | Restaurant | Cabins & Cottages | RV Camping | Tent Camping | Boating | Non-Motorized Boating Only | Fishing | Swimming | Picnic Areas |

| Trails | Horse Trails | Nature Programs | Bicycling | Golf | Tennis | Fitness Center | Playground | X-Country Skiing | Gift Shop |

Capsule Description: A large resort park with all the amenities.

Location: Southeastern West Virginia. From I-64, take the Sandstone exit (no. 139) and go south 22 miles on West Virginia Highway 20 to the park. From I-77, take the Athens Road exit (no. 14), then go east following signs to Athens on Highway 20, then north to the park.

Address: P.O. Box 150, Pipestem, WV 25979 (tel. 304/466-1800; reservations through the park number or toll free 800/CALL-WVA).

Area Contacts: Southern West Virginia Convention and Visitors Bureau, P.O. Box 1799, Beckley, WV 25802 (tel. toll free 800/847-4898 outside West Virginia or 304/252-2244 in West Virginia).

Insider Tips: The arts and crafts shop in the park sells the authenticated works of West Virginia artists and craftsmen. Most nights you can dance at the sports pub and lounge on the golf course.

Sitting on the lip of the Bluestone River Gorge, this 4,030-acre park offers a wide variety of resort amenities. The Bluestone River, once black with coal dust and sewage, now flows clear and clean through the park. A 10-mile section of the river, beginning in this park and running downstream to near Bluestone State Park, is designated a National Scenic River.

The unique name of the resort is taken from the native pipestem bush (*Spirea alba*) whose hollow woody stems were used by nine different Indian tribes in making pipes and, more recently, by settlers who used them in both clay and corncob pipes.

Activities

An easy way to get acquainted with the major facilities is to take the park's self-guided auto tour. Once you know your way around, you can go back to the areas of interest.

For a closer look at nature, there are 16 trails that travel through a variety of habitats. Most of these are short, but many interconnect so you can determine how far you want to go. The longest is the River Trail, which goes a little over 12 miles round-trip across the river and up to a rustic cabin on a ridge that's used for overnight horseback rides. This trail can be broken up into shorter segments. Along the way you have a good chance of seeing deer and wild turkey as well as smaller animals. Another trail worth the trip for the hearty hiker is the Pipestem Knob Trail; although less than half a mile, it is a steep paved trail. The reward at the end is an observation tower where you can get a view of much of the area. Mountain bikes are allowed on some of the hiking trails.

The Nature Center is open from April through December and the park naturalist conducts a number of programs during this period.

For more resort-type activities the park has an 18-hole championship golf course, a 9-hole par-3 course, a miniature golf course, five lighted tennis courts, and an archery range. There are both indoor and outdoor pools with lifeguards on duty, a fitness center, and a sauna. The riding stable has horses for rent both by the hour and for trail rides, including an overnight ride. Private horses may be brought in, but only for day use. You can rent canoes and paddleboats at the 15-acre lake, which is open for nonpowered boating only. Fishing is good for trout, which are stocked periodically, as well as bass, bluegill, and catfish.

The 500-seat amphitheater, set in a natural bowl, hosts a number of programs in the summer ranging from movies to concerts and magic shows.

For something different, take a ride on the 3,600-foot Aerial Tramway that sweeps down from the Canyon Rim Center, dropping almost 1,100 feet, to the floor of the rugged Bluestone Canyon, crossing the Bluestone River before arriving at the Mountain Creek Lodge, the smaller of the two park lodges. (There's a fee if you are not either a park guest or lodge restaurant patron.)

In winter the park offers several miles of cross-country ski trails and rents equipment. There's also a sled run with a rope tow.

The park's Child Care Center, open most of the year, offers a safe, secure, and entertaining environment for children 2 through 12.

Camping and Accommodations

There are two **lodges.** McKeever Lodge, the main lodge, which overlooks the gorge, has 113 units, including several suites, some with a gorge view, a restaurant, and snack bar. The lodge is seven stories high with the lobby located on the fifth floor. The 30-room Mountain Creek Lodge, is a remote hideaway located at the base of the 1,000-foot-deep Bluestone Canyon and is accessible only by the aerial tramway. All rooms have TV and phones. A double in the main lodge goes for about $65 in season; at Mountain Creek for about $55.

Note: If you stay at Mountain Creek, make sure you find out about the tram schedule. It's routinely out of service two afternoons and one full day a month for maintenance. Reassuring from a safety standpoint, but this can be inconvenient if you have plans for those times.

The 25 modern **cabins** are two-, three-, and four-bedroom. All have electric heat, fireplaces, TV, phones, and decks. From April through October they rent by the week for about $500 to $650, depending on size. Off-season cabins are offered on a daily basis.

About half the 82 multiuse **campsites** have three-way hookups. Of the rest, some have electric and others have no hookups. Reservations are accepted for 50% of the campsites for the period from the Friday before Memorial Day through

Labor Day with requests accepted from the previous March 1.

All reservations may be made directly to the park or by connection through toll free 800/CALL-WVA.

Nearby Attractions

If you want more water activities, just to the north is **Bluestone State Park** (tel. 304/466-2805) on the shore of the 2,000-acre Bluestone Lake, where you can swim, boat, or fish. The marina here rents pontoon boats and offers guided lake tours. A little past Bluestone Park, you can tour **Hinton's** historic district, which features 200 buildings representing a wide variety of architectural styles. This town is also one of the many places in the area where you can book white-water rafting trips with commercial outfitters. (You can also book them at the Pipestem Lodge.) Raft trips can be made on several area rivers including the famed white water of the New River, which belies its name since geologists consider it one of the world's oldest rivers. A national park follows the New River from Hinton north to Fayetteville, and the National Park Service operates four visitors centers located at Hinton, Grandview, Glen Jean, and Lansing. On U.S. Route 19, between Fayetteville and Hico is the **New River Gorge Bridge,** the second-highest bridge in the United States and the longest steel-arch bridge in the world.

Northwest of Pipestem, in **Beckley,** you can tour the **Beckley Exhibition Coal Mine** (tel. 304/256-1747), a National Historic Site that shows how coal was mined before mechanization. Located next to the mine is the Mountain Homestead, where you can experience what life was like on the West Virginia frontier, and the Youth Museum featuring hands-on exhibits for children and a planetarium. Theater West Virginia is also near this town, offering musical dramas related to the state's history.

Wisconsin

PENINSULA STATE PARK

DEVIL'S LAKE
STATE PARK

Wisconsin has 69 state parks.

Contacts

- Bureau of Parks and Recreation, Department of Natural Resources, P.O. Box 7921, Madison, WI 53707-7921 (tel. 608/266-2181).
- Wisconsin Division of Tourism, P.O. Box 7606, Madison, WI 53707 (tel. toll free 800/432-8747 [800/432-TRIP] or 608/266-2161).

General Information on Wisconsin State Parks

In 1878, Wisconsin became one of the first states to establish a state park system when the legislature set aside "The State Park," a 50,000-acre tract. But this was a false start because in 1897, again by legislative action, the land was sold to lumber companies.

The real start came in 1900 when the legislature dedicated what is now Interstate State Park. This time the action held and now the parks system encompasses 129,000 acres. The long-range goal of putting a state park within a one-hour drive of every Wisconsinite has been achieved, and the system is still growing.

Wisconsin offers a lot to visitors who enjoy the outdoors, both in and out of its parks. Bicyclists, for example, have a choice of more than 466 miles on abandoned railroad corridors that are now part of 17 designated state bike trails, eight of which include state park trails. Hikers have 830 miles of hiking trails and 60 miles of nature trails in the parks alone. In winter, these translate into almost 350 miles of cross-country ski trails and more than 600 miles of snowmobile trails. An Ice Age Trail, for winter or summer hiking, is under development and will eventually wind 1,000 miles through the state tracing the path of retreat of the great glacier that shaped the terrain of much of Wisconsin.

For boating, fishing, and other water activities, the state has 15,000 lakes and 2,200 streams.

If you want less strenuous touring, the tourism division offers a book of auto tours that will take you to all corners of the state. And, since this is "America's dairyland"—Wisconsin produces more than 35% of all the cheese made in the U.S.—close to 90 cheese factories, large and small, are open for tours.

GENERAL FEES
A one-day vehicle sticker costs $6 for nonresidents and $4 for residents. Annual stickers are available.

CAMPING
There are campgrounds in more than 40 parks with a total of over 5,300 campsites. Starting the first working day after January 1, about 30 of the parks accept reservations for the period from May through October. Fees range from $6 to $10 per

site, plus $2 if an electric hookup is provided. There's also a $3 reservation fee. Reservations are made directly to the park of your choice on a standard application form available from the Bureau of Parks, any park, or state tourist information centers.

A number of parks also have indoor and outdoor group camps, which may be reserved up to a year in advance.

Pets. Pets are permitted in most parks. They must be on a leash no longer than eight feet and under control and attended at all times. They are not allowed in buildings, picnic or beach areas, playgrounds, marked nature trails, ski trails in the winter, or any other designated "pet free zone."

Alcoholic beverages. Alcoholic beverages are allowed in most parks in the off-season. In many parks, however, they are permitted only in designated areas, such as campgrounds, from April through Memorial Day weekend.

Discounts. Wisconsin residents age 65 and older may purchase a lifetime Natural Resources Senior Citizen Recreation Card for a low one-time fee. This card permits any vehicle with a cardholder as occupant to enter any state forest or park exempt from purchasing the vehicle admission sticker. Cardholders are also entitled to free lifetime privileges of small game hunting and fishing.

Devil's Lake State Park

RV Camping | Tent Camping | Group Camping | Boat Launch | Non-Motorized Boating Only | Fishing | Beach | Snorkeling & Diving | Picnic Areas | Trails | Nature Programs | Bicycling | X-Country Skiing

Capsule Description: A large, natural park with some developed facilities.
Location: Southern Wisconsin, about 40 miles northwest of Madison. From Baraboo, take Wisconsin Highway 123 south three miles to the park.
Address: S5975 Park Rd., Baraboo, WI 53913 (tel. 608/356-8301, 608/356-6618 for reservations).
Area Contacts: Baraboo Chamber of Commerce, P.O. Box 442, Baraboo, WI 53913 (tel. toll free 800/227-2266 or tel. 608/356-8333).

Greater Madison Convention and Visitors Bureau, 615 E. Washington Ave., Madison, WI 53703 (tel. toll free 800/373-6376).

Wisconsin Dells Visitor and Convention Bureau, Box 390, Wisconsin Dells, WI 53965-0390 (tel. toll free 800/223-3557).

In 1971, the Ice Age National Reserve was established by the federal government to preserve Wisconsin's glacial landforms. This 8,700-acre park is one of nine units in the reserve. The glacier plugged a gap to enclose the basin in which the spring-fed Devil's Lake formed. The lake itself covers 360 acres and is approximately 45 feet deep. It is flanked by quartzite bluffs going up as high as 500 feet. Because the drainage basin is made up of this insoluble quartzite, few minerals wash into the lake so the water is soft, an anomaly for southern Wisconsin.

The cliffs are part of the Baraboo Bluffs, which geologists say were formed 1.5 billion years ago, making these bluffs one of the most ancient rock outcrops in North America. Because quartzite is solid rock that does not easily crack or crumble, Devil's Lake State Park is one of the best rock climbing areas in the Midwest.

Activities

A naturalist is on duty at the park all year. During the summer the naturalist conducts a number of programs and the Nature Center is open every day. The rest of the year, the naturalist and the center are available by appointment.

You can observe some of the effects of the glaciation on the 15 miles of park trails. A number of these trails are short, less than a mile, but range from easy hiking to difficult climbing trails. Among the shorter trails is the self-guiding Landmark Nature Trail. One of the most popular trails is the Ice Age Loop. Rated medium in difficulty, this four-mile wooded trail leads to some overlooks offering gorgeous views. There's one designated trail for mountain bikes, and they may be ridden on some of the other trails.

Rock climbing is also featured here, and, in winter, cross-country skiers have about 15 miles of trails available, plus there's sledding.

Among the animals you may see on the trails are white-tailed deer, raccoons, badgers, mink, and otters. More than 200 species of birds have been spotted in the park, with indications that close to 100 nest here. Eagles occasionally fly over the park in winter, and turkey vultures, an eagle-sized bird, can be seen quite frequently in summer.

Boating on the lake is restricted to electric motors only. Rowboats, canoes, and windsurfing boards can be rented. The lake is also popular with scuba divers and snorkelers and snorkeling equipment can also be rented.

There are three swimming beaches, but no lifeguards.

Fishing is good for largemouth bass, northern pike, brown trout, crappie, bluegill, and perch,

and you can rent tackle. The lake freezes over for about four months each winter, so ice fishing is popular.

Camping

Of the 406 multiuse **campsites** in three campgrounds, 121 have electric hookups. Most of the campsites may be reserved. Fees are $8 to $10 per night plus $2 for the electric hookup. There is also a group campsite.

Nearby Attractions

At **Baraboo,** just up the road, the circus is in town all summer. Big-top circus performances are given at the **Circus World Museum** (tel. 608/356-0800) located at what was the Ringling Brothers Circus's original winter quarters from the late 1800s until about 1918. Also in Baraboo is the **International Crane Foundation** (tel. 608/356-9462), where you can see pairs of all 15 species of cranes in existence. The **Mid-Continent Railway Museum** (tel. 608/522-4261), close by in **North Freedom,** features rides on trains pulled by steam locomotives.

To the north, an easy daytrip away, is **Wisconsin Dells,** an area oriented to visitors. Among the many attractions here are the **Biblical Gardens** (tel. 608/253-5091), several water parks, a model railroad museum, and a deer park. You can take normal boat tours on the Wisconsin River or opt to tour in an amphibious duck that goes from land to water and back again. Or fly over it all in a balloon.

To the south is **Madison,** the state capital. Among the places you can visit here are the State Capitol (tel. 608/266-3590), the 1,000-acre campus of the University of Wisconsin (tel. 608/262-1234), a botanical garden, zoo, and several interesting museums, including a children's museum.

Peninsula State Park

RV Camping   Tent Camping   Group Camping   Boating   Boat Launch   Fishing   Beach   Picnic Areas   Trails   Nature Programs

Bicycling   Golf   Tennis   Playground   X-Country Skiing   Snow-mobiling

Capsule Description: A natural park with some developed facilities on a peninsula in Lake Michigan.

Location: Northeastern Wisconsin, on the Door County Peninsula northeast of Green Bay. From Green Bay, take Wisconsin Highway 57 north to Sturgeon Bay, then Highway 42 north to the park near Fish Creek.

Address: P.O. Box 218, Fish Creek, WI 54212 (tel. 414/868-3258).

Area Contacts: Door County Chamber of Commerce, P.O. Box 406, Sturgeon Bay, WI 54235 (tel. toll free 800/527-3529 (800/52-RELAX) or 414/743-4456)

Green Bay Convention and Visitors Bureau, P.O. Box 10596, Green Bay, WI 54307-0596. (tel. toll free 800/236-3976).

Insider Tip: Cherry and apple blossoms are usually in full bloom in the park area from about May 15 to May 30.

Much of this peninsula, which sticks out like a thumb into Lake Michigan, is made up of Door County, a favorite vacation area for Midwesterners. The forested Peninsula State Park, Wisconsin's second-oldest park, is an equally prime vacation destination. The 3,763-acre year-round park, on the Green Bay side of the peninsula, offers both vacation-style amenities and the solitude of nature.

Activities

A good place to start your explorations of this park is the Nature Center where you'll find a narrated diorama giving an overview of park features and its natural history. During the summer season a park naturalist conducts nature hikes and other programs.

To go on your own, you have nine marked trails extending into even the most remote sections of the park. More than 70% of the park remains essentially undeveloped natural areas. Trails vary in length from the half-mile self-guided, loop nature trail, that starts at the Nature Center, to a group of interconnected hiking trails that let you go up to more than 18 miles. These vary in difficulty from easy walking to difficult with steep ascents and descents. One of the most popular is the gentle, two-mile loop to Eagle Tower. The tower was built in the 1920s and named because it was placed near the home of a breeding pair of eagles. It's 110 steps to the top of the 75-foot tower, but at the top you'll get an outstanding bird's-eye view of the park, the Green Bay island, and the Michigan shoreline. Even if you don't climb the tower, there are about a dozen overlooks along the roads and trails that give you fine views of Green Bay and the outlying islands.

Wildlife is abundant in the park and you will probably see white-tailed deer everywhere. Other smaller animals you may spot include raccoons, porcupines, skunks, and foxes. Birders have listed more than 125 species that either live in the park or migrate through it.

Fitness buffs may want to work up a sweat on the one-mile exercise trail with exercise stations;

the path winds through the forest near Nicolet Beach.

For bicyclists, there are 15 miles of bike trails and bike routes, for both standard and mountain bikes, and bikes are available for rent.

In winter, there are 20 miles of groomed cross-country ski trails, 17 miles of groomed snowmobile trails, and you can also do sledding and snowshoeing.

Most of the shoreline is rocky; however, there's a small beach for swimming. No lifeguards. One of the two boat launches is for shallow-draft boats; the other will take trailered boats. Rowboats, sea kayaks, canoes, sailboats, and windsurf boards are available for rent at the beach. One place you can boat to is the undeveloped Horseshoe Island just offshore. It's part of the park, but for day use only.

Green Bay offers a wide variety of fishing opportunities. Fish commonly caught in nearby waters include brown, rainbow, and lake trout; coho and chinook salmon; northern pike; perch; and smallmouth bass. One of the campgrounds has a fishing pier. In winter, a ramp lets you drive out on the ice for ice fishing.

On shore, the park offers an 18-hole golf course open from early May through mid-October. For history buffs, guided tours are available in the summer to the Eagle Bluff Lighthouse, built in 1868 and now on the National Register of Historic Places. A totem pole, depicting area history, and the grave of a local Indian chief are both near the golf course. Another summer special is the American Folklore Theater, which presents musical/historical entertainment in the park's amphitheater from late June through August.

Camping

Of the 469 multiuse **campsites** in four campgrounds, 100 have electric hookups. About 80% of the campsites may be reserved for the period from May through October. The rest of the year, all sites are on a first-come basis. Reservations are accepted by mail starting January 1 for this period. Sites range from $6 to $10 depending on facilities and state residency, plus $2 for electricity and a reservation fee. A group campsite is available.

Nearby Attractions

The entire **Door County peninsula** is a tourist destination with accommodations, restaurants, shops, and activities. Besides this one, four other state parks are found on the peninsula with a variety of offerings. **Potawatomi State Park** (tel. 414/746-2890), for example, includes Door County's only downhill ski area, and **Whitefish Dunes State Park** (tel. 414/823-2400) features the series of dunes it's named after.

To the north of the park, there are a number of small resort villages and interesting small museums at **Gills Rock, Ellison Bay,** and on **Washington Island.** That island—which is the northernmost island in Lake Michigan—and **Rock Island State Park** (tel. 414/847-2235) can only be reached by ferry or excursion boat.

Among the places of interest going south are the Indian Museum at **Egg Harbor;** the two National Register Historic Districts in **Sturgeon Bay,** as well as the **Farm** (tel. 414/743-6666) and other museums in that town and the boat tours that originate there; and a winery at **Algoma.**

Farther south, but still within an easy daytrip, is **Green Bay.** In addition to being the home of the Green Bay Packers football team and that team's **Hall of Fame** (tel. 414/499-4281), this is home of the **National Railroad Museum** (tel. 414/437-7623), and a complex of historical buildings at Heritage Hill State Park (tel. 414/448-5150).

Wyoming

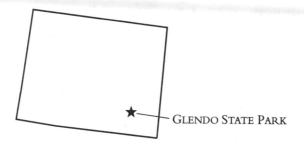

★———— GLENDO STATE PARK

Wyoming has 24 state parks.

Contacts

- Wyoming State Parks and Historic Sites, 2301 Central Ave., Cheyenne, WY 82002 (tel. 307/777-7695).
- Wyoming Division of Tourism, I-25 at College Drive, Cheyenne, WY 82002 (tel. toll free 800/225-5996 [800/CALLWYO]).

General Information on Wyoming State Parks

Wyoming is a bold state—bold in scenery and bold in attitude.

It has the second-highest mean elevation in the United States, at 6,100 feet above sea level, with the highest point at 13,785 feet and the lowest at 3,100. Which is not surprising since it is located in the Rocky Mountain section of the west. It is the home of the world's first national park, Yellowstone; the first national monument, Devils Tower; and the first national forest, Shoshone.

What may be surprising to some are a few of its other "firsts." Women were given the right to vote for the first time in our nation by the Wyoming Territorial Legislature in 1869. This was followed up in later years by the election of the first woman justice of the peace, the selection of the first women jurors, and, in 1925, the election of the first woman governor. All earning Wyoming the nickname of the Equality State.

But it is probably better known by its other title, the Cowboy State. With many times more cattle and sheep than people, ranching and cowboying is still a way of life here. Less well known is that oil is the principal fuel of the state's economy and Wyoming has the second-largest coal reserves in the nation.

As to its state parks, they are fine companions to the national parks, offering alternatives of equal scenic splendor and a genuine escape from the hustle and bustle and overcrowding that is becoming customary in those parks.

GENERAL FEES
The entrance fee is $3 per vehicle for nonresidents and $2 for residents.

CAMPING
There are **campgrounds** in a dozen parks. There are no hookups and, in some parks, no showers. All sites are on a first-come basis; no reservations. Sites go for $4 per night and stays are limited to a maximum of 14 consecutive days in one park.

Pets. Pets are permitted in most parks, but they must be under control and on a leash at all times.

Alcoholic beverages. Alcoholic beverages are permitted in most parks.

Glendo State Park

Lodge/ Hotel   RV Camping   Tent Camping   Marina   Boating   Boat Launch   Fishing   Beach   Waterskiing   Picnic Areas   Trails   Playground

Capsule Description: A large natural park with some developed facilities surrounding a reservoir.

Location: Southeastern Wyoming. From I-25, take Exit 111 to Glendo Park Road and go two miles east.

Address: P.O. Box 398, Glendo, WY 82213 (tel. 307/735-4433).

Area Contacts: Casper Convention and Visitors Bureau, P.O. Box 399, Casper, WY 82602 (tel. toll free 800/852-1889).

Douglas Area Chamber of Commerce, 318 1st St. West, Douglas, WY 82633 (tel. 307/358-2950).

Fort Laramie National Historic Site, P.O. Box 86, Fort Laramie, WY 82212 (tel. 307/837-2221).

Western history buffs will find the area surrounding Glendo State Park fascinating. The transcontinental telegraph, the Pony Express, the first Overland State Route, and the Bozeman Trail all passed through or near the park. Historic sites abound in the area, including Horseshoe Stage Station, Fort Fetterman, Fort Laramie, and Register Cliff. Two of the oldest towns in Wyoming, Sunrise and Hartville, lie just southeast of the park.

On the North Platte River, Glendo State Park (10,000-acres) surrounds a reservoir (9,000 acres) formed by the Glendo Dam. Archeological evidence from nearby digs documents that this area was used by humans at least 11,000 years ago.

Tepee rings and cultural artifacts from the Arapahoe and Cheyenne tribes, which occupied the area in the 18th century, are still found in the park. More recently, pioneers bound for Oregon, California, and Utah followed the main trails along the North Platte. Remnants of their passage can be seen in the wagon ruts, names carved in sandstone, and graves in the area surrounding the park. Some of these ruts are from wagon trains that cut across what is now the Glendo Reservoir. They can be seen heading off into the reservoir itself.

Rising out of the reservoir's east side are a series of sand dunes that stretch from the Great Divide Basin and the Green River to the sand hills of Nebraska in the east.

Activities

The reservoir and the North Platte River entering and leaving the lake are the center of park activities.

All types of boats are permitted on the lake, but noise restrictions are imposed. The park's full-service marina offers pontoon and fishing boat rentals. Four boat launches offer a total of six back-in lanes.

Fishing is good for walleye, catfish, and yellow perch. Some stocking is done, but not on a regular basis. Fishing docks are found on the trails in the wetlands areas of the park. According to park officials, the best fishing is in May and June.

The lake is open for waterskiing and most other water sports, with some equipment available at the marina. Below the lake, rafting and canoeing are popular in the river, which offers an easy float that takes about four hours. For swimmers, a large sandy beach is on the east side of the lake—no lifeguards or bathhouse. Parasailing is also popular; you need a no-fee permit from the park superintendent to do it.

One of the favorite sights for visitors is the small

bison herd near the Two Moon campground. These bison are part of a larger state herd that's kept at Hot Springs State Park in western Wyoming. Mule deer, pheasants, and pelicans are park residents, too. Occasionally golden and bald eagles soar in the skies above the park during winter.

The three designated trails in the park are all short. Two are easy-to-walk Wetlands Interpretive Trails, and the third is a three-quarter-mile hiking trail, which has parts that are rough and steep. Although these are the only marked trails, there's plenty of space to hike around the lake. Several overlooks offer views that range from the Laramie Mountains to the North Platte River. You may also want to visit the dam and power plant.

During the winter, the park is open for winter sports, but no facilities are provided.

Camping and Accommodations

The marina includes a six-room **motel,** which is open from around Memorial Day until the end of September. Rates for a double are $35 to $45. For reservations call 307/735-4216.

There are approximately 500 **campsites** in five campgrounds. "Approximately" because none of the sites are designated and each campground has some flexibility as to numbers. Some sites are multiuse while others are only for tents. There are no hookups, no showers, and no reservations. Sites cost $4 per night.

Nearby Attractions

The distances to places of interest outside the park are not small, but since most are on or near the I-25 Interstate, the driving times make for easy daytrips.

To the southeast, off U.S. Highway 20, is the **Fort Laramie National Historic Site.** This is not the famed western town of Laramie, which is much farther to the south, but the fort that was one of the most important army posts in the battles against the Plains Indians and to aid settlers on their way to Oregon, California, and Utah. Eleven of the fort's structures have been restored to tell the tale of life on this frontier post. Living-history demonstrations are given here in the summer.

On the way to Fort Laramie, you might stop at **Guernsey State Park** (tel. 307/836-2334) near Guernsey. The park museum tells the story of the impressive work of the Civilian Conservation Corps in developing some of the Wyoming parks. And nearby are the **Oregon Trail Ruts State Historic Site**—which exhibits exactly what the name says—and the **Register Cliff State Historic Site,** where thousands of pioneers carved their names into the 100-foot cliff as they journeyed west.

Douglas, to the north on I-25, is the home of the "jackalope"—the joke of a local taxidermist. A 10-foot replica of this jackrabbit with antlers stands in a downtown square. The state fair is held in Douglas, and a major year-round attraction on the fairgrounds is the **Wyoming Pioneer Museum** (tel. 307/358-9288).

Casper, the nearest large city, is farther west on I-25. Sights worth visiting here include several museums and a **planetarium** (tel. 307/577-0310).

Index

Agate Fossil Beds National Monument (NE), 152
Alabama, 1–7
Alabama Music Hall of Fame, 7
Alaska, 8–14
Alaskaland (AK), 11
Albany (NY), 186
Allaire State Park (NJ), 166–67
Alpine Loop Byway (CO), 47
Alton (IL), 78–79
Amana Colonies (IA), 93
Amarillo (TX), 258
Amicalola Falls State Park (GA), 63–64
Anacortes (WA), 275
Anadarko (OK), 215
Anchorage (AK), 14
Andrew Molera Park (CA), 37
Angel's Camp (CA), 31
Año Nuevo State Reserve (CA), 38
Anza-Borrego Desert State Park (CA), 26–29
Arapaho National Forest (CO), 43
Arcade (NY), 182
Ardmore (OK), 213
Arizona, 15–17
Arkadelphia (AR), 20
Arkansas, 18–24
Arkansas Museum of Science and Technology (AR), 24
Arkansas River Valley Arts Center (AR), 24
Asbury Park (NJ), 167
Assateague State Park (MD), 114–17
Astoria (OR), 218, 277
Atlanta (GA), 65
Atlantic City (NJ), 172
AuSable River (MI), 127
Azalea Trail (AL), 6

Backbone State Park (IA), 90–91
Bandon (OR), 222
Baraboo (WI), 286
Barren River Lake State Resort Park (KY), 98–99
Barre (VT), 265
Barrier Island Visitor Center (MD), 115
Baxter State Park (ME), 109–11
Bayou Segnette State Park (LA), 106–7

Bear Valley Ski Company (CA), 31
Beaufort (SC), 235
Beavers Bend State Park (OK), 209–10
Beckley (WV), 283
Bemidji (MN), 133–34
Benbow Lake State Recreation Area (CA), 35
Big Mountain Ski Area (MT), 147
Big South Fork National River and Recreation Area (KY-TN), 104
Biloxi (MS), 139
Bismarck (ND), 197
Black Canyon (CO), 47
Black Hawk (CO), 43
Black Hills (NE), 152
Blackwater Falls State Park (WV), 280
Bloomington (IN), 88
Bluestone State Park (WV), 283
Boise (ID), 73
Borrego Springs (CA), 29
Bourne (MA), 122
Bowling Green (KY), 99
Brazos Bend State Park (TX), 254–55
Brewster (MA), 124
Brigham Young University (UT), 262
Broken Bow (OK), 211
Bruneau Dunes State Park (ID), 72–73
Buckskin Mountain State Park (AZ), 17

Cabot (VT), 265
Cadiz (KY), 101
Calaveras Big Trees State Park (CA), 29–31
California, 25–38, 158
Camp Shelby National Guard Military Base (MS), 139
Canaan Valley Resort State Park (WV), 279–80
Cape Cod (MA), 122, 124
Cape Girardeau (MO), 142
Cape Henlopen State Park (DE), 52–53
Cape May (NJ), 53
Carhenge (NE), 152
Carmel (CA), 37–38
Carson City (NV), 159
Casper (WY), 291
Cass Scenic Railroad State Park (WV), 281

Cattail Cove State Park (AZ), 16–17
Cave City (KY), 99
Cedar Falls (IA), 91
Cedar Point National Wildlife Refuge (OH), 203
Cedar Rapids (IA), 93
Central City (CO), 43
Chaldron (NE), 152
Champaign/Urbana (IL), 82
Chaokia Mounds State Historic Area (IL), 79
Chapel Hill (NC), 191
Charleston (SC), 235, 237
Charlotte (NC), 194
Chattanooga and Chickamauga National Military Park (TN), 4
Chattanooga (TN), 4, 248
Chena River State Recreational Area (AK), 9–10
Chesapeake and Ohio Canal Historical Park (MD), 119
Chihuahuan Desert Research Institute (TX), 254
Chincoteague National Wildlife Refuge (MD), 114–17
Chloride (NM), 175
Chugach National Forest (AK), 14
Chugach State Park (AK), 11–13
Churchill Downs (KY), 86
Cleveland (OH), 206
Clifton Forge (VA), 269
Clinton, Bill, birthplace of (AR), 20
Cloudmont Ski and Golf Resort (AL), 3–4
Coast Guard Academy, U.S. (CO), 50
Coeur d'Alene (ID), 75
Colorado, 39–47
Colorado Springs (CO), 45
Columbia River Maritime Museum (OR), 218
Columbia (SC), 237
Columbia State Historic Park (CA), 31
Columbus (OH), 206
Concord (NC), 194
Connecticut, 48–50
Cooper Peak Ski-Flying Hill (MI), 130
Coos Bay (OR), 222
Cornell University (NY), 188

Corning Glass Center complex (NY), 188

Corson's Inlet State Park (NJ), 172

Corydon (IN), 86

Coshocton (OH), 205

Covington (VA), 269

Cranberry World (MA), 123

Crater of the Diamonds State Park (AR), 20

Cripple Creek (CO), 45

Cross Ranch State Park (ND), 197

Cumberland Caverns Park (TN), 248

Cumberland (MD), 119

Custer City (SD), 242

Custer State Park (SD), 239–42

Dahlonega (GA), 64–65

Dakota Territorial Museum (SD), 244

Darlingtonia Botanical Wayside (OR), 220

Davis Mountains State Park (TX), 252–53

Dawsonville (GA), 64

Dayton (MT), 147

Decatur (IL), 82

Deception Pass State Park (WA), 272–74

Deep Creek Lake Recreation Area (MD), 118, 119

Deep Creek Lake State Park (MD), 118–19

DeGray Lake Resort State Park (AR), 19–20

Delaware, 51–53

Delaware Water Gap National Recreation Area (NJ-PA), 169

Denali National Park and Preserve (AK), 14

Dennis Wildlife Center (SC), 237

Denver (CO), 43

DeSoto National Forest (MS), 139

Desoto State Park (AL), 2–3

Devil's Lake State Park (WI), 285–86

D.L. Bliss State Park (CA), 158

Dog Mushers Museum (AK), 11

Douglas (WY), 291

Douthat State Park (VA), 267–68

Dublin (GA), 66

Dubuque (IA), 91

Duke University (NC), 191

Duluth (MN), 136

Dunlop (TN), 248

Durham (NC), 191

Dyche Museum of Natural History (KS), 96

Dyer-Botsford Doll Museum (IA), 91

Dyersville (IA), 91

Eagle Creek State Park (IL), 79–80

Earthquake Park (AK), 14

Ebey's Landing National Historical Reserve (WA), 274

Egg Harbor (WI), 288

Elephant Butte Lake State Park (NM), 174–75

Elephant Rocks State Park (MO), 142

Elkins (WV), 281

Elsah (IL), 78

Emerald Bay State Park (CA), 158

Erie, Lake, 202–3, 227

Eugene T. Mahoney State Park (NE), 153–54

Eureka (CA), 35

Everglades National Park (FL), 56

Fairbanks (AK), 10–11

Fall Creek Falls State Resort Park (TN), 246–48

Fallingwater (PA), 225

Fall River (MA), 122

Farragut State Park (ID), 74–75

Fenelon Place Elevator (IA), 91

Ferndale (CA), 35

Fire Island (NY), 178–79

Flathead Lake State Park (MT), 146–47

Florence (AL), 7

Florence (OR), 220

Florida, 6, 54–61

Florida Museum of Natural History (FL), 61

Florissant Fossil Beds National Monument (CO), 45

Fort Abraham Lincoln State Park (ND), 196–97

Fort Campbell (KY), 101

Fort Canby State Park (WA), 275–76

Fort Columbia State Park (WA), 277

Fort Davis (TX), 253–54

Fort Donelson National Battlefield (TN), 250

Fort Laramie National Historic Site (WY), 291

Fort Morgan (AL), 5–6

Fort Necessity (PA), 225

Fort Niagara State Park (NY), 184

Fort Robinson State Park (NE), 150–52

Fort Sill (OK), 214–15

Fort Stevens State Park (OR), 217–18

Fort Washita Historic Site (OK), 213

Franconia Notch State Park (NH), 162–63

Fred Bear Museum (FL), 61

Fremont (NE), 154

Frost, Robert, Place (NH), 164

Gainesville (FL), 60–61

Garberville (CA), 35

Garrett State Forest (MD), 119

General Burnside State Park (KY), 104

Genesco (NY), 182

Georgia, 62–66

Geronimo Museum (NM), 175

Glacier National Park (MT), 147–48

Glendo State Park (WY), 290–91

Glens Falls (NY), 186

Goddard Memorial State Park (RI), 231

Going-to-the-Sun Road (MT), 148

Golden (CO), 43

Golden Gate Canyon State Park (CO), 40–43

Grafton (IL), 78

Grayling (MI), 127

Green Bay (WI), 288

Greenville (ME), 112

Groton (CT), 50

Groton State Forest Parks (VT), 264–65

Guernsey State Park (WY), 291

Gulf Islands National Seashore (FL), 6

Gulfport (MS), 139

Gulf State Park (AL), 4–5

Gunnison National Forest (CO), 47

Haena State Park (HI), 68–69

Hamptons (NY), 179

Handy, W. C., home and museum of (AL), 7

Harrison-Crawford-Wyandotte Complex (IN), 84–86

Hartwick Pines State Park (MI), 126–27

Hattiesburg (MS), 139

Havasu National Wildlife Refuge (AZ), 17

Hawaii, 67–70

Hawkinsville (GA), 66

Hearst San Simeon State Historical Monument (CA), 38

Heber City (UT), 261

Heceta Head Lighthouse (OR), 220

Helen (GA), 65

Henry Doorly Zoo (NE), 154

Herrington Manor (MD), 119

High Point State Park (NJ), 168–69

Hillsboro (NM), 175

Hilton Head (SC), 235

Hinckley Fire Museum (MN), 135

Hinton (WV), 283

Hochatown State Park (OK), 209–10

Holmes County (OH), 205

Homestead, The (VA), 268–69

Hoover Dam (NV), 160

Hope (AR), 20

Hopkinsville (KY), 101

Hot Springs National Park (AR), 20–21

Hot Springs (SD), 242

Hot Springs (VA), 268–69

Houston (TX), 256

Hugo (OK), 211

Humboldt Redwoods State Park (CA), 32–35

Hunting Island State Park (SC), 234–35

Huntsville (AL), 7
Hyannis (MA), 124

Idaho, 71–75
Illinois, 76–82
Indiana, 83–88
International Peace Garden (ND), 199
Iowa, 89–93, 244
Iowa City (IA), 93
Ironwood (MI), 130
Island Crossing (ID), 73
Itasca State Park (MN), 132–33
Ithaca (NY), 188

Jamestown (KY), 104
Jean Lafitte National Historical Park and
    Preserve (LA), 107
Jessie M. Honeyman State Park (OR),
    219–20
Jewel Cave National Monument (SD),
    242
Jewell Meadow Wildlife Refuge (OR),
    218
Joe Wheeler State Park (AL), 6–7
John and Mable Ringling Museum of
    Art (FL), 59
John Pennekamp Coral Reef State Park
    (FL), 55–56
Johnson's Shut-ins State Park (MO),
    142
Jones Beach State Park (NY), 177–78
Jordan Lake State Recreation Areas
    (NC), 190–91
Julian (CA), 29
Julia Pfeiffer Burns State Park (CA), 38

Kamokila (HI), 70
Kansas, 94–96
Kansas City (KS), 96
Kauai (HI), 68–70
Keller, Helen, birthplace of (AL), 7
Kentucky, 86, 97–104, 250
Key Largo (FL), 56
Keystone (SD), 242
Kings Range National Conservation
    Area (CA), 35
Kingston (NM), 175
Kirkville (MO), 144
Kokee State Park (HI), 69

Laclede (MO), 144
Lake Barkley State Resort Park (KY),
    100–101
Lake Catherine State Park (AR), 20
Lake Cumberland State Resort Park
    (KY), 102–4
Lake George Village (NY), 186
Lake Guntersville State Park (AL), 4
Lake Havasu State Park (AZ), 16–17
Lake Macbride State Park (IA), 92–93

Lake Mead National Recreation Area
    (NV), 160
Lake Metigoshe State Park (ND), 198–
    99
Lake Murray Resort and State Park
    (OK), 211–13
Lake Tahoe–Nevada State Park (NV),
    156–58
Lake Wappapello State Park (MO), 142
Land Between the Lakes (KY–TN), 101,
    250
Las Vegas (NV), 160
Laughlin (NV), 17
Laurel Caverns (PA), 225
Lawrence (KS), 96
Lawton (OK), 215
Letchworth State Park (NY), 179–82
Lewes (DE), 53
Lewis and Clark State Recreation Area
    (SD), 243–44
Lewiston (NY), 184
Lexington (VA), 269
Lincoln (Abraham) Boyhood National
    Memorial (IN), 86
Lincoln (Abraham) Home (IL), 82
Lincoln (NE), 154
Lincoln (NH), 163–64
Lincoln State Park (IN), 86
Little Ocmulgee Lodge State Park (GA),
    65–66
Little Rock (AR), 24
Long Beach Peninsula (WA), 276–77
Lost Coast (CA), 35
Louisiana, 105–7
Louisville (KY), 86
Lumberman's Museum (ME), 110, 112

McDonald Observatory (TX), 254
McRae (GA), 66
Madison (WI), 286
Maine, 108–12
Malabar Farm State Park (OH), 205
Mammoth Cave National Park (KY), 99
Manitou Springs (CO), 45
Mansfield (OH), 205
Marceleine (MO), 144
Mariette (OK), 213
Maryland, 113–19
Massachusetts, 120–24
Maumee Bay State Park (OH), 202–3
Mead, Lake (NV), 160
Memorial Indian Museum, The (OK),
    211
Mentone (AL), 4
Mercer Caverns (CA), 31
Michigan, 125–30
Minneapolis–St. Paul (MN), 136
Minnesota, 131–36
Mississippi, 137–39
Mississippi River, 91, 132, 142

Missoula (MT), 147
Missouri, 79, 140–44
Moaning Caverns (CA), 31
Mobile (AL), 6
Mohican State Park (OH), 204–5
Moiese (MT), 147
Molera Point (CA), 37
Mollie Kathleen Gold Mine (CO), 45
Monmouth Battlefield State Park (NJ), 167
Monroe, Lake (IN), 88
Montana, 145–48
Montauk (NY), 179
Monticello (IL), 82
Montpelier (VT), 265
Moosehead Marine Museum (ME), 112
Morrison (CO), 43
Morrow Mountain State Park (NC),
    191–94
Mountain Home (ID), 73
Mount Rushmore National Monument
    (SD), 152, 242
Mt. Washington State Park (NH), 164
Mueller State Park and Wildlife Area
    (CO), 43–45
Murray (KY), 250
Museum of Automobiles (AR), 24
Museum of the Big Bend (TX), 254
Museum of the Fur Trade (NE), 152
Museum of the Red River (OK), 211
Myakka River State Park (FL), 57–59
Myles Standish State Forest (MA), 121–
    22
Mystic (CT), 50

National Bison Range (MT), 147
National Farm Toy Museum (IA), 91
National Museum of Naval Aviation
    (FL), 6
National Tropical Botanical Garden (HI),
    70
Nebraska, 149–54
Nevada, 17, 155–60
New Bedford (MA), 122
New Hampshire, 161–64
New Jersey, 53, 165–72
New London (CT), 50
New Mexico, 173–75
New Orleans (LA), 107
Newport (RI), 232
New Salem (IL), 82
New York, 50, 169, 176–88
Niagara Reservation State Park (NY),
    182–84
Niantic (CT), 50
Nickerson State Park (MA), 123–24
Norfolk (VA), 270
North Bend (OR), 222
North Carolina, 189–94
North Carolina Zoological Park (NC),
    191, 194

North Dakota, 195–99
North Ocean Beach (MD), 115
North Woodstock (NH), 163–64

Oatman (AZ), 17
Ocean City (MD), 118
Ohio, 200–207, 227
Ohio Agricultural Research and
    Development Center (OH), 205
Ohiopyle State Park (PA), 224–25
Oklahoma, 208–15
Omaha (NE), 154
Onamia (MN), 135
Oregon, 216–22, 277
Oregon Sand Dunes National Recreation
    Area (OR), 220, 222
Oregon Trail Ruts State Historic Site
    (WY), 291
Ottawa National Wildlife Refuge (OH),
    203
Ouray (CO), 47
Oysterville (WA), 276

Pacific Grove (CA), 38
Paducah (KY), 101
Palo Duro Canyon State Park (TX),
    256–58
Palomar Observatory (CA), 29
Paris Landing State Resort Park (TN),
    249–50
Paris (TN), 250
Park City (UT), 262
Parker, Quanah, home of (OK), 214
Parker Dam (AZ), 17
Park Rapids (MN), 134
Parrish Art Museum (NY), 179
Parris Island Museum (SC), 235
Paul B. Johnson State Park (MS), 138–
    39
Paynes Prairie State Preserve (FL), 59–
    60
Peak-to-Peak Highway (CO), 43
Pebble Beach (CA), 38
Peninsula State Park (WI), 287–88
Pennsylvania, 223–29
Pensacola (FL), 6
Peregrine Fund World Center for Birds
    of Prey (ID), 73
Pere Marquette State Park (IL), 77–78
Petit Jean State Park (AR), 21–24
Petrified Sea Gardens (NY), 186
Pfeiffer Big Sur State Park (CA), 35–37
Pikes Peak Hill Climb Museum (CO),
    45
Pikeville (TN), 248
Pilgrim Hall Museum (MA), 123
Pine City (MN), 135
Pipestem Resort State Park (WV), 281–
    83
Pittsburgh (PA), 226

Plymouth (MA), 122–23
Point Lobos State Reserve (CA), 37
Point Sur Light Station (CA), 37
Polson (MT), 147
Porcupine Mountains Wilderness State
    Park (MI), 128–29
Portage Glacier Recreation Area (AK),
    14
Port Clinton (OH), 203
Port Jervis (NY), 169
Portland (OR), 218
Portsmouth (OH), 207
Potawatomi State Park (WI), 288
Presque Isle State Park (PA), 227
Prime Hook National Wildlife Refuge
    (DE), 53
Providence (RI), 232
Provincetown (MA), 124
Provo (UT), 261–62
Pymatuning State Park (PA), 226–27

Quartz Mountain Resort and State Park
    (OK), 213–14

Railtown (CA), 31
Raleigh (NC), 191
Rapid City (SD), 242
Reed Gold Mine State Historic Site
    (NC), 194
Reno (NV), 159
Rhode Island, 50, 230–32
Rhododendron State Park (WA), 274–75
Ricketts Glen State Park (PA), 228–29
Ridgway State Park (CO), 46–47
Robert Moses State Park (NY), 178–79
Rochester (NY), 182
Rock Island State Park (WI), 288
Rockome Gardens (IL), 82
Rocky Mountain National Park (CO),
    43
Rocky Neck State Park (CT), 49–50
Roosevelt National Forest (CO), 43
Rugby (ND), 199

Sagit Valley (CA), 275
St. Croix State Park (MN), 134–35
St. Johnsbury (VT), 265
St. Louis (MO), 79
Salt Lake City (UT), 262
Salton Sea National Wildlife Refuge
    (CA), 29
Sam A. Baker State Park (MO), 141–42
Sandpoint (ID), 75
Sandusky (OH), 203
Santa Claus, town of (IN), 86
Santa Cruz (CA), 38
Santa's Workshop (CO), 45
Santee National Wildlife Refuge (SC),
    237
Santee State Park (SC), 236–37

Sarasota (FL), 59
Sarasota Jungle Gardens (FL), 59
Saratoga National Historical Park (NY),
    186
Saratoga Spa State Park (NY), 184–86
Saratoga Springs (NY), 186
Savannah (SC), 235
Schweitzer Ski Resort (ID), 75
Scotia (CA), 35
Scranton (PA), 229
Sea Lion Caves (OR), 220
Seashore State Park and Natural Area
    (VA), 269–70
Seaside (OR), 218
Seattle (WA), 275
Selby Gardens (FL), 59
Shawnee State Park (OH), 206–7
Shelbyville State Park (IL), 79–81
Silverton (CO), 47
Sinkyone Wilderness State Park (CA), 35
Sioux City (IA), 244
Sioux Falls (SD), 244
Six Flags Great Adventure (NJ), 167
Sleeping Bear Dunes National Lakeshore
    (MI), 127–28
Smithville (NJ), 172
Snake River Birds of Prey Natural Area
    (ID), 73
Snowbowl Ski Area (MT), 147
South Carolina, 233–37
South Dakota, 238–44
South Slough National Estuarine
    Reserve (OR), 222
Springfield (IL), 82
Spring Mill State Park (IN), 87–88
Squire Boone Caverns (IN), 86
Stanislaus National Forest (CA), 31
Statesboro (GA), 66
Steamtown National Historic Site (PA),
    229
Stokes State Forest (NJ), 169
Sturgeon Bay (WI), 288
Sullivan County (PA), 229
Sundance (UT), 261
Sunset Bay State Park (OR), 220–22
Superior, Lake, 128–30, 136
Swallow Falls (MD), 119

Tabeguache Trail (CO), 47
Tahoe, Lake (CA-NV), 31, 156–58
Taum Sauk Mountain State Park (MO),
    142
Telluride (CO), 47
Tennessee, 4, 245–50
Tennessee National Wildlife Refuge
    (TN), 250
Texas, 251–58
Thousand Hills State Park (MO), 143–
    44
Timpanogos caves (UT), 261–62

Tishomingo (OK), 213
Toledo (OH), 203
Tom's Cove (MD), 115
Topeka (KS), 96
Touchstone Center for Crafts (PA), 225
Town Creek Indian Mound State
    Historic Site (NC), 194
Traverse City (MI), 128
Trenton (NJ), 167
Truman, Harry S., Library and Museum
    (KS), 96
Truth or Consequences (NM), 175
Tuscumbia (AL), 7

Uncompahgre National Forest (CO), 47
Unicoi State Park (GA), 65
University of Alaska Museum (AK), 10–
    11
Utah, 259–62
Ute Indian Museum (CO), 47

Valley of Fire State Park (NV), 159–60
Varner-Hogg State Historical Park (TX),
    256

Ventana Wilderness (CA), 37
Vermont, 263–65
Vernon (NJ), 169
Victor (CO), 45
Vikingsholm Castle (CA), 158–59
Vintage Wheel Museum (ID), 75
Virginia, 118, 266–70
Virginia Beach (VA), 270

Waimea Canyon State Park (HI), 69
Warhol (Andy) Museum (PA), 226
Wasatch Mountain State Park (UT),
    260–61
Washington, 271–77
Waterloo (IA), 91
Watkins Glen State Park (NY), 187–88
West Columbia (TX), 255–56
West Sister National Wildlife Refuge
    (OH), 203
West Virginia, 278–83
Wharton State Forest (NJ), 170–72
Whidbey Island (WA), 274
Whitefish Dunes State Park (WI), 288

Whitefish (MT), 147
Wichita Mountains Wildlife Refuge
    (OK), 214
Wild Cave National Park (SD), 242
Wilder Memorial Museum (IA), 91
Williamsport (PA), 229
Winrock International (AR), 24
Winston (NM), 175
Wisconsin, 284–88
Wisconsin Dells (WI), 286
Wisp Ski Area (MD), 119
Wolf Creek National Fish Hatchery
    (KY), 104
Wolf Creek State Park (IL), 79–81
World Kite Museum (WA), 276
Wyandotte Woods State Recreation Area
    (IN), 84–86
Wyoming, 289–91

Yosemite National Park (CA), 31
Youngstown (OH), 227

Zephyr Cove (NV), 158
Zwaanendael Museum (DE), 53